The Memory of Place

The Memory of Place

···································

A Phenomenology of the Uncanny

DYLAN TRIGG

OHIO UNIVERSITY PRESS / ATHENS

Ohio University Press, Athens, Ohio 45701
ohioswallow.com
© 2012 by Ohio University Press
All rights reserved

Printed in the United States of America
Ohio University Press books are printed on acid-free paper. ∞

Hardcover   18 17 16 15 14 13 12 11   5 4 3 2 1
Paperback   20 19 18 17 16 15 14 13   5 4 3 2 1

First paperback printing in 2013
ISBN 978-0-8214-2039-3

Library of Congress Cataloging-in-Publication Data

Trigg, Dylan.
The memory of place : a phenomenology of the uncanny / Dylan Trigg.
    p. cm.—(Series in Continental thought)
Includes bibliographical references (p. 337) and index.
ISBN 978-0-8214-1975-5 (hc : alk. paper)—ISBN 978-0-8214-4404-7 (electronic)
1. Place (Philosophy) 2. Memory. I. Title.
B105.P53T75 2011
114—dc23   2011036028

For my Parents and Brother
With Love

You must be able to think back to streets in unknown neighborhoods, to unexpected encounters, and to partings you had long seen coming.

—Rainer Maria Rilke, "For the Sake of a Single Poem"

CONTENTS

....

ILLUSTRATIONS

• •

PREFACE

· ·

TOUCHING THE PAST

> We still believe that there is a truth about the past; we base our mem-
> ory on the world's vast Memory, in which the house has its place
> as it really was on that day, and which guarantees its *being* at this
> moment.
>
> —Maurice Merleau-Ponty, *Phenomenology of Perception*

I have seen this place before. It is three o'clock on a Thursday afternoon, and
I am standing outside my childhood home. On the upper right, through the
tree, is the room I slept in. From within that room, I would be able to hear a
train in the distance. Through an adjoining alleyway on the left of the house is
the place where some children once set fire to some disused tires, causing thick
clouds of smoke to disturb the bees in the garden. If I get close enough, perhaps near enough to touch the door, I would be able to see the kitchen where I
once burned myself. Dare I trespass beyond this door? In doing so, more than
a spatial border would be transgressed. Crossing that borderline, I would risk
conflating the traces of familiarity with the presence of unfamiliarity, entering
into the scene of a different timescale, and so producing a place divested of its
intimacy with my memory but now accommodating of other people's lives. So
I maintain a distance, allowing my imagination to repair the wounds of time.
In the nooks and alcoves that have been reconstituted and altered, my involvement with the place has ended. Reduced to the outsider of my own memory,
the assurance that coincides with self-presence is undermined. After all, where
am "I" in this return? The answer is clear: partly dispersed in time, and yet
partly absorbed in place, but never actually "here." Place and time: two pillars
of identity, now bathed in a strange, even uncanny, light.

Another memory has surfaced. This time the distance is nearer and I am placed inside a house that I recently vacated and only now has been leased to another tenant. But an anomaly occurs. The new guest has yet to move his furniture and belongings in, and I encounter the place in a transitional state: deprived of my own items, yet lacking the presence of another human, and thus exposed to the strange anonymity in between.

Here, the memory of the place has yet to recede into a mythical past, has yet to be divested of its relation with calendar time. Instead, walking through the environment, feeling the light strike me in a singular way, and becoming aware of the damp air, the effect of which is a condition of the basement level, I am immediately returned not only to a specific time but also to a particular mode of embodiment. As I sit on a wooden box in the bedroom, my head must tilt at an uncomfortable angle in order to view the window above. Once more, I encounter the window primarily through its small and damaged air vent, which rotates with a gentle creaking noise. Below street level, the focus of this room is oriented toward the nameless human beings who walk above. Only their feet can be seen. Sometimes, however, a voice comes into the room before receding into silence. I confess: I had forgotten about the low-level melancholy this room invokes; forgotten, too, about the insomnia that became constitutive of my experience of failing to sleep here.

I leave, and am now in the lounge. All that remains of my former presence is the mannequin of a woman in the patio area. Too cumbersome to move, it has remained stationary, entering into a decaying existence, apathetic to its new owner. Despite this fragment of the old life, I am still able to sense my own presence in the room. When I move nearer to the French doors, the combination of feeling the draft and smelling the rotting wood returns me to a piece of writing I was finishing on aesthetic experience three years ago. As though the two events have formed one image, it is impossible for me to isolate the act of writing from the draft and rot.

Despite this arch of circular unity, something is missing in this return; namely, the other people who were brought into this place. I am not alone in this memory. Moving through the environment, the empty rooms and refurbished walls, I am followed at all times by the ghosts who continue to cohabit my memories, despite no longer existing in the material world. Putting my ear to the wooden floors, I am able to sense the presence more acutely. Hearing light footsteps, I simultaneously feel a hand on my shoulder before that same hand loses its grip and withdraws into the shadows. Further afield, in my attempt to retrieve a discarded book from a shelf, a human hand—familiar by dint of its thinness—touches my own hand.

Again, I reach out in this domestic wilderness, my hand running across the space where the bookshelves once existed. My hand stops. The coloring is a shade lighter in this recently exposed space, a testament to the accumulation of dust and dirt discharged by human life over any given period of time. All along, however, the same wall has been harvesting a life of its own, previously concealed. On this Thursday afternoon, the wall, untouched and barren, is being seen for the first time. Out of place and out of time in this underground environment, the new finding forces a further displacement: from the body. Structurally disembodied, the discovery of the untouched wall alerts me to the existence of an occult world, hidden from the eye. Despite my attachment to this environment, which varies in its attributes and intensity, the same place has covertly remained indifferent to my presence. As such, developing its own history, the house has strayed from my own past, forging a void between my body and the place.

It is becoming unnervingly clear: My relation with this place has discharged a germ in my body, such that how I comport myself could occur only *here* and *now*. And with this sedimentation, all that is different, fragmented, and absent is amplified through my nervous system. Indeed, inasmuch as I *am my body*, then, as an embodied subject with a history peculiar to this place, I have become the literal clearing ground for this difference. Only through the singularity of my own body is the anonymity of the environment articulated. Nor is the mode of articulation felt in the abstract. To be clear, the anonymity of this world is not a theoretical one extracted in philosophical speculation. Rather, it presses down upon my experience, such that I feel this anonymous materiality pulsate through my muscles, seizing my throat with tightness, before knotting itself in my stomach. Soon after, I leave this gray atmosphere and return to ground level.

To state it once more, then: *I have seen this place before.* How can we do justice to this seemingly innocuous yet enigmatic statement, which exudes a strange intimacy, while simultaneously pushing at the threshold between memory and materiality?

Each of us is held captive by a series of memories, which in their intensity and depth return us to a specific place and time. Consciously or otherwise, the places we inhabit and pass through come back to us in the present, sometimes affording a sense of familiarity in the midst of uncertainty. At other times, disturbing the course of everyday existence. However cryptic these memories are, they nevertheless attach themselves to us, just as we attach ourselves to the places in which those events occurred. Yet from the childhood house to the city square, from the attic to Antarctica, why some places become more central in our memories than others remains a source of mystery. Notwithstanding the idiosyncrasies of human memory, which is as much prone to selective remembering as it is to selective forgetting, the question of how we can begin to decipher the memory of place is at the core of this book.

But what does the memory of place mean within a philosophical and historical context? Along with time, memory has assumed a problematic if central place in the history of philosophy, partly assimilated by science and yet equally unresolved by the nature of experience itself. Explaining the actions of memory in terms of mind-body causality, such as has been the tendency from Descartes to Russell, or whether the content of memory assumes a realist or an idealist relation to the mind, and even venturing toward a neurological account of the role of the hippocampus in episodic memory—all of this, however interesting, does not abate the irreducible experience of what it is to remember something in the first instance.

The Memory of Place does not intend to approach memory as a discrete concept among many to be analyzed with recourse to the "tools" of philosophy. To do so, I believe, would be an injustice to memory. Rather, by placing episodic memory—broadly, autobiographical in nature and content—central, my interest is in understanding the role the material environment plays in shaping, defining, and constituting our sense of self and world.

Here, too, the memory of place does not assume an incidental role within the architecture of remembering. True, we can speak of various aspects of remembering, ranging from its temporality to its method of retention. We can press further into this sphere through considering the act of remembering as an issue pertaining to the philosophy of mind. However, the subject of place memory refuses to fit neatly among these distinguished branches of academia. Above all, the type of memory I shall be contending with in this book is not simply interdisciplinary in content, but in a fundamental sense, more primary in its relation to human experience than to the treatment of memory within an academic context. The memory of place forces us to return to the immediacy of our environment and to all that is absorbed, both familiar and strange, within that environment. In doing so, not only do we *feel* the measure of time pass through our bodies, but through attending to the phenomenon of place, we catch sight of how memory forms an undulating core at the heart of our being.

If our experiences of the world are founded in the depth of memory, then gaining a sense of memory's scale becomes all the more problematic. Neither beginning at one point nor ending at another, memory surrounds us from all sides. *To approach memory.* Repeatedly, we must rephrase and return to this advance. At no point does a linear gateway open in which memory's attributes can be laid out for detached scrutiny. Instead, an approach to memory can be drawn, which relies less on linearity and more on a constellation of different perspectives, mutually edifying one another. Alongside the concept "place," which I shall turn to shortly, memory diffuses itself in several different pathways simultaneously, all of which are experienced from the inside out.

Yet the movement from the inside out does not sanction a formless analysis of memory and place. Far from it. In bringing the terms "memory" and "place" together, two formal trajectories of thought immediately present themselves. First, we can identify the memory of place taken as a particular mode of remembering. With this, we remain within the realm of lived experience, pursuing a descriptive account of how the material environment shapes the content of remembering, in turn shaping our concept of selfhood. Second, we can observe the place of memory taken as a particular mode of materiality. Here, the focus is less about the texture of lived experience and more about the formation of memory within a social context, afforded by the power of place and manifest in such entities as monuments and sites of trauma.

Pursuing this distinction, we move from a concern with how personal identity is formed by the singular memory of a given place to the question of how it is possible for a place to mark an event that has already occurred in the past, existing, moreover, beyond the boundaries of an individual person. From memory to place, we are returned through place to memory. Between these distinctions, a confluence of mutual dependency emerges. Just as memory is inherently spatial, so spatiality is inherently temporal, occupying a place in the present but stretching back into the past.

How to approach this twofold movement between the memory of place and the place of memory? My suggestion is that the study of memory and place profits from a broadly phenomenological direction. As I shall spell out in detail later, the relation between embodiment, place, and phenomenology is both privileged and fluid, developing the means by which spatiality becomes both existentially and affectively meaningful. Especially privileged to phenomenology, I believe, is its capacity to mediate between place as an objective reality, presented in Kant as a transcendental form of experience, and place as a socially constructed realm of materiality and intersubjectivity. Through its attention to the appearance of things, phenomenology allows us to catch sight of the manner in which spatiality becomes existentially and intentionally meaningful from the point of departure of its being objectively real.

Where the place of memory offsets the memory of place, the phenomenological direction is strengthened with a more hermeneutic inclination. In treating the built environment as something to be "read," both the structural and the symbolic values of place are brought to the fore. Viewed provisionally, therefore, the difference between the memory of place and the place of memory forms a unifying structure, and it is to this structure that the ensuing treatment of memory and materiality will broadly adhere.

Throughout the book, a central theme—and one I shall return to—concerns *how our bodily identity is shaped through being touched by the past*. What does this complex theme signify? The phrase "touched by the past" signifies more than being merely affected or in casual contact with the past. Being "touched by the past" brings us into a region of memory and temporality that elicits the moment personal identity is marked in either an affirmative or a disruptive manner by the experience of memory itself. Coupled with this exposure to the formation of identity, the inclusion of "touch" reinforces the bind between temporality and materiality. Being "touched by the past," sets in place the centrality of place itself, implying a kinesthetic and sensual recollection of the past. The result of this bind between identity and materiality is a challenge to the idea that memory and identity are solely temporal phenomena. To this extent, my broad concern is as much with specific memories and their effect on the concept of the self as with the experience of memory as a phenomenon among many. At the same time, it is in some sense clear that certain types of memory are more pertinent to the formation and dissolution of personal identity than others. As I shall explain in chapter 1, I take place memory to be such a privileged memory, capable of heightening the interplay between self and world.

What, then, of the more problematic term "personal identity"? If being touched by the past means admitting of a relation between memory and materiality, then how can we reconcile this relation with the tendency to align personal identity with a coherence found in temporality alone, such as we would emblematically find in John Locke? Perhaps the question is misleading: Must time and place necessarily be involved in a dialectical standoff, whereby place is regarded as a deviation of time?

Such a binary treatment of identity, in which temporality and materiality are prised apart, is insufficient and naive. As suggested above, temporality and spatiality are fundamentally entwined, each implicating the other. Instead of a standoff, therefore, what is at stake in aligning place with identity is a redirection of emphasis. The question of how we account for the existential unity of life can be read as an invitation to consider how materiality sculpts time rather than how temporality alone sculpts materiality.

What does this reversal of priority mean for the concept of identity? If we are to take materiality and spatiality as primary to the formation and unity of personal identity, then the understanding of identity being employed is less about numerical "sameness" and more about existential unity in relation to the coherence of the self. Far from the largely analytical concern with deciding how entities remain strictly identical with themselves, the concern in the present context is the more ambiguous question of how we, as subjects bound by lived experience, relate to our material selves with a complex history that disrupts numerical identity. Indeed, being identical with ourselves means more than locating a singular property—memory being the most obvious candidate—that underpins the continuity of the self, such as is classically presented in Locke.

Given the difference between numerical identity and the unity of the self, the question arises: How do we begin to phrase a phenomenology not only of the memory of place, but also of the place of memory? Our question leads us away from the identity of the individual into the region of collective memory, implicating a responsibility upon the built environment to represent the past "authentically." With this imperative, a fundamental difference between the memory of place, as carried out by the individual subject, and the place of memory, as received collectivity, is conceived. Unlike the unity of selfhood, the value we confer upon certain public places is open to a plurality of contested meanings, all disposed to political, aesthetic, and ethical dimensions.

The difference between a place being a receptacle to memory and a place being built to signify a public event is marked in both cases with a relationship between the symbolic value we attach to materiality and the concurrent emergence of events tied to that materiality. This elevation of materiality to an event brings the memory of place and the place of memory together, each attesting to the peculiar power of place to seize time in its tracks. Seizing time in its tracks, what connects these two aspects in experiential terms is the treatment of memory as a genetic and phenomenal appearance in the world, an appearance, moreover, that is given primarily as an *embodied* experience.

I shall defer the discussion of the body until the following chapter, at which point the relationship between corporeality, memory, and place will justify a closer inspection.

In the meantime, a brief word about the use of photographic reproductions in the book. Overall, my intention has been to establish a distance between the images and the text, such that the relation between photography and representation is displaced. Against the notion that a photographic image can somehow "distill" the essence of an idea, what I would rather bring to light is the anonymity and strangeness of a photograph, considered in material terms.

Aesthetically, I have taken my cue for this motif from Georges Rodenbach's novel of memory, place, and loss, *Bruges-la-Morte*, which I discuss in chapter 4. Visually, the black-and-white photographs deployed in Rodenbach's *fin de siècle* novel are both sterile and richly atmospheric, a motif later adopted in the use of photographs in André Breton's (1999) *Nadja* along with W. G. Sebald's oeuvre, especially his (2002b) *The Rings of Saturn*. Bereft of human life, the scenes of empty streets, still canals, and gray skies create a mournful and haunting tone, in which time appears to have come to a standstill. Not only this, but the materiality of the buildings captured in the photographs attains a ghostly presence at odds with their apparent stillness. It is notable that in the accompanying essay to the novel, "The Death Throes of Towns," Rodenbach would describe the decline of a place in physiological terms: "dried blood," "age-old wounds," and "corpse of the lifeless waters" (2005, 141–50), all terms that play upon the decidedly inhuman quality of both the text and the images.

Yet something is gained in this lugubrious atmosphere: a density, which in its spectrality disarms the threshold between absence and presence. Despite the enthusiastic interplay between memory and loss, something remains vividly alive in Rodenbach's photographs. Indeed, what we see in these photos is something like an afterlife—literally a ghost town—a place peculiar to the medium of photography, in which all emphasis on human intimacy has been replaced with a world that is now being allowed to speak for itself. Far from being a mnemonic to aid our own memories, the use of photos in this manner frames a certain way of experiencing a given place, which has less to do with historical interest, and more with how heterogeneous features of a place can embed themselves in our memories, even—*especially*—if those features have long since died.

With Rodenbach's imagery in mind, I gesture toward two paths of thought, both of which are at stake in the current use of photography. The first concerns the relation between phenomenology and photography, while the second points to the inherent melancholy surrounding photography, especially in the context of found photographs.

Consider the first avenue. If, as I shall suggest in some detail in the following chapter, phenomenology concerns rediscovering the strangeness of things in their phenomenality, then the aesthetics of photography assumes an especially significant role. Concurrent with the phenomenological method is the space to discover things anew, displaced from environmental and temporal familiarity and retranslated into a new experience. Destabilized in this movement is the act of recapturing things as we previously knew them. Already in the structure of a photograph, this destabilization is at work. The spatiotemporality of a photograph immediately redirects our attention from the world as a whole to a world being given through the medium of photography. This prototypical phenomenological motion at once sets in place the materiality of what is being photographed while simultaneously removing that materiality from the familiarity of the everyday.

Alongside this gathering of raw experience, the photograph seizes us in our tracks, invoking the *punctum*, which Roland Barthes famously wrote about in the following way: "*Punctum* is also: sting, speck, cut, little hole—and also a cast of the dice. A photograph's *punctum* is that accident which pricks me (but also bruises me, is poignant to me)" (1982, 27; italics in original). Barthes refers to the way in which the photographic object, removed from its narrative and now placed in stasis, instills a melancholy dynamic in the heart of the viewer. Impossible to reduce this melancholy either to the passing of time or to the absence of things in the present, nevertheless, the thick permeation of this response is emblematical to the manner in which photography grasps toward a totality, despite being incommensurable with that totality. What remains is something like a damaged memory, deprived of all its reality and yet charged with a sense of that prominence becoming lost.

No doubt, it is for this reason that the experience of discovering found photographs stretches this melancholic deprivation to a limit. What unfolds in this moment is the heightened sense of the past's anonymity, an abandonment of all that was once intimate and cherished and is now relegated to a naked exposure. The encounter obliges us to reconsider the very facticity of what is being captured in a photograph. As enigmatic as the object captured is the temporality of experiencing that object in the present. Bachelard's genuinely profound and enduring question—"Have facts really the *value* that memory gives them?" (1994, 58; italics in original)—reappears in a different guise: that of the disjunction between strangers in the past and the present.

A photo is found, at once familiar and unfamiliar. A gaze—a place or a person—is returned, but now conditioned by a fundamental absence, full of empty pathos. Yet the emptiness is movement in itself, generating a dynamic animation, in which "I feel *myself* looked at by the things," to call upon a vital sentence from Merleau-Ponty (1968, 139; emphasis added). Indeed, the encounter establishes a reciprocity, marked by a shared time frame. The asymmetry shifts, and suddenly I find myself transplanted, if not to the place, then to the mutual time in which I and my subject—even if that subject remains myself—exchange a series of glances. The result is a silence, in which the living mingle with the dead, both becoming part of each other's worlds. Placed together, both of these trajectories of thought— the phenomenological and the melancholic—are entwined with the use of photographs in the current book. By refusing an explicit commentary on the photos, I hope to preserve their anonymity, if not in name, then certainly in their explication.

Thematically, this book forms a continuation to my earlier work on ruins, decay, and historical progress (Trigg 2006a). Only, while *The Aesthetics of Decay* hinted at the problematic relations between materiality, embodiment, and memory, this dynamic was essentially positioned in an overarching narrative, in which the experience of memory and place was taken as a manifestation of a broader historical movement; namely, the progressive structure of decay. In the current work, this outwardly objective approach to memory and place is modified with a direct appeal to lived experience. If there is some degree of thematic continuity between these works, marked in both cases by a commitment to the underworld of things in the world, then what remains divergent is the method employed. Indeed, insofar as the previous book deliberately oriented itself toward a broken narrative, then it can be characterized as fatalistic in its orientation. This streak of romanticism befits a book melancholy in tone and dissolute in content. If something of that residual melancholy remains in place, then today, the requirements are nevertheless different. As I shall spell out shortly, in structural terms, the current book is distinguished by a concentrated focus on the development and emergence of place memory as a singular phenomenon. What this means is that, in the current context, the topic being examined is as much at stake as the phenomenological framework surrounding that matter. To reinforce this, I shall now outline the contents of the book as a whole.

PREVIEW OF THE CHAPTERS

The plan of this book is to consider how place and memory interact from three different types of memory: everyday memory, transitional memory, and traumatic memory, with each mode demarcating a division within the work. Not only does this threefold formation define the structure of the book, it also attests to the development of memory becoming increasingly divisive, fragmented, and uncanny. Let me say a word about this narrative.

By "everyday memory," I refer to instances of the memory of place and to places of memory that are (in the least) given in their phenomenal immediacy. To this extent, the use of "everyday" is less about the banality or commonality of memory and more about a relation between memory and place that is taken-for-granted in its unified state. Accordingly, in the chapters that hold a concern with everyday memory, on both an individual and a public level, memory is thought of as occupying *a* place, even if that occupancy is open to a plurality of interpretations, not all of which can be resolved.

If the unity of everyday memory is vulnerable to a set of contested meanings, then what nevertheless remains immune to doubt is the intimate relation between memory and place. Where transitional memory is concerned, however, this occupancy is fundamentally ambiguous. In citing ambiguity as fundamental, I characterize transitional memory as the *interstitial movement of memory from embodiment to cognition to place.* Much will be said on the nature of this movement in the pages to follow. For now, however, let me say that by using the term "interstitial," I propose to argue for a model of memory that is *between* places, both the places of the body but also of materiality itself. My principal claim is twofold. First, the way in which we remember places differs in accordance with the varying emphasis cognition and corporality play in that memory. Second, this difference constitutes a threat to the stability of not only place, but also personal identity.

Experientially, this is played out in terms of the body's own memory having yet to apprehend a previous surrounding, and so being placed in a transitional zone somewhere between the objectivity of the world and the lived experience of the body. Transitional or interstitial memory, therefore, occupies a fundamentally embryonic realm, in which the experience of the past has yet to be reconciled with the unity of place and memory, resisting classification all together. This absence of unity is nevertheless in constant movement and striving toward reconciliation. If transitional memory marks an indefinite relation between place and memory, then the structure grounding that relation is one of activity and intelligibility. As I will suggest with recourse to Merleau-Ponty, transitional memory is marked by a prepersonal intentionality, whereby what remains between place gestures toward an eventual unity.

In corporeal terms, this mode of memory is evident where the role of the body is pushed to the background, such as when we experience a tension between bodily and cognitive orientation. Being pushed to the background, the body can lose presence in place through experiences as overwhelming as trauma or as seemingly innocuous as being in an airport. In both cases, the body loses its fundamental centrality in place, causing a fissure in the core of the embodied self.

In turn, this dynamic movement will be contrasted with the relative stability of everyday place memory, where memory is either taken as being incorporated into a given environment or otherwise set in place through a symbolic representation. By lacking this clarity, transitional memory exposes the self to radical contingency. At the same time, the tension between how we remember a place cognitively and the way in which a place acts upon our bodies displaces the centrality of the self. With the move into traumatic memory, this tension between the rationalization of cognitive memory and the inaccessibility of body memory reaches a deadlock.

Unlike both everyday and transitional memory, the third division necessitates an attempt at reconciling identity and materiality through attending to the symptomatic emergence of the past. Why is this move necessary? The answer is because traumatic memory is at odds with the idea that human identity strives toward temporal continuity. This assertion is realized insofar as the memory of trauma "gives" itself to consciousness only through paradoxically *not* giving itself to consciousness, a claim I shall spend some time explicating in the final chapters. To the overview, then.

The first chapter sets out to describe the structural and experiential features of place memory in a preliminary way. This task unfolds in two stages. First, with recourse to the works of Bergson, Heidegger, and Casey, I plot the basic structure of place memory as involving a gesture of offsetting a broader environment, and in the process establishing an autonomous world peculiar to place memory. Providing a phenomenological illustration of this movement through the experience of being on a train, in Las Vegas, and on Alcatraz Island, I then proceed to describe the experiences of such memories in terms of affect and embodiment. The second part of the chapter contends with the relation between memory, imagination, and preservation. Through a discussion of Bachelard's account of memory and place, I proceed to explore the tension between different instances of preserved memory, before concluding that only in the felt experience of memory as being different is the reality and dynamism of the past fortified.

In chapter 2, the ambiguity between memory and imagination is framed in the context of the relationship between spatiality and history. The overarching problem the chapter confronts is twofold. One, how can phenomenology negotiate with the idea of a public memory? Two, how does materiality augment the representation of public memory? In response to these questions, I discuss a number of issues ranging from ecstasy to trauma, before focusing more specifically on spatiality via the work of Pierre Nora. From this conceptual engagement with Nora, the bulk of the chapter concerns a phenomenological study of the materiality and silence of the Chattri, an Indian war memorial in Sussex. Constructing a dialogue between Heidegger and Levinas, the conclusion of the chapter explores how the Chattri suggests a diachronic reading of memory and history through the specificity of its texture and placement.

Chapter 3 marks the move from the theme of representation and memorialization to the lived relation between identity, place, and memory. This turn inward is structured around what I term "transitional memory." As indicated above, by this I refer to the dynamic movement of memory being between place, cognition, and embodiment. The importance of this mode of memory becomes clear in terms of a phenomenological critique concerning the notion of a "sense of place." Far from wishing to dispense with types of places simply because they appear less memorable than others, my aim in chapter 3 is to demonstrate that the bodily absorption of a place often occurs independently of the cognitive experience of that place. Through performing a phenomenological analysis of the distinction between place and non-place via a study of journeying to and from a motorway service station, I conclude by positing a mode of place I term "un-place." The distinction of this term is that it underscores the ambiguous gradients resting between place and non-place, and between body memory and cognitive memory, a claim I develop by consulting Merleau-Ponty's idea of "flesh."

The broad aim of chapter 4 is to examine how memory and imagination work together to produce a mutated past, often in tension with the anonymous reality of that past. I approach this tension from several interrelated perspectives. Beginning with an analysis of how the body is retained in place, I then proceed to consider how imagination defines the experienced reality of memory, such that our sense of belonging to the past depends on not only remembering how things were, but constantly reworking that memory in the present. This dynamic between memory and imagination is best played out in corporeal and material terms through the illustration of becoming nostalgic toward a place, a theme I develop throughout the chapter. The result of this study is that the materiality of place becomes modified in accordance with our desires and memories, accumulating a level of pathology in the case of nostalgia, which I term "spatial morphology." As fundamentally topophobic in character, the chapter concludes with a study of returning to nostalgic place, in the process producing a disruption in temporal continuity while simultaneously giving rise to what I refer to as "anonymous materiality"; that is, the indifference of a place that no longer reciprocates our memories, thus instigating an aesthetic of the uncanny.

The final two chapters concern the epistemologically problematic terrain of the memory of trauma, problematic because the memory of trauma is characterized by fragmentation, deferral, and a symptomatic emergence. Thus, whereas the first two parts of the book are concerned with the various interactions between memory, imagination, and place, in the third part, the very status of this tripartite relationship will be put to the test through attending to the phenomenology of traumatic memory.

Chapter 5 considers the epistemological impasse at the (non)center of trauma via the body. Beginning with an analysis of trauma's emblematic phrase, "unclaimed experience," I move on to relate this claim to an analysis of recognition. Establishing that "claimed experience" involves the phenomenological apprehension of what is *given* to consciousness, by contrast, a void emerges for the memory of trauma, in which an event occurs but fails to be registered. By applying Levinas's writings on death and identity to Charlotte Delbo's testimonial documents, I take the notion of the *"il y a"* to represent a figure of mediation between two sets of identities in different times. This allows me to chart the emergence of the traumatic body as the site of an anonymous memory, which I term the "phantom zone," recognized only in its symptomatic appearance.

In chapter 6, I pursue a shift from the ruins of memory to the ruins of place. Aligning the structure of Delbo's testimony and Agamben's writing on witnessing with the structure of the ruins (using Auschwitz as my lead example), I argue that the ungivenness of "unclaimed experience" can be negotiated through attending to the temporal features of the ruins. From this discussion of ruins, the question of "reading" a place in hermeneutic terms is made tenable. In the case of traumatic memory, I put forward the view that the past presents itself in terms of the ruins' housing what is absent: in effect, a non-memory. This confluence between absence and presence carries with it a dreamlike quality, which leads us back to Delbo. By suggesting that the ruins of disaster (dis)embody the notion of an architectural emergence without time and stability, the testimonial attributes of the ruins become clear: having outlived their death, the ruins occupy the spectral trace of an event left behind, serving to testify to the past through a logic of voids, disruptions, and hauntings.

The theme of spectrality is developed in the conclusion of the book, where I elicit an idea that was implicit in the previous chapters: ghosts. Bringing together phenomenology with themes torn from the supernatural, I offer readings of Heidegger on angst and Merleau-Ponty on the phantom limb in order to account for the experience of being haunted by the past.

All three divisions of the book thus form a unity, in which the placing of memory, along with the memory of place, is taken from contrasting but mutually edifying perspectives. By stretching memory between everyday, transitional, and traumatic memory, my rationale is to amplify the role of place in the formation of the past. Alongside this amplification, the movement from everyday, transitional, and traumatic memory follows the increasing inaccessibility and estrangement of memory itself. Far from arbitrary, the structure as a whole follows a genetic path oriented around the tension between cognitive and body memory, a collision played out, above all, through the manifestation and memory of place.

ACKNOWLEDGMENTS

This book has been a long time in the making, its inception beginning long before the writing itself commenced. Over the course of writing its contents, different places have cast their presence upon these pages before receding into the past. Houses, homes, and haunts have emerged with vibrancy only to fall into mute extinction. Yet no sooner did these places vanish than they once again reappeared as a memory. As much as places themselves, however, it is the people who enter those places that become fundamentally enshrined in memory. To explore the history of one's experience of place, as this work sets out to do, is to relive our relations with the people inside those places, however brief or cursory those encounters might be. As such, it is fitting that in a book about memory and place, acknowledging the people who filled those places is principal.

First and foremost, this work would not have been conceived were it not for Tanja Staehler and Paul Davis of the University of Sussex. Thanks to them, I was able pursue the research that led to this book in a supportive and friendly atmosphere. I extend this thanks to Edward S. Casey from Stony Brook, whose work remains a source of continued inspiration and guidance. Professor Casey's comments on this text were both invaluable generous, and I hope to have done justice to them.

At the University of Sussex, I would like to thank Alun Howkins and Jenny Bourne Taylor from the Graduate Centre in the School of Humanities, who kindly provided funding for several trips abroad. Robbie Robb, the philosophy departmental secretary at Sussex, has been especially kind in dealing with my queries. Finally, I would like to offer my sincere thanks to the students I have taught at Sussex, both in the philosophy department and also in the summer school, where I gave a series of seminars examining the relation between place and identity. Thanks also to my philosophy group in East Dean, Sussex, for their hospitality, warmth, and philosophical stimulation.

Beyond the tranquil grounds of the University of Sussex, it has been a continued joy making friends with others who share my concern with the idiosyncrasies of materiality and memory. Thanks to Caitlin DeSilvey, who provided me with the opportunity to visit and give a lecture at the University of Montana in Missoula, the memory of which is a source of intense pleasure. Additional thanks to Albert Borgmann from the philosophy department at the University of Montana for being a considerate host. During the writing of the middle of the work, I had the pleasure of spending some time as a visiting scholar at the Simon Silverman Phenomenology Center at Duquesne University. My thanks to Daniel Martino for his hospitality and kindness during a very rewarding stay in Pittsburgh.

The writing of the final chapters was made possible thanks to a grant from the Tauber Institute for the Study of European Jewry. My sincere thanks for their support. Sincere thanks also to Miriam Rieck, of the Ray D. Wolfe Center for Study of Psychological Stress at the University of Haifa, for her hospitality and conversation during a visit to Israel.

Several other people have been either supportive or edifying during the writing of this work, all of whom I am sincerely indebted to. These include: Iris Aravot, Jacky Bowring, David Canter, Steven Galt Crowell, Isobel Colchester, Jemma Deer, Sharron Fitzgerald, Matthew Gandy, Simon Gregg, Beth Headley, Erazim Kohák, Dalal Jazi, Mary Jeanne Larrabee, Neil Leach, Daniel Listoe, Adrian Needs, Andreas Philippopoulos-Mihalopoulos, Jennifer Pollard, Louise Purbrick, Oliver Rathbone, David Seamon, Daria Brit Shapiro, Ingrid Stefanovic, Celine Surprenant, Mark Thwaite, Karen Till, Maria Tumarkin, Laura Vaughan, Angela Voulangas. I owe a special debt of gratitude to Elizabeth Olivia Walling, who accompanied me to several of the transitional places described in this book.

Special thanks to Emma-Louise Hanif, whose friendship and intellectual camaraderie were a source of great inspiration during the writing of this book. I remain indebted.

Separate thanks to Elena Dawson, whose love, tenderness, and warmth meant that I was able to write this book in that most elusive of places, home. This book owes everything to her presence. I extend this gratitude to Milly and Rosie for filling that home with the dynamism of pure spirit, and in doing so enlightening me in the truest sense of the word. Thanks, above all, to my family for their support, humor, and love—it is to them that I dedicate this book.

For their help with the preparation of this book, I thank all at Ohio University Press, including: Beth Pratt, Kevin Haworth, Judy Wilson, Jean

Cunningham, Charles Sutherland, Deborah Wiseman, Gillian Berchowitz, Nancy Basmajian, and the series editor, Ted Toadvine.

Final thanks to my new colleagues at the Centre de Recherche en Episté-mologie Appliquée for their warm welcome, and to Dorothée Legrand and Line Ryberg Ingerslev for making me feel at home in my new city, Paris. I could not ask for a more supportive and amicable team to be working with.

For permission to reproduce their photographs, my sincere thanks to Travis Ferland, Thomas Merkle, Hannah Swithinbank, Mark Dodds, Judy Lash Balint, Thomas Herrmann, and Claus Wolf. For allowing his painting, 'Whitenoise no.4,' to be used as the cover for this book, my immense thanks to Christopher Saunders.

INTRODUCTION

· ·

PHENOMENOLOGY AND PLACE

> Memory as a place, as a building, as a sequence of columns, cor-
> nices, porticoes. The body inside the mind, as if we were moving
> around in there, going from one place to the next, and the sound of
> our footsteps as we walk, moving from one place to the next.
>
> —Paul Auster, *The Invention of Solitude*

This book is about places. More specifically, it is about the memory of places
that human beings inhabit and pass through. As bodily subjects, we necessarily have a relationship with the places that surround us. At any given moment, we are located within a place, be it in the hallways of universities, the
cockpits of airplanes, or lost in the forest at night. Over time, those places
define and structure our sense of self, such that being dis-placed can have a
dramatic consequence on our experience of who we are, and even leave us
with a feeling of being homeless in the world. Equally, the memories we acquire of the places we inhabit assume a value that is both immeasurable and
vital. Without the memory of places, memory itself would no longer have a
role to play in our conscious lives.

Yet, despite its central role in our everyday lives, coming to terms with
the nature of our relationship with place is decidedly less straightforward.
Consider the following thoughts. Place is all around us and yet not always
fully thematized. Place is at the heart not only of who we are, but also of
the culture in which we find ourselves. As invested with cultural, ecological,
and political ramifications, place does not simply designate a patch of land
without value. As proof, humans tend not to be indifferent to the effect place
has upon them. At the same time, the question of what constitutes place

brings us into a realm in which the complexity of human values are second-ary. Although we fundamentally shape our surroundings, ultimately place exists independently of human life in turn shaping us. Returning to a place after a long period of absence, we are often shocked by both the small and the vast changes, effectively alerting us to the radical indifference places have to the sentiment we apply to them. Here, our own selves can become the site of an internal quarrel as to how a place once was; by claiming to cognitively remember the feel of a place, our bodies can provide a different history of the past. The result is that a place can take on a life of its own, quite apart from the way it is experienced or remembered.

In naturalistic terms, place is taken to be so familiar as to evade all con-ceptual analysis. We are already in place. Not simply the room I currently write in, but the condition of there being a place at all. How does this room envelop me? How do I hold myself in this room? To what extent will this room become a significant aspect of my future memories? At which point did I cease feeling a visitor in this room and more a fundamental part of it? Such questions for the most part remain dormant, rising to the surface only when places either lose their familiarity or are otherwise destroyed and lost.

The complexity surrounding the topic of place is vast, and the aim of this book is to offer a contribution to the body of phenomenological work con-tending with the idiosyncrasies of memory and materiality, of which an im-pressive library is already in existence (Backhaus and Murungi 2005; Behnke 1997; Brown and Toadvine 2003; Carr 1991; Casey 1993, 2000b, 2007; Cresswell 2004; Entrikin 1991; Hayden 1997; Kolb 2008; Light and Smith 1998; Malpas 2007, 2008; Massey 2005; Mugerauer 1994; Steeves 2006; Steinbock 1995; Tengelyi 2004; Tuan 1977).

But before this contribution can begin, the methodology of the book needs to be spelled out. In particular, the relation between phenomenology and place requires our immediate attention. After all, to think in terms of a phenomenology of place, we must in the first instance think of a place for phenomenology. The reason is clear: Just as phenomenology, in its appeal to lived experience, would emerge as abstracted, partial, and disembodied with-out being situated in place, so the term "place" would be vague and cryptic without being thematized through phenomenology.

Given this hermeneutical circularity between place and phenomenology, in this book the familiar idea that definition precedes exposition will prove impossible. I point this out now, because the impossibility of this approach will be implicated from the outset. Rather than bludgeoning the reader with a fixed definition of "memory," "place," and other such key terms at the beginning, and then insisting that the reader remain heedful of those definitions throughout, I believe these themes must be returned to, forever exploring their formations and recessions. The advantage of this approach is that we move from a strictly analytical mode of accumulating static concepts and expose ourselves to the possibility that these concepts evolve of their own accord. Not tying things down in advance means allowing those things to speak for themselves.

Luckily, the refutation of fixed definitions does not entail either a postmodernist retreat into the "multiplicity of meanings" or an orientation without guidance. Rather, we must begin to work through the knots that concepts create through several different angles. As some of the knots prove permanently bound, so our task will be to redirect the emphasis, assessing indirect ways to chart the relation between phenomenology and place. First of all, then, having admitted that "place" and "phenomenology" refuse unambiguous definitions, my concession to pairing these terms is also a tacit admission that "phenomenology" as a method and "place" as a concept have potential to encounter each other in a meaningful manner. Let us explore these parts.

A PHENOMENOLOGY OF PLACE

Philosophical thinking on the topic of place tends to adopt one of two perspectives. First, place is thought of as an empirical idea, which has a reality independent of human life. Such a view tends to be marked by a scientific outlook on the environment, in which the totality of place is reduced to its parts. For these thinkers, the coherence and identity of place have a reality quite apart from the way in which it is experienced by human beings. Second, place is thought of as a constructive product of human experience, such that without human involvement, place would lose definition. In this model, place is basically reducible to a set of contingent sociopolitical circumstances.

Both of these approaches to place have their value. They each identify the subtle and complex way in which a place straddles multiple divisions. On the one hand, places can be valued by individuals, sometimes culminating in a nostalgic attachment to especially important environments. At the same time, the places we attach ourselves to are themselves spatially extended into the world. A place is not simply a cluster of discernible memories held within the core of an individual. Rather, a place unfolds in the world, and does so against a backdrop of manifold influences, not all of which contribute to an individual's attachment to that place. But neither is a place simply an isolated beacon in a mass of homogeneous space. True, both space and place are fundamentally extended. But this does not mean that a place comes into existence simply through a conversion between space and place. Place is not, after all, colonized from raw space. Such a negative definition fails to grasp the enigmatic dimension of place.

Neither of these approaches—the realist or the constructivist—is complete in itself. Experiencing place is not reducible to a set of objective properties. But nor does the experience of place depend wholly on a sociopolitical context. Instead, a third way can be mapped out, in which attention is drawn to the existential significance of place. It is such an approach that phenomenology broadly advocates in its treatment of place.

For all its internal differences, one of the features that defines phenomenology's treatment of place is a commitment to the belief that lived spatiality is not a container that can be measured in objective terms, but an expression of our being-in-the-world. For Merleau-Ponty, we find "organic relations between subject and space" (2006, 293). Spatiality is not something we are inserted into, as though it has existed all along and awaits the subject's arrival. The world does not, that is to say, constitute a series of concurrent markers placed in the earth's landscape. Rather, being-in-the-world means being *placed*. At all times, we find ourselves located in a particular place, specific to the bodily subject experiencing that place. We are forever in the *here*, and it is from that *here* that our experiences take place.

If our bodies place us in the here, then our orientation and experience of place is never truly epistemic in character but fundamentally affective. When Merleau-Ponty finds himself journeying through Paris—"the cafés, people's faces, the poplars along the quays, the bends of the Seine"—then what he experiences is united in the "city's whole being [which] Paris possesses" (2006, 328). For him, the identity of Paris is not reducible to the parts that objectively constitute the city. Rather, "There is present a latent significance, diffused throughout the landscape or the city" (328). Placed in the world of Parisian life, Merleau-Ponty discovers a texture of continuity from one place to another that is grounded in a "certain style" that all places partake of. The reason for this is that the perception of lived space

is not a particular class of "state of consciousness" or acts. Its modalities are always an expression of the total life of the subject, the energy with which he tends toward a future through his body and his world. (330)

This is a critical passage. In it, Merleau-Ponty draws our attention to the relation between a human's experience of place and the values, memories, dreams, anxieties, and other such affective states that sculpt that experience. Places are defined in their relationship with the particular subject who experiences them. To think, for example, alongside the agoraphobic's experience of public space as anxiety-making is to recognize that anxiety is relational, a shared communication that takes place neither in the body of the agoraphobe nor in the materiality of the city, but in the spark ignited between the two (Trigg 2012). In such a case, the body is the vehicle of expression for a relation with the world, thus the life of the city fundamentally manifests in the nuances of the bodily self.

In experiential terms, the affectivity of place means that establishing distance in space can be taken up only with an analysis of our embodied relationship with the world. If I am on a train and in a rush to get home in order to walk the dogs, then during that episode, home seems much farther away. Conversely, if I am under the impression that someone else is walking the dogs, then the distance diminishes. In this experience, things that prevent me from getting home, such as leaves and snow falling on the train track, are amplified in their intrusiveness, such that for every obstacle that appears, I feel my destination receding into the distance. The feeling of my home as being farther away testifies to my attachment to it, and my responsibility to ensure the dogs are walked. On the train, I place myself in the world of the dogs and seem to experience their waiting by proxy. In the desire to bypass the journey, the distance is thus accentuated. I cannot get home soon enough. Such an urgency has very little to do with measureable space. The journeys we repeat daily alter in their felt spatiotemporality owing to the mood and objects of intentionality we find ourselves immersed in. And the same is true of our relationship to nearness. When I am required to return to the train station in order to meet a friend, then the train station becomes more foreground in my field of perception. Even before it is in my visual line of sight, the station is already being perceived by my body, whereupon my body extends into the world of the train station long before the train station is a visual object for me. The feeling of the train station as being near is not an objective property of the world, not something that can be mapped out in advance. Rather, it is a dynamic relationship that varies in and through time. Lacking a reason to be at the train station, it withdraws from my bodily perception, sinks into the quiet indifference of the surrounding world.

Given its complexity, we might want to ask, What *kind* of concept is "place"? Despite the difficulty of responding to this question in a coherent fashion, a series of themes marking place's critical features can be detected. First, place is to be understood *experientially*. While it is true that we cannot reduce place to a "construct" simply imposed upon raw space, without an experiential focus and direction, place would lose what is common to the very concept: its affectivity. Thus, we experience place in an *affective* way. Our bodies orient us in place, and in doing so become the primary source of how we apprehend a given environment. Finally, because of this corporeal emphasis, place emerges as being temporally and spatially singular. We are situated in the world, inasmuch as we occupy a *particular* place. Not only is the body highly specific to a particular place—we are seldom in two places simultaneously—but the relation we have to any given place is unique and irreducible.

Experience, affectivity, and particularity are at the heart of place. Conceptually, where does this leave the term "place"? Splicing the three themes together, what emerges is a sense of place as belonging to neither the subject's constructs nor the world's reality. That places have the power to disarm our memories and electrify our imaginations is due not only to the supposed centrality of human experience. Indeed, places really *do* exist, and they do so quite independently (although no doubt differently) from the human values that are coated upon the world. At the same time, through coming into contact with the world, place becomes more than inert materiality by assuming an emblematic role in our understanding of self. Yet the hold places have on us is never absolute, and however much we attend to the world, the universe's cosmic indifference to human experience can never be fully overlooked.

In this way, place emerges as neither a realist nor an idealist concept, but rather somewhere *in between*. In situating place "in between" the world and the subject, I am implicitly acknowledging the work of J. Nicholas Entrikin (1991, 6–23), who argues that place must be understood between a detached and a lived stance. Entrikin's perspective in this relation is valuable, and his mediation between subjective and objective realms is laudable. This in-between status can be seen on a number of different levels. As Entrikin has it, the tension between "external" and "internal" vision "represents a basic polarity of human consciousness," in which each aspect is perceived as being either "real" or "unreal" (9). Consequently, Entrikin is especially strong at describing how each of these aspects informs the other, thus producing an ambiguity at the core of place, which he reconciles by bridging together seemingly contradictory claims.

However, in what follows, I want to dissent from Entrikin's account of betweenness. Ultimately, I will argue that betweenness is a concept that is fundamentally problematized by the role of body memory. As I will suggest, the cognitive space between place and world is disturbed by the independence of the flesh, which, in its intelligibility, manages to defamiliarize our experiential, affective, and particular placement—the three discernible features that contribute to place broadly. In turn, what this will mean is that the privileged observer of place standing between self and world will lose his or her bearings due to the primacy of embodiment. At such a point, understanding place between subject and object will be undermined through the observer's being torn asunder in multiple directions.

Along with space and place, time and place form another dovetailing pair. Indeed, it is only through materializing itself in place that the felt experience of time gains its powers. This experience has diverse manifestations, but the two most apparent factors are *movement* and *stasis*. Moving in place, be it from the car park to the elevator or from one planet to another, we experience time in and through place. The "in and through" motif here is essential. The movement of the body does not reconstitute itself with each new place to which it attends. Rather, moving through place means tracing an arc of time. For this reason, the felt temporal experience of a given day is inextricably bound with the movements of the body, such that the same day can diminish or expand in time according to the level of spatial activity.

Habits in place, too, can nullify or illuminate our experience of time. Consider how the habitual movement through a place can appear to swallow up lived time, such that we can never be sure of how we spent any given period of our lives in a particular place. All that we know is objective data: We occupied a certain place from one year to another. But within that time, our actions fall by the wayside through becoming assimilated into a pregiven routine. Does habit rob us of time? We may not go that far, but a habitualized routine certainly suppresses the sensitivity toward our surroundings, both spatial and temporal. In a word, we become overly adjusted to our surroundings, in the process taking for granted the very facticity of those surroundings.

At the same time, being surprised by our surroundings, especially when that environment was previously overly familiar, marks a breakage in our experience of time, such that place itself comes to the foreground. When we are locked out of our homes due to mislaying the key, then not only is our relation to the home altered in terms of being inaccessible, but the condition of attempting to resolve the situation places us, literally, in a different time-scale. Suddenly, the overlooked dimensions of the house assume a different tone, the exterior now becoming a surrogate for the interior that has become remote. This position of being on the outside of the house causes a lag in time to develop. But the drawn temporality of waiting has less to do with the objective status of the environment, and more to do with a projection toward the future. The projection has its basis in a composite of how we anticipate place and time to interact.

Here, an analogous experience takes place between the sun and the moon. As our bodies align with the movement of the earth, so the temporality of the day becomes more than an unfolding process understandable in objective terms. Instead, the temporal "distance" of the day dwells in our bodies. From the light of morning to the darkness of night, and then during the blackness of sleep, our bodies become the vehicle for the reality of the earth's movement. Without exposure to this shift in shadow and light, the experience of time would undergo massive augmentation. Think here of the movement of journeying along the horizon of the earth while aboard a plane. Forever remaining beyond touch, the endless twilight that accumulates as the sun fails to return beyond the earth sanctions a unique experience. Indeed, what can the measure of time mean when time itself, already stationed between the sun and the earth, slips away from our bodies? True, the body can gesture toward a state of tiredness, but the tiredness is now in an altered zone, at once awake and fatigued. Can we ever really trust the vague drone of a confused corporeal state independently of the visual closure of day and night? Here, too, the usual aural cues that beckon the passing of time—above all, the quieting of the world—are absent. In the cabin of a plane, with its artificially regulated air, the same hum is fixed, ever disrupted only by announcements from the cockpit.

This homogenized environment of being above the earth appears to flatten out time. But is this so? After all, our bodies are not atomic entities situated in any given place, but are exposed to the massive stream of lived time and memory. If place has the ability to shape time, diminishing and expanding it in equal measure, then it also holds the power to seize time in its tracks. One way this seizure is most viscerally and manifestly potent is through places' becoming the foreground canvas in which our memories embed themselves—the very topic of this book.

Places do this in innumerable ways. Above all, consider how it is possible to develop a relation with the places you inhabit, such that the materiality of the environment—the peeling wallpaper, reflection in the window, rustle in the branches, groan of the house creaking in the wind—becomes constitutive of who you are. Places achieve this thanks to the extension of our bodies. As our bodies reach out into the world, so a mimetic interplay arises, in which our sense of self becomes fundamentally entwined with the fabric of the world. Here, the very things that make up a given place lose their status as "objects" in the world and become an extension of the formal structure of personal identity. Being attached to a place means allowing memories to be *held* by that place. In turn, being held by a place means being able to return to that place through its role as a reserve of memories. Not only do places hold memories in a material sense—as the archive of our experiences—but those same places crystallize the experiences that occurred there. Being in place is not temporally static. Rather, our memories pursue us as we pursue place, both forming an ambiguous zone somewhere in between.

Alongside this twofold movement from memory to place and from place to memory, particular types of experience can be singled out. In nominal terms, it is the "home" that has been cited as the locus for our place memories. While we cannot dispute the origin and force of the image of the home (however real that image is), in this book, the memories we have of places do not end with the intimacy and familiarity of the home. Quite the opposite. Places can, for instance, become singular in the library of our memories through their very *unfamiliarity*. Indeed, precisely through their strangeness, places become memorable by disturbing patterns of regularity and habit. In doing so, a given narrative is broken while another one begins. Such moments tend to impart significance into our lives, even if that significance is realized only belatedly. To this extent, places become the stage setting for profound events in the life of an individual. In turn, the places where those events occurred form a union with the very environment, whether those events are strange, pleasurable, or traumatic.

BODY MEMORY

From place, we return to body. As we recall from the preface, our thematic focus concerns *how personal identity and embodiment are shaped through being touched by the past*. Having clarified the terms "personal identity" and "being touched" in the preface, it falls to the word *embodiment*, a word emblematically phenomenological in tone and yet no less problematic because of that status. As indicated above, finding ourselves in place, we discover that our bodies confer a radical specificity to the environment. We are "in" place in the particular sense that our bodies are a first point of contact for the world. This has two major implications. First, being a body means occupying a particular location in place. "Above" and "below" exist only in terms of where I am currently placed. With my bodily self as the determining force, I draw whatever is around me into my body. However, as I draw nearer to that which is above and below me, so another horizon of distinctions is established. Neither static nor absolute, these distinctions rotate and evolve in accordance with the movement of the body.

Likewise, being "here" while you are "there" is not an abstract formulation posited without regard to embodiment. We are "here" inasmuch as our bodies place us in the world. This center of orientation provides a locus for all movements, carrying with it a rich arc of sensation. In this way, the totality of experience of place begins and ends with the body. But the body is also a center in a figurative sense. Just as certain aspects of the body are more prevalent in guiding us though place, so those same features manifest themselves in the built environment. Thus, it is no coincidence that the phrase "heart of the city" adopts a bodily metaphor (Bloomer and Moore 1977, 39). The heart of the body and the heart of the city refer in both instances to a dynamic center, which has to do less with geometry and more with a gathering of force and energy.

Second, the role of the body as a center of orientation is coupled with its position as prober of material sensations. As I move through place, so my body opens itself to a thick world of sensations, all received haptically. And this haptic genesis is a source of both well-being and discomfort. My eyes, hands, ears, mouth, and nose do not simply compute the world around me, but provide the basis for how a place is received on an affective and emotional level.

When an elevator opens its doors on the world of a modern office, it is not only my eyes that feel the strain as the halogen lights greet me. Rather, the discomfort begins with my eyes but soon moves to the muscles in my arms and legs, before manifesting in a tightness in my chest. The result of this contact is anxiety. Dizziness soon follows, such that I must grip the walls in order to retain my balance. My body is unable to withstand this environment, despite attempting to reassure myself that this experience is simply a question of reacclimating myself to the light. When I move from such an environment and find repose in a dark room, then once more it is not only my eyes that are eased. An entire shift in mood takes over. The heaviness of my body is alleviated by a decrease in the temperature. Yet the temperature is not an objective property of the world, but a result of escaping from the world of light to the world of shadows. My whole body is "lightened" by the darkness, such that by feeling more rooted, the aligning reality of my body is heightened.

The body activates place. But the same is true in reverse: *Place activates the body.* Consider in this light the logical impossibly of being *no*-where. The possibility of experiencing a voided space presupposes having a body to survey that absence. Similarly, the notion of being displaced from one location requires that we are already in another place to observe that movement. We do not, therefore, encounter place as disembodied subjects, occupying an incidental relation to our surroundings. At all times, our bodies are instrumental in placing us.

This twofold motion between place and body thematizes the centrality of place in our reflective conception of self. *We carry places with us.* How can we understand this important claim? One approach would be to suggest that places habituate themselves in our bodies. Just as we become accustomed to certain patterns in the world—hiding beneath the bed when scared, gazing toward the ceiling when thinking, snarling when angry—so part of our experience of place is solidified by repetition and regularity. If I have become accustomed to writing at this desk and in this chair, then over time the surroundings of this environment will gain a normative quality for me, such that without them, my practices are disturbed. Yet the disturbance is not simply a case of finding another place at which to work. Rather, the disturbance is grounded in the residual sediment of my regular place no longer being there, despite its occupancy in my body.

This residue of a familiar place stored in the body hints at another dimension of the body's relation to its environment: Place becomes profoundly constitutive of our sense of self. In this respect, the statement "We carry places with us" gains a primordial significance greater than that indicated by habit alone. By carrying places with us, we open ourselves to a mode of embodiment that has less to do with habit and more to do with the continuity of one's sense of self. Such a mode of embodiment offers a more sustained and deeper commitment to the body's role as retriever of the past. Here, we are talking about not simply the mechanical repetition of routines, such that they orient us in an environment, but the *very facticity of the world existing through the porous retention of our bodies.*

Consider provisionally: Not only do our bodies retain habitualized patterns, but they also reproduce pleasurable, traumatic, and indifferent experiences that we have undergone in the past, all of which conspire to reinforce
or undermine our conception of selfhood. Save for Proust, nowhere is this
intimacy between embodiment and memory better articulated than in Bachelard's *The Poetics of Space*. Indeed, in Bachelard's overwhelmingly topophilic account of intimate places, everything from the "house's entire being"
to the "feel of the tiniest latch" remains in and with us (1994, 15). The
"passionate liaison of our bodies" that makes this retention possible manages to govern the unity of our lives through giving life a corporeal core. Our
bodies not only orient us, but also serve as the basis for an entire history, at
all times producing a self that strives toward continuity through retaining
and returning to places. In a highly significant passage, Bachelard states the
following:

> The finest specimens of fossilized duration concretized as a result
> of long sojourn, are to be found in and through space. The uncon-
> scious abides. *Memories are motionless, and the more securely they
> are fixed in space, the sounder they are.* (9; emphasis added)

In this passage we have the whole of Bachelard's project distilled. Bachelard's
faith in the power of place is unrivaled. By freeing materiality from the unconscious, lived place is presented as having inherent unity of its own. The
implication is striking: Time loses its privileged intimacy with memory, as
place proves itself the more effective absorber of our past. Indeed, for Bachelard, the retention of memory loses none of its vibrancy, precisely thanks to
the holding power of place. Time, on the other hand, is that through which
memory is dispersed.

Memories may well be motionless for Bachelard, but their dependence
on the body is nevertheless pivotal, as he writes evocatively: "When I relive
dynamically the road that 'climbed' the hill, I am quite sure that the road
itself has muscles, or, rather, counter-muscles" (1994, 11). Place and body
form a hybrid, each glancing toward the other for their identity and animation. Note that this is quite different from remembering my body as an
object in the world. How I remember reaching out to touch the cupboard as
a child is structurally different from reexperiencing the manner in which a
place has become part of my bodily matrix. In the first case, I position my
body as something anterior to myself. In the second case, an event appears

through my lived-body in the present. In this way, my body acts as the necessary ground for the past to reappear. Only through there being a body in the first instance is the felt density of place, in its sensuality and texture, to be relived.

EMBODIMENT AND PHENOMENOLOGY

With this provisional account of place and embodiment sketched out, it will be helpful to venture into the historical context of these ideas. With a view of assessing phenomenology's agility, let us consider how both Husserl and Merleau-Ponty have thematized the body as a center of experience, each in their own singular way.

One of Husserl's (1970) central contributions to the phenomenology of embodiment is to establish a distinction between the physical body (*Körper*) and the living body (*Leib*). In making a distinction between the physical body and the living body, Husserl thematizes the peculiarity of the body as intimate and foreign to the ego simultaneously. Thanks to its anchoring role in the world, the body is experienced experientially as a "thing" but also as a living entity reflecting on that status as a "thing," a doubling gesture that Merleau-Ponty (1968) will later rephrase in terms of the body's "reversibility" between being touched and touching. The difference between these categories is that only through the living body, "which is actually given [to me as such] in perception," are we able to "hold sway" in the world, an expression referring to the control we develop via our bodies toward the world (Husserl 1970, 107). Being able to "hold sway" means being able to orient ourselves in a kinesthetic and richly sensual way, conferring a unity upon the world that would be fragmented were the body taken as simply an anonymous and physical unit. For Husserl (103–5), the significance of the living body is that it returns us to the "life-world," a surrounding and taken-for-granted world, considered in a state of pretheoretical apprehension.

I shall have more to say on the life-world and its relationship to spatiality shortly. What I want to draw presently from Husserl in a preparatory way is the focus he places on embodiment as an active engagement with the world, such that the body becomes indispensable in the formation of the spatiality of the world, rather than simply running alongside the world. Not only does the body become constitutive of the world, but the world itself is possible only through the experience of embodiment. Because of this close alignment between world and body, Husserl comes to recognize the body as the center of experience, perception, and, above all, the kinesthetic sensation of moving in place. Only because the body occupies a specific location is the dimensionality of spatiality possible as such.

Phenomenologically, this inextricable bond between place and the embodied subject moving in that place underscores the intentionality of the body, a gesture that achieves nothing less than the vibrancy of external space. Even at this preparatory level, it is clear that Husserl's privileging of the body means that the experience of the world would be impossible through the (non)experience of a disincarnated subject. By emphasizing its active dynamic, Husserl elicits the uniqueness of the body among other things in the world; through it, we discover the constitution of the world, which in turn mirrors the constitution of the self.

If the centrality of the living body is established in Husserl, then it is in Merleau-Ponty that the implications of this role become clear. Indeed, it is precisely with Merleau-Ponty that Husserl's conception of the living body becomes *em*-bodied. This occurs through the development of a self that not only is expressed through having a body, but is fundamentally constituted by *being* a body.

Merleau-Ponty's account of body begins where Husserl's ends: with the idea of the body as being both the "bearer of sensations" and the locus of movement. Yet Merleau-Ponty dissents from Husserl in positing the body as more primary than Husserl's transcendental ego. Against the Husserlian idea that the phenomenological reduction leads us toward a transcendental consciousness, Merleau-Ponty places the body not only at the center of all things, but also at the origin of things, thus elevating the bodily self prior to cognition. In this way, being able to posit the idea of a transcendental ego, for Merleau-Ponty, already presupposes the experience of embodiment, which itself attests to the singular relationship between the "I" and the body. Given this reversal of priority in Merleau-Ponty, the consequences for the unity of experience in the life-world are pervasive. Indeed, time and again, Merleau-Ponty demonstrates that the unity of the body supersedes causal accounts provided by psychology and physiology, and instead becomes profoundly constitutive of selfhood.

Consider his discussion of "phantom limbs" as an example (Merleau-Ponty 2006, 88–102). The problem of the phantom limb is formally simple: How do we account for the illusive "feel" of a limb that is now physically absent? Three options present themselves. One is to assign an error of judgment to the belief that a limb still exists despite the empirical evidence that it is in fact absent. Yet this is clearly misleading, given that "the awareness of the amputated arm as present . . . is not of the kind: 'I think that . . .'" (94). But this does not imply, second, that the feel of the limb is simply a side effect of the body's raw sensation, a system of "blind processes" (91). Nor, finally, is the emergence of a phantom limb simply a case of the imaginary limb "substituting" the missing one in a strictly mechanical manner. In all of these instances, what is missing is the existential meaning of the limb so far as it defines our being-in-the-world. Merleau-Ponty states:

> The phantom limb is not the mere outcome of objective causality; no more is it a *cogitatio*. It could be a mixture of the two only if we could find a means of linking the "psychic" and the "physiological," the "for-itself" and the "in-itself," to each other to form an articulate whole, and to contrive some meeting-point for them. (2006, 89)

Thus, the persistence of the limb's presence pushes us in the direction of "un-Cartesian terms," in the process forming "the idea of an organic thought through which the relation of the 'psychic' and the 'physiological' becomes conceivable" (Merleau-Ponty 2006, 89). This organic idea turns out to be the body's reflexes as being able to "adjust themselves to a 'direction' of the situation" (93). The implication of this immanent direction is that all bodily actions turn out as already being involved in a "*pre-objective* view which is what we call *being-in-the-world*" (92; emphasis added). Far from a chaotic response to random stimuli, bodily movement and orientation are forever with reference to the preservation of any given world. For this reason, Merleau-Ponty is entitled to declare: "Some subjects can come near to blindness without changing their 'world'" (92). This is a telling claim. With it, the objectivity of the world as having a certain number of properties and things is dwarfed by the conduct of the embodied subject in relation to that world. Thanks to this relation, a consistency is established despite the discontinuity of the body itself. As such, something more than the materiality of the body enables the self to endure through time, asserting a fundamental "hybrid" between the physiological and the psychological.

The hybrid force between the physiological and the psychological that enables the world to retain a consistency is secured through what Merleau-Ponty terms the "intentional arc" (2006, 157). By this, he refers to the manner in which all bodily action is inherently temporal, at once projecting an orientation toward the world while simultaneously retaining the past. Because of the "intentional arc," the "unity of the senses, of intelligence, of sensibility and motility" is maintained (157). Applied to the phenomenology of the phantom limb, what this means is that the felt experience of an absent limb is to be viewed as a form of knowledge sedimented into the habitual body. Taking the "intentional arc" as that which gives a particular life its singularity and meaning, the body's role in achieving this end is unparalleled. Nothing less than a complete mode of intelligence is at stake, enveloping the discontinuous breaks in life with a thread of consistency quite distinct from abstract knowledge.

This distinction between embodied knowledge and reflective knowledge sets in a place an incipient tension between what survives bodily change and what falls from that flux despite retaining a presence in the schema of selfhood. This is viscerally clear in the case of the phantom limb. For what we are contending with is, on the one hand, the cognitive knowledge that a particular article of the human body is missing, and on the other, the retention of a life-world that no longer exists, objectively speaking. In the darkness of mutability and mutilation, the body clings to a temporal framework established in the past but projected toward the unmapped future. As a "thing" in the world, but also as the locus of all orientation and identity, the body retains an ambiguity that refuses conceptual determination. Neither solely a memory bound in the past nor simply a stimulus-response in the present, the phantom limb establishes itself as a spectral agency working between the psychological and the physiological, overlapping each domain in a confused and complex way. In Merleau-Ponty's (2006, 93) words, the realm occupies a "middle term between presence and absence."

Central to Merleau-Ponty's analysis of the phantom limb is a view that reaches far beyond the mutilation of the physical body and drops us into a thick narrative, structured by the "intentional arc." Because of this temporal context, the drama of selfhood continues toward a unity that, objectively speaking, no longer exists, as he states: "What it is in us which refuses mutilation and disablement is an *I* committed to a certain physical and inter-human world" (2006, 94). The repression of time is stipulated on a sedimented body memory that affords the mutilated subject a retrieval of a previous unity, as he writes tersely: "Impersonal time continues its course, but personal time is arrested" (96). Furthermore, this process is neither bound to the psychoanalytic unconsciousness nor ascribed to an act of volition. Rather, repression is taken to be a modification of being-in-the-world, such that we are faced with an "abstraction of [first person] existence, which lives on a former experience, or rather on the memory of having had the memory, and so on, until finally only the essential form remains" (96).

The refusal of the past to slip into oblivion is possible only on account of the tremendous intelligibility of the body. What is involved in this intelligibility transcends the Bergsonian idea of habit memory (a motorized memory obtained through the repetition of mechanical actions) and orients us toward a past that is reenacted through the body. It is this relation of memory and reenactment that is vital: It not only renders the body the center of experience, but also implicates the body's retrieval of the past as being deeply emblematic of the specificity of the self, giving the self a temporal density that would be ultimately fragmented were memory a solely cognitive affair.

PLACING PHENOMENOLOGY

With this overview of the book's themes established, our methodological pathway resumes. Here, our critical question must concern how thinking and writing can approach the topic of place and memory. More specifically, how will phenomenology, as the method employed in this book, find its place within this dynamic network of other places? So far, I have suggested that place is a fundamentally a porous concept, falling between idealism and realism. What this means is that any given place is never autonomous in its unity, but forever bleeding and seeping into other places, both those of the past and those of the future. This movement of seepage is what gives a place its ambiguous character. We are never truly "in" place without already having been in another place, and that other place is never merely left behind within a history of forgotten places. Rather, coming into a place means inserting that lived history into the present. At the mercy of our bodies, judging where one place begins and another ends is thus an artificial distinction enforced by rational abstraction.

The ambiguity of place extends also to the theory that contends with the concept. A system of thought is never alone in its quest. Rather, it enters the scene of thought within the context of an already-established arrangement of ideas and schools of thought. Just as a material place defines itself against the plastic borders of other places, so thinking opens itself to a swarm of influences, some of which strengthen the original position, while others seek to displace it.

How would we go about "placing" phenomenology? The very fact of posing this question suggests that phenomenology's placement was either taken-for-granted or otherwise in risk of becoming displaced. If phenomenology has been displaced by other factors—not least by subsequent modes of thought—then does putting it in place mean committing it to a static position? This need not be the case. Instead, to place phenomenology we would have to recognize, first, how the identity of phenomenology has been sculpted historically; and, second, what defines phenomenology as a discrete mode of thinking about place. Such is the task of the remainder of the introduction. We shall set out to discern phenomenology's special relationship with spatiality, and in the process provide an overview of the methodology as a whole. The result of this close-knit bond between phenomenology and place will be the placement of phenomenology itself.

The suggestion that phenomenology has become displaced, as though reduced to a static point within an ongoing narrative, or even pushed beyond that narrative, is a legitimate way to begin placing phenomenology. By 1963, Heidegger was already in a position to question the legacy of phenomenology: "The age of phenomenological philosophy," he writes lamentably, "seems to be over. It is already taken as something past which is only recorded historically along other schools of philosophy" (1975a, 241). Of course, the history of phenomenology, in addition to being a history of French and German philosophy, is also a history of modifications and erasures. What I mean by this is that phenomenology in the strict Husserlian sense largely (though not exclusively) survives through critical engagement with the works of Heidegger, Merleau-Ponty, and to a lesser extent Derrida. More recently, and perhaps more tellingly, Jean-Luc Marion's (1998, 2002) engagement with phenomenology exemplifies an engagement with series of pressing issues not limited to Derrida's (1998) much cited "metaphysics of presence" criticism. The modification of Husserl's transcendental phenomenology is evident, however, in Heidegger, Sartre, and Merleau-Ponty's alteration of the *epoché*, an indispensable component of the Husserlian framework.

For Husserl (1970, 135–41), the epoché would mark a fundamental rupture with naturalistic (i.e., objective) philosophy, promising a philosophy in which all existing beliefs and validities concerning the world are suspended or bracketed (*Einklammerung*). The result of this, Husserl argues, would be a radical revision of the pregiven assumptions about the world. Husserl's emphasis on what is immediately given to consciousness as an appearance testifies to the concerns of phenomenology. In its classical formulation, phenomenology is an attitude (rather than a system) framed, above all, by the primacy of *things*. As such, the epoché does not designate a denial of the reality of the objective world, but simply a suspension from, in Husserl's words, "any critical position-taking which is interested in their truth or falsity, even any position on their guiding idea of an objective knowledge of the world" (135). In effect, the world continues as it did prior to the application of the epoché; only now, theoretical judgments are reserved in advance.

The eventual result of the phenomenological epoché is Husserl's celebrated *transcendental reduction*. Reduction refers to the thematization between subjective experience and the life-world, which Husserl describes as "the world constantly given to us as actual in our concrete world-life" (1970, 51). Thus, whereas the epoché is the methodological procedure by which assumptions about the world are bracketed, the reduction—and let us note there are several reductions—leads to a recognition of the life-world *as* a phenomenon. The implication is that the life-world comes to be seen as transcendentally constituted, a condition of experience by which "transcendental subjectivity [is shown to be] always functioning ultimately and is thus 'absolute'" (153). In other words, for Husserl, the phenomenological reduction leaves open the transcendental ego that renders givenness possible in the first instance. With this move, givenness is acknowledged as being constitutive of empirical experience. The importance of this thought is that through the phenomenological reduction, appearances are shown to be appropriated by consciousness, rather than isolated in a world above or beyond experience.

Given the demands of Husserl's task (it is telling that Husserl himself would describe the commitment to phenomenology as comparable to nothing less than a "religious conversion" [1970, 137]), Merleau-Ponty and Heidegger altered the Husserlian epoché and primacy of the transcendental ego respectively, and instead turned their attention toward an existential and hermeneutic phenomenology, in which Husserl's emphasis on cognition is replaced by a concern with how the body and its moods bridge humans and their world.

For Heidegger, the centrality of Husserl's account of the transcendental ego is a shortcoming. Thus, his modification of Husserlian phenomenology has two aims. First, to prioritize Being as ontologically primary. Second, to overcome Husserl's Cartesian methodology and terminology (Heidegger's [1996, 23–34] omission of Husserl in the description of phenomenology in *Being and Time* is a clear illustration of this distance from his former mentor).

Of the first aim, Heidegger's account of the "forgetting of Being" carries with it a metaphysical distinction between the ontological and the ontic: *ontological* referring to the Being of being, and *ontic* referring to the being of Being; namely, entities, things, and humans. The distinction is important in that Heidegger's polemical stance against Western philosophy assumes a focus on the primacy of the ontic over the ontological. Since Husserl takes phenomena to be the main concern of transcendental phenomenology, Heidegger is obliged to assimilate Husserl's phenomenology within this tradition of ontic primacy, stating: "*For us* phenomenological reduction means leading phenomenological vision back from the apprehension of a being, whatever may be the character of that apprehension, to the understanding of the being of this being (projecting upon the way it is unconcealed)" (1982, 21; italics in original).

Despite Heidegger's divergence from Husserl, in the opening to his *Phenomenology of Perception*, Merleau-Ponty would cite Heidegger's *Being and Time* as "no more than an explicit account of the 'natürlicher Weltbegriff' or the 'Lebenswelt' which Husserl, towards the end of his life, identified as the central theme of phenomenology" (2006, viii). If Merleau-Ponty is correct to suggest that Heidegger's descriptions of everydayness are indeed a furtherance of the ontological precedent Husserl established with the life-world, then where does this leave the phenomenological epoché?

Merleau-Ponty's own position to the epoché and the phenomenological reduction in *Phenomenology of Perception* is seemingly clear: "The most important lesson which the reduction teaches us is the impossibility of a complete reduction" (2006, xv). Should we take this to indicate a dissent from Husserl? To do so would risk misunderstanding Merleau-Ponty's position. The impossibility of the reduction does not warrant its failure. Instead, the impossibility of the reduction testifies to its multifarious nature and endless potential. Thus, Merleau-Ponty is led to conclude that "there is no thought which embraces all our thought" (xv). Indeed, it is for this reason that Merleau-Ponty understands Husserl's return to the reduction as "constantly reexamining the possibility of the reduction" (xv). Phenomenology's incisive dynamism means resisting the determination of fixed concepts, leaving the phenomenologist as the "perpetual beginner" (xv).

Given that Merleau-Ponty recognizes both the limits and the potential of the reduction, then where does this leave the methodological epoché? Despite Merleau-Ponty's apparently receptive stance toward the reduction, in the same passage we also read:

> Philosophy itself must not take itself for granted, in so far as it may
> have managed to say something true; that it is an ever-renewed ex-
> periment in making its own beginning; that it consists wholly in
> the description of this beginning, and finally, that radical reflection
> amounts to a consciousness of its own dependence on an unreflec-
> tive life which is its initial situation, unchanging, given once and for
> all. (2006, xv–xvi)

This is a startling passage. On the one hand, Merleau-Ponty claims that the
impossibility of the complete reduction is itself constitutive of phenomenology's resistance to dogma. On the other hand, we are now told that any such
attempt at rupturing natural consciousness through attending to a perpetual
beginning is itself a mode of presuppositioned engagement. It might seem
that if Merleau-Ponty is correct, then the beginning of Husserlian phenomenology becomes untenable. But should we read the passage as a directive or
as a warning? If we are to take Merleau-Ponty as saying that radical reflection
consists in a mode of dependent reflection, then does this wholly undermine
the potential of the epoché? This answer is clearly not, given that complete
abeyance from the natural world does not negate gradients of suspension
being involved. Merleau-Ponty's argument for the dependence on an unreflective life is not, therefore, filtered out through the phenomenological epoché.
Instead, he seems to be saying that unreflective life acts as a residuum that
renders the distance between experience and reflection ambiguous, and not,
as Husserl would have it, transparent.

The impossibility of a complete reduction confers a pervasive ambiguity
upon phenomenology. As Merleau-Ponty points out elsewhere in the *Phenomenology of Perception*, "Ambiguity is of the essence of human existence, and
everything we live or think has always several meanings" (2006, 196). But not
only does the world present different meanings, those same meanings emerge
as both transitional and reversible. Phenomenology's intimacy with the genetic
patterns of emergence means that this transitional formation can be captured
without undermining the ambiguity peculiar to the appearance of things *between* other things. Further, surrounding this internal ambiguity is a broader
ambiguity caused by the tension between phenomenology's concurrent focus
on a theoretical and abstracted environment. As I will go on to state, it is precisely this receptivity toward ambiguity that marks phenomenology's force.

The transition from Husserl to Heidegger and then to Merleau-Ponty is
telling: Despite the differences between these thinkers, the movement reveals a

thematic unity. Together, both Heidegger's subtraction of the transcendental ego from Husserl and Merleau-Ponty's alteration of the phenomenological epoché carry a commitment to second seeing, the primacy of the life-world, and an emphasis on description. What I propose to do now is to survey these salient features.

1. Second Seeing

As we have seen, Husserl's emphasis on the unity of the pregiven world, accessed via the epoché, leads to a renewed apprehension of the appearance of things. The result of this renewal is not a denial of the objective world, but an increased attention toward the world. Husserl's celebrated dictum, "to the things themselves!" is thus simultaneously a *return* to those things. The twofold motion between coming-into and inquiring-back-to is central to Husserl's methodology, establishing, as it does, a simultaneous motion, to put it in Heideggerian terms, from concealment to disclosure. What Husserl tells us is that things are *immanent*; that is, the world of appearances is always "below" pregiven experience. It is precisely the immanence-of-thought-as-concealed that Husserl (1970, 113–18) reproaches Kant for ignoring. Indeed, as far as this truth remains "hidden" from Kant, then seeing things renewed becomes impossible.

The hidden immanence of things can also be said, as indeed Merleau-Ponty does, of phenomenology itself, claiming that "phenomenology can be practised and identified as a manner or style of thinking, that it existed as a movement before arriving at complete awareness of itself as a philosophy" (2006, viii). Here, too, we discover an ambiguous relation from the pregiven world to the world bracketed. Phenomenology becomes formed *as* phenomenology through disjoining from its previously unaware mode, simultaneously incorporating that unformed modality within phenomenology itself. In this way, the second seeing of things does not dispense with the pregiven world, as though the epoché somehow superseded that world. Instead, it is through the pregiven world that the second seeing of that world becomes possible. As such, the relation between the epoché and the natural attitude is fundamentally dynamic, reminding us of Husserl's emphasis on the twofold motion between coming-into and inquiring-back-to.

The phenomenological renewal of things is not limited to the visual realm. Rather, the term "second seeing" refers to the totality of sensual experience, incorporating, above all, a haptic sensibility that establishes itself in distinction to the ocularcentrism of Western philosophy (Casey 2007; Merleau-Ponty 2006; Pallasmaa 2007). Because of this openness to the smell, touch, taste, and sound of appearances, the detachment of the gaze is countered by the embodied spatiotemporality of the other senses, each of which works in tandem with vision. In the opening of *Being Given*, Jean-Luc Marion presents us with the following thought:

> The primacy of one of the senses (vision, but also any other) is important only if perception finally determines appearance, therefore only if appearance itself in the final analysis falls under the jurisdiction of perception—in short, only if appearance refers at the outset to the apparition of the thing itself, where, as in trial by fire, the apparatus of appearance and even of perception is consumed in order to let arise what is at issue. (2002, 7)

Marion's remark on the primacy of the senses underscores the demand for phenomenology to remain open to the "thing itself at the heart of its . . . appearance" (2002, 8). By privileging appearances, the dominance of vision becomes less problematic, insofar as appearances become "the sole truly decisive matter" (8). Above all, then, phenomenology as a method is marked by its reliance on things taking course, giving full weight, not to the perception of things in advance, but, in Marion's words, to the work of "travel[ling] in tandem with the phenomenon, as if protecting it and clearing a path for it by eliminating roadblocks" (9).

2. The Life-World

I have mentioned the life-world in passing. But let us consider the importance of this idea for our inquiry as a whole. In order to assess the importance of the life-world, it is important to familiarize ourselves with the theoretical background, against which Husserl's position emerges. Early on in the *Crisis*, Husserl situates the life-world as "the forgotten meaning-fundament of natural science" (1970, 48). Husserl's point is that scientific discourse, personified through Galileo's pure geometry, has replaced the real world with a "world of idealities" (48). The result of this substitution is an abstraction from "the sources of truly immediate intuition," which are transmitted into the "art of surveying" without any explicit knowledge of its idealistic constitution (49). Galileo's failure, preempting Kant's, was to overlook the "meaning-giving achievement" (49) from which geometry arose; namely, the intuited world. Husserl's claim is that the origin of geometry occurs by way of inexact shapes, which are then replaced with their ideal counterparts. This failure to attend to origins leads to the "illusion" of geometry as being an intuitive inquiry.

All this seems pertinent in theoretical terms, but does this warning against geometry have any broader significance? Husserl's rationale for this account of origins is to intervene in the "crisis," which has divorced science from life, resulting in a project without an ethical basis (a crisis Heidegger [1977] will later pursue through his striking analysis of "the Nothing," of which science excludes). In order to restore this crevice, Husserl is proposing that we perform the epoché, marking a return to the formation of the scientific method through "everyday induction" (1970, 50). In this way, the idealistic dimension of natural science will become profoundly related to the indeterminacy and vagueness encountered in daily life. Husserl's injunction to return to the things themselves, therefore, is as much a return to the transcendental significance of the givenness of those things as it is to amend the supposedly objective rationalism, which lays claim to comprehending objects.

Husserl's project in *The Crisis* is to open the life-world to an ontologically situated study, in which the static conception of abstract idealities is countered by the genetic dynamism of experience. The emphasis on genesis here is vital. Given Husserl's emphasis on the transcendental and eidetic core of phenomenology, how can this be reconciled with the mutable domain of the life-world? Indeed, for Husserl this conflict, materialized in the anthropological relativity of different life-worlds, outwardly constitutes an "embarrassment" (1970, 139). Husserl's response is to posit "a general structure" which redeems the life-world of its relativity and aligns it with the "the 'same' structures [of] the objective sciences" (139); namely, its spatiotemporal existence. Such a structure is said to occupy an "invariant" relationship with the life-world (173).

To understand how invariance can coexist with the indeterminacy of the life-world, we need to turn to §74 of *Ideas*, where we find Husserl discussing the notion of "morphological concepts" (1990, 166). Prior to Husserl's criticism of Galileo, already in *Ideas* we find a critique of "the geometer" (166). As with the critique of the abstractedness of science, Husserl wants to address the dynamic relationality inherent in ideal structures. As such, the "morphological concepts" that the geometer veers away from become "conceptually or terminologically fixed" (166). Through giving a place and a time to a concept, the emphasis on morphology presents a distinct challenge to the ideal essence, in which the seeing of things is lost. For Husserl, this is the mark of the ideal: its invisibility. In turn, the transition from the morphological to the ideal entails a qualitative loss of the thingness of the object. The discontent with the vagueness and relativity of appearances leads science to deliver appearances of their imperfections, evident in Husserl's claim that morphological essences only "approximate" their ideal counterpart, a point we will return to in the third chapter (166).

3. The Uncanny

A final but no less important reason for the centrality of the life-world is that it provides fertile ground for disturbing the familiarity of what has been taken-for-granted. The importance of this disturbance is such that strangeness and uncanniness become emblematic of second seeing, a point I briefly alluded to in my prefatory remark concerning photography and phenomenology. We will go on to explore this uncanny terrain in the following chapters, but for now let me mention how this relation between everydayness and uncanniness is thematically central to the book as a whole.

We have already sensed how the everyday world establishes itself in a pregiven way. What this means in experiential terms is that things are taken in a unified way. The world *just is*, and in it, things find their place. Without having to think about it, I am already involved in a relationship with the world, my body cojoining me with a world that is as much a part of me as I am a part of it. Here, in this human world, certain things that are valued and hold meaning stand before other things in an interchangeable relationship. Hungry, the smell of croissants assails my senses. Thirsty, the absence of water becomes a significant part of my being. In modes of melancholy and joy, the world alters, its tone and atmosphere shifting in a reciprocal exchange to my own being. But the place of things in the world is not fixed, and when experience is interrupted, then we become aware of their nothingness as a presence, a point both Sartre and Heidegger labor repeatedly. In such a moment, the world's texture undergoes change, its mood shifting. Above all else, the disruption or absence of things in the world draws our attention to the facticity of those things in the first place. This arc of facticity can range from the banality of being locked out of one's home to the trauma of losing a limb. In each case, the entrenched familiarity threatens to overthrow our expectations of how things ought to be. Such an estrangement from the natural world is, I would argue, at the heart of phenomenology. One of this book's main claims is that phenomenology's overarching achievement is to draw our attention to the strangeness of things. Phenomenology does this through attending to the natural world in an unnatural manner. In other words, through bracketing our pregiven understanding of things, those same things persist in the world in a synthesis of both familiarity and unfamiliarity. In order to render this claim clear, let us consult a passage from Merleau-Ponty, which deserves to be cited at length. In it, he is discussing the destabilizing motion of Cézanne's painting:

> We live in the midst of man-made objects, among tools, in houses, streets, cities, and most of the time we see them only through the human actions which put them to use. We become used to thinking that all of this exists necessarily and unshakably. Cézanne's painting suspends these habits of thought and reveals the base of inhuman nature upon which man has installed himself. This is why Cézanne's people are strange, as if viewed by a creature of another species. Nature itself is stripped of the attributes which make it ready for animistic communions: there is no wind in the landscape, no movement on the Lac d'Annecy; the frozen objects hesitate at the beginning of the world. It is an unfamiliar world in which one is uncomfortable and which forbids all human effusiveness. (1993, 66)

There are at least five central points in this incisive passage to consider: (1) Due to its familiarity, the everyday surrounding world assumes the impression of being unshakable. (2) Yet this impression is essentially a superimposition of value upon an "inhuman nature." (3) In the suspension of this superimposition, familiarity is effectively dislodged. (4) The result of this suspension is the strange emergence of a frozen world. (5) Finally, the reversal of the inhuman being superimposed upon the human induces the experience of discomfort.

The relation between aesthetic experience and ontological disruption is not incidental. As an aesthetic gesture in itself, the freezing of the life-world means that, what is taken-for-granted is thus shown in its transcendental givenness. This, indeed, constitutes a necessary estrangement from the world, insofar as it is precisely the everyday world in its familiar assurance that is most susceptible to sudden reversal. The "creature of another species," which stares down upon the world, does so having arisen from that world. By its very strangeness, the otherness of Merleau-Ponty's creature is an inhabitant of the world prior to its being dismantled. In this way, the reversal of the creature's perspective comes to incarnate the dialectical conflict between human and inhuman nature, so far absorbed into pregiven experience. As this intimacy between the unthinking domain of habitual thought and the orientation of familiarity is suspended, the suspension does not entail a breakage. Instead, we discover a transparency in which the otherness of being-in-the-world is amplified.

Taken in a broad light, phenomenology's perceptive relation to "creature[s] of another species" can be seen as a defining characteristic of its positive contribution to our understanding of human experience. Indeed, inasmuch as phenomenology calls our attention to the fact that there are *things* in the first instance, then its fundamental movement is oriented toward the strange and the uncanny.

Here, my usage of "uncanny" takes as its point of departure the description that emerges from Freud's famous essay on the topic: namely, a "species of the frightening that goes back to what was once well known and had been long familiar" (2003, 124). With this definition, a set of disjointed thoughts arrive. Above all, we are drawn to the fact that the uncanny is to be understood fundamentally as an effect, a felt experience that disturbs the body, resulting in a departure from the everyday. Yet no less a displacement from the everyday, the uncanny simultaneously places us in the midst of the familiar. Here a disturbance occurs: The uncanny refuses to concede to stillness, and instead presents us with something genuinely novel: *an augmented familiarity*, thus (un)familiar to the core (*unheimlich*). Close enough to be recognized as broadly familiar, the world of the uncanny nevertheless subtly manipulates that familiar screen, thus engineering a shiver down the spine of anyone caught in its rays. At the heart of this shiver is the sense that what has so far been thought of as inconspicuous in its being is, in fact, charged with a creeping strangeness.

This creeping gesture points to one of the uncanny's enduring characteristics: The term resists unequivocal definition, leading not only to experiential anxiety, but to conceptual doubt, too. Based in the *disjunction of opposed twins—familiar/unfamiliar, near/far, homely/unhomely—the uncanny circumvents laws of logic, yet at the same time frees itself from the need to be resolved of its paradoxical status. At its genesis, the uncanny takes up residence in the manifold space between experience and thought, perfectly at ease with its ability to invoke repulsion and allure in the subject experiencing the uncanny.*

The result of this disturbance: Things that are assumed present are now witnessed as absent, things hitherto thought to be homely emerge as un-homely, and entities we once thought dead materialize as being quite undead. In this way, the uncanny is a "species of the frightening" that lurks within the kernel of our epistemic desires, dismantling the very foundations of "truth" and leaving us with a porous divide between the real and the unreal. With-out the certainty that familiarity is immune to its own defamiliarization, the uncanny resists domestication, forever seeping through our clutches as it pre-pares to bleed into each and every domain of familiar life.

Experientially, the fright constitutes a moment of apprehension rather than outright terror. The uncanny is strange rather than shocking, weird rather than annihilating. Often, we fail to recognize the power of the un-canny, its workings registered only belatedly and in parched fragments. At that time, we turn to ourselves in order to ask the following question: *What just happened to me?* A feeling of disempowerment occurs. The unity of self-identity becomes vulnerable. No longer do we feel at ease within ourselves. The uncanny leaves us in a state of disquiet, unnerved precisely because we lack the conceptual scheme to put the uncanny in its rightful "place."

And no places are more conducive to the uncanny than the places that we cherish, that we hold dear to us, be it the places in which we dwell or the places of our own bodies. Both the human home and the human body breed and engender themselves toward a series of mysterious encounters, with which the following pages will begin to contend.

But how do things become effectively transformed from everyday ob-jects placed in the world to entities shimmering with an otherworldly halo, transplanted to Merleau-Ponty's "beginning of the world" (1993, 66)? Let us recall how Husserl has spoken of the truth of things being "hidden" (1970, 103–18). If things in the world are hidden, then they nevertheless remain present, spatially and temporally. Only now, once returned to phe-nomenologically, a modification occurs, such that how we previously ap-prehended an object becomes a space of distortion and incursion. Such is the power of this movement that for philosopher Graham Harman, nothing less than a philosophy of "weird realism" is at stake. Justifiably positioning Husserl within the same sphere as H. P. Lovecraft, Harman writes: "Just as Lovecraft turns prosaic New England towns into the battleground of extradimensional fiends, Husserl's phenomenology converts simple chairs and mailboxes into elusive units that emit partial, contorted surfaces" (2008, 336).

Although the premise that Husserl "converts" objects is somewhat contentious—since it is surely the case that the elusive dimension of those objects is
there all along—Harman touches on a fruitful relation between the prosaic
and the otherworldly, which is implicit in the environment of the life-world itself, and in many ways finds special fruition within the writings of Lovecraft.
As Harman goes on to argue, unlike the enigma of the Kantian noumenal
realm—which fundamentally precludes human understanding—Lovecraft's
world is terrifying precisely because of the incursion of "finite malignant beings" in a finite world (2008, 342). The reversal from a rational infinity to an
irrational finitude draws Lovecraft's own creatures into the everyday world,
conferring upon them a spatiotemporal existence lacking in Kant's noumenal
sphere. The result of this invasion, for Harman, is that "[h]umans cease to be
masters in their own house" (342), while phenomenology itself becomes the
breeding ground for horror.

Harman's claim for phenomenology *as* horror hinges upon the inextricable bind between the reality of phenomenal objects and their aligning
weirdness. As irreducible to a fixed set of properties, "phenomenal things"
are thus constantly evading definition, and instead give way to the yawning
abyss that separates the phenomenality of things from their totality. Prising
apart this unity is the enigmatic structure of intentionality, which, although
firmly placing us in the world, nevertheless stands upon a precarious interplay between absence and presence (Harman 2008, 362). Citing Lovecraft,
Harman writes:

> Intentional object are everywhere and nowhere; they "bubble and
> blaspheme mindlessly" at every point in the cosmos. Although vividly
> present as soon as we acknowledge them, intentional objects express
> their reality only by drawing neighbouring objects into their orbit,
> and these things in turn are only present by enslaving others. (362)

Because of this excess in phenomenality, things in the world remain both elusive and insufficient, calling into question all modes of apprehending those
things in an intelligible way. Harman's own contribution to this abyss is to redirect the emphasis toward the "existential threat" at the heart of intentionality. In conferring an affective quality upon intentionality, Harman thematizes
the brute weirdness unmasked through the phenomenological method.

If there was any doubt as to the visceral relation between phenomenology and the strange and weird, then consider Lovecraft's (1985) own richly

philosophical tale, "From Beyond," which, taken with the seriousness it deserves, presents a compelling contribution to the phenomenological corpus. As with several of Lovecraft's tales, the story is one of a maligned enlightenment. The protagonist and victim, Crawford Tillinghast, is a scientist attempting to gain access to "strange, inaccessible worlds" (90). But in doing so, Lovecraft sounds an ominous warning:

> That Crawford Tillinghast should ever have studied science and philosophy was a mistake. These things should be left to the frigid and impersonal investigator for they offer two equally tragic alternatives to the man of feeling and action; despair if he fail in his quest, and terrors unutterable and unimaginable if he succeed. (89–90)

Unheeded, the warning does nothing to prevent Tillinghast from questioning the reality of his surroundings, chiding in particular the limitation of the five senses, all of which fail to capture reality in absolute terms. With a belief that untouched worlds exist at "our very elbows," Tillinghast proceeds to describe the plans he has made for gaining access to those worlds: "Within twenty-four hours that machine near the table will generate waves acting on unrecognised sense-organs that exist in us as atrophied or rudimentary vestiges" (Lovecraft 1985, 90). Following this confession, Tillinghast then goes on to state that what has so far been deemed invisible—"that at which cats prick up their ears after midnight"—will become visible (90). And so in an attic laboratory the experiment dawns: Ultraviolet is cast, resulting in such a radical shift in sensory impressions that the pineal gland—celebrated for confounding Descartes—becomes an object of scientific scrutiny: "That gland is the great sense-organ of organs—*I have found out*. It is like sight in the end, and transmits visual pictures to the brain. If you are normal, that is the way you ought to get most of it . . . I mean get most of the evidence from *beyond*" (92, italics in original).

Thereafter, the narrator of the tale is overwhelmed with immemorial scenes of dead gods and black columns, eventually giving rise to "sightless, soundless space," pockmarked by the distorted face of Crawford Tillinghast, while all around him the familiar world becomes impregnated with "indescribable shapes both alive and otherwise . . . mixed in disgusting disarray, and close to every known thing were whole worlds of alien, unknown entities" (93–95). Worse still, even within this reversal of homely and alien objects, an overlapping is said to occur, such that a "semi-fluid" form emerges, leaving no room for borders and boundaries. Yet, despite this disorder, Tillinghast retains his enthusiasm for the project, stating notably: "Space belongs to me, do you hear?" (96). As is typical of Lovecraft, by the end, the events have resulted in death, madness, and a fundamental lack of narrative resolution.

Does the manner with which the world is uncovered in this short story bear anything more than a passing resemblance to the phenomenological method? That Lovecraft points us toward a hidden world already proximate to our own, and yet blocked by a fault in our sensory apparatus, orients us in the right direction. Along with this, a transition from the invisible to the visible takes place, such that "sight in the end" opens up. Lovecraft's alternative description of the "sight in the end" is "augmented sight" (1985, 95). In both cases, what is being captured is the rediscovery of appearances, which I previously termed "second seeing."

Consistent with Husserl, the "beyond" in Lovecraft's story is far from a noumenal realm, transcendental to appearances. Although strange and inaccessible, the world remains "at our very elbows," now revealed through the destruction of sensory inhibition and sedimentation. Only, in Lovecraft, what has been revealed in this second seeing is basically abject. Devoid of all form, what lies beyond comes toward the finite world with piercing clarity, distorting our accepted categories of experience. But what is singularly phenomenological about this movement is not the incursion of a malign force—which may or may not be a factor—but the modulation of the everyday world in accordance with "unnatural pryings into the unthinkable" (Lovecraft 1985, 91). *Unnatural pryings into the unthinkable*. With this, Lovecraft returns us to Merleau-Ponty's vision of an "inhuman nature," in which "nature itself is stripped of the attributes which make it ready for animistic communions" (Merleau-Ponty 1993, 66). We are witnessing something that remains "unthinkable" precisely because for the most part that thing is layered in the thick patina of human experience.

More broadly, therefore, what is being summoned in this prying is a parallel to Husserl's natural attitude, taking the natural attitude to mean "straightforwardly living toward whatever objects are given" (Husserl 1970, 144). By putting this mode into question, "a completely different sort of waking life" becomes possible, consisting of a "transformation of the thematic consciousness of the world" (144). It is especially in the late Husserl, where this emphasis on transformation becomes a recurring theme, that the correspondence with Lovecraft strengthens. Just as Lovecraft accounts the creation of a new world, composed initially from a sound, the quality of

which is of "surpassing wildness," before moving toward an intense coldness (recalling here Merleau-Ponty's "frozen objects"), and then arriving
finally at a series of "confused pictures," in which "huge animate things"
roam (Lovecraft 1985, 94). Just as Lovecraft accounts this, so Husserl (1970,
145) places us in a world of "never thematically investigated types," all of
which serve to constitute the natural attitude and yet at the same time remain
wholly obscured to that pregiven experience.

The synthesis between the natural and the unnatural is at the core of both
Lovecraft's and phenomenology's relation to the strange and weird. Above
all, what is "weird" is less a matter of content, and more the position we as
human subjects adopt in relation to that content, leading Husserl to conclude
thus: "Clearly, only through a *total change* of the natural attitude, such that
we no longer live, as heretofore, as human beings within natural existence,
constantly effecting the validity of the pregiven world; rather, we must constantly deny ourselves this" (148, italics in original).

Having ensnared a "strange, inaccessible world," the remainder of Lovecraft's work retains an additional phenomenological dimension through the
author's sober and clinical descriptions of decidedly otherworldly entities.
The conflation of the poetic and scientific, a union prized in Bachelard's reveries, establishes a tension between that which refuses to give itself over to
human experience and the singularly human response in the face of that unnameable thing. In his penetrating book on Lovecraft, Michel Houellebecq
formulates the following claim: "*The more monstrous and inconceivable the
events and entities described, the more precise and clinical the description.* A
scalpel is needed to dissect the unnameable" (2008, 79; italics in original).
Houellebecq's identification of the unnameable with the clinical creates a
mood of detachment, no longer bound by an agitated rhetoric. Mirroring
this fixed gaze toward alien phenomenon, Lovecraft's unnerving attention
on the details of those strange things only heightens their distance from our
everyday conception of things.

In a corresponding way, Lovecraft's methodology gestures toward Husserl's emphasis on returning to the strangeness of things through descriptive
precision, a motif that would later reach its literary summit in Sartre's (1969,
126) celebrated account of the root of a chestnut tree. In Husserl, this literary expression gains its origin in the philosopher's commitment to unraveling
the facticity of things in their preconceptual wilderness. Yet despite this commitment, seldom, as Harman (2008, 354) correctly points out, do we find an
extensive library of descriptions within Husserl's work. All that arises is the

allusion to these descriptions via Husserl's construction of the phenomenological reduction. Accordingly, in *The Crisis*, Husserl (1970, 120) charts the
structural relation between the "old familiar field of life" and the life-world
in terms of the former haunting the latter. "Nowhere else," so he writes, "is
it so frequent that the explorer is met by logical ghosts emerging out of the
dark, formed in the old familiar and effective conceptual patterns, as paradoxical antinomies, logical absurdities" (120). Thus, while the ingredients
are established in Husserl, it falls to later phenomenologists—especially
Merleau-Ponty, Sartre, and Bachelard—to apply those ingredients to everyday phenomenon: a connection that returns us, finally, to Merleau-Ponty's
evocation of a "creature of another species" (1993, 66).

Why have I gone to this length to place strangeness and uncanniness at
the heart of phenomenology? More than an arbitrary discursion, what is
at stake in this relation between the uncanny and phenomenology is the
essence of memory itself. Even a glance at its overall structure reveals a set
of striking phenomenon. After all, what can be fused with a greater intensity of strangeness than the experience of remembering, which by dint of
its structure, invites a no-longer-existing world, fundamentally absent in
its structure and discolored in its content, into the experience of the still-
unfolding present? What, furthermore, can be stranger than the sudden reexperiencing of a place, so far consigned to darkness, which reappears in
the present without so much as a moment's warning, less even a memento
to stimulate such a return, in the process splitting identity into several often
conflicting fractions?

Precisely because it comes to us without warning, we can thus speak of
memory in terms of its being as much bound with subjectivity as it is the materiality of objects in the world. In a word, *the places in which we live, live in
us.* More precisely, those places live in our bodies, instilling an eerie sense of
our own embodied selves as being the sites of a spatial history that is visible
and invisible, present and absent.

This doubling of experience—a theme that shall be returned to perva-
sively—points back to Freud's idea of the uncanny as involving an essential
ambivalence. After all, for Freud (2003, 132), the conjunction of *"heimlich"*
and *"unheimlich"* does not result in a Hegelian synthesis, but instead profits
from a free-floating oscillation. Quoting Gutzkow's line "We call that *unheimlich*; you call it *heimlich*," Freud writes: "This reminds us that this word
'*heimlich*' is not unambiguous but belongs to two sets of ideas, which are not
mutually contradictory, but very different from each other—the one relating

to what is familiar and comfortable, the other to what is concealed and kept hidden" (132).

The uncanny's dual nature of being hidden and familiar concurrently points to the singularly peculiar quality of the memory of place in particular. Three distinct features, all of which will be developed in turn, can be provisionally spelled out in this respect.

First, with its origins in the body, the materialization of memory can often assume an automatic appearance, thus being "hidden behind the familiar image of a living person" (135). Here, "automatic" refers to instances of recall, in which the body's recollection of experience explicitly manifests itself to the subject as a "thing" in the world, rather than an interwoven aspect of that subject's history. Faced, as we will be in later chapters, with a set of memories that submit to their own occult teleology—"occult" in the sense of hidden—each marking their presence through a set of symptomatic manifestations, the body as doing the work of memory takes on the form of an automaton. In such cases, the body begins to articulate things from the past that we ourselves as self-conscious subjects are privy to only in passing. But this symptomatic appearance of the past is not limited to instances of traumatic memory (although, to be sure, nowhere is the automated teleology of body memory clearer than in traumatic memory). Rather, the strange experience of the body's temporal workings spilling over into self-consciousness can be sensed even at the most prosaic level.

A chance encounter with an unfamiliar place can invoke a manifold response in the lived-body, the origin of which is not solely traceable to the objective features of the place, such as light, heat, and atmosphere. The place arouses something in the body, an intermingling of different sensations. Unaware of the precise orientation of the body's stirrings, the visitor to the place is left with only a vague sense of uncertainty if not anxiety. In the conjunction of body and place, something of the past is invoked, but it is not quite clear what and whose past is at stake. At such a point, the only conclusion we can make is that the body has sensed an invisible agency, of which cognition has yet to conceptualize.

Central to this anxiety is the uncertainty masking the body's work. Ernst Jentsch, of whom Freud's paper on the uncanny is indebted, writes thus: "The unpleasant impression is well known that readily arises in many people when they visit collections of wax figures, panopticons, and panoramas. In semi-darkness it is often especially difficult to distinguish a life-size wax or similar figure from a human person" (1996, 12). The emphasis here on "semi-darkness" parallels the movement of uncertainty, as our bodies creak and groan in their expression of a past not yet fully lived. The chimerical effect of this internal creaking is the experience of a life, neither present nor absent, haunting the caverns of inner experience.

Throughout this experience, the body's work is involuntary and largely noncognitive. Notably, throughout Freud's text, we read of both "unintentional returns" and "involuntary repetitions." In both cases, an agency other than our strict self-awareness is been guided by a motive concealed to the visible eye. This undercurrent of a hidden agency sets in place a menacing tone to the embodied uncanny, such that we can never be sure that the body's motivations align with "our" own. Does the body lead us astray in its desire for a unity that has since been ravished through time? Such a question will be of central concern to us. What will emerge in this body-centered study of memory is a challenge to the centrality of human experience, where that experience has so far been defined in terms of rationality and cognition. By putting in place (literally) a distinctly noncognitive mode of memory, the inanimate world of materiality will be shown as being constituted by a dormant force of alien influences, some of which are retained in the world while others situate themselves in the human body.

Second, in light of the automated emergence of body memory, the shift from the *heimlich* to the *unheimlich* can be understood as a movement of becoming conscious of the body as thing having its own independent history and experiences. This complex claim will be unpacked in chapter 3. Note at the outset, however, that alongside the uncanny quality of the body as an automaton, the relationship we ourselves have to our bodies can become one of radical estrangement. If the body operates with its own teleology, then how should "we," the self-conscious subject, be situated vis-à-vis the body's own intentionality? The question hints at a tension between different ideas of identity and otherness. Unveiled is the prospect of coming into conflict with the body as being distinctly "other" to the "I." Indeed, overarching the broad arc of the uncanny is the uncertainty of whether or not "I" am truly identifiable with my body itself.

The third mark in this tripartite relation culminates in the archetypal experience of the uncanny: returning to a place, so far held as a familiar memory. At the heart of this tension is the conflict between the body's lived retention of a place and the prepersonal, anonymous existence of that place, which, as I will argue, undercuts our human attachment to things in this world. As experience shows us repeatedly, when returning to a place from our past, the effect is invariably alienating rather than reassuring. The reason for this *verfremdungseffekt* is complex and resistant to conclusive definitions, not least because the formations of our memories of place largely comprise opaque forces working behind the scenes. As such, encountering a place from our past in the material world establishes itself in a relationship of difference and otherness to that of our memories.

Here, Freud is instructive. Discussing the "neurotic [man]'s" relationship to the female genitals, Freud offers us a rich illustration:

> A jocular saying has it that "love is a longing for home," and if someone dreams of a certain place or a certain landscape and, while dreaming, thinks to himself, "I know this place, I've been here before," this place can be interpreted as representing his mother's genitals or her womb. Here too, then, the uncanny (the "unhomely") is what was once familiar ("homely," "homey"). The negative prefix *un-* is the indicator of repression. (2003, 151)

Placing the psychosexual dynamic of Freud's study in the background, this description of the relationship between memory, place, and desire remains edifying in several respects. Reminding us that the phrase "I have seen this place before" is in fact far from a simple declaration of empirical evidence, but rather a covert doubling of memory and imagination, Freud thus locates the familiarity of returning to a place in the midst of a repressed network of unregistered desires. Even without attaching ourselves to the sexual orientation of the interpretation, Freud's passage brings to the light that our memories of place are guided more broadly by an overarching homesickness, which ties together the most disparate strands of experience into a fragmented whole. It is this tension of a fragmented whole that touches upon the prefix "*un-*," which Freud aligns with repression. A whole that is fragmented is held together only through inserting matter into the spaces that have been reduced to nothingness. In such a case, memory is not alone sufficient to confer unity upon the subject or to preserve the appearance of "home." As such, constant work modifying memory is required in order to fend off the unhomely shadow that lurks within the longing for home.

As though to prove the existence of this subterranean homesickness at the heart of memory, when returning to a place after a prolonged absence, especially that of the childhood home, the result seldom coincides with our expectations. Instead, a dreamscape tends to transpire comprising a deformed arrangement of familiar objects. Thus, things that we cherished as assuming a particular appearance—warm, imposing, intricate—tend to materialize as malformed, unsettled, overrun, and, in a word: *alien*. The world to which we had previously accustomed ourselves through memories and dreams now adopts a sinister presence, forever sliding in and out of our temporal frame. And yet, there forever remains a tension forcing the house back on its own otherness. This inevitable "and yet," thus attests to the ambiguity and allure interwoven into the uncanny house. On the one hand, a place stands before us, attesting to a material reality, which, in some broad sense, remains the same as it ever was. On the other hand, this something same is also an inverse phenomenon, now sufficiently discontinuous to exclude us from its realm. With expectations of spatial and temporal renewal, we are instead met with indifference, an inanimate and anonymous murmuring in the banality of daylight. Something remains buried beneath the house, an eerie genius loci protruding through the brick and mortar masking the house's hidden spirit. Only in the conflation between memory and experience is this strange place peculiar to the uncanny rendered explicit.

In this book, Freud's emphasis on wombs and genitals will be replaced with the prepersonal anonymity and muffled silence that haunt place, of which the body is the first to establish contact. As I shall argue from several different angles, the notion that human "value" somehow ought to be antecedent to our experience of the world is not only antiphenomenological in tone, but emblematic of a failure to speak on behalf of the specificity of things themselves. Thus, to what end a place displeases our cultural and aesthetic sensibilities is one thing among many, and not the focus of this book. Cultivating a pejorative stance toward, say, the suburban landscape, or otherwise feeling a level of affection toward a little "corner" of the world, immerses us in a community of shared values, which is subject to contestation. Such second-order judgments about how we "favor" places contribute little to the primacy of the body, which, in its appeal to an alien world, amasses a pool of data in advance of cognition.

As a rule, therefore, we would do better to counter this tendency toward "humanizing" things for the sake of preserving familiarity, and instead retain a heedfulness to the prereflective unfolding of things in their raw and strange phenomenality. In what follows, this arc of tension that I signaled above will be accompanied by an arc of strangeness and increasing anonymity. The journey from childhood home to site of trauma will be met with escalating opposition from our predisposed tendency to attach ourselves to the places that continue to reinforce our sense of self. While our treatment of monuments and trains will be relatively unaffected by the phantoms spooking place, as everyday memory is replaced by transitional and traumatic memory, a new light will creep in, increasingly at odds with our pregiven experience of the environment. We will discover that the appearance of certain places articulates the motion of a "creature of another species" fusing with the present. Along the way, the necessity of prising our cultural values apart will be determined by the intelligibility of the body, in both its humanity its and inhumanity. In turn, this conflict between the order of human experience and the (dis)order of anonymous inhumanity residing beneath that appearance will play a central role.

4. Descriptiveness

How does phenomenology begin to account for the strange and uncanny things that the life-world comprises? As we have seen, the phenomenological epoché urges that judgments regarding the causality, reality, or truth-value of things in the world be bracketed. To encourage this act, first-person descriptions of appearances and experiences occupy a pivotal position within the phenomenological framework, as Husserl writes: "[Phenomenology] aims at being a *descriptive* theory of the essence of pure transcendental experiences from the phenomenological standpoint" (1967b, 209; italics in original). Thus, what is being described is concerned neither with reality nor with the causality of an object. Description is central to the phenomenological method, since description brings together the presuppositionless starting point with the return to the things themselves. To return to a thing, we must be able to set our assumptions aside. Setting aside our assumptions means resisting making inferences in advance. For this reason, the notion of pure description is also a notion of encountering things in their given immediacy, thus elevating the role of descriptive examples to an important status. Treated with rigor, descriptive examples come to be seen as manifold appearances that disturb our pregiven apprehension of things.

One important misunderstanding of phenomenology that arises from the centrality of descriptiveness suggests that it entails an introspective description of the contents of consciousness. Whereas subjective experience indeed plays an essential role in the phenomenological method, what is being described is not a passive meditation on the affectivity of an object for its own sake, but rather how the objective world is known *through* experience. The word *through* is of central importance. In distinction to the Cartesian split between subject and object, phenomenology understands knowledge as being constituted by subjective experience. Objectivity thus stands in a peculiar relation to subjectivity, whereby subjective experience becomes the "clearing" (to use a Heideggerian term) for the disclosure of appearances. As such, the synthesis between being and world denotes an outward-looking mode of descriptiveness, rather than an invocation of subjective introspection.

So, while illustrations and examples are frequently employed in this book, their deployment is meant in more than anecdotal terms. True, we can follow Nietzsche in claiming that all philosophy is biography, and we would be no worse for doing so. Indeed, the examples and descriptions included in this book are not incidental. To be sure, their development is a result of a crystallization of fixations and possessions. But this covert expression of one's own life history is not an end in itself. Rather, by beginning with the inspection of one's own bodily and mental contents, an invitation is sent out to the reader to think alongside these illustrations and thoughts. This invitation means that the examples are not closed portals that claim to speak in absolute terms about memory and place. Instead, the gesture is meant as a spark of enthusiasm for the reader to reflect upon his or her own experiences.

In this way, I wholeheartedly follow the spirit (if not the "felicitous" content) of Bachelard's (1994) methodological "oneirism." The method can be characterized in positive terms as privileging a creative mode of reverie. For Bachelard, oneirism is the result of memory and imagination forming a hybrid. The power of this fusion is that it allows the "oneiric house"—the archetypal figure of dwelling—to superimpose itself on the spatiality of the present. In this book, archetypes fall by the wayside. But what remains in place is a commitment to the idea of "poetic image" as a guide. By "poetic image," Bachelard (1994, xvi) has in mind an autonomous and unified object, spontaneous in its appearance and causing a disturbance in a broader temporal narrative—in a word, "the flare-up of being in the imagination" (xviii).

Refusing to take the poetic image as a second-order "aesthetic" judgment, I thus agree with Bachelard that attending to things requires nothing less than an "excess of the imagination" (1994, 112). The memories that inhabit themselves in both the materiality of our bodies and in the places of the world require more than their objective and empirical standing to be brought to life. In the absence of an excess in imagination, the assimilation of the world falls to a formal mode of gathering data. "In order to surpass," so Bachelard

writes, "one must first enlarge" (112). This is a telling and significant remark. Against naturalistic causality, against sociopolitical constructivism,
and against psychoanalytic reduction, the poetic image establishes a dynamic
of "reverberation." In Bachelard's (xvi) terms, "reverberation" becomes the
figure of transportation, guiding disparate images from one place to another.
The advantage of this method is that it displaces a linear account of causality
connecting one object to another. Replacing linearity, objects appear in different parts of a given world, all contributing to the "sonority of being" (xvi)
through arriving in between different states. But in between what?

In this work, we shall follow the passage of memory as it reverberates
between memory and imagination, materiality and flesh, and spectrality and
trauma, each dyad signaling a division in the book. In all three of these instances, causal agency between each pair is undermined by a separate force
reverberating in between. This emphasis on being *between* different places
employs the motif of reverberation as a channeling device. Thus, examining
what has been ensnared by the affective hold of the poetic image means being
surprised by what comes to light, and in so doing, also discovering a strange
undercurrent to the appearance of things.

THE PHENOMENOLOGICAL METHOD

The aim of this introduction has been to outline a broad methodological and
thematic approach to the book. Given this aim, how is this objective possible
without determining the contents in advance? How, that is, can the phenomenological method proceed without tying itself down at the outset? Here, the
problem of writing becomes a problem of contending with what is taken-for-
granted in experience; namely, what is intuitively given to consciousness in
its sensuous totality. The question of the sensitivity of language—amounting
to nothing less than style of writing—is of particular concern. Appearances
alter; some things become more present than other things. In the attempt to
let things speak for themselves, we will have to stand guard against the temp-
tation to place language where appearances belong. To bring appearances
and speech together means tending to the way writing sculpts thinking. Every
language is deliberate, and this deliberation needs careful attention where
phenomenology is concerned.

Faced with these difficulties, a passage from Heidegger offers us some
guidance: "Every questioning is a seeking. Every seeking takes its direction

beforehand from what is sought. Questioning is a knowing search for beings in their thatness and whatness" (1996, 3). Heidegger's correlation between questioning and seeking returns us to the being who takes up the question. Inquiry is also an instant of intentionality, whereby empty intentions—points of absence—become embodied as the object becomes perceived. With this intentional relation, there is a teleology to what is being sought, marked, above all, by the transition from empty to filled intentions. To speak here of emptiness does not mean lack or simple absence. Instead, an empty intention is already anticipated as a filled and present intention.

Let us take an immediate example: writing this introduction. In writing this introduction, I stand in relation to an imagined future, in which empty intentions become fulfilled as the horizon of writing unfolds. Similarly, the territory already covered in the introduction designates a partial recession of presence: partial because what has been covered is already taken up in the present. The emergence of the empty and filled intentions brings us to back to phenomenology's sensitivity toward interstitial and morphological states. As intentions become filled, so other intentions subside. At the same time, we must also admit that not all phenomenology proceeds from one point and ends at another without retrospection along the way. To again take the example of writing this introduction, the fact that its formation consists of a process of writing, editing, rewriting, and further editing undermines the idea that phenomenology is an unmediated description of things. Rather, ideas are augmented, structures altered. All of this occurs retroactively, and in time. Intervals of years separate some sections of the introduction from other parts and some of those sections did not form sequentially. This retroaction appears to dissent from the supposed ideal of a "pure" phenomenology, inasmuch as it embodies a "touching-up" of content.

But can the phenomenological method ever really free itself from presuppositions? It is tempting to doubt such aspirations. But those doubts do not stand in the way of striving toward a place in which objects can speak for themselves. Merleau-Ponty offers some hope: "Since . . . we are in the world, since indeed our reflections are carried out in the temporal flux on the which we are trying to seize . . . there is no thought which embraces all our thought" (2006, xv). This movement of perpetual beginnings is one of phenomenology's great strengths. By leaving the world exposed to uncertainty, dynamism is maintained and our own place in that tension is amplified.

We can think, too, of Merleau-Ponty's earlier claim that "the most important lesson which the reduction teaches us is the impossibility of a complete reduction" (2006, xv). Thinking through this claim in light of the act of writing phenomenology, the passage can be seen as an invitation toward a horizon that is forever proving elusive. Precisely because the world proves "strange and paradoxical" is its allure secured (xv). The world to which phenomenology attends is neither static nor indifferent to the viewer. Rather, when I begin to survey the world around me, when I reflect upon how my body stretches out into the world, a dialectic forms between myself as a conductor of phenomenology and myself as a living human, with a history that trails through my body. In this respect, *I follow myself*. My past and my unlived future converge in the present, outweighing the notion of the phenomenologist as being an impersonal bystander in the world.

The structure of intentionality is thus a direct result of attending to the primacy of things. In a very real sense, the appearance of a thing—a Martian fossil, a haunted forest, a burning house—guides us in terms of what is both absent and present. We see less, but this seeing-less does not mean we are obscured by what is missing. Instead, things are contained by a potentiality, the result of which means that intentionality carries onward through a demarcated territory of absence. In this context, Heidegger's "knowing search" is a search with a direction, motivated by what was already there, but now brought to the fore. To breathe a "strange and paradoxical" life into our understanding of things is, finally, to see them anew, restored from their suspended disappearance. Let us make a first foray into those strange appearances.

Part One
From Place to Memory

• •

CHAPTER ONE

BETWEEN MEMORY AND IMAGINATION

> My memories begin with my second or third year. I recall the vicar-
> age, the garden, the laundry house, the church, the castle, the Falls,
> the small castle of Worth, and the sexton's farm. These are nothing
> but islands of memory afloat in a sea of vagueness, each by itself,
> apparently with no connection between them.
>
> —Carl Jung, *Memories, Dreams, Reflections*

"In the memory," so writes Augustine, "everything is preserved separately,
according to its category. Each is admitted through its own special entrance"
(1961, 214). If our faith in memory's ability to preserve events in a discrete
manner, as Augustine suggests, has diminished, then there is much to be said
for the notion of memory as being essentially spatial. While Augustine's notion of memory as being like "a great field or a spacious palace, a storehouse
for countless images of all kinds" (214), may have been replaced by virtual
spaces and electronic servers, we nevertheless expect memory to occupy a
"place." But is there anything inherent in the content of memory that gen-
erates a spatial structure? Do my memories "encircle" one another, some
falling into a less present "zone" than others? Similarly, do some memories
remain "dormant," awaiting their moment of resuscitation?

Implicit in the notion of memory as being stored for retrieval is the suggestion of *continuity*. Along with the familiar image of memory as a storehouse is the idea that memory remains motionless while the object itself is
not being remembered. Yet *motionlessness* does not, of course, mean transparency. Even Augustine will admit that the storehouse becomes dusty, concealed, and submerged with confused memories, stating suggestively that
"some [things] are forthcoming only after a delay, as though they were being
brought out from some inner hiding place" (1961, 214). The hiding place in

which memory recedes testifies to the significance and power of preservation: a power that continues to haunt both memory and place.

In this chapter, I will assess the status of memory as an experience preserved in time. The focus on the preservation of memory coincides with the broader emphasis on the spatiality of memory. As such, in beginning to think about the experience of memory in time, we will be in a position to gauge how space and place interact, coexist, and contribute to the formation of individual memory and collective memory. I shall have more to say below on episodic or autobiographical memory, in contrast to habitual memory, as involving a particular mode of spatiality. At this stage, however, all we need to note is how episodic memory is prima facie compelled to negotiate with an image that allows the past to be articulated. Can this relation between memory and its image be trusted?

On the one hand, as remembering agents, we are inclined to speak in such a way of having a "picture" of things in the world as the content of memory. Sometimes, I will say to myself how I can "still see the dashboard." Later on, I might be prepared to say I can "still smell the leather interior," and even that I can "still feel the touch of the steering wheel." Images, sensations, and haptic encounters persist. On the other hand, there is clearly a difference between being in a place and remembering that place. The kinesthetic, cognitive, and affective dimensions of recall delineate a division between perception and recollection.

To speak of a memory-image means questioning how the image relates to the past. An image emerges: The "feel" of the steering wheel presses down, the sight of the dashboard appears, as though reframed in its original locality. Suddenly I have "returned" to the childhood garage in which my father's car was housed. At the same time, the return is also virtual: in effect, a concurrent blending of presence and absence. In imagining myself being in a place, I join a past experience with a playful reworking of that past in the present. Because of this overlapping between remembering and imagining, the relationship between memory and its mental image becomes a foreground issue.

Pursuing this relationship will mean confronting, first, the possibility, and second, limits of a phenomenology of memory. In this chapter, I will begin with an account of the phenomenology of memory before moving on to a preliminary investigation of the structure of place memory. In this way, the purpose of this chapter is to serve as a broad theoretical foundation for the ensuing chapters. My concern, above all, is to consider how place memory differs as a unique mode of remembering, involving its own affective and conceptual tensions.

SCENE AND SURROUNDING

As mentioned in the introduction, phenomenology's receptivity toward ambiguity and process entails empty intentions' becoming fulfilled in time. The result of this is that phenomenology captures appearances as being resistant to enclosed borders and fixed points. Taken up in perception, objects present themselves to us in a manifold fashion, shifting through stages of presence and absence in time. With memory, the motif of absence gains a special quality. How, after all, can an object that is absent in one sense simultaneously be present as an intention in another sense? The singular quality of memory is realized in contrast to other worldly phenomena. Unlike the desire *toward* an object or the fear *of* a situation, both cases that are structured around a momentum of fulfillment or failure, memory presents itself, at least initially, as an appearance of what is temporally past, thus absent.

Clearly memory persists in some sense into the present. Once lived, the past does not temporally expire, even though the event itself may have ceased to exist. Instead, it stretches out into the present, resonating in such a way that personal identity and collective identity become reinforced. This gesture of reinforcement does not mean that memory is solely the province of mental content, however. Memory is not simply confined to our heads, as it were. While it is true that without our brains, recognition of the past would crumble, it is nonetheless the interaction between persons and world that provides the genesis for remembering. *Things* in the world activate our brains, directing us in different paths accordingly.

But what binds this diversity is the thematic direction of a re-collective and self-reflexive intentionality. Memory "points" us toward the past, as Aristotle states: "Memory relates to the past. No one would say that he remembers the present, when it is present" (1941, 608). But does memory really "point" us, as though the past were a landscape seen from behind our shoulders? Do we really "turn" to the past? "Pointing" and "turning" capitalize on a spatial account of memory as having been left behind. The logic underpinning this spatial language is understandable enough: Memory is thought of as involving the notion of completion, so distancing the object of remembering from experience in the present. Indeed, unless it involves a preemptive nostalgia, to speak of remembering the present is wholly incoherent.

However, when we encounter things in the present—apples, an earthquake, an eclipse—then such things provide the grounds for our remembering. Doing so, things act upon the body in the present, such that the body stands ready to express the content of memory. To say that my experience of eating an apple, to conjure something of a Proustian image, returns me to a childhood orchard is not to say that I have been temporally transplanted *back* to that lost world. Rather, it suggests that my body in the present is the ground, into which an experience is being *relived*. As the ground for a relived experience, the germs of the apple experience were there all along, only now revitalized through coming into contact with a physical object in the world. The apple contains the seeds of an experience in it, thus alerting me to a part of myself that was previously concealed.

A major implication follows: If memory is concerned with the past, then we can also think of a distinction between the *activity* of remembering and the *content* of what is being remembered. This distinction is classically phenomenological, insofar as it calls on Husserl's (1999, 86) division between the noesis of memory (the act) and the noema of memories (the what). For Husserl, the "act" and the "what" constitute the structure of intentionality, marking in each case an inseparable union. He writes:

> Perception, for example, has its noema, most basically its perceptual sense, i.e., *the perceived as perceived*. Similarly, the current case of remembering has its *remembered as remembered*, just as its remembered, precisely as it is "meant," "intended to" in the remembering; again, the judging has the *judged as judged*, liking has the liked as liked, and so forth. In every case the noematic correlate, which is called "sense" here (in a very extended signification) is to be taken *precisely* as it inheres "immanentally" in the mental process of perceiving, of judging, of liking; and so forth; that is, just as it is offered to us when we *inquire purely into this mental process itself*. (quoted in Moran and Mooney 2002, 136; italics in original)

Husserl is describing the transcendental structure of experiencing an object, *the perceived as perceived*. With this, Husserl distances the objective reality of the object in question and underscores its sensible and mental reality. The "act" of remembering concerns the mode and the form in which the past is recollected, and thus signifies nothing less than the work of consciousness. But this has a temporal consequence, too. For something to be "remembered as remembered" we must *be* remembering in the first place. This apparently obvious remark in fact highlights something that is often overlooked: The object of remembering comes to light *as* a memory only when we are in the act of remembering. The same object may pass us by or otherwise be experienced as a nonremembering act. Either way, only by the noetic act is the noematic object discernible as a memory.

Husserl's noetic/noematic distinction is helpful in establishing the formal structure of remembering. Alongside Husserl, Henri Bergson provides broader assistance in terms of distinguishing between habit memory and independent recollection. Bringing Bergson and Husserl together, we begin to get a richer picture of the specificity of remembering, as such.

Key to Bergson's analysis of memory is the question of how the past can differ from the present, given that, for Bergson (2001, 2004), consciousness is structured as a continuous and indivisible unfolding of duration (*durée*). Bergson's response to this, famously, is to establish two forms of memory.

First, Bergson describes "habit memory" (2004, 86–87). Habit memory is a practical mode of memory, which utilizes the past for the sake of being oriented in the present. "Sometimes," Bergson writes, "it lies in the action itself," while at other times, "it implies an effort of the mind which seeks in the past, in order to apply them to the present, those representations which are best able to enter into the present situation" (87). In each case, habit memory contends with the notion of putting the past into use. This means that habit memory's relation with the performative dimension of learning places it in the remit of mere survival. Moreover, the correlation between habit and survival positions habit memory as a largely automated, physiological response to stimulus. In learning to perform actions—walking, writing, talking—before repeating those actions, our engagement with the world is such that the fluidity of movement confers a sense of continuity upon our actions.

Central to this adaptable involvement with the world is the function of the brain. During habit memory, an editorial process unfolds, in which actions and movements are modified in accordance with a given end. Although immersed in the body, habit memory's special relationship with the cognitive process of the brain produces a different variant of "body memory." The primary function of habit memory is its realization in action. If that realization is blocked due to brain damage, then the existence of the habit memory is abolished. Thus, habit memory is marked not only by its dependency on being realized, but also by its need to be practiced. Should the stimulus of my habit memory disappear from the world—hills to ascend, oceans to swim, and people to speak to—then so, too, would the memory itself.

All of this is quite different from Bergson's second mode of memory: independent memory. The term "independent memory" refers to the autonomy of memory from its practical actualization. As if there were any doubt as to not only the thematic difference but also the evaluative difference between habit and independent memory, then Bergson goes so far as to describe the latter as "perfect from the outset," involving a "will to dream," which "man is alone capable of" (2004, 94–95). How does this second type of memory gain such a distinction? To answer this, we need to look at the causal basis of independent memory.

Whereas habit memory actualizes itself through practice, filtered at all times through the action of the brain, independent memory has its basis in the "memory-images," which record "all the events of our daily life as they occur in time; it neglects no detail; it leaves to each fact, to each gesture, its place and date" (Bergson 2004, 92). Furthermore, all of this experience is recorded quite independently of its potential to be employed practically. Rather than being limited to the sphere of cognition, with independent memory, we are issued a memory that occupies the entire body.

Because of its ability to prolong the past into the present independently from external stimulus, it is only this second type of memory that Bergson is prepared to term "memory *par excellence*" (2004, 95). This claim is underpinned by memory's relation with the spontaneity of the imagination. Indeed, at stake in the genesis of independent memory is the question of whether the memory-images being recalled fuse "dream with reality" (96). In contrast to the practical orientation of habit memory, Bergson is left wondering just how memory can retain its place in consciousness without inducing an "immense zone of obscurity" as "certain confused recollections, unrelated to the present circumstances," arise in the present (97). Such questions point to the depth and richness of memory as recollection. Losing their automated structure, pure memory signifies a highly personal memory, peculiar to the self experiencing it. As such, the mode of language distinct to Bergson's independent memory resists absolute clarity. Experienced from the inside out, it falls to the body to become the voice of expression for such forays into the past.

Bergson's distinction between habit and independent memory marks two ways in which objects of memory appear for consciousness. The distinction is neither absolute nor exhaustive. Indeed, within the twofold division, several subdivisions demarcating different modes of remembering present themselves (Casey 2000b, 52–64). Given the focus of this chapter, however, it will suffice to concern ourselves with memory as an affective retrieval of an episodic experience. The emphasis on affectivity testifies to episodic memory's distance to the performative dimension of habit memory. Independent memory is not simply the remembering of objective information, nor is it the processing of factual data. Instead, it embodies the meaningful retrieval of an experience, encompassing a surrounding world of place, time, and corporeality.

In Husserl, we discovered a distinction between the "act" of remembering and the "what" of memories. Having touched upon the act of remembering, our attention falls to the content of that act. In the very least, we can say that there is a "thing" being recollected. Being more ambitious, we can go on to survey such things as conversations, places, emotions, and thoughts, all of which fulfill the content of memory and vary in their presence respectively. Following Casey's (2000b, 61–67) incisive exposition of remembering, we can speak here of "remembering-what" as the category that designates particular things, which form part of a broader experience. Above all, the idea of remembering-what implicates a push toward the encompassing event. That is, the "what" emerges against a backdrop, in which the specific thing elicits a point of entry to the event being remembered, as Casey states: "This structure represents the *nominalization* of the complex, its subsumption under a description that is itself singular and without internal complication" (61; italics in original). The "what" and the "that" of remembering thus form a respective parallel to object and event, or, as Casey terms it, "state of affairs" (67).

Remembering that certain things *were the case* means situating the "what" of remembering in a context. To remember *what* she was wearing when I met her means remembering *that* we were in a different country. Object and event occupy a relation of inseparability, but mark a different emphasis in terms of intentional content. Further still, the twofold emergence of object and event are remembered in an entirely heterogeneous and qualitatively disparate manner, a disparity encompassed by what Casey terms the "memory-frame" (2000b, 68).

For Casey, "memory-frame" refers to the heterogeneous setting in which the content of memory is presented, thus producing a distinct "ambience" upon that content. Less a monolithic structure, the memory-frame emerges as a broad outline in which the content and context fuse. For Casey (2000b, 68), the presence of the memory-frame recedes and intensifies in varying ways, forever achieving the task of placing memory. Through emphasizing the spatiality inherent in remembering, Casey's idea of "memory-frame" is especially helpful. This spatial dimension is reinforced, as Casey proceeds to subdivide the memory-frame into different factors, concluding with the memory of space and time. Before pursuing spatiality generally, it will be useful to focus on Casey's first contributing factor: worldhood.

Casey's model of "worldhood" (2000b, 68–69), a term taken from Heidegger, refers to the "embrace of an environing world" (69), which situates the object and event of remembering in both a temporal and a spatial locality. The emphasis on totality in Casey's understanding of worldhood is prefigured in Heidegger's (1996, 67–83) account of the concept in *Being and Time*, as the world of Dasein occupying a particular world peculiar to it, as well as the pregiven environment in which Dasein is placed in a ready-to-hand fashion. For Heidegger (69–70), the preontological understanding of the world as an environment means that Dasein is inseparably involved *in* the world, an involvement that is discovered only as the ready-to-hand placement of the world is disturbed. In Casey's analysis of the worldhood of remembering, the same interdependence of worldhood becomes the implicit background on which the content of memory is presented to consciousness. Because of this role, worldhood retains a containing aspect, which engenders it to the role of border.

Corroborating this view of worldhood as a border, Casey goes on to make an internal division between scene and surroundings, where scene entails the "*immediate* setting for the specific content remembered" and surroundings "refer to the nonimmediate setting" (2000b, 69; italics in original). Both scene and surrounding situate the object of memory, reinforcing the particularity of what is being remembered, but simultaneously withdrawing from the main attention of remembering.

The particularity central to worldhood, he goes on to say, is made possible by the presence of the remembering agent (Casey 2000b, 69). Not only is our presence within memory the basis of all remembering, but as remembering agents, we ourselves become constitutive of the memory, as he writes: "We have internal evidence that *we were there*—there in the very midst of the remembered" (69; italics in original). With the insertion of the self, scene and surrounding are brought to a tripartite unity, sealed by the testimonial attributes of experience.

Emerging from Casey's treatment of both worldhood and memory-frame is a dynamic account of remembering, in which the presence of the self within the memory-frame is subject to flux. By employing this dynamic foundation, the memory-frame allows for the malleability of the self. As such, what is remembered can often concern less the affective experience of the subject and more the objective presentation of events within the world. And the same is true in reverse. As we shall now see in more detail, sometimes memory, self, and place fuse, producing an event peculiar to remembering as a whole.

THE MEMORY OF PLACE

From worldhood, we arrive at the gateway to place and memory itself. This development can be observed in the movement from the nonimmediate scene of memory to the immediate emergence of specific content. As we have seen, Casey's account of the memory-frame forms a surrounding border, in which the scene of memory is perceived from the standpoint of the remembering subject. Since the exchange between self and world fluctuates, with world and self each emerging and receding in its intensification, the following claim can be formulated: *Sometimes it is the case that a place provides the defining character to a memory, such that the memory becomes inextricably bound with place, thus rendering it an event.*

Note here the specificity of this type of memory. Alongside the dynamic core of the memory-frame, spatiality need not necessarily be a prevalent factor in our memories. True, all memories are placed in both space and time, but that does not entail spatiality forming a defining factor. When certain things in the world strike us in our memories, those things can exist to some extent quite apart from the environment in which they occur. A facial expression, harsh sound, pain in an ankle can force the materiality of the world to a background, nonimmediate status. But with place memory, we are concerned with a division of remembering, in which place is not simply the context on which memories hang, but the very texture of the specific content itself.

In describing place memory as an "event," my suggestion is that the "world" of place memory is self-contained, unified in its autonomy from the surrounding world of which the memory derives. Place memory's status as self-contained is possible due only to the immense hold any given place has over our memories. The hold is not so much a matter of being able to navigate our way through a given location, as though place were the mnemonic cue for our orientation. More so than assuming a navigating role, place memory gives itself to consciousness as a certain type of phenomena, existing independently of its role in guiding and orientating us spatially. This type of phenomena is instrumental not only in being the felt texture of the past but also in securing our own embodied selves within that past.

When I am given over to remembering the way in which I experienced Las Vegas during a winter some ten years ago, what emerges in this scene is not only a broad assemblage of diverse phenomena—the iconic Las Vegas sign, the dazzling neon parade of the Strip, the artificial reproduction of Venice—but a heterogeneous collection of objects and modes of affectivity, all of which play their parts in the formation of my memory. Strikingly, these established locations and motifs of Las Vegas are in fact pushed to the background, as my own experience employs them as a context for a memory that is peculiar to me as a subject. I remember less the physical and objective dimensions of driving down the famous Strip, and more the role the same site plays in cementing my first reading of Kant's transcendental deduction, since it was on this journey that I took a copy of *Critique of Pure Reason*. Indeed, when I open the pages of Kant—as I have done presently on this Tuesday morning—the annotations on the page return me to the heady ambience of Las Vegas, with its garish lighting, playful architecture, and zealous gamblers. How is synthetic a priori knowledge possible? For me, this is a question that is inextricably bound with the bright entrance to the Golden Nugget, a famous hotel located on Fremont Street.

On a bright afternoon one December, I sat on a concrete plant holder and thumbed through the pages of Kant while waiting for my brother and father, who had fallen behind, to catch up. But the waiting proved fortuitous, as it was during this particular episode that my confusion surrounding Kant's transcendental deduction was divested of mystification, the findings of which were cast over the landscape of Las Vegas. This is more than merely my memory of the place being informed by contingent circumstances. Rather, the overlapping fold between Las Vegas and my reading of Kant forms a singular event, which synthesizes the two forms. Again, this is not simply the case that Kant and Las Vegas have become mnemonic cues for one another, but that *both* form an inseparable hybrid. When I invoke this episode, all I remember is a highly specific cluster of a much broader spatiotemporal narrative. Aspects of that narrative are latent in the memory, but the specificity of reading Kant by the entrance of the Golden Nugget dislodges those surrounding properties to a hazy blur.

Figure 1: *Golden Nugget, Las Vegas. Courtesy of Claus Wolf.*

The formation of my memory of Las Vegas, as being entwined with my formative reading of Kant, focuses largely on cognitive and visual factors. But what of the body? Is the non-visual dimension of this memory somehow silent? I shall explore the inroads the body makes into memory in various ways throughout the book, but let us consider the role of the body as parallel to cognition in the emergence of place memory as a hybrid event between the self and the world.

My account of being in Las Vegas is not without a corporeal dimension. For instance, while it is physical things in the world that predominate this memory—an old copy of Kant and the entrance to the Golden Nugget—my body was there all along. My body was there when I held the book and perched myself on the concrete plant case. My body was also clothed by an incongruent duffle coat, with its collar turned up in the bright heat, the materiality of which remains as bound with the horizon of Las Vegas as Kant does. But these factors are stationed behind the visual focus of reading. Indeed, one could argue that this suppression of the body is informed in part by the relative sterility of Las Vegas as an appearance in the world. Certainly when we turn our attention to a more visceral environment, sight is augmented with an appeal to the totality of the body.

By way of a contrast, I shall invoke a memory of visiting Alcatraz, the former prison in San Francisco. As with Las Vegas, my memory here is less of the physical place in its historical and cultural significance, and more of a mood, rhythm, and atmosphere that the place facilitated within me. When I "feel" the moistness of the interior of the former prison, or when I recall the touch of the iron bars on the cells, then I am placed in a wholly different reality, a reality in which embodiment is suddenly foreground. But this foreground appearance of embodiment does not sit in an arbitrary relationship with the environment I am remembering.

Unlike the comparatively homogeneous landscape of Las Vegas, my being on Alcatraz is marked by a series of transitional zones and sites of contrasts, not least the passage from water to earth. Already in this phase of journeying, a difference in bodily regularity is afforded by the experience of being in a ferry to then being on firm land, such that I can feel myself still swaying even when on the concrete basis of the island. In contrast to the memory of Las Vegas, there is motion in this event. Once on land, I do not rest but ascend a sharp hill, which overlooks ruins now colonized by a thick patina of flora and fauna. The ruins are exposed and I am bending over a fragmented wall in order to gain a closer look, aware of the sudden drop beneath me. The tour moves ahead and I feel the pressure to maintain pace.

Farther up, I encounter the towering water tank, which looms over me like an ominous extraterrestrial entity. Despite its height and inaccessibility, arching my head back, I can see the tank is heavily rusted. The hill has leveled out and the entrance to the prison is ahead. Here another shift in bodily spatiality and rhythm takes place. From the bright surroundings of the island, as I enter the interior of the prison, a cool dampness descends from the rusty ceilings. My visual sight is still adjusting to the absence of light, but the rest of my body is already navigating its way through this new terrain. And so my senses reach out to this environment. Aurally, the sound travels quite differently within the prison walls. A cavernous boom resounds, and sounds seem to travel farther thanks to the absence of obstacles. In terms of tactility, moistness seems to creep through the brick walls, causing a porous feel to my body. The moistness is compelling and I find myself behind the caged prison door, enjoying the experience that the place inspires.

Against the memory of being in Las Vegas, the experience of Alcatraz is all together a more complex phenomenon. Now, we are confronted with a more diffuse set of circumstances and not just a highly specific instant in time. Indeed, the memory is a composite of different moments, all of which produce the unity of the episode as a whole. This is quite different from my memory of Las Vegas, where the unity of what was given was done so in a compressed instant. Along with this temporal diffusion, the concentration on visual sight is widened to the whole of the body. My whole body receives this place, with each sensory organ receiving the world in its own peculiar way. As such, the shifting between light and touch, sound and smell, marks a memory genuinely unique to my lived experience.

Despite their thematic differences, the memories of both Las Vegas and Alcatraz are bound by a parallel structure. Both demonstrate the emergence of place memory as a distinct event of remembering, in which the "world" of place memory offsets the peripheral environment, establishing a context singular to the remembering subject. The singularity of this context manifests a consistently existential dimension to it throughout. I am neither passive to the memories I recall nor indifferent to their effect on me in the present. Rather, they press down upon me, searing through my body in the present, and in the process highlighting all that has been erased or modified from the past. *Everything*, in a word, is filtered through my affective glance, from the color of the sky to the rust on the gates; none of it escapes the egocentric desires of my human body.

Peculiar to the formation of place memory, then, is the specificity of a given world. The formation "displaces place" from its surrounding environment. To draw out this strange phrase, it will be useful to bring in the Heideggerian notion of the world making itself known in its "conspicuousness" (Heidegger 1996, 68). By this, Heidegger refers to the making-present of things in their absence, disruption, or brokenness: "Circumspection comes up with emptiness and now sees for the first time *what* the missing thing was at hand *for* and at hand *with*. Once again the surrounding world makes itself known" (68; italics in original).

"The surrounding world," to repeat Heidegger, "makes itself known." But in doing so, the surrounding world was not absent prior to its disclosure, but rather revealed as there all along. Through disturbing the pregiven unity of the world, we are made aware, Heidegger argues, of the context in which things and events are situated, as he writes: "[The surrounding world] is 'there' before anyone has observed or ascertained it. It is itself inaccessible to circumspection insofar as circumspection concentrates on beings, but it is always already disclosed for that circumspection."(1996, 70). That is, by dint of familiarity, the wholeness of the world becomes available as an ontic phenomenon to be discovered. Prior to this ontic discovery, the disclosure of the world is already established as a transcendental structure of the world, thus the immanence of the world is both familiar and unfamiliar concurrently. Situating this relation between disclosure and discovery in a spatial context, Heidegger provides a fitting illustration:

> My encounter with the room is not such that I first take in one thing after another and put together a manifold of things in order then to see a room. Rather, I primarily see a referential whole . . . from which the individual piece of furniture and what is in the room stand out. Such an environment of the nature of a closed referential whole is at the same time distinguished by a specific *familiarity*, . . . and this familiarity implies that the referential relations are *well-known*. (quoted in Dreyfus 1997, 103; italics in original)

What arises from this passage is the givenness of the room as a totality. Heidegger's encounter with the room as a "referential whole" is made possible thanks to the interplay of background and foreground appearances. Notably, the interplay is neither calculated nor assessed in objective terms. Instead, the spatiality of the room appears in its "nearness" in terms of what is both familiar and present, Heidegger writes: "The structured nearness of useful things means that they do not simply have a place in space, objectively present somewhere, but as useful things are essentially installed, put in their place, set up, and put in order" (Heidegger 1996, 95). Accordingly, worldhood, be it remembered or perceived, forms an experiential context, adopted through a network of familiar, dimensional, and constantly unfolding appearances, all of which attest to a broader region.

   To relate this to place memory: Inasmuch as place memory disturbs the pregiven stillness of the contextual and everyday world, then it discloses place as a singular event, isolated from the "referential whole" of the surrounding world. Phrased another way, whereas habit memory—such as we find in Bergson as performative, bodily actions—aids in our orientation of place, so reinforcing the continuity of the world, place memory seizes the world as a singular instance, ultimately disturbing orientation.

In formal terms, the seizure constitutes a different modality of how place is given to us. Rather than appearing as a pregiven unity, the particular place that holds the past offsets, individuates, and articulates itself as a stronger and more present intention than that of the encompassing region, be it a room, a city, or a country. Structurally speaking, the formation of place memory is at the same time a disturbance of the latent world of things in their environment. As one totality is pushed to the background—the totality of pregiven experience in its "nonimmediate setting"—so another totality emerges—the totality of place memory in its "immediate setting." This transitional movement between a background region and a foreground place mirrors the phenomenological encounter with things removed from their context. Suddenly, what was so far taken-for-granted is discharged from its dormancy and forced to the forefront. As a result, the particularity of place memory—as embodied, situated, and localized—withdraws the immediacy of a location from its familiar world and resituates it as a conspicuous event.

All along, of course, my memories of places are offset by the location in which the remembering occurs. From the abandoned prison cells of Alcatraz to a recent memory of having been on a university campus, a gradient of differing relations unfolds, all of which fundamentally contribute to the phenomenological experience. Indeed, to overlook the distance disjoining myself in the present and the place I'm remembering in the past would be disingenuous, not least because a tacit residue of fragmentation seeps through all of time's polarities. I remember something that I am now removed from, and yet *I was once there*—a striking claim, fused with an abiding sense of spectrality. How I experience such a memory depends in large on the dynamic of meaningful involvement established at the outset.

Although not quite a grainy, sepia film of a distant era, there is nonetheless a patchy and vague quality to these memories, all of which are imbued with a prior and different version of my own self. True, I can remember the feel of moistness inside Alcatraz, and to some extent relive that texture on recollection, but there is a surrounding detachment to this interior experience, as though looking at myself from above. I am, effectively, a player in the scene of my own memory.

The sense of being an object of my memory rather than the absolute core is determined by my relation to the "person" in the memory. What properties still exist that bind "me" in the present with "me" in the past? This complex question is stretched over the canvas of distant and close memories, rupturing and restoring the unity of selfhood respectively. As I move nearer in time, I find more resemblance to the self that I experience from the inside out. When, for example, I see myself placed in a building on the university campus, giving a seminar to a group of students, then I still retain the felt experience of the room and the atmosphere the meeting cast. In addition, the task of teaching and performing the seminar retains a level of fluidity with my present existence, writing at a kitchen table. No significant obtrusion has entered the interval of teaching and writing to undercut my relationship to this close memory.

Yet if I reach back deeper in time and revisit the scene of Las Vegas, then the focus on a given task is displaced with a more generalized sense of simply being there. The cool December air of the Las Vegas afternoon and the reexperience of myself in a duffle coat with collar upturned is barren of all intimacy, such that the reality of this memory is never taken-for-granted. Indeed, the very existence of this memory is so familiar to me; having dwelt on it for several years it has become effectively fixed in time, devoid of the animate quality of lived experience and now more or less resembling a photograph.

All the more reason, therefore, for me to experience the physical object of Kant's book through a screen of strangeness. For here is a book that persists in time, is able to attest to my having been in Las Vegas, and has now outlived that passage of time through sitting innocuously on the kitchen table. How did the book end up here? How, that is, did it survive the journey in time from being held by me in Las Vegas to now sitting several thousand miles away in an environment so remote from that location? Having retreated into the background of my bookshelf, the book has been overlooking the course of my life without my being aware of its presence. Yet the book is here, and with its presence, all that is profoundly different about the remembering subject— myself—is brought viscerally to the foreground. I cannot remember making these annotations, and yet the handwriting is clearly my own. Nor can I remember the passages I have underlined, and yet clearly I have read them. The question is not a case of assessing how an object can *remind* us of a place, but of contending with how an object that once belonged irreducibly to a specific place and time can be rediscovered in another place and time.

Here is the "thing" of my memory, quite alive! But is the "thing" a product of my body, of time, or of the world more broadly? So much depends on this question, given that for Merleau-Ponty, "we grasp the unity of our body only in that of the thing" (2006, 375). Without the "thing," the body is "merely an obscure mass" (375). But now both the "thing" and my body standing before it are reduced to a state of stifling ambiguity. What has happened that my encounter with the book has disturbed me, revealing the book as a site of estrangement? Merleau-Ponty writes with unnerving clarity:

> Ordinarily . . . our perception, in the context of our everyday concerns, alights on things sufficiently attentively to discover in them their familiar presence, but not sufficiently so to disclose the non-human element which lies hidden in them. But the thing holds itself aloof from us and remains self-sufficient. This will become clear if we suspend our ordinary preoccupations and pay a metaphysical and disinterested attention to it. *It is then hostile and alien, no longer an interlocutor, but a resolutely silent Other.* (2006, 375–76, emphasis added)

We have returned to Lovecraft's turn toward "unnatural pryings into the unthinkable" (1985, 91). By drawing our attention to the wavering balance between everyday attention and a disinterested attention in things, in which the human subject is decentered, Merleau-Ponty uncovers the anonymity lurking within the homely. Doing so, he shows us that the domestication of things is eventually destroyed by the persistence of a more enduring force than that of its human bond: silence. Silence dissects, interweaves, and protrudes through these apparently enduring things, effecting a sense of melancholy in the very fact of their continued existence. Easier would be the thought that all materiality ceases to exist once a place is left behind. But from the doors that are closed on places, things return, forever haunting our interactions with things once familiar.

All of this, of course, points ahead toward the potential for place memories to easily slide into the region of the uncanny. Precisely through being entwined with a surrounding world of familiarity, the event of place, as becoming visible from that world, conceives a tension with the familiar. The tension is a composite between different worlds springing from the same source. Thus, the "world" of place memory, unique to the core, develops from the pregiven world, which is no less heterogeneous in its structure. That both "worlds" occupy the same space highlights the potential for each to recede and intensify in familiarity and unfamiliarity. Far from being a matter of spatial configuration (as though being a mnemonic device), and less even the disinterested memory of a place as a work of architecture (and that alone), place memory is distinguished by the correlating sense of self-presence, thus conferring an affective ambience (constitutive of personal identity) on that memory. In the following section, I shall illustrate this relation between place and self-presence through exploring the memory of journeying toward Slovenia.

JOURNEYING TOWARD SLOVENIA

When I decide to call upon my memories of having traveled through Slovenia late at night several years ago, I am immediately faced with a series of borders that enclose the place of the train carriage with the motion of journeying toward another place. The borders are not only those that generate a sense of being spatially enclosed by the carriage and compartment; nor do they simply refer to the geographical borders I passed through in order to arrive at Ljubljana, having departed from Hungary. Rather, there is at once a distinct blending of enclosed, geographical, and temporal borders. Above all, distinctive to the memory of this place is the intensified presence of having departed in one country, arrived in another, and, in the meantime, having been situated in a train peculiar to this transitional phase.

"The special attraction of the journey," writes Proust of traveling by train in the section titled "Place-Names: The Place" from *Remembrance of Things Past*, "lies not in our being able to alight at places on the way and to stop altogether as soon as we grow tired, but in its making the difference between departure and arrival not as imperceptible but as intense as possible" (1967, 310). In such an instance, the heterogeneity of the train—the distinct and localized characteristics it presented itself as having—is reinforced in conjunction with the sense of the train as being the bridge between worlds.

Once aboard, the appearance of the train as a particular appearance counters the vanishing station, where access to the train was made possible. For Proust, this is a "mysterious operation that is performed in those peculiar places, railway stations, which do not constitute, so to speak, a part of the surrounding town but contain the essence of its personality just as upon their sign-boards they bear its painted name" (1967, 310). Indeed, so far as the station embodies the door to the place memory, then I can say that while my memory of traveling to Slovenia begins aboard the train, the germs of the memory have already been established by the anticipatory gesture of arriving at the station, obtaining the ticket, and experiencing the station as emblematic of the city I am now leaving, Budapest. The registering of place memory is made possible through the interplay of heterogeneous and contrasting places, each of which surface and recede in their presence.

Due to the inseparability of the memory of traveling between places and the experience of doing so on a busy, humid, and noisy train, as central to this memory is thus my own kinesthetic perspective. Contrasting with the

Figure 2: *Keleti Train Station, Budapest. Courtesy of Travis Ferland.*

constant motion of towns, fields, and villages, all of which, although occasionally disrupted as the train stops at stations, are immediately placed in the past as soon as they have arrived—contrasted with this, is the discomfort of being stuck in a cramped and busy compartment. The discomfort is further reinforced by an inability to sleep, despite the sense that my body is prepared to do so. This inability is at odds with the motion of the train, which, in the consistency of its rhythm, provides the prima facie means by which sleep will become possible. Yet neither sleep nor comfort ensues. Instead, the motion of the train propels me toward a suspended state of sleeplessness, in which the experience of time and place is fundamentally altered.

I was there, but there in such a way that the memory of traveling on the train becomes infused with a felt corporeality, which would otherwise be lacking if the enclosure of the train were a less prevalent factor. Indeed, in returning to this journey, I do so, not from a detached perspective, as though floating above the moving train, but rather moving from inside the busy carriages, repeating the experience of trying to find a place to rest. To narrow this memory by focusing in on a specific dimension—being woken up by border control after managing to secure sleep—is to bring further details to the fore: not least, the extreme lethargy and confusion that I experienced inside the cabin of the train, having been suddenly awoken by a banging on the door. The motion of moving toward greater specificity leads to the memory-frame's being constituted by a singular object, in which the multiplicity of boarder events spawns. Such a process of enclosing inward attests to the synthesis of place and memory coexisting as a singular event. Indeed, to subtract place from such memories leaves a placeless, floating, and disassembled series of dimly connected events.

What is distinct to the formation of this memory, and indeed to place memory more broadly, is the role place plays in reinforcing the presence of the self in time. As I invoke this episode, the transition from the nonimmediate ambience of the station to the immediate enclosure of the train carriage marks a move between modes of lived duration and self-presence. Yet this transition is not absolute, as though the experience of the station as the worldhood is left behind. Here, we can recall the Heideggerian interpretation of the interplay between worldhood and place memory as being a modification rather than a negation. Where entering the train from the scene of the station is concerned, then it is only because there is some considerable overlap between these two spatiotemporal dimensions that the experience of being enclosed by the train as a visible presence is possible. Environmental relationality and temporal interdependence thus become central in the genetic formation of place memory. It is for this reason that Proust finds the "miracle" of transport a "tragic" one, stating that "we must, as we emerge from the waiting-room, abandon any thought of finding oneself once again within the familiar walls which, but a moment ago, were still enclosing us" (1967, 311). The sudden contrast between exposure and enclosure establishes the conditions by which the memory of place becomes an extraordinary event. As a consequence, coexistent with my boarding of the train is the heightened emergence of both self-presence and the visibility of the train as a place in which I am now contained.

In all of the above illustrations, place memory involves an emergence from the nonimmediate surrounding environment, whereby place is given to us as a visible event, discrete from the background context. "Emergence" here is understood as the making-present of place against an environmental backdrop, which itself contributes to the identity of the foreground place. Accordingly, the emergence of place memory occurs in accordance with the shifts in spatial borders, leading thereafter to a shift in intentionality and self-presence. Considered as broad categories, location, perception, and experience are thus brought together to constitute what is distinct to the memory of place.

DREAMING OF PLACE

Having given a preliminary account of both the structure and the experience of place memory, what remains to be said is how the memory of place finds itself in relation to temporality, and specifically how the temporality of imagination exists alongside memory. Will it suffice to assume that memory and place exist on an equal plane, especially when stretched in and through time? To be sure, the question has a significance marked by place's ability or failure to remain a constitutive part of our identities. If memory fails to retain the dynamism and experiential richness of place, then must one consider this as a lacuna in the sense of being a continuous self?

Such a question is taken up directly in Bachelard's (1994) account of memory and place in *The Poetics of Space*, an exemplary text that attests to the affective role imagination plays in retaining the existential value of memory. For Bachelard, the experience of place is not in itself enough to guarantee the temporal continuity of the memory of place. As proof of this, the expansion of memory (by way of the poetic image) highlights, in Bachelard's perspective, the fundamental insufficiency of memory: "I shall prove," he writes at the outset, "that imagination augments the values of reality" (3). Bachelard goes on to suggest that such an augmentation of reality takes place in the construction of shelter, whereby "the imagination build[s] 'walls' of impalpable shadows, comfort[s] itself with the illusion of protection" (5). The significance of Bachelard's claim in relation to the distinction of memory is rendered explicit, in that the domestic shelter makes daydreaming possible, and daydreaming is what allows the past to come forth: "An entire past comes to dwell in a new house. . . . Through dreams, the various dwelling-places in our lives co-penetrate and retain the treasures of former days" (5).

Bachelard places us in the zone of "Motionless Childhood," a zone in which the "solidarity" of memory and imagination work together to sculpt memories of previous dwelling, now reanimated in the present dwelling. Memory, then, does not make a claim to autonomy. Instead, "through poems, perhaps more than through recollections, we touch the ultimate poetic depth of the space of the house" (6). Thus, if memory and imagination are working together, then Bachelard leaves us in no doubt as to which is the more efficacious agent in returning us to "the original fullness of the house's being" (8).

This dynamic interplay between memory and imagination is realized in that place becomes the passive container of memory, whereas the imagination is raised to the role of active retriever. Bachelard's "topoanalytic" investigation of the house thus takes us into the realm of daydreams, a realm that encourages the emergence of memory from the recession of its (spatial) dormancy. Methodologically, Bachelard's inquiry into the "fragments of space" instigates a radical shift in the phenomenological formation of memory. Instead of memory's being withdrawn in abstraction, we are led back to the places in which originary experiences were conceived. This contextualization of memory means that daydreaming becomes nothing less than a halfway house between memory and imagination.

Citing the term "oneirism" for this mediating passage between memory and imagination, Bachelard goes on to state how temporal and spatial continuity is made possible thanks to an engagement with the "threshold of a daydream" (1994, 12–13). The oneiric house recalls, indeed places central, the first archetypal house in the establishment of dwelling in the present. Yet, in order to preserve its pertinence in the present, Bachelard's working of oneirism resists absolute particularity: "We orient oneirism but we do not accomplish it" (13). Instead, it remains in the "shadows," able to cast its presence over the unfamiliar landscape. In the retreat from particularity, the phenomenological content of the oneiric image necessarily becomes ineffable, as oneirism glides toward daydreaming. At this threshold, we encounter, "the very limits of memory, beyond memory perhaps. . . . All we communicate to others is an *orientation*" (13; italics in original). The topoanalytic retrieval of memory concludes, therefore, by adopting *allusion* rather than description as its methodological imperative. And so Bachelard teases the reader: "But I've already said too much" (13).

Bachelard's account of the memory-image, effective because it allows memory to maintain vivacity irrespective of its epistemological accuracy, undermines the autonomy of memory in two ways. First, by subsuming the particularity of memory to an archetypal trace. Second, by rendering the reception of memory dependent on an agency that acts between memory and imagination; namely, daydreaming.

In his attempt to retain the past into the present, Bachelard necessarily circumvents the fragmentation of that same past undergoing alteration. If the past is preserved, then it is at the expense of hollowing out its original content. Indeed, elsewhere in the book, Bachelard makes a confession: "Great images have both a history and a prehistory; they are always a blend of memory and legend, with the result that we never experience an image directly" (1994, 33). We never experience an image directly because the same image is altered by the creative imagination, and for Bachelard, this is how memory is spatially renewed.

The tension between creative renewal and epistemological certainty is a problem peculiar to the interplay between memory and imagination. The interplay precludes the autonomy of memory, and renders the imagination the guiding agent. In Bachelard's reading, the creative dimension of image-making marks an aesthetic dimension to place memory. The aestheticization of memory is not incidental to the act of imagination, as Casey writes in his account of imagination: "To imagine authentically is to be creative, whether or not this creativity is embodied in a work of art or any other tangible product" (2000a, 185). The question of "where" memory has receded to in this active exercise of the imagination, and whether we are entitled to term the memory-image "memory" as such, is complicated, in that the boundaries between memory and imagination, as well as those between perceptive consciousness and passive daydreaming, are blurred.

MEMORY AS A REDISCOVERY

Do memories of places risk erosion through being in touch with imagination? For Bachelard, the answer is clearly no. Far from bringing about the destruction of either memory or selfhood, the achievement of involving the imagination is to keep the memory of place alive. In and through time, memories are reworked, reconstituted, and reconfigured to suit the constantly changing self that exists temporally. This relationship between the flux of time and the work of imagination points to the significance preservation plays in our experience of places.

Why preservation? Already in Bachelard, we have discerned the movement from the original experience of being-in-place to the imagination's augmentation of that experience. Bachelard's reason for introducing the imagination into memory is to maintain existential unity for the dwelling subject. After all, without the house, "man would be a dispersed being. It maintains him through the storms of the heavens and through those of life. It is body and soul. It is the human being's first world" (Bachelard 1994, 7). Given the immense value Bachelard places on the house, the issue of maintaining the presence of that center becomes pivotal, lest the subject is exposed to ontological dispersion. Yet the content of memory does not remain unaffected by the passing of time. Instead, it is precisely through being vulnerable to time that our relationship with memory needs constant heedfulness. By attending to the persistence of memory, the transition from the original experience to an imagined version of that experience becomes clear.

To approach this shift from experience to difference, we shall adopt a problem established through Ricoeur's reading of Plato's *Theaetetus*. The question has a simple form: "If a man has once come to know a certain thing, and continues to preserve the memory of it, is it possible that, at the moment when he remembers it, he doesn't know this thing that he is remembering?" (quoted in Ricoeur 2004, 8).

Plato's question concerns the relation between memory and storage, an issue with which we opened the chapter. In Waterfield's translation of the passage, "preservation" is translated as "lodged securely in the memory" (Plato 1987, 51), in the same fashion that Bachelard describes memory as "lodged in the houses of the past" (1994, 184). The containment of memory stands in close relation to the spatiality of storage. Yet far from remaining intact, uncertainty surrounds the identity of both the memory and the remembering consciousness. The doubt intensifies as Socrates asks the following question: "Does one remember something or nothing?" (Plato 1987, 52). After Theaetetus concedes to the "something," Socrates retorts, "Even when one's eyes are closed? Or does that make one forget?" (52).

The invocation of sight is notable. By equating unconsciousness with the erasure of memory, the suggestion is that memory decays through not being watched. In that blindness, memory is thought to go astray, so producing an altered and unrecognizable memory, evident only as the eyes reopen. Such an alignment between sight and recognizability cements the relation between knowledge and perception, resulting in the striking possibility of "remembering without seeing" (Plato 1987, 52). *To remember without seeing*. At stake in this thought is the question of whether memory can maintain its identity through a mediation that takes place in the present. The initial passage from the *Theaetetus* emphasizes the effort of preservation. The man "continues to preserve," implying the engagement of work and volition. But what takes place such that through a lack of sight, memory falls beneath the threshold of recognition? The question points to the centrality of preservation.

Central to the logic of preservation is an action that is neither intrinsic nor necessary to the formation of memory. Instead, the preservation of memory is attached *only after* the memory is temporally complete, typically as a result of ascribing meaning and value to that memory. As the present falls into the past, so a totality is gained, and only then is that totality judged in terms of value, which determines its persistence. That preservation is neither necessary nor intrinsic to memory means that it can be thought of in terms of degrees. For this reason, preservation gains the status of being an "art" in its ability to preserve the "original" past. As a result, the relationship between memory and preservation is contingent and dynamic, establishing the possibility of overpreserving or underpreserving the original experience. With this twofold axis of overpreserving and underpreserving, the result is the production of variants of the same memory, with an allegedly "original" experience outlasting faults in perception and recollection.

The disjunction between contrasting presentations of memory, one located in the past, the other represented in the present, becomes realized only when two or more collide—that is, when the eyes reopen and find that what we thought was the past is, in fact, altogether *different*. Difference is essential to the knowledge and experience of the past: the difference of a past, which is nevertheless recognized as being the *same* one we remember. Difference is felt in the flesh when the preserved past misaligns with our pregiven expectations of that past. In this way, memory thrives on incongruities, disruption, and estrangement. If our sedimented notion of the past places the image of the storehouse as ideal, then memory's differences render that storehouse unfamiliar and other, a place now barren of its homely quality. Forcing itself into the present, we come into contact with the felt reality of the past, a past that has less to do with a "representation" of memory and more to do with the revival of an already-experienced moment in time.

Tellingly, the structure underpinning the difference of what is being preserved reappears where involuntary memory is concerned. The sudden and unexpected encounter with an experience that was so far consigned to an apparent void reminds us that our duration in time is constituted by several factors resting beneath the threshold of consciousness, invoking the possibility of "remembering without seeing." We need only think of celebrated passages from Proust to realize that the affective involvement of involuntary memory depends on the existence of a previous voluntary image of the past, which is prepared to be dismantled. The joy of the discovery is at once a joy of the depth of remembering, as contrasted with the presentation of the past as a still image.

In his study of Proust, Deleuze is undoubtedly correct to point out that what is missing in this mode of remembering is the sense of "the past's being *as past*" (2000, 57; italics in original). It is precisely because difference is effaced that memory is assimilated as a static image. Static, and thus *timeless*. No doubt for this reason, Plotinus is prepared to say that "being rooted in unchanging identity cannot entertain memory, since it has not and never had a state differing from any previous state" (1991, 278). The self-continuity of a "divine being" is its own form of an atemporal void, with the lack of difference commanding a "memory outside of time" (279). For mortals, however, difference engenders itself toward the vanity of life on earth, with the memory of oneself as being different engineering the experience of moment in time. The result is something of a temporal synthesis, producing what Deleuze refers to as an "internalized difference, which becomes immanent" (2000, 60). The immanence of difference is thus the condition by which the preservation of memory can be dislocated from its given place.

In its difference, silence, and otherness, memory reminds us that regardless of our attempts to put the past in place, that same past resists the confinement of the storehouse, forever standing ready to catch us off guard. Doing so, memory evades the watch of the open eye and instead takes form through an indirect mode of communication. Of this indirect communication, the seeds of the uncanny are already detectable in the body's retention of a past that is not only different, but also *opposed* to the subject's remembering. In what follows, this escalating tension will be placed in the relation between memory and history.

. . . .

CHAPTER TWO

MONUMENTS OF MEMORY

It is better to form one's memory *loci* in a deserted and solitary place for crowds of passing people tend to weaken the impressions. Therefore the student intent on acquiring a sharp and well-defined set of loci will choose an unfrequented building in which to memorize places.

—Frances A. Yates, *The Art of Memory*

We move through places and in the process gain a wealth of memories, some of which return to haunt us while others fall by the wayside. Yet our memories do not begin and end with the idea of a center, less even of a "home." Nor, for that matter, is our own experience the sole province of remembering. As we move beyond the close-knit world of our own remembered past, so we expose ourselves to a temporally jagged world, in which the present sits alongside the depth of the past. This disjuncture between the past and the present sets in place a responsibility peculiar to place and memory: How do we commemorate events outside our experience without modifying the structure and content of that event? Such is the question we will be asking in the current chapter.

The question emerges from a tension conceived in the previous chapter. There, we were led from an analysis of place and memory to an understanding of memory as being both present and absent concurrently. What resulted from this tension between absence and presence was the broader involvement of the imagination, a trait we discerned, above all, in Bachelard. Through bringing imagination into the scene of memory, the identity of what is being remembered comes under question. We remember a thing from the past, but augment that memory in order to preserve its presence. In doing so, the relation between the original experience and the preserved version of that experience draws an increasing distance. In time, we may adjust ourselves to the distance and lose sight of the original experience altogether. Indeed, on an individual level, the experience of this distance may amount to nothing more than a vague estrangement from one's own past. Publicly, however, a different set of problems is at stake.

This gap between experience and recollection is embodied publicly when, as in one example, the past becomes articulated through the figure of a *monument*. On the surface, the monument offers no simple clues for how it embodies the past. How can a chunk of materiality deposited into the ground claim to speak on behalf of another person's memory? Moreover, how can such a block of mass assume a role in the public's imagination, such that the construction of a "public memory" is inaugurated? These are complex questions and will require a careful negotiation between the lived experience of a monument and the hermeneutic attention to interpret what the monument embodies. In this chapter, just as we will move from a concern with individual to public experience, so a broader shift will occur from memory to history.

FROM MEMORY TO HISTORY

Let me begin with a methodological problem. Until now, we have focused solely on the phenomenology of individual experience of place and memory. This has been taken up through a consideration of the structural emergence of place memory, and enforced through the role imagination plays in preserving the past. The blending of memory and imagination marks a broader tension between memory and history, whereby the past becomes articulated indirectly. In the previous chapter, we considered how the ambiguity of a preserved memory was partly resolved by the rediscovery of memory as being different from that of the pregiven experience. Within this context, the account of memory and place as an event in the world occupies a narrative verifiable (to varying degrees) by the remembering subject. Such a narrative attests to the gradual formation of memory, and so to an underlying temporal unity. Where history and memory are concerned, however, this phenomenological foundation seems to reach a limit.

To get right to the point, the problem can be phrased as a question: How can we phenomenologically observe the past in the built environment insofar as that past is external to our lived experience? To be sure, in the face of the built past, the distance is both spatial and temporal. Not only does the past come to articulate something detached from my own experience, but often the articulation signifies an event before my life span, so marking an event in history rather than memory.

With individual memory, we are in the region of a highly specific frame that is brought alive through recall, remembrance, and the imagination. Individual memory is irreducible to experience, yet fundamentally rooted in lived experience. Individual memory, moreover, is forever in process, constantly modifying its contents as the remembering subjects themselves are modified. Lived from the inside out, individual memory obtains a deep affective quality by dint of its intimacy with the rememberer. We are, after all, seldom indifferent to memories, despite their familiarity and recurrence.

History, on the other hand, appears to objectify and render the individual aspect of memory external. History does this by articulating the past into an ordered unit, allowing us to confer the title of "event" upon the past. The demarcation between memory and history is reinforced, in that from the perspective of the historian, memory becomes the "raw material" with which history works (Le Goff 1992, xi). In order to make this transition from memory to history, departing from the lived experience of the individual subject appears as a prerequisite. As far as the past is represented in the world, then it appears for us as a phenomenon among many. Questions of how such an appearance is inscribed with the temporality of the past, how the past is accessible if represented, and if a phenomenology of history is indeed possible will lead us to attend to the phenomena of monuments. Before then, we need to consider the transition from memory to history, and more broadly how phenomenology will negotiate that shift from the internal to the external, and then from the individual to the public.

But first, a clarificatory point. By employing the phrase "public past," I am proposing to make a distinction between a past that exists independently of the subject, and a historical, cultural, and social context in which the subject is located, spatially and temporally. The distinction between a past that is embedded within a social matrix and a past objectively present within the world is neither absolute nor autonomous. Both the publicness of history—the objective occurrence of events—and the cultural conditions that determine how that representation materializes are thus entwined. Methodologically, however, my concern is not with the cultural conditions surrounding representation but with its appearance as an object related to the past.

The public past is also a collective one. The past does not simply float discreetly amid a collection of individual subjects, against which those subjects either become aware of that history or turn away from it. While it is true that

a public history is assimilated through encountering it as a source of knowledge, the same history is not, as it were, confined to archives and libraries.
Individual memory finds itself situated in a historical environment, and the
untangling of complex and repressed individual pasts is often exacerbated
by broader understandings of the working of memory (Antze and Lambek
1996). Accordingly, the decision to commemorate events is seldom an arbitrary one. Rather, the spatialization of the past carries with it a sentiment
broader than the idiosyncrasies of the object representing that remembered
event. This responsibility to a social framework means that the practice of
remembering a public history is, above all else, a form of communication, in
which the success of the representing object depends on its ability to transmit
the past.

What, then, of the interplay between the individual and the social? In
my previous account of the structure of place memory, the emergence of
the event of place memory presented itself as a singular experience to be
revisited. With this account, all that can be described is a discrete set of circumstances that constitute a wider set of relations. The emergence of place
memory is at the same time an objective experience in the world, carried out
by other people. At all times, my experience is placed alongside those who
coexist with me in the same space. Given this relation between coexistence
and lived experience, the structure of place memory appears as an event not
only for me, but for others, too. Alongside this simultaneous coexistence,
the memory in question offers itself up as a journey that can be experienced
and remembered in the future. Both the past and the future, therefore, are
brought together as a possible experience, distributed and shared in time.

Two implications follow from this relation between lived experience and
communal experience. First, as spatial movements are repeated within a given
location, a process of assimilation occurs between place and the persons who
collectively perform those movements, such that worldhood becomes the receptacle of a social experience. To say that a location becomes assimilated
by a group of people is not to say that a group is a product of a place. To
be clear, I am not arguing for the causal emergence of social groups. Nor
am I putting forward a deterministic account of general behavior in space.
Rather, I suggest that a given location delimits, encloses, and facilitates the
possibility of an experience being a shared one, even if the recognition of that
community is unregistered. The result: First-person experience of a place becomes constituted by the intersubjective character of that place. The bodily
routines of a specific group situated in a location effectively lend themselves

to a localized gathering of specific bodily practices, the result of which is the assimilated sense of a collection of people as having an identity.

Tellingly, playful reconstructions of historic identities tend to result in certain bodily positions supposedly peculiar to that sensibility (Connerton 1996). Equally, bodily gestures not archived in history also come to form the cultural identity of a group of people. Speaking of the body language of East European ghetto Jews in New York, Connerton writes: "The gestures cannot be itemised as 'saying' something; they communicate only to someone who understands the accompanying words, particularly if they are familiar with the meanings of certain stereotyped intonational forms characteristic of Yiddish" (1996, 81). Of course, that these gestures are often comically exaggerated or otherwise misappropriated for political exploitation may well be the case. However, such reconfigurations of bodily practices do not efface the alignment between embodiment and collective identity, but only amplify it.

Above, I described the formation of a spatial community through the performance of repeated and sustained movements, exchanges, and actions. Out of this involvement, a transition was activated from the individual to the public. The second aspect following on from the correlation between lived experience and communal experience concerns the compression of time being enclosed through either shared ecstasy or trauma, the impact of which loosens the border between self and other.

In both trauma and ecstasy, there is a literal standing-outside-of-oneself, a dissolution between self and other (we can recall here the celebrated etymology performed by Heidegger of the word *ecstasy*, as referring to Greek *ek-sistence*, and meaning "standing out into the truth of Being" [1977, 230]). "Standing out" also means stepping away from oneself. Where ecstasy and trauma are concerned, an event occurs, whereby the insulation of the self is shattered, so marking the arrival of a memory rooted in the public sphere. Because of this enclosure of the past, the compression of time is reinforced by the shared experience. As the event takes place, so it becomes enmeshed in the surrounding environmental area, such that an affiliation between different people is broadly constructed. By remembering an event of heightened proportions, therefore, we simultaneously invoke a broader region of properties, places, and objects that remain implicated within that event. The memory is not mine alone, despite its being taken from a singular perspective. Instead, the image is bound by a relation of other remembering agents, each of whom constitutes and is constitutive of the event itself. The result of this is the formation of a "we."

When a community is bound by joint suffering or joy, then the surrounding world draws in, together with the people who occupy that world. Doing so, the shared experience of a place establishes a thread of continuity between self and other. Community becomes possible thanks to the holding power of place. Not only this, but the event occurring is itself an instant of materiality, stretched over the wood, stone, and brick of any given location. For this reason, the commonality of sharing the same world is determined and brought to the foreground by the events that occur there. Because of this dynamism, becoming aware of the other as also occupying that world depends in large part on to what extent a shared attention is directed toward a singular event. This gathering of attention implicates the particular spatiality of the world as an interweaving, involving place.

In its converse image, consider how the violence inflicted upon a place through terrorist attacks serves to punctuate the area, in both spatial and temporal terms, where the event occurred. The transformation of lower Manhattan in September 2001 to what has since become "Ground Zero" is not simply an instance of materiality being razed to the earth. Nor, for that matter, is the creation of a site of mourning for a gathering of people incidental to the ruins themselves. Mourning is not only a private affair. Instead, the need to mourn collectively became prevalent, and was facilitated, furthermore, by the ruins of the World Trade Center acting as a beacon for the bereaved. Out of such an event, a center is established through the destabilizing of previous centers. This structural tension is entirely concealed where the everyday passage of the city urges movement and commonality in a tacit but largely taken-for-granted relation. There, the continuous bodily practices that ground orientation and regularity tend to flatten out the relationships between individuals and others by rendering those relations implicit. Continuity and regularity diminish the emergence of uncertainty and volatility. As such, it is precisely against constancy that an event is formed in a discontinuous and disruptive manner.

As with the individual experience of place memory, the emergence of a public memory is relational, arising against an antecedent context that serves to offset the formation of the event *as* an event. Indeed, insofar as an event can be spoken of as being memorable, then it is only with reference to other less memorable occurrences. At its most expressive, this gradient of memorability involves the explicit unification of the individual in relation to others. Even if contested, the affiliation forges a network of mutually conceived memories of an event. Remembering an event collectively means reinforcing the presence of the event, such that the formation of the past becomes a code-pendent and coresponsible concern.

PLACING NARRATIVES

So far, we have considered the idea of public memory. What has been lacking in this discussion is an explicit consideration of the spatiality of memory as it relates to history. What will be required is an investigation of the formation of history by considering how the built environment of memory alters the status of the past. The writings of French historian Pierre Nora are helpful here, because they are emblematic of a certain perspective on memory and place, framed, above all, by an association between forgetting, erasure, and representation. For Nora, the consequence of the assimilation between history and memory is an annihilation of the particularity of memory at the expense of becoming a historic entity. Accordingly, Nora invites us to think about "the disappearance of peasant culture" (1989, 7). For him, "mass culture on a global scale" entails the "end of societies that had long assured the transmission and conservation of collectively remembered values" (7). If the notion of "collectively remembered values" strikes an ambiguous tone, then the description of real memory, on the other hand, is unequivocal: "Social and unviolated, exemplified in but also retained as the secret of so-called primitive or archaic societies . . . a memory without a past that ceaselessly reinvents tradition, linking the history of its ancestors to the undifferentiated times of heroes, origins, and myth" (8).

Fundamental to the life of memory is its exclusivity, as he puts it: "Memory is blind to all but the group it binds" (Nora 1989, 9). The distinction between private (if simultaneously collective) memory and public memory reinforces Nora's opposition between memory and history. For this reason, Nora's claim that history "belongs to everyone and to no one" (9) is central, since it exposes the form of the past: able to morph with time, but lacking the particular content of memory, which would temporally bind the past to a specific point.

This logic of loss is compounded with his analysis of the "acceleration of history," in which history shatters "the warmth of tradition" (Nora 1989, 7). The result compels "an increasingly rapid slippage of the present into a historical past that is gone for good, a general perception that anything and everything may disappear" (7). Not only this, but the "rupture of equilibrium" emerges in "particular historical moment[s]," constituting "a turning point" (7). This concurrent emergence of rapidity and loss, Nora goes on to say, disturbs the conception of memory and history as involving a degree of "equilibrium." Further still, the "rupture of equilibrium" exposes the difference between cultivated memory, manifest in the "site" and archived historically, and real memory, "ceaselessly [reinventing] tradition" (8). For Nora, the opposition between memory and history extends to the point where we are now faced with nothing less than an "eradication of memory by history" (8).

The strength of Nora's position is that it allows us to see what is essential to the relation between memory, history, and materiality in an amplified way. What his argument lacks in balance, it compensates for in establishing sharp polarities, which methodologically, can be treated as stepping-stones to an experiential perspective on memory and materiality.

Consider here his depiction of memory as being colonized by representation, assimilated by the velocity of history, and divested of presence. In place of memory, we discover the relativity of history, aided by the *lieux de mémoire*, which he defines as a "significant entity, whether material or nonmaterial in nature, which by dint of human will or the work of time has become a symbolic element of the memorial heritage of any community" (Nora 1996, xvii). The word *lieux*, variously translated as "place," "site," or "loci," signifies not only the physical articulation of the past, but also symbols of memory, such as flags, commemorations, and calendars, all of which form critical sites of representation. For Nora, the representation is neither transparent nor peculiarly intimate with the past. Rather, his sites of memory are solely mimetic, "reconstituted" images of the past. As a result, the *lieux de mémoire* come to occupy a critical presence, preserving the presence of traditional memory while simultaneously submitting to the limitations of critical history. The "exterior scaffolding and outward signs" that constitute the substitution of real memory in turn are mistaken for their lost counterparts, so conferring a new identity on memory. With a tone of fatalism, Nora writes: "Its new vocation is to record; delegating to the archive the responsibility of remembering" (1989, 13). What emerges from this focus on archiving is a homogenization of the past, whereby the amassing of data displaces the ritual of remembering, leading to Nora's celebrated claim: "Record as much as you can, something will remain" (14). Divested of its origins, the object of memory is literally displaced (in the museum), reconstituted (in the archive), or otherwise represented (in the monument), so that the life of memory exists outside the *lieux de mémoire*.

Complicit with this mournful tone is an implicit (and often explicit) nostalgia toward the "quintessential repository of collective memory" (Nora 1989, 7). In *The Future of Nostalgia*, Svetlana Boym corroborates this view by arguing that "Nora's own view is fundamentally nostalgic for the time when environments of memory were a part of life and no official national traditions were necessary" (2001, 17). Following Boym, geographer Stephen Legg, in a nuanced treatment of Nora's nostalgia, suggests that the centrality of the *milieux de mémoire* results in a rigid concept of memory, "as being of another order to the symbolic" (2005, 500). Because of this insulation of genuine memory, the "lived experience concerns subjectification: the role of the individual in capitulating to subjugation or in taking up technologies of the self. . . . In failing to consider this order, Nora's nostalgias are not forced into sufficient contact with the situations that could challenge their imaginary origins" (500.).

Yet it is a nostalgia that meets an impasse, since the fixed image of the past, evident in the notion of a "dictatorial memory," refuses to be negated by the traces of history (Nora 1989, 8). Instead, both memory and history come to assume an absolute position, thus susceptible to an insidious dogmatism.

What is useful in Nora, then? Above all, his view contests the notion that memory's assimilation to history is both continuous and congruent with the past in its original status. For Nora, the very materiality of the past—"high fidelity and tape recording" (1989, 13)—disrupts the possibility of memory being lived as a bodily practice. Moreover, his demarcation between memory and history involves what looks like a realist framework, as though the division were unambiguous. Strangely, then, Nora speaks of *lieux de mémoire* as involving "an interaction of two factors," and equally a "mixed, hybrid, mutant, bound intimately with life and death, with time and eternity; enveloped in a Möbius strip of the collective and individual, the sacred and the profane, the immutable and the mobile" (1989, 19). If such a mutation causes the erosion of the past, then Nora does not clearly mention what is produced in this hybrid other than a negation. Due to his vilification of *lieux de mémoire*, nowhere is this interaction between memory and history treated as anything less than absolute. Phenomenologically, however, the polarization central to this view is subject to contestation and in need of a lived perspective. Now that we have established the scope of the problem, we need to venture out toward experiencing monumentality in the flesh.

A PHENOMENOLOGY OF THE CHATTRI

Several hundred feet above sea level, in the middle of a field overlooking Brighton and Hove, located on the southern coast of Britain and accessible only via a bridleway, a memorial to Sikh and Hindu soldiers who died in the First World War has been built. Meaning "umbrella" in Hindi, Punjabi, and Urdu, the *Chattri*, an octagonal, domed monument unveiled in 1921, stands in an enclosed area, surrounded by fields and cattle and flanked on each side by a tree-lined pathway. This decidedly rural setting is played out against a backdrop constituted by a more built environment. Visible from afar, the Chattri's presence as a visual appearance is both enigmatic and striking. Below the steps leading to the monument, three stones have been laid to mark the funeral pyres where the bodies of the soldiers were cremated, their ashes then scattered in the sea beneath. On the side of the monument's base, an inscription reads:

> *To the memory of all the Indian soldiers who gave their lives in the service of their King-Emperor this monument, erected on the site where the Hindus and Sikhs who died in hospital at Brighton passed through the fire, is in grateful admiration and brotherly affection dedicated.*

In approaching the Chattri, three different aspects can be detected: the relation between the landscape as a given area, the production of meaning within that landscape, and the embodiment of memory beyond that area. Let us begin with the first aspect.

When experiencing the Chattri, the relationship between background and foreground places is assisted by the fact that journeying toward the monument is possible only on foot, and even then, locating it is a matter of catching sight of it in the distance rather than navigating in advance. From the enclosure of the bridleway, the land opens itself to spacious fields, framed by an increasingly open view of the city beneath. Throughout the journey, the level of ascent intensifies, such that the physical effort involved in reaching the monument also increases. Coupled with this heightened physical concentration, the isolation of the walk is countered by the presence of cattle, the company of which establishes a border between the open fields and the pathway leading up to the Chattri.

Given the emergence of the Chattri as an appearance in the world, how does the materiality of the site interact with the making of memory? By

Figure 3: *Chattri Memorial, Sussex. Photo by author.*

placing particular emphasis on the role of the monument as disruptive of the broader landscape, we can, I would argue, approach the Chattri as a discrete object, imbued with a heterogeneous series of symbolic and temporal features. Consider at the outset how the monument finds itself in relation both to the comparative sparseness of the surrounding fields and to the heavily built environment below the monument. Sparseness and density entwine to frame and hold the monument in place. The result of this double enclosing is that the monument negotiates with both foreground and background places, simultaneously able to redefine perception between both modes. Structurally, this oscillation establishes the Chattri as a place in its own right, irrespective (at least initially) of what is being memorialized.

This formal characterization of the monument as a breakage in the landscape gains a temporal and representative depth as the site becomes a place of meaning, a meaning that is informed by the relationship between silence and memory. In what follows, I take these two aspects to be inextricably bound with the act of commemoration, and thus implicated in the monumental structure.

To phrase the presence of a monument as an embodiment of silence risks conflating metaphor with materiality. Yet it is precisely the appearance of the monument as an aural and more broadly sensible event that I wish to refer to. Indeed, this relationship between memory, silence, and commemoration is a *lieux de mémoire* in its own right, as Nora rightly puts it: "The observance of a commemorative minute of silence, an extreme example of a strictly symbolic action, serves as a concentrated appeal to memory by literally breaking a temporal continuity" (1989, 19).

Given this ritual of breaking time as a bodily practice, we might consider how this dynamic between continuity and discontinuity is transferred to the external body of the monument. With the commemorative minute of silence, the seizure of time accents the content of what is being remembered. In other words, in stopping to remember, attention is not drawn toward the past, as though the past were located spatially and temporally in the elsewhere. Rather, the presence of the now is shown to be constituted by the persistence of an event that has already occurred. The formation of silence is at once an attentive and physical gesture, whereby the cessation of activity informs the emergence of memory. In turn, this reliance on a contextual break in time allows the emergence of silence to become possible. No longer bound by a particular location, the collective silence transcends space, implicating a response far wider than that of a specified location.

Figure 4: *Holocaust Memorial Day, Jerusalem. Courtesy of Judy Lash Balint.*

It is for this reason that the visual appearance of collective silence correlates with a sense of the uncanny: presenting a sentiment ritualistically performed, which at the same time disturbs the order of a given timescale. The
synchronicity of the action leads to both a diminishment of subjectivity and
a suspension of social regularity. Taken together, these forces produce a scene
in which the limits, lawfulness, and legitimacy of place are shown to be ultimately contingent. What has so far been regarded as occupying a normative
state—above all, motion and distance—suddenly disperses. In the dispersion,
the existence of others assumes a presence rendered explicit in the silence. To
commemorate means to be joined with others in a nonanonymous mode of
collectivity. As a result of this gathering of public intentionality, the unfolding of the present is momentarily suspended. In its place, the past is given
room to breathe into the present.

If the world stops to remember, then how does the monument breach the
regularity of the landscape, obligating the viewer to literally stop in his or her
tracks? Any response to this question must attend to the structural relation

Figure 5: *South Downs, Sussex. Photo by author.*

between the presence of the landscape and the incision of the monument. As the monument finds itself within a given context, so it establishes itself in a relationship of difference with that context. Despite the lack of activity and comparative absence of sound, the fields surrounding the Chattri do not in themselves constitute a space of silence or of absence. Rather, due to the stability of the scene, a presence emerges in which the absence of sound itself becomes an audible presence. Through becoming familiar with the grooves, paths, and textures that mark the broad character of the Downs, so those features conspire to swallow up the silence of the space, in the process producing a thick ambience peculiar to the landscape.

This thick atmosphere engenders itself to a state of regularity and rhythmic continuity, such that the body's own rhythm of navigating the terrain becomes defined by the physical attributes of the landscape. Because of this relation between regularity and rhythm, as the Chattri becomes visible, the phenomenon of fullness and continuity is broken. Without knowing the significance, history, or symbolism of the monument, phenomenologically, a dynamic is established, in which attention is refined and refocused. Disinterested engagement in the surrounding world, underpinned by the subtle modulation in textures, collides with the radical subversion of that texture. In place of the flat gradient of rolling hills, the monument emerges as an object wholly other to the environing world, and the emergence is both symbolic and structural.

Structurally, the monument offsets the world. Symbolically, this offsetting disrupts the constancy of the world, effecting a different mode of engagement in the viewer, in which the atmosphere of steadiness is displaced by the singularity of a nonuniform and synthetic object. The appearance of the Chattri attests to the fact that the structure is neither an accidental arrangement of materials nor the ruins of a site. Rather, given its location, the monument's disruptive potential, as both symbolic and structural, is conditioned by its being a deliberate structure, in Alois Riegl's celebrated term, an "intentional monument" (1982). This twofold disruption is framed by the gateway to the monument, which serves both to limit the objective borders of land and to enclose the entrance to the site as an event within the encompassing environment. Put aside from the surrounding world, yet simultaneously looking toward the encompassing world, in spatial terms, the monument balances between inclusion and exclusion: inclusive of the city central to its commemoration, yet exclusive of a memory independent of the city. As a result, the interaction between the world beyond the enclosed gate and the place that opens itself up within the gate underscores the predetermined significance of the monument.

The relation here between the monument as a place and the monument as expressing meaning deserves a closer inspection. In his late essay "Art and Space," Heidegger proves instructive:

> Sculptured structures are bodies. Their matter, consisting of different materials, is variously formed. The forming of it happens by demarcation as setting up an inclosing and excluding border. Herewith, space comes into play. Becoming occupied by the sculptured structure, space receives its special character as closed, breached and empty volume. A familiar state of affairs, yet puzzling. (1973, 3)

For Heidegger, the animation of space occurs due to its delimitation. Indeed, precisely because space is closed is it also defined, for Heidegger a legitimate source of perplexity. What, then, of the "special character" of space? Pursuing an "emergency path," Heidegger aligns space with the motion of "clearing-away" (*Räumen*) (1973, 5). For Heidegger, "clearing-away" marks the opening of dwelling, whereby "a happening at once speaks and conceals itself. . . . Clearing away is release of places" (5). The release of places, Heidegger goes on to say, is also a form of "making-room" (*Einräumen*) (6). By "making-room," Heidegger means the "twofold manner," whereby a thing is "admitted" and then given the space to "belong to their relevant *whither* and, out of this, to each other" (6). Making-room is at once a mode of arrangement within the world and also the manner in which spaciousness becomes possible. Because of this process, "the yielding of place happens" (6).

It is within these terse but dense pages that Heidegger offers us his account of what constitutes place itself: "Place always opens a region in which it gathers (*Versammeln*) the things in their belonging together" (1973, 6). Belonging together, Heidegger suggests, secures ontic security. The power of place, for Heidegger, is not that of the strictly Aristotelian notion of containment, but an opening of regions, a "free expanse" (6). The term "region" here connotes the "aroundness," within which, so Heidegger writes in *Being and Time*, "the regional orientation of the multiplicity of places belonging to the ready-to-hand" forms (1985, 136). The region gathers as gathering forms the region. With this action, we can understand Heidegger's talk of gathering and regions as the particular, concrete, and unified whole, in which a multiplicity of discrete and divergent elements coheres.

Can we characterize the emergence of the Chattri as a description of the opening of a region, where region refers to, in Heidegger's terms, the gathering of "the things in their belonging together" (1973, 6)? I believe we can. If we take region as a primordial but inconspicuous structure of experience, then by encountering the monument, the continuity of place, in its pregiven "aroundness," is broken up into different aspects. The result is that the "interplay of places" is brought into a critical relationship as a thing discovered in the world.

The word *discovered* emphasizes the seeing of the monument within a phenomenal landscape, an intentionality that contains both possibility and the objectivity of presence, Heidegger writes: "With the phenomenon of the region we have already indicated that for which space is discovered beforehand in Dasein" (1996, 102–3). That region is a thing discovered in the world thus separates it from place. At the same time, however, place and region unite by establishing a directional environment, in which region gains a qualitative character provided by place: Place shapes regions as regions open themselves up toward place.

What, then, of silence? We have seen how the relation between place and region establishes a series of borders, in which the dynamic appearance of things in their objective presence becomes possible. It is this emphasis on the presence of things (and equally of the *presencing* of things) that literally "makes-room" for the embodied materiality of silence. Applied to the Chattri, this embodiment has the result of producing an "ontological amplification" (to borrow a term from Bachelard). Thus, as the broader landscape is met with the monument, the resultant effect is not limited to the borders of the monument. Instead, the encounter emits a presence with implications for both the monument and its surroundings. In concrete terms, as the Chattri comes into sight, so the thick ambience of the encompassing scene fragments, elevating the monument to the foreground. As a result the presence of the surrounding world is diminished, producing an aura of silence, around which the monument resides. As the monument stands aside from the surrounding world and forms a presence distinct to that of the broader world, so it becomes silent in its lived presence. The encounter is, ideally speaking, a disjunction, a moment of discovery in which the world is broken up, so writes Lefebvre of monumentality and space, "with the fullness of swelling curves suspended in a dramatic emptiness" (1991, 224).

Phrasing the monument as both a presence and an absence concurrently evades logical incoherency if we understand that this embodied absence is possible only against a backdrop of potential plenitude, as Heidegger writes notably: "But absence also concerns us in the sense of what is not yet present in the manner of presencing in the sense of coming toward us" (2002, 13). Heidegger's correlation between absence and potential brings together the phenomenality of presence with its immanence. To speak here of the monument as silent means giving a dynamic presence to place, dynamic because the emerging monument plays off the diminishment of the world, such that the formation of silence becomes intertwined with the emergence of depth and presence.

The close relation between commemoration and silence marks the entwinement of place and region. The enigmatic quality of this emergence is emblematically phenomenological, insofar as we are returned to the emanation of things in their strange facticity. That the phenomenological emergence of things holds the power to stop us in our tracks affirms the gap that arises between place and region. Relying on these gaps to invoke the depth of time, the monument offers a visible unconcealing of the silence that surrounds all phenomena.

MEMORY, MEANING, MATERIALITY

The preceding emphasis on silence reinforces the affective power of the monument in its relational difference to the world. While we have concentrated on the phenomenal emergence of the monument as an object that disrupts and offsets the world, what we have yet to touch upon is the hermeneutic dimension of this appearing. A focus upon the relation between meaning, materiality, and memory is thus needed. Here, our issue concerns to what extent the building of memory simultaneously *embodies* memory. In making this distinction between building and embodying, a difference between materiality and representation arises. The materials employed in the construction of a monument do not, of course, necessarily result in the fulfillment of a conceptual design. Insofar as a monument signifies something other than itself, then its representative role is subject to ambiguity. How do we assess if a monument has achieved its given objective of marking, preserving, and commemorating a specific event in time and place? In the least, with the failure to achieve their design objective, some monuments become reduced to spatial markers, fixed in the ever-changing present rather than making-room for the opening of time. In this sense, monuments occupy a peculiar responsibility, whereby the relation of representation and embodiment is intensified. How can we understand this relationship?

In his *Ethical Function of Architecture*, Karsten Harries assigns a "pictorial" role to architectural representation, stating: "To understand the representational character of a particular building, we have to understand just how it pictures, that is, the form of representation employed" (2000, 99). The implication of this claim is the foregrounding of a hermeneutics of the built environment.

Throughout his writings on representation and symbolism, terms such as "imitate," "connotation," and "metaphorical" are used to convey the relationship between architecture and representation (Harries 2000, 98–115). Identifying an "inherited code" that allows us to recognize certain buildings as being a particular type of building—the example of a church is given—Harries proceeds to bind the temporal distance between representation and conception under the rubric of an "ideal," writing how "this ideal presided over and informed the evolution of medieval church architecture. It provided something like an invisible theme on which generations of church builders composed countless variations" (103).

This "invisible theme" permeates the link between materiality and meaning, establishing an architectural language, in which representation and embodiment appear to unite. But how is this permeation translated into written language? In the case of the church, Harries maps out the link (or more precisely analogy) between materiality and the representation of the Heavenly City, or City of God (2000, 105). As tied by analogy, we come to understand the appearance of the church as equivalent to a manifestation of a "heavenly paradigm," such that a normative foundation is established, in turn conferring a heterogeneous, indeed, supposedly special quality on the structure of a church. As to the origins of a specific architectural motif, the "divine plan" guiding the construction of churches leaves us with only a "faint literary trace" (110). Despite this obscurity, the persistence of form is carried out, so Harries argues, only by appeal "to human nature" (112).

There is a curious similarity here to Tevye's account of the origin of tradition in *Fiddler on the Roof* (1971), where he asks himself: "How did this tradition get started? I'll tell you. I don't know. But it's a tradition, and because of our traditions every one of us knows who he is and what God expects him to do." Nothing less than an invariant structure, to invoke Husserl, guides the continuity of such claims, a structure that relies less on the Platonic inception of how things ought to be and more on the human demand for the stability of identity. Thus, tradition lingers as an adaptable presence, bordering a collective identity from other such identities.

Alongside this orientation, particular microcosmic features cement the relation between embodiment and representation. Harries takes gold in this regard as being a "metaphorical device" parallel to the "golden halos that encircle the heads of saints," allowing the observer "to transport . . . from this world into 'The True Light'" (2000, 107–8). The connection between metaphor and transportation is particularly telling, since by the power of metaphor, not only is a different place opened, but so, too, a different time. Given this bond between place, time, and metaphor, the church as a built structure combines the blending of light, texture, form, and representational content to reinforce the sense of the church as being a transformative place distinct from its broader surroundings.

The mention of a broader environment reminds us of the culturally temporal context of representation: "No longer," Harries writes, emphasizing a tone of lamentation prevalent throughout the book, "can we take seriously conceptions of the church as representations of the Heavenly City" (2000, 110). Does this rupture undermine the affective role of architectural representation, endangering it to either kitsch or nostalgia? The cultural distance between representation and materiality, evidenced by the reassignment of churches to social spaces (and that alone), would seem to instill a close relation between the loss of origins and the advancement of progression, so returning us to Pierre Nora's lamentation over the erasure of ritualistic memory. Indeed, in this respect, there is a strong thematic link bringing Nora and Harries together. Both, for instance, are concerned with architecture as the means through which the natural is protected, and a sense of collectivity is preserved. In both thinkers, this unity is presented as being under constant threat from a process of homogenization, the result of which is the purported effacement of an object's essence. The question of essence and its relationship to the arbitrary here is critical. Indeed, in an earlier article, Harries runs directly into Nora:

> We may know much more about history today than ever before, but precisely in making the past an object of scientific investigation, the sense of belonging to the past is lost. We have removed ourselves too effectively from the past to still belong to it. Time has been reduced to a coordinate on which we move back and forth with equal facility. (1993, 47)

The lack of belonging, loss of the past, and reduction of time crystallize the problem of arbitrariness. Representation, for Harries, is precisely the problem of negotiating with the "dreams of an ideal architecture" (1993, 48), in a time where those dreams have been usurped, largely by (post)modernity. The result is the employment of architectural practice as a matter of convention, rather than necessity. It is a project, moreover, carried out through modern architecture, which Harries is decidedly wary (and seemingly weary) of.

Given the problematic nature of architectural essentialism—the propensity to exclusion, the overemphasis on boundaries, and the implicit nostalgia that holds essences in place—must we dispense with architecture as a form of re-presenting the past? Note that the relation between representation and re-presentation is one of temporal emphasis. If representation concerns the language that enables the past to be transmitted into the present, then the re-presenting of the past accents the doubling of the transmission. In other words, re-presenting points to the return of the past, its resurgent repetition within the present. Given this relation, the question we must now ask is *what* is being re-presented through representation?

The disquiet Harries experiences in the face of modern architecture appears to be due to the erasure of the ideal essence, so undermining the affective potential of representation. Yet this is hardly surprising given the rigid tension between representation and the ideal incarnation of what is being re-presented; namely, the nonarbitrary essence of a specific building. The reliance on architecture as occupying a temporally continuous lineage—a lineage that preserves the original essence of a given building—serves to only delimit rather than strengthen the power of representation, diminishing, in Gadamer's terms, the "mysterious intimacy that grips our entire being" central to the relation between aesthetics and hermeneutics (1977, 95). Indeed, Harries's emphasis on the "telos" of architecture entails a plea to "natural symbols," understood as transcendental features of spatial experience (1993, 53–54). Hermeneutically, the re-presentation of symbols in the built environment buckles under the pressure of what is lost or otherwise "granted to univocity" (Harries 2000, 132). Consequently, for him, the effacement of architecture's transcendental properties renders contemporary representation veering toward outright nihilism—for him, a free-floating emergence of unhinged "metasymbols" (132), symbols marked by their playful interplay of surface forms.

This dichotomy between the natural language of symbols—a "system of symbols that architects could presuppose and therefore did not have to invent" (Harries 2000, 133)—and a nexus of metasymbols, each of which affirms its arbitrary playfulness through posturing ironically, is contestable, reductive, and, above all, wholly unreceptive to the relationship between representation and contingency. This omission of contingency is an invitation to think anew the relationship between architecture and representation. Disrupting the relationship between architecture and essentialism does not necessarily mean simultaneously rejecting architecture as the gesture of representation as re-presentation. Rather, it means making-room for the emergence of representation as an ambiguous rather than ideal re-presentation, a claim I will now develop by turning to the materiality of the Chattri.

A TEXTURE OF DEATH

Beyond the analysis of the Chattri as an object that displaces the landscape, how does this object come to invoke a particular way of attending to the past? More specifically, under what conditions is it possible for an object to not only mark the landscape, but to also signify the narrative history of that landscape? Let us take text and texture as the main themes as we interrogate this question.

Textually, the inscription framing the Chattri sanctions a specificity peculiar to the monument and its setting. In this way, the given themes in the inscription—memory, sacrifice, death—literally re-collect what is necessary to the emergence of the monument: as a place of commemoration and a place where Hindus and Sikhs were themselves cremated. Nothing more is said, no broader history portrayed. Yet what results from the text, concise as it is, is nothing less than a confirmation of the continuity of the past through the death of those being remembered, as Casey observes incisively: "Commemorative language not merely replaces the loss effected by death; it is a substitute for death that allows death to come forward as death" (2000b, 232). What is paradoxical about this language is that it renders the abstract dimension of death void precisely through providing a distance between representation and the event. Coming forward "*as* death" means retaining a dynamic narrative, in which the event of death perpetually springs toward the present rather than being consigned to the stasis of nonactivity. Indeed, it is precisely because commemoration occurs through text that death can be assimilated as an enduring event.

Coupled with this framework, the texture of the monument presents itself as solidifying the union between silence, memory, and meaning. Just as the practice of collective silence stabilizes the presence of the past in the present (and also the future), so the durability of the material serves to bind time with place, establishing a reliance on the monument, against which the effects of weathering and erosion falter. As located within a given place, the temporal centrality of commemorative silence is transferred to a fixed location, a practice that would otherwise be undermined were the monument physically dispersed. Because of this immovability, the past, as carried forward into the present, occurs through the interplay between ritual and durability.

Thanks to this entwinement between texture and commemoration, the aesthetic dimension of the monument plays a significant role in its symbolic emergence. Above all, the monument's resistance toward mutability forms a complicity with the sublime, not least because the confrontation with the unbound—Pascal's "terrifying infinite space"—mirrors the Kantian articulation of rational sovereignty. In this way, it is through engaging with, and being constituted by the transience of materiality, that the monument overcomes the flux of becoming. "A cyclopean wall," so writes Lefebvre, "achieves monumental beauty because it seems eternal, because it seems to have escaped time. Monumentality transcends death" (1991, 221). This direct exchange between texture and death empowers the monument, generating an intensified ambience, in which durability coincides with the appearance of the transcendental. For Lefebvre, of course, the emphasis on the transcendental as an affective rather than an ontological category attests to the voluntary "will to power," led by the figure of the "architect as demiurge" (133). Representation as re-presentation thus forms a circular path, whereby the "illusion" of durability returns to the desires and fears of the lived-body in its own diminishment. The return is telling, since it implicates the role of the individual self as both finite and contingent within the collective arrangement of a public past. How can we phrase this relation between public memory and individual death?

The individual human subject stands before the monument. The object is neither passive nor indifferent to the viewer. But nor is the meaning of the interaction clear from the outset. A relation between self and world opens, whereby the monument not only empowers itself as transcending death, but also presents itself as an object to empower the viewer as a finite entity. Thanks to this dynamic, affective experience is framed by the aesthetic attributes of the monument. The monument becomes a site of affirmation and introspection, at once pointing to the anonymity of death but also to the singularity of individual finitude.

In this respect, Lefebvre's "will to power" reduces the monument to less a public memory and more an ornament positioned as an indirect but glorified memento mori. If this movement toward the self is only hinted at in Lefebvre's account, then from a Heideggerian perspective, this appeal to individual experience can be understood within the framework of Dasein's potential for an authentic being-toward-death. Such an approach is taken up directly by Janet Donohoe in an article dealing with dwelling and monumentality (2002).

For Donohoe, the marking of a successful monument is its ability to "keep us mindful of our death," together with its potential to "remind us of an open relationship to the world that resists presuppositions or the imposition of meaning" (2002, 237). Given this twofold operation between death and indeterminacy, Donohoe (237) comes to the view that "totalitarian" monuments built in honor of (and under the eyes of) dictators, effectively undermine death as a space of potential. On the one hand, Donohoe's distinction between totalitarian monuments and a monument that "resists order, resists ideology and inspires the telling of personal histories" is laudable (237). In light of the distinction, a framework is provided, in which meaning and memory are directed to the viewer rather than toward an abstract conception of this relationship. On the other hand, the additional alignment between indeterminate monuments and the imperative to remain "mindful of our own individual death" by inducing anxiety is contentious (238).

Above all, the main concern regarding the tension between the public emphasis of the monument and the individual relation toward death can be framed as a question: If it is the case that the interaction between self and monument is one of potential for the self as a finite subject, then where does this leave the memory of the past, given that a "successful" monument appears to become the medium for uncertainty, anxiety, and ultimately a call toward "our attentiveness to the human condition" (Donohoe 2002, 238), rather than encouraging a critical dialogue, not between Dasein and death, but between memory and history?

Quite apart from the legitimacy of Heidegger's argument for an authentic being-toward-death, the question arises whether a monument can point toward the past while simultaneously orientating itself toward death as a future event, if only as a polarized memento mori. Whereas the relation between monumentality, death, and dwelling concerns bringing the past into the future via the self, such a lineage, nonetheless, privileges the present as an event for Dasein. In turn, the objectification of death is subjected to an ontic appeal. Not only this, but the temporality of the monument places the self in a privileged location, insofar as time becomes re-presented in and through the self. Because of this, even the "spontaneous quiet" that descends upon the visitors to monuments forces a return to the opening of anxiety rather than remaining a fluid interplay of different spatial and historical structures.

To clarify, I am not denying a thematic and corresponding link between the monument as an object of death and the viewer as subjected to death, a link that undoubtedly reinforces the affectivity of the monument within a given space, such that being "reminded" of our own death in a mindful way marks an intimacy between monument and self. Such a connection, however, is discrete from the appearance of the monument in both its textural and textual complexity, as an object of relation to the re-presentation of a past event.

How can we accommodate the relation between subjectivity and monumentality if not through an appeal to the existential facticity of the self? One alternative route toward this relation can be mined with recourse to Levinas's (2005) account of nonegocentric temporality. To situate this approach in context, let us recall that in the Heideggerian reading, the presence of the self in the face of the monument has been framed by the monument's ability to disturb our relation to death. By way of contrast, for Levinas, the re-presentation of the past through the "egological" self attests to the treatment of time as an objective presence parallel to individual memory. This tendency is incipient even within the act of intentionality, as he writes: "But intentionality also indicates an aspiration, finality, a moment of egoism or egotism and, in any case, 'egology'" (98). His sense that intentionality is also an "aspiration" has significant implications for the alterity of time, given that "presence or being is also a temporal modality" (98). Ethically, this leads to the danger of converting otherness into the same, a conversion that takes place through the reclamation of the past: "To comprehend the alteration of presence in the past and future would be a matter of reducing and bringing back the past and future to presence—that is, re-presenting them" (99). From this "alteration of presence," the "*I think*" assumes a magisterial stance, conferring a unity upon time through its own governance.

At the heart of Levinas's understanding of time is his anxiety about "synchrony" (2005, 99). For what this involves is an effacement "of the other [*Autre*] to the Same, synchrony as *being* in its egological gathering" (99; italics in original). Temporally, the assimilation of otherness is understood in Levinasian terms as the future. Reducing otherness to sameness, a linear timescale is produced, which leaves no room for a past outside of an already-established narrative and seizes the dialectical unfolding of time in its tracks. Indeed, for Levinas, this assimilation is led by the "search for the presence of what is already past or of what has not yet come about, and then recall them, foresee them, or name them, by signs" (100). In the relation between memory and history, the egological approach refuses to be interrupted "even when presence, beyond the re-presentation accomplished in memory and imagination, is assured by the investigations of the historian and the futurologist" (101). Against the work of the ego, objective knowledge falters, while history is reduced to the province of the self.

The synchrony between the self and temporality can be witnessed in the Heideggerian attempt to affix the anxious subject with the appearance of the monument, such that the monument already establishes a relation with the self in advance. In a Levinasian context, the result of this self-monument hybrid is the erasure of responsibility, as time, in its difference and otherness, is seized by the ego. It is precisely this subjugation of history toward an egocentric limit that is occurring in the Heideggerian reading of memory and monumentality as an invitation for Dasein to realize (and remind itself of) its potential toward an authentic being-toward-death. Given this orientation from the monument to the self, what follows is a gathering of the past, which is thus transformed into an anticipated, rather than unknown, future.

But here Levinas stages a turning. For only within the light of what he terms an "immemorial past" is synchronic time replaced by diachronic time, thus establishing the basis for an ethical responsibility toward history: "In this responsibility I am thrown back toward what has never been my fault or my deed, toward what has never been in my power or in my freedom, toward what has never been my presence, and has never come into my memory" (Levinas 2005, 111). This radical exclusion of time leads to a negative concept of history. For this is a decentered part, "an-archic" in its structure and without reference to a self attending to it. Without any personal attributes to attract the ego, the immemorial past signifies a "*nonintentional* participation in the history of humanity*," such that the "I" becomes anonymous (111; italics in original). The immemorial past is anonymous, given that what is being represented is outside human experience, and necessarily precludes ever being present.

The peculiarity of Levinas's position is realized when contrasted with the Heideggerian account of death and monumentality. What is taken in a Heideggerian context as the gathering of Dasein, for Levinas, is witnessed as the subjugation of history, a subjugation only deferred by the time of the Other, which, in its refusal to be re-presented, issues an "ethical vigilance" toward my "responsibility for the Other" (2005, 112). Levinas's "imperative" renders the Other the simultaneous futural-past event, unable to be recuperated in the present or raised as a presence, and instead serving to disrupt the egology of the self.

Instead of phrasing the monument as a reminder of mortality, I would prefer to speak alongside Levinas of the monument as an anonymous presence that re-presents, not simply the spatial and symbolic interruption of the landscape, but also the irreducibility of the past, taken at the limits of its materiality. In this sense, the monument articulates a borderline between history and memory, meaning that what is being returned to is both absent and present concurrently: absent as an "immemorial past," but present as the "imperative" toward the responsibility of that past.

In the view—indeed, the *face*—of the monument, the restoration of a past event is not achieved; presence is not returned in its originary state. Nor is the monument's representative power ultimately capable of returning the past to the present, such that what is being re-presented occupies a privileged relationship with place and time. Rather, what is being re-presented is the struggle of the past to be met in the present. This struggle can be sensed in Levinas's account of "the 'difference' of diachrony," in which the ideas of totality and closure are ruptured (2005, 118).

In the subject's relationship to the monument, closure is usurped by the legacy of an event that exceeds the spatiotemporality of the present. Through its text and texture, the gesture of offsetting is evident as the environment of the monument undergoes a dislocation of time. Time and place become pressurized in this light, while the ego simultaneously loses its bearings in the world. Through exposing ourselves to the monument's durability, what comes to the surface is not the singular incarnation of a prescribed history, but the anonymity of a "time before the beginning" (Levinas 1994, 88). Before this immemorial time, otherness incurs upon my desires, decentering the spatiotemporal self. With this decentering, the I experiences an estrangement before the monument; through its very phenomenality, a rupture is forged in the midst of everyday being.

Because of this rupture, the certainty masking the historical past is met with radical uncertainty. In so doing, Levinas sounds a warning to our tendency to ally ourselves too closely to habituated narratives of memory, history, and experience. In the experience of the monument, this warning is articulated: Through attending to it phenomenologically, the demand to remember becomes invested with a reluctance to find "closure" on the past. From a Levinasian perspective, the monument does less to affirm our fortitude in the face of death, and more to shatter our egocentric bond with mortality. The result of taking materiality and monumentality in strictly phenomenal terms is thus a challenge to our attempt not only to "place" the past, but also to place our own selves within relation to that past—a theme I shall now give full reign to.

Part Two
From Flesh to Materiality

. . . .

CHAPTER THREE

MEMORIES OF THE FLESH

The aggressive stylization of this mass-produced cockpit, the ex-aggerated mouldings of the instrument binnacles emphasized my growing sense of a new junction between my own body and the automobile, closer than my feelings for Renata's broad hips and strong legs stowed out of sight beneath her red plastic raincoat. I leaned forward, feeling the rim of the steering wheel against the scars on my chest, pressing my knees against the ignition switch and handbrake.

—J. G. Ballard, *Crash*

In a hallway pockmarked by dark green organic spores, a wooden door has swung open. Through the door is a room that I have yet to set foot in. Already, however, my body is in the room, stretching its sensory organs toward the horizon of this strange new world. At the forefront of this dis-covery is my visual sight, which is gazing, glancing, and glaring at the room from the safety of the doorway. A high ceiling is in a state of disrepair, and all around me I catch sight of various artifacts eroding. Chairs are upturned and tables have been piled on top of one another in the corner. Not only this, but I can also *see* the room from different angles. A glitterball remains perched precariously on the ceiling, and from it, I can view the room from above. But other senses soon follow. Before long, my nostrils and ears are exposed to the smell and sound this particular room invokes. Everything has succumbed to a musty hue, and the sound can be heard of a trapped bird flapping its wings frantically. Although I have yet to move within this space, something peculiar can be discerned in my limbs: My body has begun to "touch" this place in advance. Even at the doorway—*especially* at the doorway—I can feel my hand trace the curtain on the other side of room, by the derelict stage.

THE LIVED-BODY

How does my body, this "mass of tactile, labyrinthine and kinaesthetic data" (Merleau-Ponty 2006, 290), sense this abandoned ballroom before "I" have actually set foot in it? To phrase the question in this way seems to presuppose that the "I" is an entity autonomous from my body, as though the body wanders in the dark while the cogito remains in place. Yet my experience of the ballroom is characterized by a preemptive movement on behalf of my body, as though my hands had eyes of their own, and in which processes and actions are occurring in advance of my abstract formulations. Does my body really reach out toward the world before my mind is prepared to do so? This is a complicated question, which appears to run contrary to our phenomenological expectations that the self consists of "one's own body" (115), a body that is presumably temporally coexistent with cognition. If movement in place is only possible thanks to the fact of being "one's own body," then by forcing a crevice between bodily space and cognitive space, we seem to have fallen short of the classical phenomenological subject, inasmuch as my consciousness is somehow "left behind." Worst of all, however, is the impression of a Cartesian account of experience, in which the materiality of my body occupies an incidental relationship to my genuine "self."

Yet this impression is misleading. After all, when I stand at the doorway of an abandoned ballroom, then what is foremost in this action is not the supposed sovereignty of consciousness, but the primacy of the body. This is clear in that my body's intelligibility extends beyond the reach of my cognition while at all times being entwined with my rationalization of space. "Motility," writes Merleau-Ponty correctly, "is not, as it were, a handmaid of consciousness, transporting the body to that point in space of which we have formed a representation beforehand" (2006, 161). When faced with the ballroom, it is not enough for me to remain within the space of the doorframe. Instead, this particular presentation of phenomena is an invitation for me to reach out and touch the textures that make up the room. I do so because the room asks itself to be experienced. But touching does not always involve tactility. Rather, I am able to figure this world out from afar, literally gaining a sense of it without yet moving.

Where does this leave us? On the one hand, my body—the core of both lived experience and a site of physical activity in the world—is wholly identifiable with myself as a subject in space and time. On the other hand, myself as a subject in space and time is vulnerable to a shift in emphasis, such that how I experience things can waver between an emphasis in cognitive and bodily focuses. Does this difference in emphasis between the intentionality of the body and the intentionality of consciousness constitute a tacit dualism? An objection to this claim might well be that the consciousness *is* embodied and that embodiment *is* conscious. This is certainly true, but there is a further complication.

Consider how we can plot a different movement in space and time through *emphasizing* how a corporeal and cognitive response to experience produces diverse findings. The stress on *emphasizing* is central here. Although guided by what Merleau-Ponty terms a "primitive spatiality" (2006, 171), the embodied self is nonetheless engaged in an ambiguous relation with how rational and abstract formulations of those experiences are constructed in light of that primitive presence. By emphasizing the cognitive or the corporeal dimension, we need not posit metaphysical dualism to the mind-body interaction. Emphasizing how I rationally appropriate or perform an experience does nothing to detract from the anchoring role of my body. My body is there all along, consistently rendering my actions possible. Only now, my body has come into conflict with the difference in how that experience is understood in a less corporeal manner.

If we can emphasize our cognitive and embodied responses to the world, such that one dimension is heightened at the expense of the other, then what of memory? Can we, for instance, remember a place in two quite dissimilar even opposing fashions? The broad task of the current chapter will be to contend with this significant question. What is presupposed in the question immediately forces a distance from the earlier chapters. First, we found ourselves attending to the development of place memory via the kinesthetic sensibility of the body (chapter 1). Second, our concern shifted to the representation of the past through built materiality (chapter 2). In each of these cases, it was taken for granted that the memory being attended to had already been located in its environment.

But let us suppose that it is possible to remember a place in such a way that we are cognitively unaware of that memory; that is, to open up the possibility of "remembering without seeing," as Plato would have it. Where would that lead us? No doubt faced with a paradox: Precisely through experiencing something in a cognitively perceptive way, that same experience becomes blind to the act of remembering. At least, blind to the *volitional* recall of that event. But a memory that evades consciousness does not equate a void in experience. Rather, through circumventing the demands of an

impatient consciousness, memory only embeds itself deeper in the noncognitive body, in the limbs and sinews that refuse to rationalize experience into
past, present, and future. Does this mean our conscious awareness of that
memory has fallen prey to blindness? The answer hinges on what is meant
by "blindness."

To be cognitively unaware of an experience does not mean that the experience goes wholly unobserved. For instance, there are many experiences
and moods, such as generalized anxiety, that are taken up and materialize
through the body prior to cognitive intentionality being wholly receptive to
the unfolding activity. Indeed, one could argue that of all emotions, anxiety
is the only one that bypasses abstraction and self-distance. In those initial
stages, all we might feel is that something in the world is slightly disjointed,
without having fully ascribed that peculiarity to an effect of the human body.
Later on, however, we sense that far from an atmosphere floating in the air,
the discomfort derives from a precognitive action the body has committed
itself to. The result of this realization is something like an uncanny tremor,
as it becomes evident that a part of our lived experience has broken off from
being an immediate focus of attention.

This orientation toward the bodily reception of things pushes us in a new
direction, in the process catalyzing a new series of problems concerning the
phenomenal quality of places in relation to the unity of selfhood. The problem can be phrased as a question: Do mental and bodily phenomena exist
independently of one another? The classical phenomenological response
would be to answer in the negative. Merleau-Ponty speaks of the "synthesis
of one's body" (2006, 171). Doing so, he describes an overlapping movement, in which all the parts of the body tacitly work together to perform any
given action. At no point is the action split into dissectible compartments,
ordered by a separate agency termed "cognition." The same is true of the
visual aspect of the body, as he states: "Thus the connecting link between
the parts of our body and that between our visual and tactile experience are
not forged gradually and cumulatively" (173). Instead, the body as a whole
performs the visual and tactile actions simultaneously, both folding into the
same zone. The result of this, for Merleau-Ponty, is that visual observation
and embodied experience coincide with each other, meaning that "we are the
unifier of these arms and legs, the person who both sees and touches them"
(173). Like a work of art, the body has a meaningful unity, which is immediately given through its phenomenal and lived appearance. Just as we seldom
approach a novel or poem in terms of the parts of which it is composed, so

the body is a "nexus of living meanings" (175), whereupon visual and tactile data fuse together.

Where does this leave my experience of the derelict ballroom? If Merleau-Ponty is correct in saying that the body is a "nexus of living meanings," each of which coincides with the other, then the idea of my body moving in a pre-emptive way *prior* to my rational mind being ready seems untenable. Rather, what we are presented with is the total schematic movement of the body as a whole. In this way, the integration of the body is less a manner of utilizing its parts conceptually and more a question of the embodied self placing itself in the world in an anticipatory way.

But here something key happens. With the anticipatory gesture of the body placing itself, we come into contact with the notion of a "motor intentionality" (Merleau-Ponty 2006, 127), which is distinct from mental intentionality, not least because, unlike mental phenomenon, motor intentionality is devoid of reflective beliefs concerning the world. At the door of the ballroom, reflective reason alone does not prevent me from immediately setting foot on the damp floorboards. Instead, my body grasps the appearing world *through* my body.

Once again, then, we are straddling a line of ambiguity. Not only is this ambiguity torn between my body as being identifiable with myself, and my-self as being exposed to a different emphasis in cognitive and corporeal ex-perience—now we see that two modes of intentionality at once unify the self, but simultaneously place the body in a state of relative autonomy. This autonomous status has already been detected in Merleau-Ponty's account of the phantom limb, which we discussed above, and we shall return to it time and again.

In such a case, the body's reflex movements prove themselves as being "never blind processes," but "adjust themselves to a 'direction' of the situa-tion" (Merleau-Ponty 2006, 91). Seen in light of "motor intentionality," the body is presented as a mode of persistence in the world. The world endures just as it did when all the limbs were intact. But this endurance is not reduc-ible to psychological repression or habit. Rather, the body intervenes in its own materiality, providing a bridge to our being-in-the-world that would be damaged were it the case that human beings were solely mental substances.

When faced with a new room, our bodies exceed the view of our vi-sual perception. The overview is not only topographical, but haptic, too. My body is the receiver of this vast space, just as I self-consciously inte-grate the room into my memory and imagination. Overriding the complex ambiguities of the human body, then, is the anticipatory gesture of the living body, as its inhalations and exhalations reach beyond the realm of visual sight, traveling far into the unseen alcoves that are blind to the eyes but visible to the perceiving body. "Prior to stimuli and sensory contents," so writes Merleau-Ponty, "we must recognize a kind of inner diaphragm which determines, infinitely more than they do, what our reflexes and perceptions will be able to aim at in the world, the area of our possible operations, the scope of our life" (2006, 92).

If there was any doubt as to the body's primacy, both spatially and temporally, then in this passage, Merleau-Ponty renders the body's secret "inner diaphragm" clearly—a primacy that extends to the very "scope" of a life.

But just as our hands can exceed the range of our eyes, so our eyes can exceed the reach of our hands, as Merleau-Ponty remarks: "While I am overcome by some grief and wholly given over to my distress, my eyes already stray in front of me, and are drawn, despite everything, to some shining object, and thereupon resume their autonomous existence" (2006, 97). Not only are the eyes already in front of me, but their direction is oriented toward a meaningful horizon, which imparts itself upon my present existence. And this occurs from the most trivial of details to the boldest endeavor to preserve a life-world made vulnerable in the contingency of space and time.

**

The direction we have steered toward has thematized the body as expressing a world peculiar to its own sensibility. In short, the body's understanding of the world is unique *to* the body. In what follows, this understanding will be applied to the tension between the experience of place and the memory of place.

Consider the following thought: Our bodies experience places according to certain contingent dimensions—cultural, economic, aesthetic, and so forth. At the same time, our bodies also open themselves to a wholly different memory of that same place, purely phenomenal in structure, serving as nothing less than a platform for *embodied hermeneutics*. The phrase "embodied hermeneutics" plays upon Merleau-Ponty's distinction between mental intentionality and motor intentionality, in the process affirming the terrain occupied between these poles. My body reveals itself as having two sides, that of a lived organ of perception and that of being an object in the world, receiving the world in its own unique way. As the center of perception and my world, the "sight" of the body is nonetheless autonomous from this center; beyond the visual realm, my body's intentionality works of its own accord, finding its way in the indeterminacy of any given environment. This is the power of embodiment, as the body sets the path for all dimensionality.

But understanding this mode of intentionality does not necessarily generate unity with the contingent aspects of a place, such as sociopolitical dimensions. When faced with an urban wasteland, I might be inclined to formulate a response as to how this place merits restoration. Doing so, I would factor in manifold social and economic issues in order to best achieve that status of renewal without damaging the broader environment or undermining the history of the area. All of this, however, is a matter different from how I experience that same zone of land through my body. Before this abstract formulation is made, my body has already apprehended the rugged terrain, ingesting the wasteland's surfaces and counters through the body's own textures.

Here cognition and corporeality have the potential to clash, effecting a disturbance in place that was absent in the previous chapters. After all, it is not necessarily the case that how I experience a place culturally will reconcile with how I experience a place corporeally, a difference I shall return to in time. This is made clear provisionally if we again consider how the train and the monument from the previous chapters emerge as highly distinct in their emphasis on experience and representation, with each emphasis demarcating a comparatively unambiguous region of discourse and experience. What I will suggest in this chapter is that between these distinct poles, a third process occurs, whereby we can phenomenologically attend to the space in which the body becomes the site of an experience that is independent from and at odds with our abstract assessment of that same experience. As stated in the preface, I term this motion "transitional memory." My reason is as follows: *Transitional memory is a memory that, while originating in the body, has nevertheless yet to be formally registered as becoming part of the self as a unified whole.*

As I shall go on to argue, such a memory has a special relation with certain ways of experiencing an environment and is especially pronounced when there arises a strain between visual memory and body memory. One particular way in which this strain is articulated is through being in places that themselves share in this ambiguous and transient status. Here, I am referring to locations, commonly termed "non-places," such as airports, motorways, and waiting rooms—places that, broadly construed, contribute to a sense of being disembodied. My overall aim in this chapter, however, is to argue that far from being opposed to our conception of what constitutes a "sense of place," these ambiguous environments are as much a factor in the formation of identity as are domestic and domesticated places.

INSIDE AND OUTSIDE

The task we have assigned ourselves is to examine how the body's intentionality has the potential to receive the world in a manner that confers a tension upon our cognitive and cultural experiences of the world. how does the term "place" fit into this discussion? How can we begin to chart this dialectical movement from the body to culture without already finding our way in place? Such a question is compounded by the introduction of the term "non-place," which has a gained a cultural legacy despite several significant shortcomings, all of which shall be addressed soon. While we have broached the question of what "place" is in the previous chapters, by contrasting it with "non-place," a more detailed analysis of what makes the identity of place is required. Indeed, without this clarificatory move, the main critical thrust of the chapter—that place and non-place are fundamentally ambiguous— would lose its clarity.

By suggesting that place has an identity, I am not arguing that this identity is either static or absolute. As I have argued in the introduction, place is a decidedly elusive notion. Yet if not place itself, then the *formation* of place, nevertheless, deserves to be characterized in broad terms. Otherwise, we are left with an ungrounded assertion as to the limits and scope of the very term "place." Particularly pressing to this question is the supposed distinction between place, non-place, site, and space: terms that, considered as interrelated, warrant critical engagement.

As outlined in the introduction, we understand place to be composed of a complex texture, as rich as it is irreducible. Exclusively neither a subjective construct nor an object incidentally in the world, place is somewhere in between—fundamentally a hybrid concept. By straddling the line between realism and idealism, it becomes possible to contest the identity of place as an already-formed category, which is posited as being transcendental to experience.

Place forms in time. This much we can say. Nonetheless, other desires, not least the desire for a home, encroach upon the indeterminacy of place, affording a line of continuity. Desire stretches out toward the world, at the same time returning that world to the self. With this motion, place is both gained and lost in time, as our desires collide with the reality of things. How can we trace this emergence of loss and gain?

The question seems to suggest an encounter with place, as though finding place was a matter of locating it in the world, distinct from space, and informed by a distinction between the insideness of place and the outsideness of space, where insideness refers to the everyday, meaningful immersion in the surrounding environment (Bachelard 1994; Relph 1976; Seamon 1979; Tuan 1977). What would such an encounter signify? Undoubtedly, we are faced with an archetypal distinction between inside and outside, which relies on the primordial image of shelter, and thus becomes the elemental motif in all built spaces. Indeed, given the relationship between shelter and insideness, it is difficult to conceive of dwelling as involving anything less than an unequivocal division between inside and outside. While the question of encountering the inside of place is an important one, the encounter cannot be understood without proceeding from the temporal perspective of where place has come from; namely, *outside*.

But how do we approach a phenomenology of being outside a place without already finding ourselves inside a place to conduct that glance? The bind reinforces the overarching importance of being somewhere in place. At no point do we find ourselves wholly displaced, in a region without any discernible features to orient us. The very fact of being embodied undermines such a stark reality. It is no doubt for this reason the images of centrality and unity are associated with the enclosure of being inside place. If transgressing the limits of being somewhere in place prove to be solely the dream of Gnostics, then we can nevertheless conceive of being at the *threshold* between inside and outside.

Phrased another way, if, as phenomenological geographers such as Edward Relph and David Seamon suggest, the experience of place-insideness, marked by a sense of belonging and homeliness, is where meaning and stability are attained, then where does the outside stand in this relation? Against the impulse to polarize these modes of experience, note that even within the most explicitly topophilic context, inside and outside acquire a dynamic status. I am thinking here of Bachelard's incisive discussion on the "dialectics of outside and inside" (1994, 211–31). For Bachelard, the relationship between inside and outside is fundamentally dialectic in structure, meaning that "it has the sharpness of the dialectics of *yes* and *no*, which decides everything" (211; italics in original). More than this, however, there is a conceptual scheme at work alongside the positive and the negative. Recognizing that inside and the outside is understood philosophically as a division between "being and non-being," Bachelard proceeds to align these two aspects with "here" and "there" respectively (212). The significance of these dimensions does not mean that the "there" of non-being retains its distance from the "here" of being. Instead, Bachelard invites us to think of these dimensions as "always ready to be reversed, to exchange their hostility" (218). This is a promising move, which compels Bachelard to consider the ambiguity at the heart of inside and outside. All of this, however, requires an experiential focus to breathe life into this distinction. Accordingly, we need to (re)turn to our own situation within place.

THE ABSOLUTE HERE

We start from the position of possibility. The word *position* here is revealing, because what is peculiar to place is not an abstract, geometric position, but a set of different and complex directions. One need only think here of Merleau-Ponty's account of directionality as involving "an absolute 'here' which can gradually confer a significance on all spatial determinations" (2006, 288). The "gradual" movement of gaining spatial determinations coincides with the lived experience of a place that is situated in relation to other places, and other regions within a place. The relationality of place is thus evident in that we can employ terms such as "left/right," "near/far," "above/below," and so on.

When I experience the room that I am currently in, I orient myself with reference to the surroundings of the environment. The term "surrounding" emphasizes the complex formation of the room. From the hallway, I am required to pass through the living room before arriving at my desk. In my corner, a wall of books creates an enclosure around me. At my desk, I am also aware of two other walls of books behind me. The enclosing influence of the walls of books is offset by the window, which is situated at the end of my desk. At the same time, the border between my desk and the world beyond it is further emphasized by my neighbor's windows, which peer directly down into my room. Being aware of the distance between the external windows and my own, I keep the shutters half-closed in order to retain my intimacy (in spite of never seeing anyone else in the windows opposite my own).

Here and there, far and near, left and right, thus constitute a fundamental set of binary opposition that leaves little room for ambiguity, but enough

Figure 6: *Neighbor's window, Brooklyn. Photo by author.*

space for vagueness. In other words, my references to the distance of the bookshelves, the external windows, or the scarf in the hallway, which I am contemplating collecting, are all mediated by a multiplicity of factors, and all prey to a flux of degrees of concentration. The proximity of my neighbor's windows, for example, is experienced as nearer the more I expose my own window from the shutters. Feeling the neighbor's window press down is the result of a greater attention I pay to it, which is brought about by the dual influence of daylight and the gradient at which the shutters are open.

Combined, the daylight and the sight of the neighbor's windows through the shutters leave minimal opportunity for distancing what is often a concealed presence. By contrast, the complete closure of the shutters at night brings about an almost total erasure of my awareness of the external windows. The erasure is not only an absence of seeing the windows, it is also recognition that my experience of this room no longer stands in relation to the windows that exist beyond the interior of place.

The same intensification of presence, informed by a sensory experience of that presence, is also true of "above and below." The felt spatial distance between my flat and the flat above me, for example, is mediated by the intensity of sound and vague creaking from above. The experience of the flat enclosing itself is the result of becoming aware of the environment as a discrete space beyond the limits of my immediate surroundings. The otherness of that space, in distinction from the place I have established down below, establishes a sharp opposition that not only is dependent on the intensity of sound, but also varies in accordance with *when* that sound occurs.

Thus, the retreat from my neighbor's windows at night brings with it an increased awareness to sound and to the surrounding environment from where that sound comes from. Yet the awareness is not a spontaneous discovery, but a reminder of what was there all along. Experiencing my flat at night, I am reminded of what is less conspicuous during the daytime. Only now, the awareness marks a shift in the experience of the total region. Darkness carries with it a creaking in the floorboards and a groaning in the walls. When trying to fall asleep, these sounds can penetrate the flesh of my body, such that I shudder when lying down. These sounds, with their primordial origins, seem to carry through the very center of my being, and at times, the slightest whimper from the floorboards can assume the impression of things trapped beneath the surface of the room. When the night recedes into the day, those same sounds no longer appear so prevalent, having been consumed by other forces, not least birds outside or the sound of the water heating up. Do those voices from the night sink further into the floorboards as life is resumed in the morning, or are those voices felt to be alive only during the night due to quieting of the broader world?

In being reminded of the otherness of the things outside my world, I simultaneously become aware of my own centrality within that dialectic.

Accordingly, in direct concordance with the reception of sound, the reverberations of sound within my own environment also become amplified. The amplification of sound is not determined by the objective level of output, but by the dual role of recognizing the otherness of space and the time in which that otherness occurs. In both cases, measurable space stays motionless, whereas lived place reveals its dynamic structure.

In a telling passage, Merleau-Ponty offers us the following account of his own flat:

> When I walk round my flat, the various aspects in which it presents itself to me could not possibly appear as views of one and the same thing if I did not know that each of them represents the flat seen from one spot or another, and if I were unaware of my own movements, and of my body as retaining its identity through the stages of those movements. I can of course take a mental bird's eye view of the flat, visualize it or draw a plan of it on paper, but in that case too I could not grasp the unity of the object without the mediation of bodily experience, for what I call a plan is only a more comprehensive perspective. (2006, 235)

Merleau-Ponty's description of inhabiting his flat outlines the salient features of how experiencing place depends on the totality of the body. The body's cohesive intelligence—its ability to attend to multiple directions without comprising orientation—means that place and body coexist alongside each other. Indeed, so tacit is bodily intentionality that we are accustomed to referring to it as "habitual." Yet the habitual routine of bodily experience does not entail passivity. Instead, the constantly projecting "here," which "confer[s] a significance on all spatial determinations," is a movement outward, toward the encompassing world in which the body is placed (Merleau-Ponty 2006, 288).

In conjunction with the activity of the body, the surroundings of place gain a greater sense of their very presence. Contrary to the view that habit dulls our sensible experience, considered from the perspective of experiencing place through time, accustoming ourselves to a specific region results in the background animation of that region. In other words, the taken-for-granted consistency of place allows for both surroundings and body to suffuse one another. The result is that the experience of place is heightened as the body, through its active but tacit engagement, literally absorbs the contours and textures of an environment.

Applying Merleau-Ponty's use of "absolute here" to the above account, what emerges is a confluence between place and body. Experiencing the room does not entail positioning myself "here" in abstraction. Instead, it means becoming placed by a series of felt directions, each of which stands in relation to where I am within place. In this way, the "here" is perpetually altering. Within this scope of dynamic fullness and particularity, the body carries with it an intelligibility, which becomes central to our experience of being here.

A sense of being "here" is thus peculiar to the experience of being placed. As proof of this relation, it is notable that the experience of disembodiment coexists with a lack of orientation. The diminishment of being-here, such as we may experience after not sleeping for several nights or when we fall ill, usually results in the inability to retain the continuous unity of bodily presence. Indeed, if the absence of sleep or illness is compounded with an expanse of space, then the destabilization is heightened. Consider the drama the body must undergo when traveling from one country to another while simultaneously gripped by illness. It is not simply that our bodies suffer from the symptoms of illness, such as fatigue or fever. Rather, the whole world is mediated through the ill body, so that place and time assume a highly singular appearance that conforms to the strains of the human body. In such a case, the body's intentionality places an extra demand for presence to be animated. With that demand, the intimacy between self and world, so far assumed as a taken-for-granted given of the life-world, is experienced as a self-conscious lack. In the same way, when a part of my body is injured, the presence does not retain a localized isolation, but instead disturbs the surrounding presence of my whole body. The disturbance is as much an explicit presence of my body *as* an objective body as it is the discomfort of the injury.

THE MEMORY OF AIRPORTS

"Body," "time," "world": With these terms, the "absolute here" of being in place gains a defined structure. But if we have so far focused on the relationship between world and body, then let us now consider the involvement of time within this matrix. To demonstrate the role place plays in shaping time, I suggest we consider an environment in which time is compressed: an airport. In doing so, let us consider how the duration of a single day differs in accordance with manifold environmental contributions. By performing a phenomenology of the experience of exiting an airport, we will see how

Figure 7: *Missoula International Airport, Montana. Photo by author.*

place forms a marker of temporal movement. In this way, movement in space becomes identifiable with movement in time. From one place to the next, we follow and pursue a thread of time, remembering where we have been and imagining where we are going. Enclosed within a day, the role movement plays in determining the unity and discontinuity of that day is absolute.

Let us imagine ourselves in the baggage-claim zone of an airport before the day has fully begun. Let us imagine that we have entered the space after a long international flight, the experience of which has left our bodies feeling heavy and slow in its mobility. Our bodies pause. Even if we travel on a regular basis, then the movement from exiting the plane before proceeding to customs is full of the drama of our bodily being. Above all, our first grasp of the environment beyond the cabin of the airplane is filled with the atmosphere peculiar to the region we have arrived in. Sometimes we are struck by a humidity that pierces the walls of the arrival gate despite the glass protecting us from the air. We *feel* the place around us even before leaving the airport itself. Since the flight has been international, this moment of reappearing in another country gains a peculiar, magical dimension.

On arrival, it is as though the actual experience of being airborne was more a void in time than the means of objectively covering ground. After all, we do not see the ground at eye level when we fly, but we see it as an abstracted canvas from the window of the cabin. This isotropic angle removes the details of our shared planet and instills an otherworldly, nonterrestrial aspect to flight. Having arrived at the airport from the plane, the anticipation of moving beyond the airport is heightened. Unlike the moment of waiting to depart, the adjoining action of arriving occupies a very different spatiotemporal scale. All the more so if we have arrived at the same airport we left from, since we risk being reunited with the ghost of our previous self, a self that had yet to experience the journey, which, for us, is rapidly becoming a memory. That this return should be charged with a sense of melancholy is entirely logical. At the root of this feeling is the radical difference stretched over the axis of leaving and returning. We have arrived, arrived at our homeworld, only to find it cloaked in an atmosphere of world-weariness. In light of this, the focus becomes one of anticipation and movement. In short, we seek to escape from this interstitial space as swiftly as possible. Because of this orientation toward the future, the appearance of the baggage claim becomes intensified as an intermediary space, an obstacle through which our exit depends. And yet before we leave, we must contend with the strange act of reclaiming our luggage from a slowly moving belt situated in the midst of other slowly moving belts.

How does time proceed as we await our luggage? At first glance, the question looks as though it is asking us to negotiate with the experience of impatience. Do we get agitated if the luggage takes too long to arrive? Is our experience of flying easier if we find our luggage already revolving on the belt? Such questions are soon conflated with the broader phenomena of crossing different time zones. Does the movement of the belt accelerate and slow down according to how jet-lagged we are? Likewise, does the experience of jet lag on our bodies—itself an action that deserves a lengthy treatise—influence how we encounter the experience of waiting? No doubt these questions have an overarching significance, but we must probe at a more enigmatic thought, and ask: Does the baggage claim offer itself as the spatial link between one place and another?

Here, the baggage as a material object becomes intrinsic to the question. Visually seeing the baggage eject from the tunnel before landing on the rubber track, we encounter an object that simultaneously reminds us and assures us of our previous place. That an object we deposited in one country should then arrive in another, without our seeing the logistics of how such an operation is possible, affirms the very reality of our presence here. Strikingly, this emergence evades all the marks of the uncanny, such as we would experience when finding a forgotten note in a book from a lover who is no longer with us. The luggage lacks this spectral dimension through still being a basic part of our life-world. In this way, (re)claiming the luggage, we are simultaneously reclaiming and reinforcing temporal continuity. To phrase it unequivocally, we reclaim our very *selves* through this act. Indeed, when the baggage claim belt is emptied of its contents and our belongings fail to appear, then the dismay is not due simply to the inconvenience of lacking items in the world. Rather, the experience of disquiet is bound with the irresolution of a part of us occupying a nonterrestrial space.

But here something odd occurs. As we move beyond the airport and return to our homes, the memory of the baggage claim becomes invested with a peculiar centrality, such that the experience of the day gains its orientation

Figure 8: *LAX International Airport, Los Angeles. Courtesy of Thomas Merkle.*

thanks to the earlier experience of waiting for the baggage. Away from the airport, space and time become jagged, caught in the prism of an experience that has yet to settle into the earth. At home, the baggage claim is still with us, sliced into the pockets of our flesh. Together, this fusion between experience of an intermediary space and the action of suddenly leaving that space for a final destination serves to create an impression of time's being protracted. Often, enough of the feel of the airport remains within us to retain the sense of where we have been. We are home, still unpacked, the suitcase consigned to a corner, and yet something else is beside us. A waiting, a memory, a visitation.

Even the great power of jet lag to confuse and disorient time and space remains limited. Thrown between different and disparate time zones, we nevertheless remain rooted by the pivotal experience of being linked from one place to another. Sometimes, however, jet lag does get the better of us, and when we are unable to fend off sleeping in the afternoon, then we enter a different temporal horizon. In giving ourselves over to the lost time of unconsciousness, a new rhythm is conceived, composed partly of the former remnants of the experience of the airport but now shadowed by the confusion of being back in our own homes. Sleep has intervened, and now the baggage claim, customs check, and window of the airplane risk being colonized by the work of dreams. What survives this night in the midst of day ends up becoming memory itself, that which binds us to another place. Until that event has formed, however, then our fall into sleep serves to demarcate one time and place from another. And this genesis of awaking into our homes is a privileged moment. A distinct instant, analogous to musical modulation, is acted out. The atmosphere has altered, our bodies have caught up with us, and fatigue will soon set in. Similarly, whether sleep produces a temporal tabula rasa is not what is important at present. At stake is the expansion and estrangement we feel from the past, as the rhythm of time loses its place in the present, until the memory of baggage claim becomes entangled in a curiously atemporal plane.

Concerning the spatiality of being-in-the-world, Heidegger writes as follows:

> Even when we use more exact measures and say "it takes half an hour to get to the house," this measure must be understood as an estimation. "Half an hour" is not thirty minutes, but a duration which does not have any "length" in the sense of a quantitative stretch.

> This duration is always interpreted in terms of familiar, everyday "activities." (1996, 98)

Heidegger's point makes it clear that lived time and objective time are at all times at the mercy of everyday experience, which is immune to all but the most ambiguous modes of measurement. The experience of time comprises not simply what occurs in any given stretch of time, but also the very affectivity of those occurrences. Moods such as boredom, enjoyment, familiarity, and unfamiliarity all conspire to undermine the notion of time as being homogeneous.

"In its countless alveoli," writes Bachelard characteristically, "space contains compressed time. This is what space is for" (1994, 8). Compressing time, place becomes more than a geometrical marker in our experiences and instead becomes the very ground of how time is given form and definition. The relationship is complex because through our experience of place, our own bodies become entangled within our surrounding environment. Doing so, places become plentiful, full of the temporal vibrancy of our bodies, stretching back into time and reaching out to the future.

AGAINST NON-PLACES

Place marks time, as time marks place, with each passage carried out through the lived-body. Thematizing this claim, four points can be made: (1) The directionality of place, articulated through the movement of the body, is distinct to the experience and temporality of place. (2) The experience of directionality confers a heterogeneous and qualitative frame upon place. (3) The heterogeneity of place is temporally and spatially particular. (4) Finally, the insideness of place is peculiar to the intentionality of the body and directionality taken together.

In order to make these four points clear, we need to consider not only how embodiment, place, and temporality define the experience of plenitude and continuity, but also how ambiguity lies at the heart of this threefold relation. To do this, I will present the idea of "un-place," which the rest of the chapter will now investigate. Before immersing ourselves in the thick texture of un-place, let me preface my investigation with some methodological points.

One reason why I employ the phrase "un-place" is to avoid a rigid dichotomy between space and place, where space would refer to an ontological tabula rasa prior to place, and presented as a passive possibility for place to be carved (Sack 1997). Broadly construed, the proceeding criticism of various spatial dualisms is not an attack on binary divisions simply because they employ dualisms. Advancing a prejudice toward dualisms is to already enforce a pregiven nature upon place. Moreover, the general vilification and equal fixation toward binary oppositions, symptomatic of a certain mode of elapsed academic thought, leave us no closer as to the experience of things than a dogmatic insistence that concepts of place and self consist of a singular property. My response to these tensions is to begin from the middle ground, ambiguous in character, before then stretching out to the shifting framework surrounding that terrain. In this way, we can hope to penetrate the nebulous formation of experience in its prime, rather than returning to a fully formed image of that experience already established.

Above all, the problem with the distinction between space and place is that it avoids the ambiguous threshold between different textures of place. Instead, it relies on the notion that space is antecedent to place, thus situating place in a causal relation to space, whereby the natural order of space is colonized by place-makers, thus producing a space-place compound. Yet space is not the raw material of place, as this view suggests. Instead, place, as we have seen, is a triadic relationship between body, time, and world. Space is not beneath place in this sense, but is a necessary condition for place to occur. Thus, that we can speak of placelessness, but not spacelessness, highlights the necessity of location, but does not mean that the absence of place give rise to raw space.

As an alternative, the term "non-place" similarly employs various problematic dualities between place and what is characterized as an anti-place. Most obviously, the term has come to designate a homogeneous landscape of supermodernity, characterized by temporally compressed, indistinguishable, and transient spaces. Marc Augé's description remains exemplary if equally problematic: "If a place can be defined as relational, historical and concerned with identity, then a space which cannot be defined as relational, or historical, or concerned with identity will be a non-place" (1995, 77–78).

Associated in particular with the anthropological research of Augé (although the term was in use earlier; Webber et al. 1964), the term reappears in Deleuze as the "any-space-whatever" (2005), features heavily in Virilio's writings on the "facelessness" of the city (2004, 2005), appears as an ethically pernicious statement of the encroachment of homogenization to be lamented in several urban theorists and architects (Katz 1993; Kunstler 1994;

Duany, Plater-Zyberk, and Speck 2001), has an established history in the work of phenomenological geographers and philosophers, most often as a risk to the stability of identity, memorability, and place (Bloomer and Moore 1977; Relph 1976; Seamon 1979; Casey 1993), and has appeared recently as "thinned-out places" in the work of geographer Robert Sack (1997).

At stake in this survey of different treatments of place and non-place is more than a series of opposing views to cultural and geographical hegemony. Rather, what is fundamental to this move is the gesture of voided space encroaching upon the concrete presence of the spatiotemporal present. Spatially and temporally, we are confronted with logic of annihilation, a displacement of place, and a reconstitution of orientation. Indeed, this low-level anxiety toward the encroachment of place from an outside source is as prevalent as it is in Pascal's celebrated invocation of "terrifying infinite space" as it is in Lovecraft's description of the void, which surely deserves to be quoted at length:

> Perhaps I should not hope to convey in mere words the unutterable hideousness that can dwell in absolute silence and barren immensity. There was nothing within hearing, and nothing in sight save a vast reach of black slime; yet the completeness of the stillness and the homogeneity of the landscape oppressed me with a nauseating fear. (1985, 12)

Lovecraft's visceral account of the void in *Dagon* touches on what is central to this topophobic tension: The dichotomy between voided space and plentiful place, each of which conflicts with the other. The "nauseating fear" gripping Lovecraft's protagonist is less a mode of affectivity directed toward the features of the landscape and more the result of a failure of appropriating discernible aspects of that landscape. This failure to incorporate non-place within the sphere of place itself constitutes the basic worry that place itself is vulnerable to ontological decomposition.

While I recognize that the homogenization of place is indeed a culturally prevalent feature of what Augé terms "supermodernity," with significant implications for the erosion of a human community, the qualitative experience of place, and the assimilation of difference into the category of sameness—with individuality registered in bureaucratic terms alone—*nevertheless*, the radical dichotomy between place and non-place has two contestable outcomes.

First, coexistent with the place-placelessness distinction is the construction of a hierarchy of placeness, where "thinned-out places" combat "thick places" (Casey 2001a). Indeed, for Casey this exchange leads to "the compensatory logic of loss," which instills a reinforced desire toward "thick places" in spite (or because of) the growth of thinned-out places (685). As proof of this logic, Casey invites us to think about how the attractiveness of places such as movie theaters and bookstores has increased alongside the availability of "online superstores" and a "proliferation of movies on video" (685). The tacit reasoning in Casey's claim is that the perseverance of place is based, if on a logic of loss, then also on a logic of negation, whereby place becomes defined in terms of what it lacks. Thus, the thick place of the cinema punctures the thinness of "virtual space," affirming the solidity of place by dint of invoking a desire for what existed prior to that place.

The retrospective motion of Casey's argument, as obligating us to recognize what existed *before* thinned-out places were as prevalent as they are today, leads to the second main outcome: Placelessness comes to be viewed as inconsistent with both memorability and formation of identity. The result is that the distinction between modes of place and placelessness does not lead us to the middle ground of place's temporality, which is where we gain a deeper understanding of the ambiguous relational balance between body, time, and world, but instead leads us to *either* its plenitude *or* its destitution. Throughout, we read of a desire to "reclaim place" (Relph 1993) from "standardized landscapes" (Relph 1976), which induces "alienation [and] decrease[d] attachment to particular places" (Duncan and Duncan 2001), and ultimately forces us to ask: "Where have all the real flowers and the actual wild places gone?" (Casey 1993, 259). Coupled with this fragmentation, Casey is especially insistent on the lack of memorable features in non-place, or what he terms more appropriately "site" (1993, 1997, 2000b, 2004). Referring to site's absence of "points of attachment onto which to hang our memories, much less to retrieve them" (2000b, 186), Casey's explicit hostility toward site is summarized in what he regards as the incompatibility between nature and site, producing a "desolated" space, in which "[t]rue place is elsewhere. Real life is missing" (1993, 269).

In an earlier paper on place and site titled "Getting Placed: Soul in Space," Casey provides a clear outline of features that will become especially significant for his later philosophy. First, in distinction to the priority of place, a defining feature of site is its contingency (Casey 2004, 302). As proof of this contingency, site is presented as a "modification" of place: "Site," Casey writes, "is non-unique and replaceable" (302). The implication of this is an assimilation of site into the category of nondifferentiation; with every site essentially the same, and thus replaceable, site becomes seen as pernicious to place, indeed, "levelling [places] down, razing them, making them indifferently planar" (302). Together with this leveling down, sites become a location for a disembodied experience. Whereas place, Casey (302) argues, requires the total involvement of the body, measuring site, by contrast, is achieved for instrumental reasons alone. Without the body's presence, site disembodies experience, reducing its presence to the mere "indices of memorable places" (303). The pervading theme of Casey's cogently argued case for place's priority over site is thus the universality of site (empty of form, contingent, geometric) against the particularity of place (filled with content, unique, and experienced qualitatively).

The strange situation of site's universal contingency would seem to emphasize the strain it places on body, time, and world. For Casey, peculiar to place is the role it plays in cohering personal identity, a process that occurs in and through *time*. But whether or not place colonizes personal identity at the expense of site remains contestable. On the one hand, following Casey, there is certainly a qualitative difference between types of place, whereby particularity, difference, and bodily receptivity all conspire together to what might be termed a "sense of place." In this respect, Casey is correct, and his treatment of the plenitude of place is comprehensive, consistently incisive, and phenomenologically exemplary. On the other hand, simply because place is plentiful and particular does not mean that it is constitutive of personal identity. Indeed, the strength of Casey's argument for the power of place depends on the assumption that the unity of personal identity necessarily revolves around temporal continuity. But is this so?

The emphasis on temporal continuity is evident in Casey's employment of Pierre Bourdieu's notion of *habitus*, which Casey cites is a "figure of the between" (2001a, 409). Precisely what is being united in this mediation is self and place. With this act of mediation, place becomes stable and regulated, and above all, constitutive of the temporality of the self, as Casey writes: "The generativity of habitudinal schemes is at once placial and temporal, and because of this double-sidedness, the geographical subject is able to insinuate himself or herself all the more completely into the place-world" (411). As proof of this association between coherence and temporality, a central attraction of place's magnetism, in contrast to site, is its ability to contain and hold its contents, a gesture Casey terms "in-gathering" (2004, 303). Through its ability to ingather, place stands in contrast to time's "dis-closing" momentum, which dissolves boundaries rather than preserving them. Such is the power of place, however, that it stands ready to seize time, hence Casey's vital claim: "Place conserves while time destroys" (303).

If place conserves time, then site is such that it retains a fundamentally *untimely* relationship with place, encouraging the dispersion of personal identity. This can be seen in how a site is able to reappear anywhere and at anytime. Think of any derided institution of capitalism, from Starbucks to Walmart; nearly all of them are defined in terms of spatial density rather than their temporal legacy. The legitimate presence of these places is due to their sheer spatial mass in any given urban environment. Occupying space, the appearance and then the reappearance of such sites attest to their strange temporality. As so often happens, when a cluster of cafés, supermarkets, or clothing stores descends on the built environment, then the rhythm of that clustering tends to accelerate: Each Starbucks becomes closer to another, with the experience of time *between* these locations more or less suspended. The life of a place, as having a particular history, is usually absent in such a case. Instead, a site never diminishes as such, but rather reconstitutes its absence through reconfiguring its presence. Complicit with the "dis-closing" motion of time, site lacks the consistency, continuity, and coherence of place. Thus, Casey's (2004, 303) conviction that "time takes us out of ourselves—out of our mind and body, of our place as well" is entirely applicable to site: The site is seen to disembody what place restores.

WILD BEING

Having dealt with the space/place, place/non-place distinctions in conceptual terms, we must now also consider these divisions in cultural terms. Indeed, so integral is the tension between appearance and culture to the project of un-place that without this discussion, the integrity of this central chapter would lose its bearings.

Until now, the clearest engaged attempt to disrupt the oppositional structure of place and site has been carried out through poststructuralist and postmodernist geographers, the central critical focus of which is to decenter what these thinkers deem as static and foundational structures (Bontana and Protevi 2004; Doel 1999; Hubbard et al. 2002). Two very broad trends result from this. The first is a paranoid exposition of the city as an organ of power and terror, against which there is an imperative to think "new ways of explaining complex systems as only geographically-minded individuals, teetering on the balance of human and non-human, can achieve" (Bontana and Protevi 2004, 39). The second trend, though now losing its sway, is to aestheticize placelessness through the figure of the postmodern *flâneur*, manifest through a mode of irony, playfulness, and mass culture celebration (Baudrillard 1989, 1990, 1995).

In his account of place and placelessness, Edward Relph (1976) insightfully preempted postmodernity's celebration of placelessness in terms of an appropriation through "kitsch," where "kitsch" would mean a detached posture, indirectly receptive to an environment. Furthermore, for Relph, a kitsch appraisal entails an "inauthentic" relation with place, where inauthentic refers to an "uncritical acceptance of mass values" (82). Having retreated into submissive resignation, *kitsch* carries with it a tone of irony and passivity. From a postmodernist perspective, the detached spectatorship of homogeneous place, evident in its assimilation as an academic novelty to be canonized, is indeed a clear illustration of a failure of thought mediated by kitsch. Both of these positions fail to confront the significance of place on its own terms. Through demonizing and aestheticizing homogeneous place respectively, poststructuralism and postmodernism defer an engagement with gradients of place through isolating configurations of the urban landscape as autonomous entities, and thus remain complicit with the view of non-place as less "real" than place itself. By contrast, let us proceed to approach this distinction from a point between place and non-place.

Following my analysis of place and non-place, two points of intersection emerge. The first is place understood as a cultural product. We have seen this in how non-place has been vilified as a threat to the originality and plenitude of place. The vilification occurs against several social, economic, and cultural factors, global capitalism being the most apparent. The consequence of this surge in placelessness, in Relph's terms, is "the undermining of the importance of place for both individuals and cultures, and the casual replacement of the diverse and significant places of the world with anonymous spaces and exchangeable environments" (1976, 143). In conjunction with this experiential diminishment, place is said to fragment the involvement of the body, and thus personal identity as a whole.

One problem with this connection between subjectivity and culture is that it belies a place-prejudiced framework in which *culture precedes experience*. As a result, homogeneous and heterogeneous properties are established in advance. From a phenomenological perspective, this prejudice is an oddity. The consequence is a radical dichotomy between place and non-place, whereby non-place is reduced to a static understanding. Yet if place is such that its formation is a relational movement, in which the interaction of the self gives form and plenitude to place from the *inside out*, then to argue that the cultural and spatial features of site are incompatible with "true place" seems to approach place as an already-formed object, which exists outside of experience. The implications are that place exists "there" while the subject retains a position "here": a position untenable for phenomenology.

But here we must recognize the cultural impact upon our experience of place. Let us, for instance, grant that our immersion in place is varied and dynamic. Let us also agree that certain places come to assume a centrality, whereby associations of nativity, centrality, and locality are reinforced. But let us dissent from the notion of place as polarized and instead consider a model of ambiguous gradients, which form a more indeterminate notion of place. In order to achieve this, we would have to dispense with the view of site as a deficient mode of materiality, evident, for example, in Casey's view on the memorability of site as "transformed into a memorable place by the erection of a distinctive house upon [an indifferent building lot]" (2000b, 186). Such a transformation from site to place appears to forge an arbitrary criterion for the value of place, judged in terms of preference alone.

By contrast, we wish to remain open to place as a source of strangeness rather than being determined in advance. In the phenomenological treatment of place and placelessness, two omissions are prevalent. First, owing to a supposedly transcendental structure, locations defined as "non-places" have been precluded from the scope of place as meaningful and memorable. Second, as a result of this preclusion, a phenomenology of points *between* place and non-place remains incomplete. In opposition, we wish to channel the very fabric of place, irrespective of its aesthetic and cultural merits, through the flesh of our bodies. As such, the question concerning an "ethics of architecture" is fundamentally removed from the fact that there are architecture, buildings, and places in the first instance. But how can we gain a foothold in this liminal area?

In one of the more enigmatic texts of his working life, Merleau-Ponty gives us a clue with the idea of "wild being" or "brute being" (*être sauvage*) (1968). For Merleau-Ponty, in the radical ontology he developed late in his life, the task of philosophy is to "interrogate [the] world without presupposing anything" (123). Yet this is a move beyond the ontology established in his (2006) earlier *Phenomenology of Perception*, given that what was presupposed in that work was the unity and existence of subject and object. There can be no doubt that by the time we get to the final chapter of *The Visible and the Invisible*, titled "Preobjective Being: The Solipsist World," this unity is no longer taken for granted.

At stake in this chapter is an ontology that must be accessed largely through an "inverse route" (Merleau-Ponty 1968, 157). Whereas the *Phenomenology of Perception* sought to unravel the structure of being via the lived-body, in this latter work, the very fabric—or, as we shall see shortly, "flesh"—linking the world to the body comes into question. Indeed, everything given through perception, including perception itself, is at issue in this late thinking, as he writes: "We will not admit a preconstituted world, a logic, except for having seen them arise from our experience of brute being, which is as it were the umbilical cord of our knowledge and the source of meaning for us" (157).

As the umbilical cord of our knowledge, the brute world stands prior to perception, operating on a different "layer," in which "interrogation itself" is unknown in advance. In fact, Merleau-Ponty presents this wild being as a world without discernible, singular identity. Overlapping, "the flesh of the world" installs itself in all things that have yet to surface to the realm of subject and object: "Like the natural man, we situate ourselves in ourselves *and* in the things, in ourselves *and* in the other, and at the point where, by a sort of *chiasm*, we become the others and we become the world" (1968, 160; italics in original). Nothing is admitted in this wild being, except that there is a "thing," which has yet to attain the status of being an object.

Brute being is thus the being that stands beyond, outside the "habitual world," including that of the cultural world. It is a world that evades every familiar trajectory of thought, existing in an anonymous "prehuman" realm so much so that "we do not yet know what to see is and what to think is" (Merleau-Ponty 1968, 158). In positive terms, all that can be posited is an "encounter between 'us' and 'what is'—these words being taken as simple indexes of a meaning to be specified" (159). *There is a thing*. Such is the starting point for Merleau-Ponty's late thought. The thing is nameless, mute, and anonymous. Yet it has presence, a unity. In handling a shell, Merleau-Ponty speaks of it as having "a power *de jure*, a legitimacy" (161). There is a thing, but there is also silence, a transcendence of things, which avoids direct sight. Things exist precariously, as fractures maintained through desire and the sedimentation afforded by human narcissism with its insistence on naming things of the world. At this point, we have been dislocated by otherness: "The thing thus defined is not the thing of our experience, it is the image we obtain of it by projecting it into a universe where experience would not settle on anything" (162). And then, suddenly and without warning, Merleau-Ponty's late text stops. The void a testimony to the problematic task of gaining entrance to the brute world from the point of being situated "in the heart of the visible" (130).

Taking Merleau-Ponty's enigmatic idea of brute being as motivation rather than a direct prescription, we are able to get a sense of the conceptual maneuvers required in order to strip away the veneer of aesthetic and cultural residue determining our prejudice toward the environment. If we are to regard the body as the "zero point" of all orientation, capable of discerning the environment in advance of cognitive intentionality, then we must allow corporeality to take lead, thus situating us in the midst of the "ontogenesis" of place itself, a horizon into which culture is displaced by the body's own *wild being*.

The importance of undertaking this phenomenological investigation is threefold. First, through attending to the ambiguities within and between place, we will appreciate the role different environments, and not only those that are archetypal, play in contributing to personal identity. The aligning result of this will be a challenge to the notion of place as unequivocally able to assimilate the past.

Second, via the transformation of "non-place" to the category of "un-place," the value of a phenomenological method toward place will be exemplified. This will be achieved thanks to phenomenology's ability to estrange us from culturally sedimented ideas about how a place *ought* to be given. Through pursuing a phenomenology of place via the primacy of the body, all accounts of cognitive and rational experience will reveal themselves as second-order judgments, fragmented in light of the wilderness that is raw phenomena.

Finally, in contextual terms, the motive for plotting this journey into the wild being of place is to respond to phenomenology's emphasis on the lived experience of inside rather than outside. Phenomenology's tendency to have a fairly controlled access to the environment, both built and natural, has left an entire terrain of the world unchartered. To be sure, while much of this terrain has been picked up in other disciplines, what remains to be said is how overlooked places are in fact central to our embodied experience. By widening this direction to include places outside the insular realm of individual experience, we can take our cue from postphenomenological thinkers, not least Michel Foucault, whose enigmatic concept of "heterotopia" proves instructive (1986, 22–27). Let me briefly touch upon this broader context.

What is notable about the concept of heterotopia, as Foucault presents it in his essay "Of Other Spaces," is the temporal history of the concept "place" (1986, 22–23). Foucault invites the reader to join him in performing a genealogy of place. In doing so, we arrive at the concept of "site" (otherwise translated as "emplacements," thus distancing site from Casey's usage), which he defines as "relations of proximity between points or elements; formally, we can describe these relations as series, trees, or grids" (23). What Foucault wants to underscore with his notion of site is the formal features of spatiality, which establish a network of links with other places. It is into this spatial network that Foucault places himself in opposition to Bachelard. In an important passage, he writes:

> Bachelard's monumental work and the descriptions of phenomenologists have taught us that we do not live in a homogeneous and empty space, but on the contrary in a space thoroughly imbued with quantities and perhaps thoroughly fantasmatic as well. The space of our primary perception, the space of our dreams and that of our passions hold within themselves qualities that seem intrinsic: there is a light, ethereal, transparent space, or again a dark, rough, encumbered space; a space from above, of summits, or on the contrary a space from below of mud; or again a space that can be flowing like sparkling water, or space that is fixed, congealed, like stone or crystal. Yet these analyses, while fundamental for reflection in our time, primarily concern internal space. I should like to speak now of external space. (23)

Foucault's turn toward space that "draws us out of ourselves" reminds us that ultimately "we do not live inside of a void," such as Bachelard would have it, but rather must contend with the "space that claws and gnaws at us" (1968, 23). In this way, Foucault's characterization of phenomenological space as being invested with an interior space plays upon the contrasting idea of "heterotopias" as a fundamental contradiction: containing both the reality of lived place but being simultaneously mythical and transcendental to interior space. Cinemas, prisons, gardens, asylums, mirrors, and, above all, ships, all cement the reality of heterotopias in varying ways. But what they all have in common is the quality of spatial ambiguity.

This element of ambiguity becomes clear in the sixth principle characterizing heterotopias, as Foucault writes: "[Heterotopias] have a function in relation to all the space that remains. . . . Their role is to create a space that is other, another real space, as perfect, as meticulous, as well arranged as ours is messy, ill constructed, and jumbled" (1968, 27). Foucault is fundamentally describing an "elsewhere" where certain rituals and rites are practiced. Furthermore, this elsewhere emerges between the residue of space and the production of culture, developing a polarized space, in which the reality of place proper is shown to depend upon heterotopias for its identity.

By ending his essay with the example of a ship, Foucault capitalizes on this ambiguous relation between the "space that claws and gnaws at us" and the interior experience attending to that disruptive gesture. Thus, Foucault describes a ship in paradoxical terms as "a floating piece of space, a place without a place, that exists by itself, that is closed in on itself and at the same time is given over to the infinity of the sea" (1968, 27). With Foucault's description, we gain sight of a constellation of different ambiguities, each of which is fundamentally implicated in the others. The ship stands apart from the land, but at the same time does not lose its spatiality because of that distance. Yet that distance places the ship in an infinite space, linking all other places within its grasp, thus marking the heterotopia par excellence for Foucault. Enigmatically, he concludes thus: "In civilizations without boats, dreams dry up, espionage takes the place of adventure, and the police take the place of pirates" (27).

As closed and open simultaneously, we can discern a fundamental trait in Foucault's ship: It gives itself over to stasis and mobility in equal measure. This is significant, as it forces us to step beyond our phenomenological footing to see places not from inside out, but from outside in. Through this motif of disruption, our attention is redirected not simply to a renewed understanding of what constitutes a sense of place, but of how we get to those places in the first instance. Forced outside of the "void" that Foucault identifies in Bachelard, place itself could not be understood without embarking on the journey to and from any given environment.

**

Before setting sail into the world of wild and liminal place, a final preparatory detour must be made. In order to establish a basis for decentering the cultural legacy of place and non-place, we must first map out a mode of experience that restores the world to its partial wilderness. We shall do this through aligning Merleau-Ponty's idea of "wild being" with Husserl's concept of "morphological essences."

As we have seen, the concept of "site" emerges in an untimely relationship to place. Doing so, the spatial and temporal reconstitution of site marks its difference from the particularity of heterogeneous place. What this means is that the "aura" (to borrow a significant term from Walter Benjamin) of the localized place—the café, the greengrocer, the shoemaker—is distinguished by its irreproducibility (Benjamin, 1977). The irreproducibility is both spatial and temporal. When we enter a foreign city, we seldom expect to encounter the same place that is peculiar to the city we have come from. Nor do we expect particular places to emerge in the future. Instead, we take it for granted that a given place belongs to its surrounding locality, where belonging means contributing to the enduring character of an environment. The exception to this, of course, is when a local place makes the transition from one place to multiple places. How can we phenomenologically chart the felt experience of Starbucks as it shifts from the particular place on the corner of one's street to a global brand (Trigg 2006c)? The problem is not an objective one, but an experiential one. As soon as a place becomes global, then it loses sight of its original sensibility, such that the very atmosphere can alter. The place becomes something else, tarnished by the fact of being multiplied, and no longer peculiar to "we" who inhabit it.

What does the assimilation of place tell us about the experience of place? On the one hand, the movement involves a logic of loss, where place is destroyed by forces outside of itself. But is the "spirit of place" usurped through repetition and reproduction? Phenomenological geography and architecture have tended to reproach aspects of modernity such as mass communication, global capitalism, and consumerist culture, all of which engender the production of homogeneous and atemporal "flatscapes" (Norberg-Schulz 1974; Relph 1976). The argument against the assimilation of the particular has a rich philosophical lineage, of which our discussion of the dialectic between place and non-place is but one illustration. On the other hand, the alteration of an environment suggests that temporality is a defining but not determinate feature of place. When a place exceeds its origins, then our qualitative experience alters, knowing well in advance that this "same" place exists elsewhere.

If the temporality of place is basically contingent, then the very idea of a "timeless place" merits reappraisal. Do some places transgress the weight of their own history, ascending beyond the bulk of their materiality, and thus serving as a beacon of something essential behind the flux of the world? To suggest otherwise would mean implementing a system of gradients in which timelessness suddenly becomes otherwise.

In asking this question, the relational rather than static structure of place is reinforced. And here we discern an opening. If the experience of a place is altered through the very fact of its production, repetition, and erosion, then what constitutes a "sense of place" must be seen as transitional and ambiguous. At no point does an inaccessible core peculiar to a place stand with immunity to its broader surroundings. Rather, as a place exists in time, so it makes itself vulnerable to the spatiality of its own being, instilling a foundational dynamism.

Being dynamic, the identity of place is what Husserl would term "morphological" (1967a, 207). As I have stated in the introduction, Husserl's distinction between ideal and morphological essences pertains to a distinction between the scientific perspective and a fundamentally phenomenological perspective. Ideal essences are abstractions of their morphological counterparts, which are seen only in the life-world. And it is phenomenology that brings us into the region of morphological entities through attending to the formation of appearances. Applying Husserl's invariant morphology to place, what emerges is a movement of disparate "approximations," each place never entirely settled, but instead orientating toward a specific form, which, nonetheless, proves imperfect. The emphasis on imperfect dynamism means that the division between place and non-place is essentially arbitrary in structure, deriving from habitual experience rather than the objective identity of place itself.

How does an airport attain the status of "non-place"? Clearly, there is more at stake than a fear that singular, particular, and localized places are at risk of being colonized by globalization. If we follow Husserl, the answer is that the very category of "non-place" is an abstraction of our experience of the airport. The airport is a thing in the world, malleable, ambiguous, and in flux, affecting our bodies in a multiplicity of ways. Yet at no point does this arc of ambiguity attain the status of being "ideal," and thus able to be described in mathematical, abstract terms, establishing a limit to the thing that is an airport. Despite this, the discourse on places such as airports treats them as already defined in advance, with exact formulas covertly included in aesthetic and cultural judgments.

Phenomenologically, this conflation of the ideal and the experiential is a deep error and requires rethinking. The implication is that the derision toward certain places is due not to a reflection on the experience of the things themselves, but to the predetermined stance on the objective status of a place. In a word, things of the world become ambassadors for other causes, in the process consigning those things to a mute void. The task to be addressed requires prising the objective identity of place apart from its culturally sedimented incarnation.

This presentation of experience as having an objective and cultural focus should not, however, imply that we are dealing with a fixed opposition. As Merleau-Ponty warns, "The distinction between the two planes (natural and cultural) is abstract: everything is cultural in us . . . and everything is natural in us" (1968, 253). Yet, at the same time, the relationship between culture and the natural (i.e., *wild*) is in some sense intimate if symbiotic, as Merleau-Ponty asks: "How can one return from this perception fashioned by culture to the 'brute' or 'wild' perception?" (212). The symbiotic element of the relationship, for Merleau-Ponty, already gestures toward a unitary phenomenon. He speaks of a "carrying over," a movement in which different modes of perception interbreed with one another. At stake is not the restoration of a lost unity, or a forgotten mode of Being, as Heidegger would have it (Merleau-Ponty writes tersely: "If Being is hidden, this is itself a characteristic of Being, and no disclosure will make us comprehend it" [122]). Rather, "the search for the 'wild' view of the world" entails recognizing that otherness and self-presence coexist, with each overlapping into the other (182). Here it is worth spending a moment to consider more broadly the relationship between wild being and culture.

What Merleau-Ponty shows us is that wild being is ontologically prior to the "alleged *objective* condition" of appearances (1968, 200; italics in original). Placing this condition as intrinsic to experience, the "disturbance of the relation with the world" is thus divested of its reality (200). Yet, as Merleau-Ponty shows us repeatedly, it is within the area of disturbances and cracks that the layered depth of the visible comes to the foreground. And it is a depth pregnant with an "ontological vibration," from which the question of "what the world is before it is a thing one speaks of and which is taken for granted, before it has been reduced to a set of manageable, disposable significations," gains an urgent appeal (102). Pushed to a threshold, therefore, Merleau-Ponty's philosophy of wild being takes "things" in a provisional sense, yet to attain the mastery of being objects proper (162).

This language of "prior," "before," "beneath," and "layers" points to the immanence of wild being. Wild being inheres and adheres to all things, forever lurking in the "there is" of all things. Forever lurking yet also close; indeed, identifiable with the surface. After all, "this environment of brute existence and essence is not something mysterious: we never quit it, we have no other environment" (Merleau-Ponty 1968, 116–17).

How, then, to approach wild being without prescribing an essence to that being in advance? I have said above that, for Merleau-Ponty, wild being constitutes a symbiotic relationship between culture and world. What this means in conceptual terms is that access to wild being is possible only through the conjunction of contrasts, between the horizontal and the vertical, and the visible and the invisible. Culture is the reflective space of wild being, as wild being in turn opens the ground of culture. He writes: "This event [wild being] is that a given *visible* properly disposed (a body) hollows itself out an invisible sense" (200). Hollowing out the visible within the invisible: With this formula, Merleau-Ponty can speak freely, as he does in "Eye and Mind," of "a prehuman way of seeing things" (1979, 63). In turn, this would mean a suspension of consciousness and an opening of infinite perspectives, each of which is taken up in "wild perception" (Merleau-Ponty 1968, 213). Indeed, within these enigmatic and incomplete working notes that Merleau-Ponty leaves us, a glimpse into a methodology is conceived:

> The key is in this idea that perception qua wild perception is of itself ignorance of itself, imperception, tends of itself to see itself as an *act* and to forget itself as latent intentionality, as *being at—* (1968, 213; italics in original)

We are faced with a thought, abandoned before logic, and constitutive of a paradox immune to resolution. Perception, as Merleau-Ponty has it, is at the same time a turning-away, a blindness from which sight emerges. It is as though Merleau-Ponty is seeking to capture thought in action by turning ignorance in and on itself. This "latent intentionality" is emitted through the very darkness that "natural perception" stretches toward.

Methodologically, the answer to the question of encountering wild being is to diminish the centrality of the subject while focusing toward the "mute life," which "[takes place] among the *artefacts* and products of culture, as an instance of them" (Merleau-Ponty 1968, 102; italics in original). In these taken-for-granted products, wild being is imbued with a special vibrancy. Perception assumes its normal path, only now aware of itself as ignorant, thus indirectly communicating with the "latent intentionality." The "mute life" that is at the center of our world is at the same time an audible presence, and that presence announces itself in the equality of all objects. As equal, no one object takes precedence over another; the subject's gaze now mirrors the gaze of its own otherness.

Applied to our tension between place and non-place, the following three points can be made. First, the conviction that the "spirit of place" "seems to rest in itself" can be viewed only in strictly provisional terms. Experiencing place is not reducible to a finite set of properties. Rather, all experience of the environment carries with it a persistent uncertainty, an overarching ambiguity, framed in the depth of wild being.

Second, at no point is any given place immune from a radical reversibility, in which all that has become "fixed" in its stability is suddenly and discontinuously altered. Irrespective of the cultural, social, and political aspects of an environment, built or natural, there always endures a wilderness immanent to that place. Resisting domesticity, "once we have entered into this strange domain," so Merleau-Ponty writes, "one does not see how there could be any question of *leaving* it" (1968, 152; italics in original).

Third, the relation between culture and wild being is to be seen not in hierarchical terms, but in terms of a gesture of mirroring contrasts. As intertwined, wild being and culture serve as two sides of the same thing rather than a mode of revelation given over to a fallen state of representation. Culture is that from which the blindness of vision renders the "mute world" possible, in the process, evincing the possibility of what Merleau-Ponty terms a "phenomenology of 'the other world'" (1968, 229).

JOURNEYING TOWARD THE SERVICE STATION

By joining Merleau-Ponty's idea of wild being with Husserl's idea of morphological essences, what emerges is an account of the appearance of place both beyond and before an environment in the lived world is marked as either homogeneous or heterogeneous, homely or unhomely, place or non-place. If our methodology is correct, then we would instead be faced with a vague "approximation" of place, accessible only through an "inhuman" analysis. Such is the third place, existing literally in the in-between. The morphological essence finds its place *in* between wild being and our sedimented experience of things. Not, as Edward Casey rightly argues in his recent paper on edges and the in-between, simply "between" points, but "something much less determinate" (2008, 5). This less determinate mode involves an ambiguity, whereby a thing "'settles in,' gets acquainted with a place, takes up residence there, and comes to know it from within" (5–6). As such, the in-between is a place in its own right, rather than being defined in terms of orientation toward a point either far away or close by. Were we to conflate the outer edges (i.e., place and non-place) without situating ourselves in the ambiguous ground within, then a rigid determination of place would transpire. And it is such a conflation that results in the abstraction of place, producing a sedimented notion of what divorces place from its otherness. Yet place is neither fixed nor exact, and before cultural, ethical, and sociological judgments are applied, the genesis of place is initially a *phenomenal appearance* in time and space.

But how does this in-between place materialize? The answer, which I will now explicate, is through the *interstitial receptivity of the lived-body*. What this means in provisional terms is that through the body, we catch sight of things in their incipient being becoming visible. As I shall argue, the body gives us a first vision to that, which, in turn, becomes familiar and assured but, at first contact, retains a sufficient aura of strangeness.

In order to prove this dense claim, I will invoke the experience of journeying toward a service station (variously termed "rest area," "service plaza," or even "highway oasis"). I have chosen the example of a service station, since it has become emblematic of the culture of "non-places." Indeed, precisely its status as being a particular type of place—diminished and transient—is the grounds for its renewal made possible. By beginning with the orthodox assumption that a service station is an incidental site on the journey toward place—and nothing more—a systematic unfolding of ambiguity can be obtained. The conclusion of this journey will be to demonstrate two things. First, that our "sense of place" is in fact a mutant concept, forever evolving under the watch of cognition. The second conclusion will show that motor intentionality and mental intentionality have the power to rupture the unity of the "I" once those different modes of intentionality collide.

I will document this voyage in three stages, the aim of which will be to give an account of the narrative structure of what I have provisionally termed "un-place," the definition of which can be secured only retroactively—once the journey has ceased. At first, I will phenomenologically attend to the experience of journeying in a vehicle on a motorway. Second, I shall pause at the service station, giving particular consideration to how the experience appears for us as a spatial event. Finally, I shall return to the vehicle, exiting the service station and assuming that the journey reaches a final place. Let us, then, begin this expedition into the everyday and the strange.

We can begin by imagining/remembering ourselves seated within the spatiality of a vehicle that enables us to journey between places. As both mobile and static concurrently, the interior of the vehicle (let us commit ourselves to journeying by car) is a medium receptive to what has been termed "place-insideness." Through acting as a space in which the body is situated, the interior of the car, so often a cinematic image of seduction, gains a sense of place by dint of its ability to reinforce the unity of the self. As located in a transitory space, the self becomes embodied in the car precisely through being disembodied from the surrounding world. Far from signifying an exclusion from the social world, however, this detached attention, played out through the border of the windscreen, or windshield, marks a heightened involvement with the world. Much in the same way that the hotel lobby establishes the possibility of disinterested attention, so the car presents itself as a space in between the private and the public (Trigg 2006b).

As Robert Mugerauer (1993, 107–8) has argued in his account of the domestic porch, peculiar to this privileged space is the encouragement of lingering. For Mugerauer, lingering is made possible thanks to a limited vulnerability, which positions us near enough to the natural world to remain within it, but close enough to the inside to merit the porch's being "an intermediate site" (108). It is with the possibility of lingering that worlds are connected. Because of this dynamic exchange, the space in between the world is modified as a place in its own right. "*The porch*," Mugerauer writes, "*marks a threshold*" (119; italics in original). But a threshold to what?

This world in between other worlds underscores and enhances the extension of the gaze. From one place to another, the world striding between spaces is a privileged position, allowing unmediated access to multiple perspectives. Moreover, because the space in between worlds occupies a location of distance and proximity, the gaze toward things is unbroken by the intrusion of conflicting gazes. In effect, the gaze lingers on a field of appearances, which, were the space in between worlds less ambiguous, would otherwise prove impossible.

Here, the threshold of the windscreen is central. Thanks to the windscreen, the projection of the self and car is met with the introjection of the world. In particular, given the ocularcentrism of the car, the in-betweenness of driving revolves around the notion of an unreciprocated glance. The view gained through this glance is thus fundamentally detached. In the same way that certain spaces encourage asymmetrical observation if not outright voyeurism rather than a reciprocated exchange, so the car compels outside appearances to emerge as visual manifestations of a broader, if anonymous, world.

The result of this meeting of a discrete car and a broader environment is the production of a seamless world, operating from the centrality of sight, but also having the power to absorb the world on a kinesthetic level. Indeed, unlike the computer or the television screen, the windscreen does not efface touch or smell, but rather establishes the circumstances in which smell and touch can be moderated from a place in between, as architect and theorist Juhani Pallasmaa states: "Computer imaging tends to flatten our magnificent, multi-sensory, simultaneous and synchronic capacities of imagination by turning the design process into a passive visual manipulation, a retinal journey" (2007, 12).

While we cannot overlook the distance established between the car-inhabitant and the non-car-inhabitant, it seems to me that there is a sensual difference between the gaze of the computer screen and the gaze of the windscreen. Indeed, despite the essentially cocooning environment of the car, the car nevertheless remains exposed as a social object among many.

About this threshold between inside and out, Virilio writes thus:

> Arranged before the eyes of the driver this instrument panel forms a totality: the agent of displacement will by turns observe the

Figure 9: *Car windscreen, New York City. Photo by author.*

approach of objects which will not fail to hit the windshield (images—but also insects, gravel, feathered creatures) and also diverse
movements which will animate the gauges and counters. In this driving fascination begins a double game of lining up the inside and the
outside of the car. (1998, 12)

In bringing together the windscreen with the motion of things in approach,
Virilio's remarks emphasize the symmetry between the centrality of the car
and the dynamic temporality of things passing through the car, ultimately
turning the driver into a "voyeur-voyager" (1998, 13).

The synthesis between the detached spectatorship of appearances and the
traveler in the midst of an appearance reinforces the dynamic enclosure of the
car. Instead of being an objective holder or a simple transportation device, the
car's dynamic motion imbues the vehicle with a theatrical magnetism played
out, above all, through the windscreen. Virilio again: "The opening of the
windshield is therefore not a window but a kind of glass door through which
the passengers pass non-stop, a glass door by which the voyeurs-voyagers en-
gulf themselves in the attraction of arrival" (1998, 15).

To say that the car is an in-between place, allowing motion and stasis to
entwine, does not mean it is a diminished place. Instead of being a collection of separable parts, the car forms a total image, present to the body that
inhabits it. As a result, the relation between car and body is entirely heterogeneous. The felt experience of being-in-the-car, without even driving it, forms
a unique synthesis marked by the sense of belonging to the car.

While the term "belonging" clearly implies both possession and the sociality of ownership, belonging also underscores the reciprocal formation of the
car as a place and the driver who experiences that place. Thus, the small domain of the car interior becomes magnified through being assimilated by the
tactile sensuousness of the body. In effect, body and car interior merge (producing the weary Freudian image of the car as a phallic extension, but also
the more compelling vision J. G. Ballard [1995], and in a cinematic guise,
David Cronenberg [1996], establish in *Crash*). As proof of this crossbreed,
driving is often said to be intuitive, an act carried out with the habitual assurance of walking. The implication being that the car acts as a limb of the body,
receptive to the exterior space through which it travels.

Here, the notion of habit as merely a mechanical response bearing no
affective or existential counterpart can be outlawed. As Merleau-Ponty has

shown tirelessly, the human body's ability to form habits attests to a broader "grasping of a significance" (2006, 165). Thanks to this grasping gesture, "free space" is won, as he writes in reference to driving: "If I am in the habit of driving a car, I enter a narrow opening and see that I can 'get through' without comparing the width of the opening with that of the wings, just as I go through a doorway without checking the width of the doorway against that of my body" (165).

Enlarging the body beyond its own objective edge, things in the world take on the sensibility and nervous system of one's own being.

Coupled with this embodied emergence, the interior of the car simultaneously gives itself over to an imagined landscape. By using the phrase "imagined landscape," the role the passing landscape plays in forming the continuity of the self and car becomes central. This twofold temporality, between self and landscape, in time, leads to the dynamic production of an internal landscape, fortified by the intimacy of the car as, to phrase it in Bachelardian terms, "an alcove."

Again, instead of simply being a transportation device, the car's constant sense of becoming-toward leads to the formation of a place as being a retreat from the immediate present and a projecting toward the unmapped future. Indeed, so central is this image of temporal escapism that the cultural relation between the car and freedom remains inseparable. But this inseparability not only entails the freedom of space, such as that of journeying between places; it also invokes the freedom of time and, more precisely, the freedom to rearrange time.

Consider, as an illustration of this temporal manipulation, the following passage from Paul Auster's *The Music of Chance*:

> Nothing around him lasted for more than a moment, and as one moment followed another, it was as though he alone continued to exist. He was a fixed point in a whirl of changes, a body poised in utter stillness as the world rushed through him and disappeared. The car became a sanctum of invulnerability, a refuge in which nothing could hurt him anymore. As long as he was driving, he carried no burdens, was unencumbered by even the slighted particle of his former life. That is not to say that memories did not rise up in him, but they no longer seemed to bring any of the old anguish. (2006, 10–11)

At least two salient points are evident in this passage. First, we appear to be faced with the enclosure of lived experience as being the absolute center of things. The experience of driving through place, disrupted only by the intensification of traffic, means that different places emerge as a residue, or a stream of discontinuous fragments, taken in by the driving-subject and simultaneously left behind in a horizon of disappearances. Second, this motion between gathering and dispersing leads to the car as being a refugee, marked by the car's ability to constitute a breakage in time: "Nothing could hurt him anymore," so Auster writes notably. Memory remains in a literal state of deferment, noncommitted to either the past or the present. Instead, the car's becoming-toward structure has the consequence of emphasizing the notion of the car as an escape, from place and time. Yet a curious outcome emerges from this temporal noncommitment: Through traveling beyond time, Auster's driving-subject proceeds to go no-where, or rather *no-when*. The insulation of the moving vehicle has the consequence of slowing down time, enforcing the cocooned temporality of the car interior. Motion becomes simulated; memories become fabricated.

Figure 10: *Parking lot, Missoula, Montana. Photo by author.*

lIGHT, SHADOW, TEXTURE

From the experience of being both behind the windscreen and beyond time, we can observe a fulfillment of the body-self-car relation. Together, this relation marks the car as being a distinct place among a matrix of other places. With this matrix in mind, let me shift the motion of driving to the second stage of our account: leaving the car and entering the service station. The transition from the interior of the car to the car park marks a shift in rhythms not only temporally, but for the spatial gestures of the body, too. In particular, exiting the vehicle to find the whole body permitted to stretch itself into space designates an instant of bodily renewal. On departing the car, the very openness of the car park is framed as a space, in which bodily intention orients itself, such that the expanse of the car park becomes a countermeasure to the inhabited place of the car. Now, the very flatness of the concrete lot opens as an uncluttered space of motility and extension. Instead of remaining as a "site" to be transformed, the car park gains a richness in its own right, so bringing together a differing sensibility from that experienced in the car. This difference of sensibility constitutes an emergence of foreground-background involvement, with the car and the car park overlapping each other. My body is no longer set against the car park as a scene in which other exchanges occur. Rather, the car park rises up, so that objective space is effectively blurred with a past established in the moving vehicle. And so, the particular features of the car park—ranging from the humidity of the air to the gray concrete of the floor—become imbued with a peculiar ambience, at once full of the plenitude of tactility while also retaining a distance established by their transitional status. After all, I am standing in the car park in order to move beyond the service station, which I proceed to do.

The electric doors close, and I am beyond the screen leading to this unchartered terrain. All around, wooden chairs are flanking small circular tables. Their colors are light and the surfaces clean. Some tables have umbrellas stationed through their center, as though to protect the diners from the lights above. Of the lights above, at least thirty-six halogen lamps with steel casings shed their rays on the world below. They are powerful, and if one looks too long at the center of the light, then intense disorientation ensues when returning to the place as a whole. Here and there, clusters of people wait motionlessly around the tables, only occasionally swooping to the gelatinous

Figure 11: *Service station, Grantham, UK. Courtesy of Mark Dodds.*

mound of food beneath them. But their eyes are fixed and their expressions glazed.

Others line up in an orderly queue, waiting to collect their food at the end. When returning to their tables, some people must avoid the yellow beacons placed in the middle of the tiled floor, warning that this particular patch of earth has just been cleaned and is now a hazardous zone. There is no center to speak of, other than a stream of continuous travelers collecting food before consuming and departing. But this center is elusive, and instead of providing the source of orientation, the service station seems, rather, to be dispersed in several directions simultaneously. What remains is a center arranged in what appears to be arbitrary terms. Chairs, tables, and televisions scatter the place without any discernible link connecting these isolated entities.

Coupled with this arbitrary placement of things, much can be said for the sensual atmosphere in the environment. Although not windowless, the windows either are too high to gaze out of or lead only to an enclosed view of the immediate surroundings, chiefly the car park. Other windows lead to the petrol station, and to the slow crawl of cars filling their bodies with energy. Beyond these vistas, visual sight is automatically reverted back to the food plaza, with its hungry banqueters keenly consuming their dinner. The air is thick with the smell of cooked oil and food items that have been out since dawn, resting either on the metallic shelves or within the steel trays used to contain more hearty goods such as sausages, eggs, and a pool of dark-red baked beans. Having had enough of the food court, some travelers loiter around the periphery of the central space, taking advantage of the gambling machines that are widely available to all who pass through. They make little sound and move infrequently, other than when new coins are collected from their pockets before being inserted into the electric machines ready to present them with hope of a fortune to come.

As I step deeper into this world, I begin to recognize that being here, eating here, lingering here is fraught with anxiety: an anxiety placed by the violence of the light, which establishes itself as entirely contrary to the intimacy of being behind the windscreen. Indeed, at times, I can feel myself gesturing toward the exit, hankering for that intimacy of the car's dashboard, sealed at

Figure 12: *Villa, Mijas, Spain. Photo by author.*

all times from this world of brutal consumption by my own mobile terrain. But there is too much to learn from this raw light to retreat, and attending to the spatiality of the service station in terms of lighting alone would constitute a contribution to the phenomenology of transitional places. So I remain, with the hope conceived of gesturing toward that contribution.

How does light affect our experience of places? It is customary to think that a blending of light and shadows brings places to life (Chang 1981; Millet 1996; Pallasmaa 2007). The revelatory aspect of light as *enlightening* space carries with it the surfacing of texture, depth, and form. Architecturally, the employment of light shapes a building in such a way that form and matter are radically altered in differing conditions of shade and light. Such a rhythm of textures literally opens space, creating a passage in which the inhabitant is either drawn or repelled. The light that marks the interior of the domestic home, for instance, is at once homely and distant thanks to the darkness from which the lighting is offset. Void and presence entwine, allowing the body to be surrounded by a place with attributes distinct from the outside. As a result, the lighting of place is at the same time the means by which place becomes dynamic. Indeed, such is the centrality of light to the formation of place that Junichiro Tanizaki, author of the seminal *In Praise of Shadows*, is prepared to state: "In making for ourselves a place to live, we first spread a parasol to throw a shadow on the earth, and in the pale light of the shadow we put together a house" (2001, 28).

The association between shadows and the originary house reinforces the thick temporality of light, darkness, and architecture. To think here with Bachelard, "the flame of the candle summons reveries from memory. It provides us occasions, in our distant memories, for solitary vigils" (1988, 23). The contemplative aspect of shadows, such as those found littered in de Chirico's landscapes, instills a depth in place, whereby materiality becomes animated.

A shadow emerges from elsewhere, and in casting itself on a wall, it does so from a different point in time. At times, detecting the origin of a shadow proves elusive, and we are thus left with a strange spectral presence that both unsettles and settles us, situating us in and out of time. Fallen from time, the shadows on the walls and cast upon the floors are also an invitation for further exploration, an opening, into which human desire is invariably drawn.

In this way, the intrusion of the elsewhere situates place in time, leading Tanizaki to describe how Japanese design orients itself around "neutral colors so that the sad, fragile, dying rays can sink into absolute repose" (2001,

Figure 13: *Garden, Mijas, Spain. Photo by author.*

30). The emphasis on the neutrality of space as a platform on which shadows form underscores the dynamic texturing of surfaces as not simply being in time, but also having the potential to morph time.

This confidence in depth, darkness, and mystery is, of course, largely obliterated in today's sanitized urban environment. Bachelard states ironically: "Dreamer of words that I am, the word 'lightbulb' makes me laugh. Never can a lightbulb be familiar enough to take a possessive adjective. Who can say 'my electric lightbulb' in the same way that he once said my 'lamp'?" (1988, 63). His transition between lamp and lightbulb might well prove obsolete for the present study, but the onus on a loss of specificity and a gain in standardization is instructive. The "age of administered light" (64), which Bachelard laments emphatically, is irrefutability upon us.

For Bachelard (1988, 64), the dichotomy between light that is on and light that is off is enough to dehumanize light and extinguish the flames of imagination. This process of dehumanizing the environment follows on from the action of divesting material of its organic worldliness. Erasing depth and texture, place is simultaneously divested of its powers to arouse memory and dreaming. More than this, however, for Bachelard, the absence of attention involved in the flick of a switch redeems the phenomenologist of his or her responsibility for attending to things in a considerate and deliberate manner. As a result, an argument can be made for the "age of administered light" as producing less-cautious phenomenology, no doubt obliging Pallasmaa to re-mark whimsically, "The human eye is most perfectly tuned for twilight rather than bright daylight" (2007, 46).

I point out this trajectory of thought because it highlights a transition of presence and absence, while occupying a dialectic between humanized and dehumanized worlds. In other words, what emerges from this discussion of light and texture are certain prejudices aligning a particular configuration of the environment with the concordant divestment of human presence. The trajectory is helpful, since it pushes these assumptions to the foreground, es-pecially where the experience of intensely administered environments is con-cerned. However, since my intention is not to judge light in qualitative terms but to describe it as sheer appearance, I need not join Bachelard and Pallas-maa in lamenting the standardization of lighting. Far from it. For the present purposes, I shall put aside the history of lighting, and turn, instead, to the shadowless environment of the service station as it appears in the present.

So far, the relation between place and lighting has depended on an in-teraction between surface and form. As shadows are cast upon a space, so that space is illuminated as a depth. The significance of depth is thus that it projects a rich dimensionality to the environment, which establishes itself as distinct and singular. But the flourishing of light and place is not simply constrained to the visual realm. Rather, the combination of a homogeneous geometry and stark lighting instills an environment, which, though chan-neled through vision, affects the entire bodily experience. Thus, in the ser-vice station, or any other place that precludes varied and dynamic lighting, the eyes do not detach themselves from the rest of the body, but instead filter the affective dimension of the lighting—harsh, cold, and sterile—through the entire body.

In the face of industrial-scale halogen or fluorescent lighting, the play of surface and form is undermined by the erasure of diversity. Because of this harshness, finding our way in a shadowless environment proves awkward. "The lighting," writes Merleau-Ponty, "directs my gaze and causes me to see the object, so that in a sense it *knows* and *sees* the object" (2006, 361; italics in original). To know and to see the object means being able to place that object within a given context. He goes on to say:

> If I imagine a theatre with no audience in which the curtain rises upon illuminated scenery, I have the impression that the spectacle is *in itself visible* or ready to be seen, and that the light which probes the back and foreground, accentuating the shadows and permeating the scene through and through, in a way anticipates our vision. (361; italics in original)

Thanks to the phenomenality of light, the framing of place serves to enforce a scene of visibility, even when that content of that vision is missing. As such, light gives form, and so preempts our navigation into and from place. By contrast, at the service station, the aggressive lighting renders an appearance without form. In effect, all that is being lit is the presentation of a place deformed by the very light that aspires to impose a form upon it. This "Nothing of Revelation," to borrow a term from Gershom Scholem, certifies the appearances of the service station as a place in which the presence of the body is diminished (quoted in Agamben 1998, 53). Without form, without texture, and without the shadows that lead us into place, the site disembodies, disperses, and disturbs the relation between body and world, such that Merleau-Ponty's "absolute here" must ultimately be called into question.

Calling into question the being-here of the service station means, above all, confronting the displacement of the body from its center. Without the depth of shadows to guide us, movement itself undergoes doubt. No longer do we feel intuitively compelled to find our way in place. Instead, a thinking must occur, such that this formless world is brought into order. The result of this emphasis on visual thought is that far from imaginatively projecting myself into the general ambience of the service station, *the environment splits my body into disunited parts, causing a separation from both spatiality and mental intentionality.* Owing to its importance, this point requires detailed analysis.

ANXIOUS EMBODIMENT

We are in the midst of a strange world, shadowless and standardized in its appearance. Accustomed to sensing itself through place, in this world the body finds itself partially divested of its powers. Now, tremendous effort is required to maintain existential security and spatial orientation. Within the low hum of the human body, a strain begins to appear. My body is tense, anxious. For a while, I feel a need to sit down, and yet I lack the inclination to commit myself further to this place. Alongside this, the palpitations of the heart serve as a constant reminder that there is such a thing as the human body in the first place. The presence, however, is one of alienation and radical contingency. Because of this heightened sense, I have suddenly become aware of my body as a thing in the world, operating, to some extent, of its own accord. My body presents itself to me, has become *self-aware*.

Where am "I" in this spatial anxiety? Objectively speaking, I am "here" inasmuch as I occupy a specific place. Were someone on the other side of the service station to recognize me, then I believe they would say that I am over "there," within the far corner of this environment. And yet—if I am "here," then I am nonetheless reluctant to speak of being "inside" this place. Something in this service station is preventing being "inside" and being "here" from coinciding. Due to this ambiguity, my body is weakened through being in the service station. Not only is it weakened, it is also made aware to me as an object of which I have suddenly become conscious. My body is "here," and still I remain on the periphery. The hesitation testifies to the strange nature of the place, a strangeness with far-reaching implications.

Here, a shift occurs: My body resists this scattered environment, employing its intelligence to absorb the surroundings despite the failure to conceptualize this place as a whole. Emphasizing motor intentionality, we are led back to Merleau-Ponty's account of bodily synthesis. My body works to achieve a certain telos "against the double horizon of external and bodily space" (Merleau-Ponty 2006, 115). Space is forever oriented with respect to my body, and not only this, but my body "actively assumes" space and time, "takes them up in their basic significance" (117). At all times, my body sets out to absorb an environment, not in "relation to axes of co-ordinates in objective space," but within the "domain of the phenomenal" (121). These "intentional threads" that allow me to be guided through the world do so in a prereflective fashion, affording an arc of unity peculiar to the lived-body.

Within the service station, bodily perception takes on a new dimension, as visual sight fails to comprehend the immediacy of the space. Here, thanks to its heightened intentionality, the body as a visual thing in the world becomes amplified. Although never fully reduced to one object among many, my body nevertheless becomes thematized in objective terms. "The body catches it-self," writes Merleau-Ponty, "from the outside engaged in a cognitive pro-cess" (2006, 107). But this insight folds back upon my body as the center of lived experience; indeed, the only perspective of experience. Catching it-self from the outside, I simultaneously experience that gesture of catching as it occurs. In turn, this ambiguity instigates a tension with my movement through the service station.

Beginning to walk from one end of the service station to the other, I become aware of a certain awkwardness and irregularity in my gait, as though I am forced to calculate how many steps are required to proceed from one point to the next. The absence of fluidity does not deter my body from moving, but the movement appears as an experience distant from a previous and remembered unity, such as I experienced in the car and also in stretching my body beyond the car. Now, movement becomes automated and mechanized, laden with a dense pressure, as though my body could give way at any time. At times, I feel my skin grow pale, the blood beneath the surface shivering under this brutal lighting.

Alongside the spatiality of this movement, experience of time is also augmented. As my visual perspective discerns where to go in advance, the body seems to follow through the veil of a time lag. Without the interplay of shadow and light from whence ontological security emerges, an increasing reliance on abstract and orientation ensues. Often, I will feel the need to hold on to the nearest wall in order to walk from one corner of the station to the other, as though I were floating quite freely in both space and time. When I turn my head to each side, then I feel my vision follow shortly after, delayed by some invisible force along the way. It is as though my body has literally seized up. With some form of anxious energy pulsating through each and every organ of my internal body, the notion of intuiting myself through this environment, as I would when at home, becomes ineffably distant.

Here, Merleau-Ponty is instructive: "The normal function which makes abstract movement possible is one of 'projection' whereby the subject of movement keeps in front of him an area of free space in which what does not naturally exist may take on a semblance of existence" (2006, 128). Merleau-Ponty's "semblance of existence" points to the power of projection, a power that presents us with a unified space quite apart from the objective status of space. Yet where the environment overpowers the body's projection, then we can speak of abnormal functioning, characterized by the failure to forge a "semblance of existence" from the "free space." Normal functioning ceases, and the surrounding world takes on a liminal, amorphous appearance.

Figure 14: *Service station, Grantham, UK. Courtesy of Mark Dodds.*

To speak of space as "fitting" the body would thus be misguided. In exchange for a language of containment, the service station engenders itself toward diffusion rather than tightness. Even if we were to describe the service station as occupying a "loose fit," then such a fit would immediately be contested by the body's displacement, which presents itself as unsuited to the anodyne environment, despite the attempt of visual sight to reconcile body and space.

The tension between motor intentionality and mental intentionality is disarming: The farther we move into the station, the greater we distance ourselves from the unity of the body. In effect, space and light work in tandem to position the body outside itself. Through encouraging the experience of seeing at the expense of the other senses, this disembodying motif is enhanced by the sense of being *overwhelmed* by the place. At no point do I truly feel as though I am here within this place. Instead, my experience of my body is one of passivity rather than activity. The seeing of the service station does not entail its being oriented. In being seen, the environment only remains where it is: as a flat appearance, in which the body is positioned in the objective "here" but not existentially placed. As overwhelming, the lack of a dialogue between my total self and the surrounding space means that my body has become detached from cognition; the dream of embodiment has been shattered by the failure to incorporate corporeality into subjectivity.

Beyond movement within the service station, the very circumstance of entering the world is conditioned by its relationship to the motorway. That the moment of entering the service station is not a respite from journey but an instant of anxiety is proof of the service station's disturbing temporal affectivity: a disturbance that attests to the apparent contradiction between the motionlessness of the site and the motion of the motorway. Now, we find ourselves in a spatial impasse: between place and outside of time. The middle of the afternoon and the middle of the night are swallowed up in this mute horizon: both reduced to the same murmuring presence. Indeed, given the presence of the service station within the sphere of a broader environment, place itself seems to be colonized by the pervasive power of the site. References to specific places within the service station fail to reconcile; cities outside the remit of the microcosmic world of the service station—New York, Beijing, Havana, Tokyo, and Paris—appear as otherworldly entities, remote, inaccessible, and mythological in their possible being.

***

We can distinguish between different modes of place: one contained in the interior of the car, the other dispersed in the service station. Already we can see that the experience of the service station takes place against the backdrop of the car environment, which, in turn, establishes a destabilizing tension emphasized by the disjoining of these places. Yet, as we leave the white noise of the service station and return to the safety of the car, the place does remain as a location experienced in the sealed-off past, thus resolved to the finality of time. The reason for this is as follows: Because our experience of the service station was effectively disembodied, it follows that *not only was the experience digested as a partial memory, but the memory itself was only partially digested.* Let me explain this.

When in the service station, my embodied self as a normal functioning network of projecting internationalities was suspended. In its place, an abnormal relation between visual and non-visual perception emerged, such that the "plenum of the world" lost its assurance. Experienced as anxiety and dizziness in the body, a disordering of space ensued. Together, this anxious affectivity was coupled with an acute awareness of the facticity of my body as both a thing in the world and a center of experience. That the body undergoes anxiety in certain places is notable. Following Heidegger, what this means is that where spatial anxiety is concerned we are never truly *present to ourselves*; rather:

> We "hover" in anxiety. More precisely, anxiety leaves us hanging because it induces the slipping away of beings as a whole. This implies that we ourselves—we men who are in being—in the midst of beings slip away from ourselves. At bottom therefore it is not as though "you" or "I" feel ill at ease; rather, it is this way for some "one." (1977, 103)

Heidegger's claim that anxiety leaves us hanging presents us with a depersonalized subject, to some extent disconnected from the world of things. The "one" who survives anxiety does so less as the subject who entered it and more as an indeterminate subject exposed to nothingness. Spatially, the anxious subject is able to experience an environment in only a partial sense. Hovering over the world, the harmony of visual and non-visual perception is literally put out of sight.

And yet: Simply because the anxious subject is now hovering above the service station does not mean that the body ceases its prereflective perception of the world. Quite the opposite. As abstract thought fails to find its way, the body nevertheless carries on, as though a blind phantom wandering in the dark, to absorb and claw the particular features of the location. For this is the very essence of the embodied subject. With its focus on the "intentional arc" of existence, the lived-body never ceases in its attempt to synthesize world into a meaningful whole, even if that arc tends to go "limp in illness" (Merleau-Ponty 2006, 157). Against the danger of the service station, the body endures, actively stretching toward place with the aim of bringing about "unity of the senses, of intelligence, of sensibility and motility" (157).

Yet against this unity, Merleau-Ponty also speaks of space and perception as "saturating" consciousness, writing that "the instability of levels produces not only the intellectual experience of disorder, but the vital experience of giddiness and nausea, which is the awareness of our contingency, and the horror with which it fills us" (2006, 296). Merleau-Ponty's alignment among contingency, nausea, and horror is exacting and beyond refutation. The vitality of giddiness serves as a reminder of our own contingency, and a contingency that is placed in the very midst of our bodies. A returning question reappears: Where am "I" in this nauseating horror? There is no clear answer, and this lack of clarity means that an incipient dualism is created between the prereflective projection of my lived-body and the cognitive apprehension of my body as an objective thing.

As to how the experience of the service station is unified in the same subject, the answer lies in the body's reanimation in a previous place—for us, the cocoon of the car. Once reinserted, the reconciliation between experience and orientation is neither instant, automatic, nor transparent. Instead, as the journey toward the final destination commences, a gradual and irregular emission of what the body has previously absorbed comes to the foreground, by way of an embryonic body memory. In the car, I feel disquiet. Something has altered, and it is as though I can still feel some trace of the service station on my skin, even though I am not fully aware of the extent of this trace. Not only does the car feel different, but so, too, does my body. I grip the door handle with excessive force, attempting to replace myself in a world that existed prior to the onset of anxiety. I place my head on the headrest and close my eyes. My rhythm has been subjugated by an outside force, effecting a level of exhaustion throughout. In fact, the difference between my body before and after entering the service station is so immense that I am prepared to say that my experience of spatial anxiety served as a threshold between altering ways of comporting myself in the world.

If the body inhabits space and time, then no amount of disharmony with the world can thwart the body in its unconscious experience of being. "At every movement," Merleau-Ponty writes, "previous attitudes and movements provide an every ready standard of measurement" (2006, 161). And these standards are actualized only in the relationship of difference to new movements. Placed in contrast to a different environment, an entire span of time comes to be relived. Yet from the service station to the car, the emission of a previous place is so gradual that the recognition of that dovetailing is deferred. Only as the final destination in the journey becomes visible as a material presence is the recognition of what the body has undergone in the past acknowledged in the present. In such an instant, the body exhales the weight of its own experience, and thus surveys the different modulations it has undergone since beginning the journey.

And so we face a synthesis, whereby the bodily gestures of the service station—the feel of the lighting, the touch of the wall, the jagged pathway of the food plaza—materialize as a residue of what was only partially experienced in the present. The familiarity of the car does little to abate the sense of incongruity: The strange world of the service station is now with us, in the car, permeating the interior, infusing the homely atmosphere with a decidedly unhomely aura. The encroachment of an elsewhere serves to undermine the clarity of journeying toward place as a unified whole. In contrast to the clear unfolding established at the beginning of the journey, now, continuity has been broken while identity simultaneously loses its assurance.

With this loss of assurance, we are reunited with Auster's account of driving. Only now in the narrative, the protagonist has suffered an inexplicable experience—that of being held to build a wall against his will—and is now faced once more with the car, which before had been the place of escape but has now been transformed into a phobic symbol of anguish: "He saw the red Saab parked in the driveway, and the moment he understood what he was looking at, he felt himself go numb with grief. The thought of riding in it again made him sick, but there was no way he could back out of it now" (Auster 2006, 189–90).

The combination of fatalism and transformation merges to produce an experience, in which both the present and the past become irreversibly altered. This incursion means that the self takes in multiple textures of place, in both a cognitive and a bodily manner, and not only those that reinforce the continuity of place. In particular, the involuntary absorption of liminal and transitional places saturates the self with the otherness of place. As a result, the memory of having been in a leveled-out zone disrupts the radical duality between place and non-place through bringing both realms into a third place; namely, the strange place of the body, the receiver of both foreign and native places simultaneously, and thus, fundamentally a mutation, which we can now term "*un-place*."

ALIEN FLESH

Within the dark walls of the car, my body has emitted an encoded distress signal. Although I am unable to fully decipher its code, I sense internal tension beginning in the coldness of my hands and extending to the disquiet in my stomach. From my expedition into the service station, with its shadowless landscape and exotic colonies of life, my body has been the recipient of an experience, which has yet to be fully registered. That I am now beyond this experiential marshland means that we can begin to formally assess the theoretical significance of what I have termed "un-place." Along the way, we must evaluate two of our initial objectives. The first objective concerned the relationship between mental and motor intentionality. More precisely, the question we asked ourselves was: Does the way the body experience the world establish a tension with that of cognitive apprehension? Alongside this trajectory, another demand emerged: to demonstrate the interweaving ambiguity between "place" and "non-place." Let us pursue this latter point first.

In contrast to the notion that place is split into modes of "place," "non-place," and "site," we can now see that such divisions are essentially fluid, each supposed division forming one texture running through the materiality of the human body. As I enter the realm of the service station, my "pre-personal body" (a key term that I shall come back to) does not single out this place as being "culturally" deficient. The work of aesthetic and cultural evaluation is left largely to the sedimented values manifested rationally. All my body experiences, in its primal intentionality, is a phenomenal plane to be understood and oriented with regard to its own perspective.

Such an entanglement with the body undermines the notion that place exists "there" while non-place is positioned "here," and vice versa. Indeed, to speak phenomenologically of "here" and "there" as occupying modes of place is untenable. The result of this is that un-place forges a receptivity to complex *layers* of place, some familiar and others unfamiliar, rather than discrete blocks of spatiality situated in abstraction, all of which retain a familiarity to the subject. Un-place is porous, ambiguous, and opposed to the language of "place" and "non-place" in advance of experience. Instead of being formed in advance and then remaining in place, these divisions serve only to impose an ideal grid of abstract references upon our experience of the world.

In this respect, the prefix "un-" reflects the absorption of other places, and not only those that reaffirm my sense of self. Whereas "non-place" suggests a deficiency in certain culturally produced spaces, "un-place" puts aside the status of place through attending to its experience as a whole. The result of this is a recognition of the body's role in disturbing the cognitive, cultural, and aesthetic distinctions superimposed upon the world. Such second-order concepts, though vital to an understanding of place in a local context, are divested of their certainty through the incursion of a prereflective experience of place. For this reason, it is especially where liminal and transitional places such as airports, hotel lobbies, and waiting rooms are concerned that the

MEMORIES OF THE FLESH

power of un-place proves most fertile. In such cases, the apparent invisibility and homogeneity of these places prove illusive and elusive. Because of this ambiguity, an event is established that positions itself in opposition to the abstraction of place.

But here a tension needs to be addressed. While we can freely emphasize the role of the body's perspective in distinction to other modes of perception, what cannot be overlooked is the body's experience and memory of other places, which, in turn, are already laden with aesthetic and cultural values. To be in place is to have already established what is other than place. Are we ever, after all, really purely embodied subjects of perception, divested of the cultural values that somehow precede the world of abstract thought? Our earlier engagement with Merleau-Ponty's idea of "wild being" has taught us to be cautious of binary divisions between "nature" and "culture." But Merleau-Ponty can also help us approach the manifold ambiguities placed between embodiment and abstraction with his enigmatic notion of "flesh" (1968).

We know from our engagement with Merleau-Ponty that the principal aim of the *Phenomenology of Perception* is to describe the world in distinction to intellectualist and empiricist idealizations. Rather than leading back to a transcendental ego, however, Merleau-Ponty instead posits an embodied subject as the necessary condition of experience. The enduring contribution of that work was to render circular the relationship between being and world, with each overlapping and folding into the other, and thus forming a coherent system. In the late ontology of Merleau-Ponty, the unquestioned status of the embodied subject in relation to the world will come into question from the philosopher himself. Indeed, in a final working note the following criticism is made: "The problems posed in *Ph.P.* are insoluble because I start there from the 'consciousness'—'object' distinction" (1968, 200). The classical opposition employed in Merleau-Ponty's earlier work proves inadequate, for what is missed is the question of "the common stuff of which all the structures are made" (200). Precisely because the world is approached via the intentionality of the embodied subject is a radical phenomenology of intentionality omitted.

Already, however, Merleau-Ponty had hinted at the radical ontology that was to later follow in a usage of Husserl's "touching my left hand with my right hand," as he writes:

> When I touch the left hand I also find in it, too, series of touch-sensations, which are *"localized"* in it, though these are not constitutive

of properties (such as roughness or smoothness of the hand, of this physical thing). If I speak of the *physical* thing, "left hand," then I am abstracting from these sensations. . . . If I do include them, then it is not that the physical thing is now richer, but instead *it becomes Body, it senses.* (Husserl 1990, 152; italics in original)

In Merleau-Ponty's (2006, 106) reading of this passage, a "double sensation" is identified, from which the knowing subject who is body and flesh is molded. Touched and touching, each hand is ready to exchange its role through collapsing into the same space. Doing so, the body begins to reflect itself as a sentient thing, stretching into the being of the world.

By the time of *The Visible and the Invisible*, the taken-for-granted status of embodied intentionality becomes the point of departure for a critique of the visible world itself. "The visible about us," so he writes, "seems to rest in itself. It is as though our vision were formed in the heart of the visible" (Merleau-Ponty 1968, 130). The result of this intimacy between the visible world and the subject attending to that world is a literal *con*-fusion, whereby the gaze of the subject clothes the world in a language already formed in advance. When the world appears for me, then how does it gain its depth simply in the glance of an eye? (Casey 2007). What enables my body to touch the world beyond me, as the same world touches me? How is it that when I look at things, then what I experience is not chaos, but things? "What," finally, "is this prepossession of the visible, this art of interrogating it according to its own wishes, this inspired exegesis?" (Merleau-Ponty 1968, 133). There must, Merleau-Ponty suggests, "exist some relationship by principle, some kinship, according to which they are not only, like the pseudopods of the amoeba, vague and ephemeral deformations of the corporeal space, but the initiation to and the opening upon a tactile world" (133).

The answer to this puzzle is clarified with the Merleau-Ponty revision of the touched-touching distinction. There, he identifies a "crisscrossing within it of the touching and the tangible, its own movements incorporate themselves into the universe they interrogate, are recorded on the same map as it" (1968, 133). On the same map, now we are in a realm of more than simple circularity and instead moved to a position, whereby the lived-body "cannot possess the visible unless he is possessed by it, unless he *is of it*" (134–35; italics in original). This idea of the subject's being "of it" is critical: It demonstrates not simply the circularity between subject and world, but also their shared existence in the same "flesh." Thanks to the "thickness of flesh," an "intercorporeal" nexus between body and world is established, dispersing the division between subject and object and forming an interstitial "ultimate notion" (135). Into this notion, the "thickness of the body" does not establish itself as a rival to the world, but is "the sole means I have to go unto the heart of the things, by making myself a world and by making them flesh" (135).

How the "flesh of the world" is set in place is primarily through the lived-body. Having the capacity to touch and be touched at once, the body embodies the reversibility between the visible and the invisible and so disrupts the distance between "subject" and "object." The double play between touching and tangibility retains a singularity, in which neither becomes indistinguishable from the other. In this respect, the body's flesh is both privileged and peculiar. Thanks to its sensing-sensible structure, the body stands aside from other things through being sensible for itself. Yet the body "*is of them,*" of the single reality prior to appearances and simultaneously constitutive of all appearances.

What Merleau-Ponty's emphasis on touching and tangibility helps us to realize is that the emergence of the world as a visible appearance is taken as nothing less than extension of the place of the body. "As soon as I see," he writes in an important passage, "it is necessary that the vision . . . be doubled with a complementary vision or with another vision: myself seen from without, such as another would see me, installed in the midst of the visible, occupied in considering it from a certain spot" (1968, 134). In seeing myself "seen from without," I simultaneously experience myself from within, the result of which is that seeing things themselves is invariably with reference to the body that stands in a concurrent relation of distance and closeness to the world.

And so, Merleau-Ponty poses the question: "Where are we to put the limit between the body and the world, since the world is flesh?" (1968, 138). With the world as flesh, the atomic subject is replaced with a carnal intentionality, whereby the seer already finds himself or herself immersed in the world, just as the visible world already finds itself within the seer. But not only does this reflexivity attest to a circular correspondence between "subject" and "world"; rather, the ontology of the flesh means that body and world, seer and visible are different modalities of the same fabric, securing both their coherence and their opposition. Moreover, the being of the flesh means that body and world do not stand in a static and oppositional mode of existence, but continuously intertwine, creating "a quality pregnant with a texture, the surface of a depth, a cross section upon a massive being, a grain or corpuscle borne by a wave of Being" (136).

What Merleau-Ponty wants to elicit in his writing on the "flesh of the world" is the manner with which the visible becomes defined as such. Rather than presenting itself as a "chunk of absolutely hard, indivisible being," he asks us to approach the visible as a "sort of straits between exterior horizons and interior horizons ever gaping open, something that comes to touch lightly and makes diverse regions of the coloured or visible world resound at the distances" (1968, 132). The immanence of the flesh is ultimate, therefore, since it forms "a strange adhesion of the seer and the visible," of which "there is no name in traditional philosophy to designate it" (132). Indeed, he will go on to say that "flesh is not matter, is not mind, is not substance. To designate it, we should need the old term 'element'" (139). As an element, the flesh is immanent to the subject, and transcends the Husserlian division between noesis and noema. For this reason, the flesh is a "*general thing*, midway between the spatio-temporal individual and the idea, a sort of incarnate principle that brings a style of being wherever there is a fragment of being" (139; italics in original). We can see now how the elemental status of the flesh links with Merleau-Ponty's adjoining idea of "wild being": Both terms refer to the world prior to things, from where depth and meaning are excavated from an invisible presence.

What can Merleau-Ponty's ontology of the flesh tell us about the spatio-temporality of journeying to and from a service station? There are two points to make. First, given the elemental status of flesh, at all times I remain within a world of depth and meaning despite any such attempt at classifying the world into different orders. The flesh unites me to the world, of which places ranging from intimate homes to nocturnal motels have a shared coexistence. That I was able to apprehend the service station as a coherent appearance testifies to the fleshy adhesive, which renders even the most inhospitable environment consistent and continuous with my presence. In this respect, the flesh of the world is an important notion for redefining our relationship to the environment, and a concept that has proved central for environmental philosophers working in the phenomenological tradition (Abram 1997; Cataldi and Hamrick 2007; Evans and Lawlor 2000; Toadvine 2009). What all of these approaches tend to have in common is the idea that flesh can be employed as a site of critique for the human-world relationship, challenging the anthropomorphic approbation of the natural world through emphasizing the chiasmatic entwinement of flesh.

Merleau-Ponty's contribution to environmental phenomenology is thus rich and enduring. But what has been underplayed in this engagement with

Merleau-Ponty is the question of whether the elemental hold the flesh has on us is immune to disruption. Phrased another way, if flesh is the "formative medium of the object and subject" (Merleau-Ponty 1968, 147), then does human subjectivity risk being displaced from its element, and thus rendering the flesh *visible*? But how would the flesh become visible? For is the flesh not simply the condition for my experience of the world, the invisible fabric binding bodies and things, and thus everywhere and nowhere? Never present, never visible: "This strange domain to which interrogation properly so-called, gives access" (140). Yet later on, Merleau-Ponty makes an exception to this "strange domain." Writing on other bodies, he refers to an "*anonymous visibility* [that] inhabits both of us, a vision in general" (142; emphasis added). For Merleau-Ponty, the anonymity of vision is the wild being preceding the split between subject and object, self and other. To this end, it is a transcendental condition of experience, subtending to the particular articulation of vision.

Yet a question can be voiced in this ontology: What is "my," the individual subject's, relationship to this transcendental anonymity? Do I ever experience the anonymous visibility that makes up my bodily vision of the world? How does my particular body experience this "*general thing*," termed "flesh"? Merleau-Ponty says very little about the *experience* of anonymity. Despite the importance of anonymity within Merleau-Ponty's late and early philosophy, no answers are presented to these questions. Before us, however, an opening into this hidden anonymity has been forged. For we have been covertly plotting with our expedition into the service station the ingredients for a phenomenology of flesh's anonymity, *as experienced*. Let us remind ourselves of this journey.

With the backdrop of Merleau-Ponty's late ontology in mind, we can rediscover this journey in five distinct stages. First, when entering the service station, my body underwent an anxious modification, instilling a disembodied mode of affectivity. Because of this anxious embodiment, my experience of the place was not only fragmented, it was also in tension with my attempt at rationalizing space. My failure to bring this space to order led to the neutralization of my own subjectivity, experienced in terms of being objectively "inside" yet existentially "outside."

Second, as this tension ensued, my body, in its clawing grasp of the "intentional arc," persisted toward a unity that "I" myself as a rational agent was not fully aware of. All around me, the environment of the station was being incorporated into a prereflective scheme, yet to reconcile with the life-world. This is the power of the body. Through its own perspective on the world, the body is able incorporate things into the world prior to our conceptualization of those same objects. In turn, the orientation of this schema is toward familiarity and enclosure, at all times reinforcing the solidity of the embodied subject in its interdependent relation with the world.

Third, not only is the service station as a particular thing in the world absorbed, but so, too, is the singularity of the service station's flesh now developing a "circle of the touched and the touching" (Merleau-Ponty 1968, 143). Into this circle, my own body forms an "opaque zone" with that of the service station's body, such that we both partake of the "anonymous visibility" that inheres in "the secret folds of our flesh" (118). In this respect, the "flesh of the world" is indicative of the unconscious bodily immersion into the world, a striving toward a continuity beyond that of my personal body.

Fourth, thanks to the reversibility between things, the flesh of the service station interweaves in the "fundamental narcissism of all vision" by reverting its vision back on the subject. Suddenly, "I feel myself looked at by the things," and in particular, I feel myself looked at by the world of the service station (Merleau-Ponty 1968, 139). That the service station is able to see me is possible inasmuch as my bodily perception of the place is at the same time the experience of the station *touching me*. When moving within the place, the place acts upon me, perceives *through* me. This does not mean that the service station depends upon my existence, as though we had reverted to a form of transcendental idealism. Nor does it entail a crude animism. Rather, the place becomes *animated*. Animated not only through the movement of things, but because the place's being articulates itself through the human who is receptive to that genesis, with each being overlapping into the flesh of the world.

Finally, experientially, this reversibility of the flesh is felt after leaving the service station. Once in the car, the personal body comes back from a state of dormancy, now able to partly communicate a truncated message from beyond. This experience carries with it an uncanny sensibility. There, a vague memory acts upon the body as a virus incubates itself within the moist walls of its host. Indeed, it is only because the sedimentation of memory discharges itself beyond the threshold of the body that the reunited self becomes aware of just *where* the body has been: subject to the "alien flesh" of a place that is located in the anonymity of the body but invisible to the personal self.

The phrase "alien flesh" singles out the ambivalence placed between the anonymity of the flesh as an element and the reflexivity of that flesh as experienced. As I have sought to show, in certain environmental conditions—especially those involving anxious embodiment—the ontology of the flesh becomes destabilized, in the process disclosing the anonymous infrastructure of that which is touched and that which does the touching. In such a case, a duality of experience unfolds. On the one hand, we are faced with an anxious, fragmented partial experience of a place. Such an experience is taken from the perspective of "one's own body," and remains consistent with my embodied subjectivity as a whole. On the other hand, something else is revealed in this disquiet: another "subject" for whom there is an existential difference to my self-reflexive "I."

Yet the disclosure is necessarily belated, indirect, and manifest when two or more experiences collide. The emphasis on deferment and incompletion forces a lacuna in the relation between place, time, and memory. Only in the disjunction of different places is the alienness and anonymity of this experience brought to the fore, no doubt causing Merleau-Ponty to write: "But once we have entered into this strange domain, one does not see how there could be any question of *leaving* it" (1968, 152; italics in original). In the car, at home, in the abandoned country retreat miles from the city center, not only is another place felt to be moving through my flesh, but so, too, another presence is felt within the heart of my being, and a presence of whom unfamiliarity is the abiding characteristic. In such a case, alien flesh becomes defined as *the lived-body becoming the host for an interstitial memory foreign to the cognitive experience of that event.*

Alien flesh is thus characterized by the experience of "one's own body" being subject to another subjectivity. Such a subjectivity is in some sense *not my own*. This is evidenced by the fact that the experience of alien flesh is one of estrangement and uncanniness. Thus, if un-place is the overlapping of places within the same body, then alien flesh is the recognition of the body as the host for that overlapping. Together, the result is an uncanny effect. Precisely because alien flesh involves a concurrent blending of absence and presence, it follows that the delayed recognition of having been in a place is thus a *re-recognition* of that experience. Doubling, (un)familiarity, and strangeness conspire to create an experience that refuses to fit into the notion of place and identity as forming a continuous duration. Rather, what is pregiven as tacit—the body—suddenly loses its inconspicuousness, forcing a shift from the virtual to the actual, and thus drawing attention to the body's own awareness of its history, as *having* a history.

But is this subjectivity a modification of my own, a subspecies of the service station's flesh, or the phantom of an altogether different life-world? After all, if it is the case that we can feel ourselves being "looked at by the things," then assessing whose vision is at stake becomes ambiguous, as Merleau-Ponty writes in "Eye and Mind":

> Visible and mobile, my body in a thing among things; it is caught in
> the fabric of the world, and its cohesion is that of a thing. But be-
> cause it moves itself and sees, it holds things in a circle around itself.
> Things are an annex or prolongation of itself; they are incrusted
> into its flesh, they are part of its full definition; *the world is made of
> the same stuff as the body.* (1979, 58–59; emphasis added)

Encrusted into its flesh. With this, Merleau-Ponty commits himself to a radical ontology, adjoined with a deep sense of phenomenal ambiguity if not
outright strangeness. With the world made up of the same stuff as the body,
a weird animism ensues between the watchfulness of the world and myself as
aware of that sensibility. But far from instigating a premature environmental ethic, the existence of this correspondence only amplifies the urgency of
establishing whose subjectivity coexists with "my" own. To answer this, we
need to revert back to the earlier Merleau-Ponty.

Lurking within Merleau-Ponty's *Phenomenology of Perception* is a largely
uncharted yet sparse library of references to the phenomenon of the "prepersonal" body (2006, 296). In various ways, we have implicitly touched upon
the basis of this idea throughout the chapter, ranging from the experience of
the derelict ballroom to the anxious spatiality of the service station. In each
case, a difference in subjective emphasis came to the fore. Thus, the anxiety
of the service station led to a split within experience, with my body taking
over as "I" hovered in anxiety. How this dual experience is possible is a question Merleau-Ponty confronts directly in the *Phenomenology of Perception*.
In a passage, the significance of which cannot be overstated, he writes:

> There appears round our personal existence a margin of *almost* im-
> personal existence, which can be practically taken for granted, and
> which I rely on to keep me alive. . . . It can be said that my organism,
> as a prepersonal cleaving to the general form of the world, as an
> anonymous and general existence, plays, beneath my personal life,
> the part of an *inborn complex.* It is not some kind of inert thing;
> it too has something of the momentum of existence. It may even
> happen when I am in danger that my human situation abolishes my
> biological one, that my body lends itself without reserve to action.

> But these moments can be no more than moments, and for most of the time personal existence represses the organism without being able either to go beyond it or to renounce itself; without, in other words, being able either to reduce the organism to its existential self, or itself to the organism. (2006, 96–97; italics in original)

This passage is as striking as it is important. Merleau-Ponty is effectively claiming that the unity of embodiment is made possible thanks to an anonymous subject existing "beneath" my personal existence, such that I am kept "alive" by this absent presence. How am I kept alive? In certain cases, my body "lends itself without reserve to action," establishing a continuity that would otherwise be dispersed were I simply a cognitive agent. This we have already witnessed in the experience of anxious spatiality: The bodily perception of things is accented, as an unconscious body is summoned to action. Not only this, but for the most part, impersonal existence is "repressed" by personal existence, as though avoiding the status of being an organism, and that alone. At no time is the "anonymous and general existence" of which I am constituted freely available to my personal being. Only in certain "moments" is the anonymous architecture of being visible. And the reason is clear: *Experiencing* the prepersonal, anonymous body carries with it an enigmatic quality, into which reason and cognition fail to apprehend. Yet such moments are reported to exist, whereupon my personal body comes into contact with this anonymous field of force "beneath" but also *within* me.

In our account of un-place and alien flesh, I believe we have discovered an initial foray into this encounter between the personal and prepersonal body. Defining itself as a peculiar mode of experiencing the world, un-place sets in motion the multifarious entwinement of different places within the same body. In light of that entwinement, the experience of alien flesh stands as the recognition of "another subject beneath me, for whom a world exists before I am here, and who marks out my place in it" (Merleau-Ponty 2006, 296). That I can experience this other subject only fleetingly testifies to the dynamism of alien flesh; its structure is mutable and mutating, expressing itself through the indirection of the body's self-reflexive awareness of its own history. And what is revealed in that history is something other than my strict sense of self; it is the "captive or natural spirit [which] is my body . . . the system of anonymous 'functions' which draw every particular focus into a general project" (296).

How, then, do we experience the body as an anonymous presence? Phrased another way: How do I experience my personal existence as the "resumption

of a prepersonal tradition" (Merleau-Ponty 2006, 296)? Does the world
cease to be once the personal body reaches its own end, its own edge? What
is the world for the impersonal body, this "pre-world in which as yet no men
existed" that Merleau-Ponty (376) alludes to?

The answer to these questions must surely lie in the nature of *body memory*. From anonymous to personal and then back to anonymous, the body's
ontogenesis is a narrative definable only as a memory. For through the experience of our bodies' remembering, we come to see a world that was hitherto
silent now assume an indistinct visibility within our own being. The vision
of this anonymous body is necessarily indirect, as we remain limited to the
symptomatic appearance of a past that manifests itself in a vague sense.
But in those moments in which I feel fundamentally dis-placed, dis-eased,
dis-connected, and dis-quieted, then it is clearly because I have fortuitously
caught sight of the presencing of an impersonal life-world at work, which
removes me, the subject, from its flesh.

But this is not only the memory of particular places and things. When I
am made aware of my body as "lending itself without reserve to action," then
what is occurring here is not simply a difference in how I experience a given
place. Rather, what unfolds in the alien flesh is a genetic memory of a "world
more ancient than thought" (Merleau-Ponty 1968, 296). More ancient than
thought, I experience the very transcendental structure of what it is to have a
body—not *my* body, but the "inhuman" body, yet to figure itself as belonging
to the world of particular things. Touching this dark side of being, the result
is a primal experience of uncanniness. At times, "my life slips away from me
on all sides and is circumscribed by impersonal zones" (386). No wonder,
therefore, that Merleau-Ponty speaks of "repression" as a chief factor in our
relationship to the prepersonal body. The knowledge that within me dwells
another self, ambiguous and ancient, of which I am only partially conscious,
is a thought more attuned to the sense of being possessed by another body
rather than the sense of possessing our own bodies. Indeed, in the chapters
that follow, the germ of alien flesh will develop into nothing less than a model
of uncanny horror.

· ·

CHAPTER FOUR

THE DARK ENTITY

New York was an inexhaustible space, a labyrinth of endless steps, and no matter how far he walked, no matter how well he came to know its neighbourhoods and streets, it always left him with the feeling of being lost. Lost, not only in the city, but within himself as well.

—Paul Auster, *The New York Trilogy*

"He needed," so writes Georges Rodenbach of the widowed protagonist in *Bruges-la-Morte*,

> a dead town to correspond to his dead wife. His deep mourning demanded such a setting. Life would only be bearable for him there . . . in the muted atmosphere of the waterways and the deserted streets, Hugues was less sensitive to the sufferings of his heart. . . . In this way the town, once beautiful and beloved too, embodied the loss he felt. Bruges was his dead wife. And his dead wife was Bruges. The two were united in a like destiny. (2005, 30–31)

Rodenbach's fin de siècle depiction of loss and love in a decaying Bruges plays on the thematic entwinement of embodiment, memory, and mimesis. In the process of mourning his wife, Hugues Viane establishes a "spiritual telepathy between his soul and the grief-stricken towers of Bruges" (2005, 60). This structural device, central to the novel, provides the opportunity for Rodenbach to explore the affective power of memory and imagination, manifest as actions able to morph a location to mimetically resemble the object of desire. The "sense of resemblance" prevalent in the book leads the protagonist to seek refuge in Bruges, in which his grief and loss are personified in the stone and material of the city.

What is peculiar to this reading is the extent to which place is assimilated by memory. The "thousand tenuous threads" that link the past with the present occur thanks to the specific environment of Bruges itself, which facilitates the spectral emergence of the dead wife through the figure of another woman, an actress named Jane. As a result of this meeting, Viane proceeds to clothe the actress, with the aim of modifying her behavior in accordance with the memory of his wife. Indeed, the strangeness of this story is precisely the reconfiguration of the past in another imitative guise, such that the familiarity of the past becomes dislocated by the alteration of the present. "Resemblance," Rodenbach writes, "is the horizon where habit and novelty meet" (2005, 60). But resemblance, as Rodenbach presents it, never deviates from the position of the protagonist. Rather, Bruges the city becomes a spatial and temporal extension, and so expression, of Viane the subject, recalling Nietzsche's account of the "antiquarian man": "The history of his city becomes for him the history of himself; he reads its walls, its towered gate, its rules and regulations, its holidays, like an illuminated diary of his youth and in all this he finds again himself, his force, his industry, his joy, his judgment, his folly and vices" (Nietzsche 1997, 73).

This narcissistic relation to the city is at the same time the necessary means for Hugues Viane to retain temporal continuity. At the expense of this commitment, objective temporality becomes fundamentally altered. Accordingly, by the end of the story, Viane's misappropriation of the actress and the city as counterparts to his dead wife ends in abject histrionics, as the illusion of the past being preserved into the present gradually comes undone:

> Hugues had suffered a great disillusionment since the day he had had the strange caprice of getting Jane to put on one of his dead wife's outmoded dresses. He had gone too far. By trying to fuse the two women into one he had only succeeded in lessening their resemblance. (Rodenbach 2005, 86)

In this passage, the form of the past disjoins with the content of the present. Effectively, the two aspects fail to merge, so producing a mutant, which breaches the walls of Viane's illusion. Another way of considering the confluence between habit and novelty, and between form and content, is to consider the power of place as the power of preserving a singular conception of the past, and yet a conception that ultimately resists becoming fixed by memory. In this way, the emergence of place gains the associated role of sealing absences and points of discontinuity. Rodenbach's novel, despite its stylistically untimely embellishments, is exemplary in exploring this act of projection, whereby the world becomes a mirror of the history of memory and the body.

I resurrect this story in order to establish the thematic focus of the chapter, namely: how personal identity depends as much on memory as it does on the constant modification of that memory through being integrated with imagination. What we glimpse at in the above summary of Rodenbach's novel is the role the imagination plays in preserving (and thereby failing to preserve) the continuity of the self in place. The outcome of this failure to bind identity with place is a dispersed being, alienated from his or her environment. At stake in this emergence of an alienated environment is the tension between memory, imagination, and the embodied self.

The broad aim of the chapter is to critically assess to what extent the imagination contributes to the continuity of the memory of place, and thus the unity of the bodily self. Seen in this way, the current of the present chapter extends the work done in the previous chapter, by demonstrating the vulnerability and contingency of the body being the receptacle of the past. Only now, we shall modify this focus in relation to the spatiotemporal continuity of personal identity. This aim occurs against the backdrop of the view that memory and imagination, as Bachelard (1994) would have, work in "tandem" to produce a "felicitous" image of the past. What is missing in this formula, however, is an analysis of the relationship between time and place taken in their difference. In this chapter, I will challenge the notion that place memory retains its affective unity by positing the notion of place memory being in conflict with imagination. To achieve this, I will turn to Bachelard and Freud, developing a phenomenology of nostalgia, and finally positing the notion of "anonymous materiality," place comprising the uncanny remnants of both memory and imagination.

PLACE-MAKING

In the previous chapter, we considered how place is elevated to the event of memory via the body. Our task now is to assess how place retains its persistence as a singular event, especially where that persistence is stretched through the course of time. As we have seen, the singularity of place assumes an intimate role in becoming identifiable with personal identity. Because of this intimacy, inhabiting place does not simply mean coexisting alongside and within the materiality of an environment. Rather, it means cultivating a fundamental identification with place. By this, I refer to the absorption of the external world through the primacy of experience, such that self and world form a corresponding and synthetic relationship of resemblance.

This is evident where our habits intercede between place and world, allowing the body to become a receptacle of the world but also encouraging what Merleau-Ponty terms a "renewal of the corporeal schema" (2006, 164). As places alter, so our bodies take the time to master the environment, and the objects that inhabit that environment. In the previous chapter, this mastery centered on the interior of the car, but the synthesis between person and thing does not end with particular things but spreads out in a multidimensional way. Thus, for Merleau-Ponty, the blind man's stick is not a "tool" to be employed in the objective world, but becomes an "area of sensitivity, extending the scope and active radius of touch, and providing a parallel to sight" (165). More than a substitute for sight, the blind man's stick actually assumes the role of sight, discerning the world with its own unique sensibility, the power of which descends from the body of the blind man, and, indeed, is incorporated into the "bulk of our own body" (166).

In turn, this extension of the body extends to a broader absorption of place and world, with body and world contributing to each other's shared identity. Merleau-Ponty writes: "To understand is to experience the harmony between what we aim at and what is given, between the intention and the performance—and the body is our anchorage in the world" (2006, 167). With our bodies as anchors, *in*-habiting the world becomes the task of comporting ourselves in the world, as the world comports itself into the grooves of the body. Thus, the accented "in" within *in*-habiting attests to the developmental interplay between ourselves and the places we find ourselves.

The result of this shared inhabitation is the hybrid of place and self. Ontologically, the flesh of the world conjoins body and world into the same stuff. Ontically, this conjoinment takes place on an experiential level. Places are felt to be moving in and through the human body, as human bodies are experienced within those same places. The body's inhalation and exhalation concern more than the elements we breathe. With its pulse, the body opens itself to the heterogeneity of a particular place. Indeed, thanks to the body, place gains meaning *as* place. Doors, ladders, beds, and tables all invite the body to comport itself in a specific way, varying with each entity the body encounters. As windows lull us to glance beyond our immediate place, so chairs ask that we find repose in a room. With these intuited movements, things of the world, objects and places, cease to be anonymous in their presence, and instead become invested with the potency of human value. Elevated to the center of our lives, over a period of time, the tables and chairs we encounter in passing transform to beacons of our own existence. Experiencing the tables of this world, we simultaneously experience our own selves as sitting at those tables, joining in the ritual of a life suited to dwelling and habitat. At such a point, the table is never truly "external" to the body, but already constituted by a proximity to its presence.

Having developed a relationship with place, in turn, we expect a place to reciprocate the feelings and experiences we share with it. Cultivating a sense of affection for one's corner of the world is expressive of more than vanity. Appealing to our desires for self-affirmation, the places we dwell and reside in assume the equivalent role of interpersonal relations, requiring the same level of care and attendance. And when places fall from this care, as when things break down in the house, then there is considerable ambiguity resting on whose fault the breakage rests: ours or that of the place itself. In a word, this act of place-making testifies to the very organic life of a place, situated, as it is, within the same earth that human bodies dwell in.

Here, however, a critical tension can be discerned: Given the interplay between place and self, an adjoining correspondence ensues between the materiality of the world and the temporality of the self. If the world is incorporated into the self, then the agency binding these mutually dependent aspects is at the same time vulnerable to alteration and disruption. As an inseparable hybrid, both the dynamism of the self and the staunch materiality of the world are nonetheless thrown into radical contingency once memory enters the scene. That memory plays a fundamental role in uniting self and world is already clear. Yet presupposing that this unity is necessarily given to harmony is contestable.

With this tension in mind, a question can be formulated: *How does place retain its meaningful, absorbing, and dynamic presence in time without succumbing to a static image of memory, whereby the lived past is* superimposed *on the still-unfolding present?* The idea of the past being "superimposed" here is central. What I have in mind involves less an active projection of the past on the present and more a covert movement of the body as it strives toward an existential unity in the present. Dramatically shifting in time, the places we inhabit seldom remain untouched by their own existence. Places grow; flourish in the summer of their plenitude, then fade in the autumn of

their being, before receding into the winter of their annihilation. Throughout
this span of time, we ourselves retain a relationship to the places we dwell in.
The life of the human is as equally ravished by the "taskmaster with a whip"
as the stone and mortar of places are (Schopenhauer 2000, 292). Because
of this mutual erosion, human life must adapt to its surroundings, which,
at all times, is thrown into contingency and sudden destruction. The shared
equivalence between dwellings and dwellers is brutal and brief, and unless
the imagination can modify what time augments, then our memories remain
alien to our experiences.

As we have seen in Bachelard, the prevention of place slipping from our
timescale elevates imagination to the role of preserver of the past. As preserver of the past, the imagination is the agent that reconciles the otherness
of the world with the insideness of the subject. More specifically, the imagination can be seen to blur the division between inside and out, meaning
that "belonging" to place is not interrupted by the discontinuous breaks in
memory. In this way, the imagination orients itself fundamentally toward the
future. Whereas memory *gathers* place, imagination appears to *disperse* the
origin of place by throwing it outward and ahead of time. With this dispersion, imagination enters the realm of aesthetic discourse, so partially diverts
from the reality of lived memory.

In an article in the London *Times* on travel books and memory, Jeanette
Winterson writes on the temporal liberation invoked between the conflation
of memory and imagination. Citing the subjective domain as being in tension
with the objective, she writes:

> A private landscape in a public place can only happen imaginatively.
> An old map and a long-forgotten guide can re-open a place to its
> own past, and give a sense of continuity as well as romance. It is
> not necessary to stand dutifully on a preserved ruin or to visit a
> museum to feel the history of a city; it is better to find the layers
> for yourself—a kind of virtual archaeology where whatever you dis-
> cover will be yours to keep. (2006, 3)

Possessed by place, in turn place becomes the container for our obsessions
with a thematically incomplete experience. For Winterson, the void between
the past and the perpetually fragmented present does not preclude unity. Instead, "to evoke a place imaginatively is to find it through its many layers
and strange incarnations" (2006, 3). To become part of a place is, thus, to

undergo a temporal risk. This risk gains a clear form if we ask the following question: In the relation between the two, are the remembering body and the object of that memory equal in their temporal duration? If not, then we are led to consider how place gains temporal stability. Here, imagination shows itself to be an act of place-making for the future, a resistance against time, in which the preparation for the loss of place is established. About this resistance, Bruce Janz writes:

> Much of the impetus for place-making imagination comes from dissatisfaction with existing accounts or experiences of place. Sometimes, the places we experience are narrated in a very restrictive fashion. Place-making imagination can be an act of resistance, an attempt to broaden the narratives we give to place. That resistance may simply be a matter of multiplying possibilities about place, or even fictionalizing it. Imagining place as an act of resistance may mean little more than providing alternate story-lines in an effort to unseat or destabilize a dominant account of place. (2005)

Janz points to the aesthetic dimension of a "place-making imagination." Doing so, he suggests that places are re-discovered, due to some previous dissatisfaction or boredom. In this way, the imagination maintains the affirmative role it occupied in Bachelard: retaining the unity of the self as it provides ground for place to adapt to the modulations of the self. Yet agility is open to gradients. The reworking of place expands and contracts in terms of how well the imagination can integrate it. Failing to assimilate place successfully means producing an excess in imagination. However, without a place to return to, the movement of memory and imagination simply turns on the self, highlighting in each case the distance between desire and the world. Contending with a "place-making imagination," this distance must be attended to.

To redirect the faith in memory and imagination, then, let me propose the following formula: Against Bachelard (1994), who posits the motionlessness of place memory (securing the original place even after "twenty years" of absence), and contending Casey (2000b), whose faith in place to "hold its contents steadily within its own embrace," means that "memory connects spontaneously with place," by way of contrast, let us consider memory and place as existing on disparate planes, each contesting the reality of the other's existence. The purpose of this trial will be to establish to what extent place can survive the contingencies of the self and also to what end the self can survive the contingencies of place.

A PHENOMENOLOGY OF NOSTALGIA

So far, I have emphasized the theoretical conflation of memory, imagination, and place. In order to demonstrate how this conflation is played out experientially, a phenomenology of nostalgia will enrich our understanding of how the imagination renders place timely but simultaneously altered. Why nostalgia? My point of departure is the following claim: The fragmentation of the world we are nostalgic for presents us with a privileged temporality, which brings together, in a particularly vivid manner, the limits of imagination in the face of the diminishment of memory. This tension between timeliness and unreality is central to the logic of nostalgia. Indeed, the power of nostalgia depends as much on the evocation of place as it does on the time in which that memory occurred, forcing an image of the past in which time is literally held in an unreal place. One way in which we see this is how nostalgia relies on an image of the past as temporally isolated; that is, as *fixed*. The fixture means that place, as a temporal episode, singular and irretrievable, is preserved. Fixing place in time, place is thus fixated on. As we will investigate, the bind between fixing and fixation intensifies as the integration and continuity of the past undergo a loss of transparency.

To defend my opening claim regarding the relation between nostalgia and a privileged mode of temporality, what I propose to do now is attend to the temporal formation of nostalgia before situating that structure firmly in place. One of the peculiar temporal features of nostalgia we can immediately observe is the ambivalent role the past plays in contributing to the personal identity in the present. Characteristic of the structure of nostalgia is the pronounced fixation, qualitatively positive or negative, of an image that binds the self to a place and time. In material terms, what this means is that because place gains vibrancy through being temporal, nostalgia flourishes as the place either withdraws into the spatiotemporal distance or is otherwise altered in the present.

Take the first movement. We see this as the emblematic motif of nostalgia: Once a considerable distance, spatial or temporal, has been forged between the object under consideration and the subject attending to that object, a transformation occurs. Primarily, this transformation is evident in the experience of a value being renewed. Indeed, the concurrent yearning affixed to the experience of nostalgia could be thought of as having its origins in the difference between the manner in which a thing gives itself and the process of then subjugating that givenness to a desired state. That the eventual realization of desire is invariably thwarted does less to diminish the yearning and more to enflame it. Suddenly, the receding distance of what was once intimate and stable ignites a moment of heighted self-presence, especially if that object played a significant role in the development of the self, such that without it, a partial loss of the self would ensue.

By contrast, the second trajectory plots a more compressed temporality. Instead of retreating into the darkness of the past world, the same object undergoes terminal change in the present, becoming fundamentally alien to the subject attached and bound with that environment. In sight of this alteration, a renewed value is conferred upon a given object. Only now, the tone is less of lamentation and more of preserving what remains of the past, with such an effect to conceal the erosion of time and space. This inclusion of hope pushes this second mode of nostalgia more toward what the Portuguese would term "saudade," a modified version of nostalgia, in which the lamentation of loss is displaced with a projected reclamation in the future. As such, we are concerned less with what is absent in the past and more with what is missing in the present, or, has since disappeared but may soon reappear again (See 2008). This dynamic between absence and disappearance conveys a sense of nostalgia's ambiguous structure. Entwined with the past, that same past is reexperienced in the present as one of presence and absence simultaneously. In both cases, therefore, the altered or distanced past renders what was previously continuous with the self, now discontinuous, leaving the existential unity of human identity uprooted.

Alongside this twofold structure, a further observation emerges: As the distancing and alteration of the past begins to be recognized, the self that has invested its unity within a given environment attempts to forestall the process through centralizing an amorphous—indeed, almost *oneiric*—point in time. I emphasize "oneiric," because what is central to the temporality of nostalgia is an ability to mutate, transfigure, and shift forms. As James Hart points out in his important paper on the topic, "Nostalgia is not about passing time but about eras, seasons or aeons. It is not about dates but about 'times' . . . which are enshrined in a kind of atemporal (i.e., non-fleeting) dimension" (1973, 406). Hart is right, I believe, to emphasize the atemporality of nostalgia. As with Bachelard's murky, shadowy first house, the object of nostalgia covertly

protrudes into the present, refusing all specificity of a set time and so allowing the imagination to clothe the object in an idealized light. What Hart calls
"aeonic time" (406), therefore, can be seen at work in the interplay between
memory and imagination. Thanks to the distancing of set time, the reality
of memory takes second place to the preemptive gesturing of imagination, a
role that is facilitated by the elevation of the past to a mythical status.

***

Having given this circumscribed sketch of nostalgia, a provisional sense
of its core unfolds. Structured in a threefold way, we have seen, first, how the
object of nostalgia undergoes a transformation, such that the affectivity of
remembering becomes infused by a mode of desire. In the second case, the
same structure becomes modified with a plea to reconstitution rather than
dissolution, establishing a link between affectivity and praxis. Finally, we saw
how nostalgia is structured by a peculiar temporality, which has less to do
with pastness and more to do with the atemporality of the nostalgic object
under question. Three questions need to be asked in light of this provisional
structure. First, how can we distinguish between nostalgic memory and non-
nostalgic memory? Second, how does nostalgia gain its status *as* nostalgia?
Third, what is it that we are nostalgic for? Only when these questions have
been thematized will we be able to situate nostalgia properly in place.

If the question of how nostalgia differs from non-nostalgic modes of remembering risks engineering a false dichotomy, then we can nevertheless attempt to plot their differences in structural terms. Situating this direction
within the context of the previous chapters, a leading motif is that the acts
of recollection described are all, in some broad sense, voluntary. Reminding ourselves of this trait, the memory of a childhood place, traveling on
a train, and visiting a monument were all marked by a mode of volitional
intentionality. Only in the corporeality of un-place was this claim to possessing the past disrupted. In that case, the cognitive unity of remembering was
subjected to the independence of noncognitive memory. In effect, producing
a double memory. It is this gesture of the past acting upon the self that forces
a clear structural distinction between modes of remembering to appear.

We can, I would suggest, approach this double memory in parallel terms
as the distinction between voluntary and involuntary memory. Further still,
we could raise the question of whether or not nostalgia occupies a special
relation to involuntary memory and, resuming the thread of thought started

with the idea of un-place, if such a relation is privileged to body memory. In asking these questions, I take my cue from Hart in positioning nostalgia as fundamentally distinct from "intellectual memory," as he writes: "The advent of nostalgia is less like (reproductive) memory and more like retention in that it is not a special deliberate act of turning to the past or re-presencing the past. Like retention it occurs without an act on our part" (1973, 401). Hart's distancing of nostalgia from a "special deliberate act of turning to the past" underscores the structure of nostalgic remembering as one of spontaneity and independence, both of which produce an involuntary act.

As I argued in the first chapter, the affective modality of involuntary memory depends upon there being a previous idea of the past in the first instance. The gesture of displacing the past with a revised version is less about the production of a new representation of memory and more a case of a reexperiencing of the same past through returning to it, primarily in an embodied manner. In a word, acting upon memory would seem to determine that content in advance, thus erasing the "internalized difference," which Deleuze spoke of as being peculiar to involuntary memory (2000, 60).

In a similar light, we can think here of a passage from Cézanne that Merleau-Ponty quotes in his essay on the painter. We read: "If I paint 'crowned' I'm done for, you understand? But if I really balance and shade my place settings and rolls as they are in nature, you can be sure the crowns, the snow and the whole shebang will be there" (1993, 64). Cézanne's remark reminds us that volition and cognition have a peculiar relation to each other, such that the selectivity of perception is the result. The idea of undercutting a representation of "crowned" means, to repeat Cézanne, returning to the "place settings and rolls as they are in nature." Returning to the place settings means, above all, being oriented in both a spatial and a temporal way. In this way, the limited horizon of a solely cognitive memory gives way to a more comprehensive account of memory oriented in the haptic realm of embodiment.

Applied to the phenomenology of nostalgia, the key to the enigma of involuntary memory is manifestly located within the body. Consider how the alignment between involuntary memory and nostalgia crystallizes the role of the body in nostalgic recollection. Acting upon us—emblematically through the sensual encounter with a mnemonic object—nostalgia retains its dynamism through storing itself in the body. With this, the body acts as a focal point, out of which an entire world is cast, complete with its own peculiar atmosphere and associations, its own ghostly actors and stage settings, and its own space for the ruins of the past to reappear and disappear. No longer held in time, the past reanimates itself through the radical heterogeneity of the human body. And so we follow the body—follow our *own* bodies—in leading us toward the rich texture of the past, as it was then in its original corporeal incarnation. Prised apart from the prism of everyday memory, the body loses its status as an instrument of orientation but gains the role of being a threshold to the past.

But here we arrive at an impasse: If a phenomenology of nostalgia depends upon a dual phenomenology of involuntary memory, then how can we undertake such a task without willing that spontaneity in the first instance, and so undermining it? Conversely, to contrive the experience of nostalgia through placing ourselves in a supposedly nostalgic "mind-set" (or better still, *body-set*) would be to absorb the "internalized difference" into the realm of cognitive representation. True, we can take our cues from objects situated in the world, placing those objects in such a way that our powers of recall are somehow heightened. But all that would remain is a simulacrum of the experience of nostalgia. Unable to will the nostalgic moment directly, we stand adrift in a constellation of different memories, all of which hold the power to return us to the pure moment itself. Our phenomenology, therefore, is a memory. Not a phenomenology *of* memory, but phenomenology *as* memory. This retrospective emphasis allows us to phenomenologically attend to the moment, in which we catch sight of the past seizing us in its grip before once again returning us to the world of the living.

We have attempted to differentiate between nostalgic and non-nostalgic memory. Into this nascent division, embodiment and spontaneity have proven themselves to be essential in the formation. But if this consideration has so far pursued a structural emphasis, then we now need to begin attending to the figurative content of nostalgia in its relation to the self. My question is simple: What is involved in the experience of nostalgia that is peculiarly nostalgic, *as such*? Historically, the response to this question has emphasized the role of "algos" (pain) in the Greek "nostos" (Boym 2001). Under such a treatment, the nostalgic dimension of nostalgia has focused on the physical separation from one's home, whether that home is manifest as either a place or a person. Understood in this historic way, "homesickness" has come to assume a central importance, defined by a longing for nominal unity that has since come undone but is now being preserved by the intentionality of a peculiar mode of remembering. Coupled with this tension, the quality of *algos* in nostalgia is marked by the impossibility not only of being reunited with the home as it was originally experienced, but also of recapturing the time in which that experience was lived. Both enemy and ally, place and time serve to distance the nostalgic body from its home but at the same time become the means to foster a desire for that home.

Time and again, the question reappears in different guises: Why does the past suddenly act upon us, emerging without any visible stimuli before affecting a mode of nostalgic reverie located deep in the human body? If we phrase the physical separation at the center of nostalgia as a symptom of history and culture rather than an invariant quality, then what remains of an experience, such that we can term it distinctly "nostalgic"? In pursuit of this question, let us return to the figure of Hugues Viane. Earlier, I characterized Viane's attachment to the decaying city of Bruges as relying on a threefold fusion of mimesis, embodiment, and memory. Given *Bruges-la-Morte*'s emblematic treatment of nostalgia as a pathology of time and place, are we able to place this threefold division at the intermittently beating heart of the nostalgic body? To this question we now turn.

Viane's mimetic identification with Bruges depends on a dual gesture of absorption and desire. Absorbed are the material features of Bruges itself, which, in their aesthetically parallel appearance, reinforce the reality of Viane's desires. This reversible narcissism, played out through the solitude of mimesis, establishes a space where details of a given world are able to be modified in accordance with the active desire of the nostalgic ego. As much as the city itself, of course, it is the figure of Jane, the doppelgänger of Viane's dead wife, who becomes subjected to this process of mimetic (re)discovery:

> A disturbing apparition! An almost frightening miracle of resemblance that went as far as identity. Everything: her gait, her figure, the rhythm of her body, the expression of her features, the inwardness of her look, things not merely of shape and colour, but expressions of a person's spirituality, movements of their soul—all this was given back to him, had returned, was alive. (Rodenbach 2005, 36)

Viane's itinerary of bodily resemblances not only attests to the active mutation of his surroundings, but also serves to place the protagonist as spatially and temporally central to those surroundings. Indeed, key to this mimetic gesture is the desire for the temporal continuity of the self, despite that continuity's having been broken by the absence of a central element: Viane's wife. Recall: "An almost frightening miracle of resemblance that went as far as identity." Just whose identity is being referred to here is left ambiguous. On the surface, the reference appears to be to the reconstitution of his wife's identity through the figure of the *doppelgänger*. But the term "identity" could just as easily refer to Viane's own reconstitution of his previous self, until now frozen in the dying landscape of nostalgic reverie. In both cases, however, we are faced with a process of mutation and manipulation. As I shall argue shortly, mimesis is basically *morphological* in tone. Already, however, this dynamic is clear in the dual metamorphosis of the actress and the city, both of which encourage the past to reappear in resembling guise.

Mimetic identification thus forges a morphological bond between the body and the world, such that a halo of singularity is conferred upon the identity and reality of the self. If we cite this as a feature peculiar to nostalgia, then how is it possible for embodiment to aid in this formation? Rodenbach gives us the following clue: "The two were united in a like destiny. It was Bruges-la-Morte, the dead town entombed in its stone *quais*, with the arteries of its canals cold once the great pulse of the sea had ceased beating in them" (2005, 33). The passage forces the affective experience of time to the foreground. At stake in Rodenbach's dead town is the cessation of lived time and, in effect, the production of a posttemporal world. All that matters in such a world is the development of a frozen image of the past, abstracted from the life-world and displaced to a mythical realm: mythical in terms of being idealized but also as being *beyond* time. Here, there is no death and no decay. All time has been contained by the reclamation of a lost world, so far consigned to the underworld. And so the twilight of memory endures, exceeds its own mortality by reinventing itself through the human body, a privileged vessel of time and space.

By placing the body at the center, materiality and memory conspire to hold the past in place, at once conceding to the erosion of time but simultaneously denying that process. This delicate ambivalence between presence and absence can be seen as underscoring the *algos* in nostalgia. As a protest against time, this stance frequently collapses into a black melancholy, shattering the solitude of nostalgia and exposing the self to the estrangement of the present. No simple resignation to failure, this dissolution only encourages the flames of imagination and memory to be reinvented anew.

What, then, of memory and nostalgia? Having identified mimesis and embodiment as coconspirators in the formation of nostalgia *as* nostalgic, memory emerges as the ground of this experience. Yet the account presented in Rodenbach's novel is far from a direct reexperience of the past. Rather, what is suggested is that nostalgia's relationship to memory is one of distance and proximity, affecting a sense of resemblance to the object but at the same time retaining a degree of caution to avoid the outcome of splicing together two different objects. At no time does a dialectical assimilation between the past and the present occur in *Bruges-la-Morte*, despite the apparent desire for such a motive. To this end, Rodenbach invokes a wavering desire between the form of the past and the distance from the content of that past. This oscillating movement manifests itself in terms of Viane's temporal continuity with the past (and so with his own self) being reinforced and disrupted respectively. Although the voice and bodily gestures of the actress strengthen the reality of a mythical cessation of time, the same body becomes a site of alienation and spatiotemporal discontinuity, as memory and imagination fail to seal the differences between the dead wife and her *doppelgänger*. Dressed in the wife's clothes, the image produced is nothing less than that of a mutant:

> He had the feeling he was watching a distressing masquerade. It was the first time the spell cast by the physical likeness had not been strong enough. It was still working, but in reverse. Without the resemblance, he would have found Jane merely vulgar, with it she gave him the horrible feeling he was seeing his dead wife again, but degraded, despite the sameness of face and dress. (Rodenbach 2005, 70)

The reverse formulation places us in a different narrative. Rather than assuming an ever greater likeness to his dead wife, by touching the borders of materiality, the image loses its mythological status through overlapping with an extinct narrative. The collision of the living and the dead establishes a lunar narrative, neither fully visible nor invisible but instead hovering in a zone of fragmented familiarity and radical estrangement. Such is the relation between the form of nostalgia and the content of memory: Only when a sufficient distance is forged from the imaginary and the real is the ambivalent desire of nostalgia cared for, as Rodenbach writes whimsically: "True, she still had the same eyes. But if the eyes are the windows of the soul, then it was certainly a different soul that appeared in them than had in those, still present, of his dead wife" (2005, 86).

Notably, as Viane's temporal narrative comes undone, so he returns to a dependency on materiality, at once affirming the consoling grip that the city of Bruges affords. With this return to the city, the narrative is resumed but only now in a material guise: "Now that Jane no longer appeared absolutely identical to his dead wife, he once more began to resemble the town. He felt at ease on his constant monotonous walks round its empty streets" (2005, 89). Central here is how the protagonist "once more began to resemble the town." Revealed in this line is the contingency of mimetic identification, serving as a reminder that what establishes existential unity in the world is less about specific objects themselves and more about how those objects either reinforce or disrupt temporal continuity.

We have surveyed the tripartite relation between mimesis, embodiment, and memory. In doing so, we have been led back to *Bruges-la-Morte*. Whereas the structure of mimesis has revealed a morphological trait to nostalgia, embodiment has proven to be central in holding time in place. Giving mimesis and embodiment their affective force, memory enters the scene of nostalgia in a profoundly ambivalent way, acting as the basis of desire but at the same time retaining enough ambiguity for the imagination to reign supreme.

What renders nostalgia *nostalgic* is the peculiar interplay between memory and desire, such that the proximity of the past is never entirely oblivious to the present but at the same time occupies a covert hold through the body. Seen in this way, that the past should appear to "suddenly" act upon us, as though without any prior warning, is a misleading thought. Instead, defined in its relation to nostalgia, involuntary body memory simply discloses what was already present all along; namely, that the body hungers for temporal continuity as much as cognition does in formal and abstract terms.

***

We are now prepared to consider the final question: What is it in the world of nostalgia that we are nostalgic for? Considering the question as a whole, the inclusion of "world" has a special significance. As we have seen in the first chapter, for Heidegger (1996, 59), "world" can be taken to refer to the pregiven environment, into which Dasein is inextricably bound and lives. As we have also seen in connection with Casey's analysis of the act of remembering, scene and surrounding refers respectively to the interplay between the immediate and the nonimmediate content constitutive of a given world, and eventually central to the structure of place memory itself. Accordingly, if we take "world" to be central in the formation of place memory, where place emerges as the defining event of a memory scene, then where nostalgia is concerned can we assume an intensification of the distance between scene and surrounding?

To answer this question, let us recall how the structure of place memory involves a gesture of displacing place from a surrounding environment, such that memory as a whole becomes "conspicuous" in its presence (Heidegger 1996, 68). Applied to the context of nostalgia, this formal distance between the inconspicuous realm of things situated within a pregiven context and the things concurrently torn from that context is wholly amplified. Already this has been evident in my account of nostalgia as involving a tripartite relation between mimesis, embodiment, and memory. Above all, what this relation thematizes is the radical distance of things taken in their unmediated phenomenality, with those things then transported and mutated in a wholly different guise. In a word, nothing less than a *double world* is at stake where nostalgia is concerned; a world at once phenomenally present but at the same time spooked by the world superimposed upon those appearances.

In formal terms alone, the world of nostalgia has a unique significance attached to it. Like no other act of intentionality, the act of being nostalgic toward a thing involves a complete dissociation from the objective status of things in relation to their transformed reappearance. Approaching this dynamic as a unitary phenomenon, Casey's treatment of a "world-under-nostalgement" is instructive (1987).

Casey takes the world-under-nostalgement to refer to an original world, which, in its radical anteriority, resists all reduction to the content of memory itself (Casey 1987, 365). Strikingly, for Casey, such a world breaks with a timeline of identity, since the "past which has never been present" signifies, above all, incommensurability between memory and experience. Casey's characterization of this dynamic as one of "lingering" is telling, therefore, insofar as the nostalgic past is not totally inaccessible, but neither is it wholly present as an experience to be relived. Rather, the same past reappears in fragments alone, never once again reunited as a whole, having never "given [itself] in *any* discrete present moment" in the first instance (366; italics in original).

Considered in terms of world alone, all nostalgia presupposes a gesture of departure and returning. Whether such a return is to the materiality of place or to the temporality of a certain conception of self, the desire of nostalgia is oriented toward returning to what was lost. In Casey's view, the return is to a "mode of absolute, irreversible pastness: a 'world-under-nostalgement'" (1987, 377). What is notable about Casey's emphasis on world is that it absorbs the total ambience of an experience, taken up primarily through the materiality of place, but nevertheless resistant to "isolated recollections" (377).

In contrast to Casey, for Hart, the nostalgic return is "to the time when the wishes and hopes which constitute our present were fresh and before the wishes and hopes were battered and bruised—but which wishes and hopes still constitute our life-project" (1973, 408). Is Hart right to place an emphasis on a loss of vibrancy in the shadow of effervescent aspirations? Hart's dualism between a "fresh" hope and a battered "hope" hints at a linear timescale, in which the old self seemingly reflects upon the vibrancy of youth. While the image of old age being a time of wistful reverie populates a certain common image of nostalgia, I would contest this in claiming that the motif of return has less to do with the objective passing of time and more with the felt duration of change and transition.

Seen in this way, there is nothing inherently more given to nostalgia in youth than there is in maturity. Rather, what is more pressing is how these stages in a life reconcile—or fail to reconcile—with each other. To this end, Hart is right in aligning nostalgia with a meaningful "life-project." By "life-project," he has in mind an idea "akin to 'the heart's desire,'" an enduring desire that takes the place of desiring for something in the world, and becomes, instead, a desire *for* desire's sake, even if that motif is concealed to the nostalgic ego (408–9). Guiding this arch of desire, the life-project assumes a unifying role, such that who we *are* is somehow confirmed in the retention of this presence. For Hart, this presence achieves a temporal synthesis of past, present, and future, thus "comparable in richness to the personal presence" (409). Concurrent with this unity, however, is the distance between the imagined or remembered unity of our lives and the way in which that unity is dispersed in reality. Expectation and experience collapse, causing identity to fall back on itself while the germs of nostalgic desire are born again.

Let us summarize this relation between nostalgia and the unity of life as a narrated whole. Already I have referred loosely to the strands of "existential unity" holding a life together. But what can this existential mode of unity mean for a phenomenology of nostalgia? One observation is immediate: The attachments we feel toward things is less a question of their objective status and placement in the world, and more a question of how we meaningfully respond to the changes in those objects as they proceed to challenge our notions of selfhood. When I experience a nostalgic attachment to a particular place, time, or thing in the world, what is being invoked is not the objective spatiotemporality of that thing, such as remembering that it was four years ago and in the loft that the event occurred. Rather than a linear timescale, what I experience is the gradual unfolding of concurrent events, each of which is bound within a singular constellation. So, while the nostalgic experience is anchored with a central point of fixation, this same point is surrounded on all sides by a mutually edifying aura. In this way, the object of my nostalgia never ends with that object in itself, but works its way slowly through the microcosmic world of things contained both inside and outside that focal point.

The movement of nostalgia is one of a *seeping* orientation. Having drifted into the aeonic time of a past world, that gliding gesture now allows me to become absorbed by the cocooning environment, which, in its singular detail, pushes at the threshold of memory and experience. The world for which I have become nostalgic is no longer placed in the temporal distance, as though time were able to be measured spatially, but sits alongside me in the present, *felt* in its immediate (corpo)reality.

Nowhere is the seeping, bleeding, and aeonic movement of nostalgia better articulated than in Andrei Tarkovsky's film *Nostalgia* (1983). Structurally, the pursuit of memory in this film follows an interweaving, overlapping narrative, which fuses the texture of the everyday world with the imagined memory of the past. Citing this slow wave of movement as "oneiric" is more than a mere figure of speech. This is especially the case if we conceive of oneirism in Bachelardian (1994, 13) terms as the shadowy region between memory and imagination, played out as a reverie. Indeed, what Tarkovsky shows us time and again is that the entwinement of memory and imagination is literally a mercurial exchange of different rhythms, images, and scenes, all of which usurp the notion of memory as belonging solely to a location spatially and temporally known as the "past." Folding in and over itself, the representative contents of Tarkovsky's nostalgia disrupt the distance of pastness in its supposed detachment from the present. Rather, the seeping motif of nostalgia points to a pivotally seamless transition from different temporal edges.

One clear illustration of this seamless divide is visible in a scene from *Nostalgia*, in which Andrei Gorchakov—a Russian writer on study leave in Italy—has returned to his hotel for the night. From a wide shot of the room, the camera proceeds to slowly move toward the bed, on which Gorchakov is falling to sleep. As this motion is slowly unfolding, the light in the room shifts toward darkness with such a measured rate of progression that it becomes impossible to discern at which point the two worlds invoked by this shift occur. As proof that the movement of light and darkness correlates with the entwinement of inner and outer, dream and reality, a dog—the

emblematic oneiric figure in Tarkovsky's corpus of work—appears from
beyond the bathroom door. Already seen in the sepia visions of the past
depicted earlier in the film, the presence of the dog in the hotel room marks
its reality through knocking over a glass in the room, attesting to its material
extension in space. Yet Tarkovsky is not signaling the presence of the dog as
a ghost with mass. Rather, what we observe in this scene is the transgression
of borders between memory and imagination, past and present, and reality
and unreality.

Tarkovsky's (1986, 64–66) account of the art of cinema as a process of
sculpting in time cements this act of redefining the structure of narration,
which relies less on the objective status of linear time and more on the com-
position of experiences within that space of time. In the case of *Nostalgia*,
Tarkovsky's mode of sculpting in time produces an affinity between temporal
movement and memory, such that what we have seen termed "aeonic time"
becomes wholly visible in Tarkovsky's cinematography: "Time and memory," so he writes, "merge into each other: they are like the two sides of a
medal" (57). This allusion to the doubling of time and memory is clearly at
stake in the work of nostalgia. Rather than a movement of turning "toward"
the past, it is the ever-elusive time of the present that becomes the site of an
immemorial memory, as Tarkovsky writes enigmatically: "Time cannot vanish without trace for it is a subjective, spiritual category; and the time we have
lived settles in our soul as an experienced placed within time" (58).

If nostalgia is characterized as involving a seamless bleeding of time, then
can we still speak strictly of an "object" to which intentionality is directed?
The response to this question hinges on the affective role of the object in
question. What I experience nostalgically is not so much a nostalgia for
a given object in the world—the loft overlooking a square, the fire escape
overlooking the church, the painting of wolves sleeping—but the roles these
things play in my conception of who I am. What is being animated in these
objects is the spirit of what has since become distant from my grasp, and
thus elevated to the form of a ghost. I "see" not the red wallpaper, skylights,
and sewing desk in the loft, but myself as I *was* flanked by those objects. I
see myself again, but through the prism of the loft that has become my focal
point.

This distinction between the objective presentation of the past and the
subjective experience of temporal change brings us to an ancient problem,
famously invoked in the Greek puzzle regarding the ship of Theseus. Familiar
though it is, Plutarch's account remains instructive:

> The ship wherein Theseus and the youth of Athens returned had thirty oars, and was preserved by the Athenians down even to the time of Demetrius Phalereus, for they took away the old planks as they decayed, putting in new and stronger timber in their place, insomuch that this ship became a standing example among the philosophers, for the logical question of things that grow; one side holding that the ship remained the same, and the other contending that it was not the same. (2001, 13)

Far from an exercise in formal logic and that alone, Plutarch's story of the ship of Theseus captures the ambiguity inherent in how we attempt to nostalgically seal ourselves within an (imagined) memory of the world. Things return from hibernation, having traveled afar, but in a different state than how we remember them. Thereafter, the line between sameness and difference becomes increasingly amorphous, and indeed interchangeable. Yet if the interchangeability of the ship of Theseus before and after its restoration signifies the persistence of matter, then it also attests to the rupture of memory. Is it enough that the past endures as a simulated replica, held together merely as an imagined world? If so, at which point does nostalgia cease being a memory, becoming, instead, a mutant hybrid between memory and imagination? Such questions rely on the idea that the decay of memory can be mapped out, as though laid flat in a line of continuity, ready for our inspection. Yet clearly this is inaccurate. It is surely less a question of the measurable status of an object and more an issue with the affective and embodied relationship we have with the past, as we experience its becoming absent.

This experience of the past's becoming absent is where an objective emphasis on spatiotemporality shatters and the clarity of our affective experience toward memory's unexpected vagaries forms. Into that disruption, the role of a life-project resumes its importance. Indeed, so privileged is the experience of a life-project—more broadly the sense of oneself as *being* a self—undergoing transformation, that for the most part the intensely heterogeneous quality of being a self in time resists all uncertainty. The peculiarity of nostalgic phenomenon is that it forces us to consider the discontinuous lacuna in our sense of self. Stranded from the present, the attachment toward a given experience relies on that experience's fundamentally damaging or reinforcing who we are. This movement of a seeping displacement pushes identity toward a horizon. Within this horizon, the taken-for-granted experience of unity is dissected to reveal a discontinuous constellation of different spatiotemporal events, all of which fail to produce a coherent account of selfhood. At the same time, however, the momentum of nostalgia is not forestalled by the experience of fragmentation. Rather, the moment at which identity is touched by the world becomes the gathering space for rebinding what has since lost its defined place.

To this end, Steven Crowell—with Tarkovsky's evocation of memory as a "spiritual concept" in the background—is surely right to identify "sublimity" at the core of nostalgia (1999, 94). For Crowell, both Casey's and Hart's treatments of nostalgia lack "the nonpresentability of existential identity" (94), which Crowell places under the category of the sublime. With the Kantian heritage in the background, Crowell touches upon an ineffable, indeed, *mystical*, dimension of nostalgia, not simply resistant to remembering (as Casey would have it), but fundamentally in tension with experience itself. Crowell says: "As Kant was perhaps the first to notice, the affect of the sublime (like nostalgia, a peculiar combination of pleasure and pain) must be traced to a bifurcation within the *subject* of experience" (95; italics in original). Placing divergence central to the experience of the sublime, we are able to formalize this claim in terms of the subject's being unable to apprehend a given experience, due, in Kantian terms, to a state of indeterminate formlessness. At the same time, however, the failure to apprehend experience already constitutes an intimate relation with that nonexperience, such that it remains outside the realm of rational appearances.

But there is more to this trajectory of thought than a parallel between the sublime and the nostalgic. The bifurcation of subjective experience points to a broader desire, of which nostalgia is only symptomatic; namely, the absence of unity between the finite subject and the imagined/remembered whole, of which the subject nevertheless remains conscious. Such a dialectic of finitude and infinity has a revered philosophical legacy, most obviously manifest in Hegel's account of "the pathway to despair" and Kierkegaard's own appropriation of Hegel through the "unhappiest man." Reapplied to the context of nostalgia, what materializes in the distance is a condition of homelessness that has less to do with geographic distance in the world and more to do with the distance slowly unraveling through the body of the nostalgic subject.

The emphasis here on slowness is central. Thanks to its power to slow—but never *seize*—time in its tracks, nostalgia resonates with the ambivalence of demonstrating a unity that is ever glanced at only from afar. And yet this ambivalence ultimately evades satisfaction, given that the nostalgic body and the non-nostalgic body remain fundamentally alien to each other, despite their mutual dependency on the past. Strictly speaking, I am never entirely *myself* during the experience of being nostalgic. Rather, my body in the present becomes overridden by an irreconcilable desire to reinvent itself, such that who I *am* must be called into doubt.

Calling myself into doubt, we are once again assailed by a "bifurcation within the *subject* of experience" (Crowell 1999, 95; italics in original). Only now, we should be prepared to suspend our belief that this split occurs "within" experience. While I remain within myself as the locus of spatio-temporal orientation, my body has broken from its anchor, departed into a realm of aeonic time, and so has fundamentally become *beyond* myself. At the expense of slowing down time, something has gone awry: My body has become the site of an *autoscopic* experience—an experience of myself as a detached body. As a result, the sublimity of this experience is crystallized in the image of physically surviving the attempt to transgress the borders of flesh and time. Seeing myself from outside, the result is that the lived-body and the physical body form a hybrid somewhere in between.

Situating this hybrid within the above-mentioned dialectic of finitude and infinity, Kierkegaard is instructive. Placing us at an open grave, where the body is missing, he asks us to consider the unhappiest man: "Did he find not rest, not even in the grave; does he perhaps wander restlessly about in the world? Has he forsaken his dwelling-place, his home, leaving only his address behind?" (1971, 217). Not only is the dwelling-place of his death an appearance of absence, but so, too, is the unhappiest man an embodiment of that absence. As with the nostalgic body, the unhappiest man conjures a paradox of materiality: "He is always absent, never present to himself" (220).

Further still, both the unhappiest man and the nostalgic body carry an absence framed by the failure to *be* in the present. Beyond time, both find themselves living in a region that smolders the present, tears it asunder, and renders it a liminal place, in which both bodies are merely visitors. What arises in this terrain is a realm of the already dead. For both the unhappiest man and the nostalgic body, the undead retains a dynamism that the living lacks. It is a place divested of hope, but grounded in the structure of a false promise. Under such conditions, it becomes impossible to distinguish what actually exists in the present and what has been seized from the past and thrown into the present, forcing Kierkegaard to finally ask: "Is this a real being, or is it an image, a living person who lives, or a corpse who lives? It is Niobe. She lost all at a single blow; she lost that which gave her life" (225).

Just as the world of nostalgia is a double world, in which the spatiotemporality of the present is haunted by the superimposed appearances of the past, so the nostalgic body occupies a parallel relation: Temporally absent to itself, in material terms, the flesh of the body nonetheless remains intact, inviting the spooks of the past and present to reconstitute themselves in the place where the nostalgic body "is always absent, never present to himself" (Kierkegaard 1971, 220). If, as I have argued, that nostalgia is a movement of seeping returns, then upon returning from the world of nostalgia, can we readily assume that the body is left untouched by its autoscopic voyage? The return is as much to the world of the temporal present as it is to the body that has now become partly colonized through its own internal disjunctions. Characteristically described as "bittersweet," in this light, the gesture of departing and returning assumes an essentially ghostly quality, in which nostalgic "poignancy" is replaced with a logic of spectrality, and, as I shall shortly suggest, morphology.

HOMESICKNESS

At once familiar and unfamiliar, embodied and disembodied, nostalgia breeds a peculiar ambiguity. Such ambiguity pushes at the threshold of appearance and reality. Alongside phenomenology, psychoanalysis can help us in understanding the psychodynamic drama at the heart of this ambiguity. Accordingly, it will be worth voyaging into the Freudian backdrop, from which nostalgia's relationship to mourning is given credence, thus propelling the philosophically rich concept of "homesickness" to the foreground.

In his short essay simply titled "On Transience," Freud is in conversation with a "well-known poet," who was evidently Rilke. "He was," we are told,

> disturbed by the idea that all this beauty was bound to fate, that it would vanish through the winter, like all human beauty and everything beautiful and noble that people have created and could create. All the things he would otherwise have loved and admired seemed to him to be devalued by the fate of transience for which they were destined. (2005, 197)

Freud's response to the poet's world-weariness was to counter his anxiety by insisting that beauty's value is heightened precisely through being transient.

To his surprise, however, this thought offered no consolation to the poet, simply affirming that "there must be a strong affective element disturbing [his] judgement. . . . It must have been the psychical revolt against grief that devalued the pleasure of beautiful things" (2005, 198). With this, Freud puts forward a dialectic of beauty and grief, which forms a more generalized theory of mourning. At stake in the theory is the idea that "objects . . . are thus to an extent absorbed into our ego," whereupon once the object is destroyed, then the "libido clings to its objects and does not wish to abandon those which are lost even when a substitute is ready and available" (199).

Freud's terms "revolt," "absorbed," and "clings" point to the tripartite genesis of mourning. On a structural level, the ego comprises the objects absorbed into its being. No great effort is required to see how the body works in an identical fashion, at once opening itself to an intersubjective formation with other things in the world, both animate and inanimate. Once these things are under threat, the revolt begins. Seeing himself within the transience of the world, the poet resists the revised aesthetic view put forward by Freud. And so, the stage of clinging ensues, marked not only by an attachment to residual objects, but also to the world more broadly, extending to the "love of the fatherland, the affection for our neighbours and pride in what we have in common have been suddenly reinforced" (2005, 199). This final act of conferring pride is thus the birth of nostalgia, defined as the elevation of an object crystallizing the self's place in time. Phenomenologically, such a fixation is possible only through an estranged relationship to both the present and the future. Once retreated into a state of hibernation, by forcing the present and the future aside, the presence of the past is given an exaggerated tone. With that reinvention of the past, the failure of the present opens itself to modification, at once allowing the nostalgic subject to rediscover himself or herself in the renewed present.

In this respect, the psychoanalytic treatment of nostalgia supports the phenomenological emphasis on a felt absence. Consider here a section from Freud's (1984, 314–15) *Introductory Lectures on Psychoanalysis*, titled "Fixation—The Unconscious," where he makes an important distinction between spontaneous neurosis and traumatic neurosis. Peculiar to traumatic neurosis, so Freud argues, is the fixation to the temporal event. During episodes in which the trauma reveals itself, it is the time of a particular place that emerges, as Freud writes notably: "It is as though these patients had not finished with the traumatic situation, as though they were still faced by it as an immediate task which has not been dealt with" (315).

Applying Freud's account of traumatic neurosis to the case of nostalgia, the unconscious force, to reinvoke Bachelard's notable concept, forms the determining contributor. But here a tension arises; namely, how can we reconcile the notion of an unconscious mind within a phenomenological framework? Would it not be phenomenologically unsound to project a subsection of consciousness that was somehow less visible in intentional terms than a supposedly more conscious part? If so, how can we genuinely account for a phenomenology of fixation while retaining a strictly intentional structure of consciousness?

In an appendix to Husserl's (1970) *Crisis*, Eugen Fink, Husserl's research assistant, confronts this question directly. In doing so, Fink questions the legitimacy of positing the unconscious "according to the methodological means for understanding consciousness" (385). Fink's response to this tension between content and method is to assess the unconscious as it relates to the natural attitude, ultimately absorbing "the problematic of the 'unconscious'" into a phenomenological reduction (387). With this gesture, Fink's polemical stance against the unconscious is to position it as "pregiven" to phenomenon, covertly employing a duplicitous mode of reasoning that depends upon an "implicit theory of consciousness" for its identity (387). For Fink, only via the phenomenological reduction can this complicit insertion of an unconscious be clarified.

Fink's contribution to the phenomenology of the unconscious helpfully clarifies the formation of the concept. But does this help us in placing the Bachelardian notion of the "unconscious force"? Returning to Bachelard's concept with Fink in mind, can we still maintain the centrality of this idea? To answer this question, we need to consider the movement of this force more broadly. Formally speaking, Bachelard begins plotting the development of the concept by referring to the unity of memory and imagination as a movement that "keep[s] turning" (1994, 16). Contrasted with a positivist account of memory and place, Bachelard's turn toward dreams mirrors the turning of memory itself. What is being recalled is less an object located in the hidden realm of the Freudian unconsciousness and more a corporeal expression of a movement working behind the scenes of intentionality, such as we saw in the previous chapter with Merleau-Ponty's notion of "motor intentionality." This is clear if we consider the relevant sentence as a whole: "It is our unconscious force that crystalizes our remotest memories" (Bachelard 1994, 16). The force makes itself known as a dynamic creation, which is then felt experientially—that is, through the experience of oneirically reliving memory. Seen in this way, Bachelard's notion of the unconscious force places us in an interstitial zone, in which memory itself is given neither content nor an encrypted meaning, but rather the motive to reinterpret itself creatively.

As for the unconscious force at work in nostalgia, the desire for unity is symptomatic of a visceral homesickness, an impasse set between two different points in time, neither of which invites resolution. Protracting time, nostalgia simultaneously reshapes time. This reinvention is critical to the slow pulse of nostalgia, given its resistance to letting the past slip away. In a word, the relationship between mourning and nostalgia becomes one of transition and reinvention. Just as Bachelard's oneiric house invites an overlapping synthesis of dream, memory, and imagination, all with the aim of protecting the dweller from the outside, so the nostalgic relationship to memory and place encourages a profound spatial-temporal ambiguity, which is guided throughout by the body's encounter with loss and sorrow. Describing the psychoanalytic work required to resolve this loss, Freud writes as follows:

> Some particular mental processes should normally have developed to a point at which consciousness received information of them. This, however, did not take place, and instead—out of the interrupted processes, which had been somehow disturbed and were obliged to remain unconscious—the symptom emerged. Thus something in the nature of an exchange has taken place; if this can be reversed the therapy of the neurotic symptoms will have achieved its task. (1984, 320)

As we will go on to see, the unconscious force toward modifying the past is disarmed, or "reversed," to use Freud's terminology, as different modes of time and memory come into contact with one another. In Freud's account of traumatic neurosis, psychoanalysis takes on the task of bringing the unconscious to light, so disturbing the imbalance between resignation and resistance. Phenomenologically, the idea of an unconscious force can be redirected toward the lived-body, which continues to unravel in its complexity. For us, the felt attachment to a particular place runs in parallel to Freudian neurosis, which refuses to disperse until the "interrupted processes" are resolved.

Until such time as a fixed attachment to place is relieved of its hold, the borders between the end of place and the persistence of place remain vague. Place endures through the lived-body, at once forming an interwoven texture with the self. Yet this mode of spatiotemporality is fundamentally questionable in its scope, given that experience of place is reduced to the domain of the subjective ego, thus exposing itself to the charge of a morbid psyche. The pathological undercurrent of this attachment does not imply plenitude, but exclusion and confinement. Indeed, the basic character of the nostalgic attachment to a particular place is a *topophobic* relation to other places.

Here, "topophobic" refers to a form of spatiotemporal homesickness that is fundamentally disturbed in character. This disturbance is evident in at least two ways.

First, the apprehension of boundaries within a topophobic framework is subject to an extreme ambiguity, such that marking differences between places is blurred. For the ego attached to a place that has been lost or altered, a phobic trepidation with regard to other places is the logical outcome, given that it is through the otherness of place that absence is thematized. As Heidegger suggests, a boundary is not "that at which something stops but, as the Greeks recognized, the boundary is that from which something *begins its essential unfolding*" (1977, 332; italics in original). Understood temporally, the "essential unfolding" of which Heidegger speaks is placed within a distinct location, around which its force and presence are maintained. Returning to that enclosed place, the genesis of the self is established. In such an instant, the boundary acts as a root, a source of all that ensures continuity and unity.

But under certain conditions—not least those of becoming nostalgic toward a lost place—this boundary line becomes restrictive rather than freeing, as Heidegger would have it. In this respect, the topophobic understanding of boundaries marks the shift from a creative synthesizing of memory and imagination to a homesickness, in which other places present themselves as not only accenting their non-home status, but also colonizing the spatiotemporality of the self. For this reason, Freud's account of Rilke's melancholy centralizes the act of "clinging" to things "all the more intensely" (2005, 199). Clinging to that which assures us of a sense of selfhood, the division of boundaries becomes a frontier between the I and the non-I. Indeed, the more the residue of the former place is clung to, then the more a sense of intimate belonging is protracted, even if that protraction is fundamentally contrived in its duration.

Second, this elevation of the boundary within topophobia carries with it an experiential force, defined by anxiety, sickness, and an abiding sense of derealization. At the heart of this malaise is the following question: How is it possible to dwell in one place while simultaneously feeling bereft of another place? The affectivity of this question, at once full of desire, hope, and loss, exists in a fundamentally discordant relation with the Heideggerian idea of dwelling as "a staying with things" (1977, 329). Staying with things entails cultivating a relationship with the broader environment, allowing the indeterminacy of place to grow within us as we adapt to a world of new horizons. Not only this, but staying with things also forges a reciprocity with the movement of the self, suggesting a sense of nativity. All of this presupposes a certain harmony between mobility and rest, between nearness and remoteness, and between gathering and freeing (332). In a word, the idea of dwelling in a place of which phenomenology has become familiar with is framed by a dynamic core, in which differences are synthesized to a more unified whole.

Where homesickness is concerned, this synthesized unity is augmented with a sense of spatial and temporal incompletion. "Home" is thought of as a thing to be salvaged from the wreckage of memory, there to be reinserted into the living self, as though it had accidently fallen by the wayside but now demanded recollection. The implication: Deviating from this desire instigates the sense of being a visitor to a particular place, even if that place is the house currently occupied. At no point does duration furnish the world with any degree of intimacy or attachment. Instead, all intimacy is forsaken by an incapacity to be resituated. At the same time, the homesick relationship to place becomes characterized by disquiet and anxiety, as the phenomenal reality of the world loses its assurance. "The knowing animals," so writes Rilke in the first of the *Duino Elegies*, "are aware that we are not really at home in our interpreted world" (Rilke 1987, 151). Pierced by loss, the transformation of the world to an "interpreted" phenomenon carries with it a vertiginous contingency, forever exposed to a sudden loss of familiarity, as the foundations of things lose all their bearings.

This is the "psychical revolt against grief" of which Freud (2005, 198) spoke. Taking homesickness as a "psychical revolt" against the loss of place, the relation between topophobia and dwelling thus becomes a question of how movement in space is possible without the experience of motion sickness. After all, what movement in space involves, above all, is the experience of *dispersal in time*. This mention of "dispersed" time points back to Bachelard's insistence that "without [the house], man would be a dispersed being. It maintains him through the storms of the heavens and through those of life. It is body and soul. It is the human being's first world" (1994, 7). The elevated place of the home is at the same time its own ruin. Raised beyond brutal materiality, the value forged in the daydream of dwelling sets in place a standard, which reverie and oneirism can only approximate at a distance. And yet: "The house we were born in is physically inscribed in us" (14). Physically inscribed, the sickness peculiar to homesickness takes shape in the solitude of inner space, a low-level humming that accords with the memories of home, which, to quote Bachelard, "reconstitute themselves in a new day-dream" (6). Against its better intentions, this oneiric overlapping does less to integrate time and more to alienate the present from the determination of the past. In short, the very condition of being placed is identified with the experience of no longer being home, both spatially and temporally.

The adjoining sense of being homeless in time distinguishes homesickness as involving the complete absence of a future. Taking its place: a clustering of different modalities of the past, forever turning back on themselves to give the appearance of progression. Time is understood as a resurfacing, a reprising, and a revisiting of already-lived experiences, now sufficiently confused in its depth to constitute a circular movement. In reality, however, time has frozen, and movement has been divested of its powers. Without a future, without direction, time becomes the province of a solitary mood, a pathological wait for the vital spirit to be reawakened.

In the strictest concrete terms, the dialectic between inner space and outer space manifests itself in the core of the lived-body's encounter with the phenomenal world. Crossing the threshold from inside to outside—be it from the door to the street or from the hallway to the window—a simultaneous encounter with anxiety can be witnessed in the phobic body. Indeed, anxiety literally takes place at the boundary of familiarity, disturbing the reality of a self-enclosed world privileged by memory. The reason for this becomes clear if we remind ourselves that homesickness is structured around a dynamic precluding dwelling in one place through the continued and felt loss of another place. Moving from one place to another, we are reminded that beyond the scope of narcissism, another landscape exists, and a landscape that is no longer coincidental with one's own (Merleau-Ponty 1968, 141).

This tension brings about a hypersensitivity in the experience of movement, as though the memorial anchor that orients the homesick body is forever disorientated in other places; such is the anchor's gravitational hold. As we have seen from Bachelard, beyond an atomic point in space, the home is an ontological center, the site of the self's own being. The interweaving of home and self forms a hybrid entity, constituted by the materiality of both parties. When separated, movement loses its bearings, emitting an anxiety within the subject. In one of the many strange and poetic accounts of schizophrenic experience in Jaspers's *General Psychopathology*, the following is reported:

> I still saw the room. Space seemed to stretch and go on into infinity, completely empty. I felt lost, abandoned to the infinities of space, which in spite of my insignificance somehow threatened me. It seemed the complement of my own emptiness. . . . The old physical space seemed to be apart from this other space, like a phantom. (1997, 81)

The patient felt "lost." Space exceeded its objective bearings before developing its own dark agency, at once folding back upon the subject. In facing this account, the reader must contend with two spaces, both of which occupy the same time. Together, the two spaces overlap, with each rupturing the solidity of space as a whole. And yet: The room remains where it is, untouched by the immateriality of emptiness. Into this void, a "phantom" intervenes, neither body nor world, masking the surface of space with a drifting motion. In another report, an even more foreboding anxiety ensues:

> Suddenly the landscape was removed from me by a strange power. In my mind's eye I thought I saw below the pale blue evening sky a black sky of horrible intensity. Everything became limitless, engulfing. . . . I knew the autumn landscape was pervaded by a second space, so fine, so invisible, that it was dark, empty and ghastly. . . . It was wrong to speak only of space because something took place in myself; it was a continuous questioning of myself. (Jaspers 1997, 81)

Again, the report points to "limitlessness," "second spaces," and space as being an anonymous, lurking movement in the world. A loss of control comes to the foreground, and the self as the site of perception is usurped. More than this, however, the subject of this report tells us of a "continuous questioning" of himself. As to whether space undermines the subject or the subject undermines space, we are left no better off. In each case, however, space becomes the stage setting for a fundamental dis-ease with the world, expressive of a broader ontological insecurity central to subjectivity.

But this spatialization of sickness is not solely the province of a particular type of phobia, whether it be agoraphobia, kenophobia, nyctohylophobia, or even nostophobia. Rather, what is at stake is a generalized anxiety with regard to the reality of space more broadly. This is especially the case for the topophobia at the heart of homesickness, where security is predicated on the reality and persistence of a home. Elevated to a vital place within the structure of the self, the loss of and then yearning for home invokes a disintegration of reality in other places, as though those places were somehow the detritus of memory rather than places in and of themselves. If streets and buildings are felt to be swaying in the wind, then this is entirely consistent with the insecurity of a reality with no center, less even a place to call "home." Likewise, if color and depth are torn from space, then the derealized world that survives that fragmentation only reinforces the damaged reality of memory itself. Inner space is overwhelmed with outer space; boundaries buckle, and intimacy is invaded by the nothingness of an alien landscape, which, in its anonymity, proceeds to absorb the vulnerability of the self. The result: an acute awareness of the difference distancing the longing for home from the indifferent reality of that home.

All of this leads us, then, back to Rilke's "demand for eternity," of which Freud (2005, 197) reports in his essay on the poet's melancholy. The tension in Freud's account between desire and loss, between decay and beauty, forms an equivalent parallel in the homesick body. Staying with Freud's account of Rilke, what comes to the fore in light of the preceding inquiry into homesickness is a desire, offset by the disbelief "that all these wonders of nature and art, of our emotional world and the world outside, should dissolve into nothing" (197). Rather than malign the halo of the home's beauty, however, the home's proximity to the void only serves to frame its irreducible value. For Rilke, the "demand for eternity" is at the same time a "claim to reality" (197), a reality that is threatened as things are witnessed as folding into oblivion.

For Freud, Rilke's sorrow was ultimately expressive of a "state of mourning" (2005, 199), which in its resistance and revolt, forever protracted a final conclusion. The failure of Rilke to consume his own loss may well point to a narcissistic relation to that loss in the first place (Von Unwerth 2005). Loss is the source of its own energy, and the unreality that feeds into our experience of reality is a creative dynamic, which ensures a communion with "home," even if that home is, as we shall now see, a mutation of its original form.

SPATIAL MORPHOLOGY

In the previous section, we saw that nostalgia's inherent vulnerability with respect to the world leads to a topophobic mode of experience. Indeed, nothing less than a fixed image of the past is required for the self to retain unity in the contingency of time. But if we have so far focused on how time is sculpted according to the nostalgic worldview, then what remains neglected is the materiality of this sculpted world. In particular, the question of how nostalgia gathers memory through and in place requires a firsthand exploration. Already the foundations for this analysis are laid down in the very spatiality of memory itself. With nostalgia, however, the role of time and place in the constitution of the self undergoes a radical amplification, such that we can no longer speak of the self without reference to the places inhabited, as Casey writes: "The laying down of memory traces creates lasting psychical localities comparable in durability to towns or regions—to those very external places that instigate nostalgia in its classical, homesick format. The deepest layer of such traces is set down in primal repression, a fixation of all fixation-points" (1987, 372). Understood temporally, Casey's usage of the Freudian "primal repression" embodies the transformation of objective time to a timescale determined by the solitude of individual experience. This constant holding-in/holding-on gesture domesticates the radical indifference of time and place; a movement, moreover, clearly at work in the history of nostalgia.

Consider the historic transformation of nostalgia, from a medical condition resolved by the return to native place, to an intrapsychic state played out in the landscape of the unconsciousness—throughout, nostalgia maintains the centrality of a fixed point, since rendered absent, against which time and memory in the present revolve. In each case, nostalgia discloses the desire for what is lost, either through invoking the possibility of return or by withdrawing the past into the present. This dynamic between temporal compression and temporal mutation ultimately serves the same purpose: to subjugate objective time to the influence and determination of lived time. Seen in this way, the time of nostalgia is basically pathologized, held in place by the passion of the subjective ego. Allying with this resistance against temporal dissolution, the preservation of the identity as being continuous-with-the-broken-past depends on the imagination fortifying in material terms that to which memory can only tenuously testify.

As we have seen, the success of nostalgia depends on the renewal of the past, with imagination gaining a primacy over memory. In light of the temporal focus of this "primal repression," a fundamental shift in the experience of place unfolds: *Thanks to its ability to sculpt and seize time, nostalgia's grip on materiality becomes complicit with the imagined alteration of the past.* What this means is that memory, imagination, and place conspire together, serving as homogeneous platforms for the nostalgic body to impose and identify itself. The idea of the memory-imagination-place hybrid as being homogeneous is central. If we take nostalgia to be a mode of responding to the past, such that the affective reply is anchored by a fixed image, then anything that counters this bearing constitutes a threat to the unity of the nostalgic subject. To this end, "homogeneous" does not refer to an absence of features, but to features that contribute to the fulfillment of a lost image.

We have witnessed this balance between specificity and homogeneity throughout *Bruges-la-Morte*. There, a delicate balance between desire and loss expressed itself through familiarity and unfamiliarity colliding with each other. Too close to the image of the thing lost, the fabric of an imagined reality is ruined. Hence the elusive quality of the nostalgic object: not reducible to a singular thing, yet able to permeate singular things. A key moment ensues: When conjoined with the imagination, the experience of specific material features in the present can invoke an imagined return to a past, which, objectively speaking, no longer reciprocates the contents of the desiring mind.

With an uncanny prescience that looks toward the work of trauma theory, Lovecraft poses the following question: "Was there a special type of delusion afflicting those who had suffered lapses of memory? Conceivably, the efforts of the subconscious mind to fill up a perplexing blank with pseudomemories might give rise to strange imaginative vagaries" (1994, 477). Lovecraft's "strange imaginative vagaries" is a requirement in the bridging of a disunited self. For what is involved in this move is the creation of a world that is set apart from a nominal reality, and at all times grounded in the preemptive gesture of the unconscious self, be it of the mind or of the body. In each case, the objectivity of the world is subjected to a "special type of delusion," which renders place and self coexistent with each other.

Such a position is one of pure solitude, straddling two points of place and time simultaneously. In the present, place is experienced as indeterminate and constantly unfolding. This is the realm of life, of freedom, a spontaneity carried out in the drama of the everyday. Place is open, life is possible. But that freedom gains a secure identity only by reconstructing what the remembering subject lacks in the present, and the method of reconstruction is embodied in the thickness of the lived-body. In effect, the materiality of the present undergoes unconscious mutation in order to adopt the impression that the previous self—that is, the self who is now lost—remains part of place in the present, and a place that continues to thrive.

Figure 15: *Staircase, Brooklyn. Photo by author.*

So we turn to that strange environment, now a composite of different eras. And what we see is both banal and supernatural, a mixture of the placid face of life and the murky underworld ascending toward that face. Above all, the liminal surroundings of place—banisters, doorways, bridges, window frames, hallways, ledges, lighting, chairs, and staircases—offer themselves as indexical place-holders, which encourage a similar bodily interaction in a place experienced before. A staircase becomes less a linear pathway from one point to another and more the means for oneirically restoring the past. How does the staircase do this? How does the staircase summon the past? By inserting its grooves into the flesh of the human body, at once providing the means for the body to synthesize the "immemorial and recollected" (Bachelard 1994, 5).

Nostalgia occupies a precarious line between the lived experience of the past and the augmentation of the memory through the dynamic activity of the imagination. That materiality assists in this augmentation means that felt experience is forever on the brink of unreality, a dream that refuses to end and instead has eloped into the "real" world. Moreover, that we are made aware of this persistence of tactility often by surprise demonstrates the role touch plays in bringing out the layering of memory traces.

Consider how the feel of stairs outlives their immediate environment, reconstituting itself into other such stairs. The application of memory in the present amounts to more than the formation of a network of associated spatial experiences. Instead, the emergence of the stairs, in both its kinesthetic and temporal dimensions, constitutes an opening into the lived past, whereby past and present places effectively fuse.

In this way, the staircase creates a portal, and by attending to that space of mediation, the preservation of temporal continuity is reinforced. At its core nothing more than base materiality, yet in the hands of the nostalgic body, the staircase becomes a channeling device, used to commune with a previous mode of the self. The possibility of place becoming readapted in accordance with the fixation of time gathers particular strength in the face of transitional space—hotel lobbies, departure lounges, shopping malls, and so forth—where temporal particularities are countered by interchangeable qualities.

Far from obscure, a nostalgia for an airport testifies to the possibility of homogeneous space gaining a highly specified ambience. And the airport is advantaged in this respect. Through its global homogeneity, it is impossible to be tied to one particular place, despite the airport's being bound to a particular location. Yet at no point does the objective status of the airport encroach upon its role as a gateway for dreaming and remembering. For what matters is the strange chemistry, which removes us from the present and strands us in an ambiguous past.

Such places open themselves to reinterpretation and the possibility of being anywhere at any time. Anywhere, anytime: Between these poles, a

Figure 16: *JFK International Airport, New York City. Photo by author.*

space is created in which memories and dream can overlap. Here and now: a fusion that is only possible when enough of the localized features of a place recede, so preparing a clearing for the body of the nostalgic body to affirm itself. Thanks to this opportune clearing, a moment of crystalline oneirism develops, into which the sounds, smells, textures, and tastes of a place conspire to reunite the nostalgic body with its lost place.

Alongside the experience of place, the question of how body memory contributes to this process of morphological adaption also merits attention. Consider, for instance, how the body contributes to this spatiotemporal re-enactment by allowing us to repeat gestures and movements that were previously embedded in the past, and indeed peculiar to a particular memory in the past. Standing, sitting, walking, leaning, breathing, shouting, crying all carry with them a particular temporality, which is rooted in the body's capacity to incorporate the past into the present. To find our bodies embodying the past by way of repeating actions in the present is to instill a distance, if not a dualism, between what persists in the body and what has asymmetrically diminished in the mind, a tension we looked at in the previous chapter but will now consider over a longer duration of time.

Certain chairs, not least, can encourage a particular way of sitting in place, which in turn may partially inform how that place resides as a memory. The partial involvement of how we sit in a chair with our bodies contributes to (but does not entirely fulfill) the wholeness of a memory. That this relation between the chair and the entirety of the memory is only partial is important, since it invites the possibility of body memory only semirecognizing the experience of place. By speaking of semirecognized experience, I am calling upon a phenomenon already familiar to us, whereupon the body experiences the past ahead, and to some extent independently, of the remainder of the self, such that what emerges is nothing more than a vague murmur of the clarity of total recognition—all of which was termed "alien flesh" in the past chapter. How can we begin to phenomenologically account for this half-recognized experience over a longer stretch of time?

It is a cold afternoon in October 2006, and I am sitting in the lobby of the Herald Square Hotel, New York City. I have never been to this specific hotel before, but I am familiar with the surrounding area and have spent a considerable amount of time absorbing the layout of the Manhattan

Figure 17: *Herald Square Hotel, New York City. Photo by author.*

streets. The hotel is standardized and nothing in particular catches my eye, other than a derelict coffee machine. Having checked in, I am waiting for my room to be prepared. Instead of lingering by the reception desk as this process unfolds, I opt to make my way to the communal sitting area. Being fatigued, I find relief in observing strangers going about their private business. Divested of the burden of having to communicate with others, I thus sink into reverie.

During this state, my body responds to the chair in a highly singular way. As though by some occult power, the chair holds my body but at the same time redirects it to a distant elsewhere. Just where this other space is, I could not say. And yet the precise manner in which the chair holds me, together with the posture I have adopted in this chair, has established a reciprocal pathway, tending to a hitherto unrecognized body memory of having experienced this pathway previously. Binding this moment is the affectivity of the imagination, which vaguely encircles the mood of nostalgia cast by the chair. Thanks to this scene of animation, I experience my powers of memory in a heightened scale, such that I am able to *touch* the past with greater veracity than were I simply strolling in the street outside. Far from anchoring me in the present, the situatedness of the chair beckons a distance between my embodied and cognitive states, with each prying for the other's spatiotemporal bearings.

More than simply attesting to the power of body memory, what we can draw from this illustration is that the embodied reception of the past creates a baseline for the imagination to sketch what cognitive remembering cannot itself complete. Advantageous to the nostalgic body, this relationship points to the body's own attempt at grasping an existential unity, so far thought to be chiefly the domain of mental intentionality alone. But we can take this embodied desire further still through speculatively redirecting it toward the idea that body contains its own *temporally synchronized memorial patterns*. Let me unpack this notion.

I take as my cue the idea that the events toward which we are nostalgic are in some sense heightened as we pass them by annually. Often that moment of recognition is vague, even noticed on hindsight. Nevertheless, the affectivity of recognizing that it was x amount of years since I underwent the experience for which I am now nostalgic means that the marking of distances through an awareness of anniversaries plays a significant part in the structure of nostalgia. As each anniversary passes, my nostalgia either diminishes in time or becomes enflamed by the passing distance. But either way, the convention of calendar time is inherent in the affective experience of time. If we take this to be a significant component of cognitive memory, then can we not expect that body memory should also operate by a similar, albeit covert, logic?

The result of this embodied pattern is that we feel tremors of past places with greater intensity as they are repeated annually. In this way, the body becomes its own memorial to past events, its own haunting ground for creating smoke signals to previous episodes. Moreover, all of this takes place quite independently of cognitive memory. The duration of the body marks an underground lineage of unobserved territory resurfacing in the present, spurred by the cognitive recognition of calendar time. It is in this way that involuntary body memory is necessarily fuzzy, at best a vague sense of being kinesthetically touched by the past, such that Hart spoke about with reference to "aeonic time."

If the embodiment of the past can produce a strange variant of memory, then the same is also true of the body as a place that represents time itself. The memories we have of our bodies as objects existing temporally sanction an inconsistency between the space of the past and the time of the present. Mental and bodily memories thus inform but also oppose one another, creating a temporal landscape in which different heterogeneous inscriptions of time converge.

It is surely not surprising, then, that in light of the body's material discontinuity, tremendous effort is invested to blur the threshold between the past and the present. In a scene from Thomas Mann's *Death in Venice*, where Gustav von Aschenbach is lamenting his "aging body," the desire to restore continuity is played out through the expression of vanity and melancholy:

> "Gray," [Aschenbach] said with his mouth twisted. "A bit," the man replied. "It's all because of a slight neglect, an indifference to externals—quite understandable in the case of important people, but still not altogether praiseworthy, all the less so since just such people ought not to harbour prejudices in matters of the natural and the artificial. . . . Gray hair can in certain circumstances give more of a false impression than the dye that some would scorn. In your case, sir, you have a right to your natural hair colour. Will you allow me to give you back what is rightfully yours?" (1994, 58)

Applying this claim to the experience of memory, association and resemblance serve to build and simultaneously preserve the diminishing past. The barber's question: "Will you allow me to give you back what is rightfully yours?" testifies to the normative foundation of the past, as though the theft of youth were an accidental property, a side effect of unobserved time. Coupled with this reclamation, the barber's insistence that "[g]ray hair can in certain circumstances give more of a false impression than the dye that some would scorn," suggests paradoxically that artifice (deriving from lived time) cements temporal continuity more than duration itself (deriving from objective time).

AN UNCANNY RETURN

From the composite of memory and imagination, a strange place has formed, neither as yet belonging to the past nor solely a chimerical invention. Somewhere between these poles, the place of nostalgia dwells. Having been divested of a dynamic relationship with time, the nostalgic place enters into a warped timescale, becoming subject to the desires of the nostalgic self. If we have so far determined that this morphological conflation of memory and desire is liable to disruption, then what remains to be said is how the materiality of the remembered place fits into this nostalgic worldview. In particular, we need to consider the privileged moment in which the memory of place (re)turns to the physical environment, from whence the memory arose. Privileged because what will transpire in this return are the very elements that provide place with its genius loci but also serve to estrange us from that spirit. In what follows, our task will be to instigate a shift from the familiar memory of place to the reexperience of that memory in an unfamiliar world.

Deep in the wounds of the nostalgic body, an anchor has been dropped, around which all time now revolves. Up above, the horizon has been marked with the fallout of an incomplete experience, to be resolved only in the earth below. This arc of magnetism begins with time and memory, and soon extends to the material world, affecting a morphological structure upon the world. In its refusal to recognize the alterity of space and time, nostalgic thus operates with a topophobic logic, domesticating otherness into the realm of the same.

The magnetic powers of the nostalgic body do not end with the body itself, however, but rather forever exceed their own limits, with each transgression inviting further exploration. Owing to this accumulative power, it is inevitable that through time, a gravitational pull will form, into which the nostalgic body will be drawn back to its physical origins. As Freud observed, the neurotic fixation toward "a particular phase in the past" compels repetition and "obsessional action" (1984, 315–16). As we have seen, this obsessional gesture is fundamental in the phenomenology of nostalgia. Far from remaining content as an imagined world, the nostalgic body grows hungry, its desires for the flesh of the world exceeding the domain of its own psyche. Soon, the body's melancholy grows weary of gazing at the interior of its own experience. A calling is heard from the outside world, a desire to repeat, reenact, and return to the scene of the self's conception in time.

In a parallel world, we sometimes read and hear of criminals and their victims' compulsion to return to the scene of the crime, "as though," to again repeat Freud, "they were still faced by [the traumatic situation] as an immediate task which has not been dealt with" (1984, 315). What is gained by that return? One thing is clear: The return is a performance that invites risk, of raising suspicion in the perpetrator's case, and of reliving the experience in the victim's. But a performance of what? If place is said to be charged with events in the past, then the vibrancy of that presence depends on a mutual relationship between place and embodiment. Revisiting the crime scene is thus a disclosure of the meaning conferred upon place and the compulsion to align an event with that place. For the victim of crime, there may even be some degree of psychological clarity in testifying to the place in which trauma occurred. Understanding the event, therefore, means being able to place that event.

The same logic correlating event with place is inverted for the perpetrator. Instead of seeking an end to a temporal event, that same event is sought to be stretched out in time. In an essay dealing with the spatiality of crime, geographers Warf and Waddell write:

> Serial killers frequently attach ritualistic meanings to the places where they commit the murder and where they dispose of their victims' bodies. Some, for example, revisit the site of the murder repeatedly, especially if they have failed to find a new victim, as the locale evokes the thrill of power so central to their motivations. (2002, 339)

Here, place as a container gains an insidious and dark undercurrent. Returning to the locale enables the killer to reexperience the memory of the event in its visceral reality. The confirmation of what occurred in place is psychologically central not only to the return to the scene of the crime, but also to an understanding of the crime itself, as being contained in place.

To what extent is there a structural alignment between the compulsion to return to the scene of a crime and the need to return to a place of nostalgia? The answer can only be speculative in focus. Logically, however, we are in a parallel universe. The momentum of nostalgic memory is not static, and the drive is not abated by reverie and desire alone. As the interplay between imagination and memory diminishes, the felt presence of what is absent intensifies. With that development of intensity, the attraction of originary place gathers momentum, emitting a gravitational pull, in which all sentient life capable of dreaming and remembering is vulnerable.

I have seen this place before. It is four o'clock on a Thursday afternoon and I have moved to the entrance of my childhood home, having now transgressed the general locality in which the house continues to dwell. The sign reading "Twitchels" remains affixed to the gate, its inscription having eroded in time. Unable to resist the allure, the door to this former life has beckoned me. A stranger's car is parked in the driveway; their flowers have been growing for many years. The windows are intact, and the rooms have remained in

Figure 18: *Childhood home, Hertfordshire, UK. Photo by author.*

place. New gates have been erected, no doubt to ensure certain safety precautions that were not a pressing issue when I lived in this place. I have turned the corner and am now within the property. A massive tree remains in place, its presence a beacon of unparalleled continuity. The bark is moist to the touch, and its warm color offsets the clouds that have begun foaming on the horizon.

To move beyond this space, it is inevitable that I will be seen by those who now dwell within this old house. Venturing out, I recognize that I must now establish contact with this alien life-world. My hand is pressed to the door, and in doing so, the handle sounds a muted groan toward me: the shiver we experience together, a testament to the amorphous spirit now sensing my partial return. And I remember this handle, too. Its materiality places me in time, and its carefully controlled downward swoop returns me to a former incarnation of myself. "The feel of the tiniest latch," so writes Bachelard, "has remained in our hands" (1994, 15). Bachelard is right: My hand clamps around this latch in a familiar and reassuring way, as though the latch were also reaching out to me. Greeted by the new inhabitants of the house, I will explain that owing to some peculiar curiosity, I am

Figure 19: *Childhood home, Hertfordshire, UK. Photo by author.*

compelled to retread my old footsteps. Having conceded to my reasoning, I am roaming the gardens, able now to peek quite intently into some of the windows of my childhood.

There are other people in this garden; two children, one with a red hood and the other without a hood, seemingly oblivious to the fact that a perfect stranger is walking into their nest. Save for a few new ornamental novelties, nothing on the surface has changed too radically. Over time, the very specific features of the garden—the large windows from where I would sit and read, a shade beneath the tree, and the tree house—have cemented themselves in my memory with an affectionate tone, such that who I am is in some sense rooted in the materiality of this place. Indeed, I will often find myself thinking of this childhood sanctuary, almost able to relive the smell of the place.

And now, beneath gray skies and light drizzle, I am near enough to the surface of this world to touch its being. I do so, my hand now against the brick of this house, no doubt to ensure that by dint of touching it, its reality would somehow be secured. Yet a turning occurs: My hand seems to glide through the very wall that stands before me in its bold presence. I touch it again, only to suffer the same disarming fate. It is as though something outside of this place exceeds the material presence I face, as though this place resists the very act of being touched.

I think of Bachelard and his passionate commitment to the twenty years he spent within "anonymous stairways," only to find the "first stairway" waiting for him in the house in which he was born: "The house's entire being would open up, faithful to our own being" (1994, 14–15). To what end Bachelard was able to force a communion between his childhood house and his successive life, we can only guess. The engraving that Bachelard finds when he turns inward is one of continuity and plenitude, a womb of "delicate gestures" unmarked by the brutal passage of time. For him, all bodily gestures remain "faultless" in their reprisal, as we become the logical and phenomenal extension of the home itself, so much so that "the house we were born in," he writes epigrammatically, "is more than an embodiment of home, it is also an embodiment of dreams" (15). But here, that dream has collided with a semiformed reality. In this reality, sections of the past endure but are now battling against the peculiar dark spots with which my memory, in its refusal to recognize the otherness of this world, is now in contact.

Figure 20: *Childhood home, Hertfordshire, UK. Photo by author.*

My hand remains on the wall of my childhood house. Like so much, I have seen it before. But here there is no reciprocity, no time regained: only the cold indifference of time departing from the materiality of place, leaving the residue of an altered place where my memories stood. Despite standing on the grounds of my home, the home remains simultaneously absent. This place cannot be touched, cannot be experienced save as a pure sensation, which resists all modes of affectivity except estrangement.

"Every sensation," writes Merleau-Ponty, "carries within it the germ of a dream or depersonalization such as we experience in that quasi-stupor to which we are reduced when we really try to live at the level of sensation" (2006, 250). Is Merleau-Ponty sounding a warning? Is this not the beacon of things that dwell beneath the surface; a depersonalized daydream, oneirically folding over into the landscape of the present? Here, Bachelard's great faith in the power of dreams and memories easily crosses over into the dark terrain, where that porous domain becomes infected by the very thing from which it sought to incubate itself: anonymity.

I decide to venture inward, assessing if the spirit of this place has been confined to the interior of the home. After all, if Bachelard is misguided in his faith in the power of place, then perhaps he is right to suggest that "memories of the outside world will never have the same tonality as those of home" (1994, 6). Testing this hypothesis, I am standing in the hallway of the home, with the portentous door slowly closing behind me. The carpet has been removed and the wood exposed. A bench from my own era remains in place, either too attractive or too unwieldy to consign to the flames.

I turn the corner and am in the lounge, or living room, now surrounded by the clutter of an unfamiliar life, with only the fireplace enduring through the seismic shifts in space and time. Everything in this room has been divested of its familiar attributes, save for the placement of the windows. Truly, I must exert considerable effort to resituate my former self within this room. That nothing has survived my departure is hardly surprising. But that such an erasure should entirely disorient my memories comes as a shock. It is as though the pink sofas and elephant-themed curtains have curtailed my own past, forcing a lacuna in my identity.

The second lounge is also no longer recognizable, and when I position myself in certain corners of the room, I may as well be in a different country. Yet were I to close my eyes in this room, I could quite easily reexperience myself in this old haunt, hiding under the coffee table as a boy in order to avoid speaking to my parents' visiting friends. For a second, I begin to wonder if this room is not an entirely new extension to the house. But the room occupies a central place in my memories. After all, beyond the front door, this smaller living area gained a ritualistic role in the sequential order of my memories. When retracing the phenomenology of remembering the home, I would invariably pursue a particular route, which allowed me to extract richer experiences than were I to focus on the rooms as separate entities. Yet this method is failing me; this room is refusing to "settle." This room has annexed itself from my spatial awareness, and in the process lost its animative dynamism. Rilke, for whom the longing for home was an idée fixe, writes of remembering a "strange dwelling" in the following way:

> Here one room, there another, and here a bit of corridor which, however, does not connect the two rooms, but is conserved in me in fragmentary form. Thus the whole thing is scattered about inside me, the rooms, the stairs that descended with such ceremonious slowness, others, narrow cages that mounted in a spiral movement, in the darkness of which we advanced like the blood in our veins. (quoted in Bachelard 1994, 57)

Rilke's fragmentation testifies to irretrievability of home. Such irretrievability is the result of the home's departing from position of the self. The scattering of which Rilke speaks thus hints at the removal of the subject from the place, with the place now floating in the zone of resembling scenes. "It is as though," writes Bachelard, "we sojourned in a limbo of being" (1994, 58). Too much is lost in this return to preserve a strict sense of continued realty. Rather, unreality intrudes, uprooting the home from the soil, and thus damaging the duration that once inhabited that place. In need of orientation, I move to the ontological center of the home, the kitchen.

The blue AGA stove, flanked on all sides by red bricks, has not budged, its sturdy presence unwavering in fortitude. Seeing this mass of blue flesh again is startling, a piece of fiction that has transgressed its own borders. Indeed, in a literal way, my body and this AGA are united by a small scar on my chest, where I burned myself while clumsily removing some toast from the chamber. The blue surface of the kitchen, which also derives from my own time, has proved attractive with the current family, too. The materials have endured well. A windowsill looks out to the front garden. I have sat here before. I, too, have looked out on the garden, and on one afternoon I repeated the word *mountain* until the same word no longer made sense. I must have been eight years old. Later on, the kitchen table would become the site for a series of significant events in my life, all framed within the peculiar aura of this room, and all gravitating in one way or another to the blue AGA.

Here is the heart of the home, with its warmth creating flames of illusive comfort in the midst of this Thursday afternoon. Everything is in place, and yet nothing is placed. I am here, in this crystalline familiarity. Strands of my own past have survived intact, massive chunks of deposited life. Other dimensions have been overlapped by the passing of time and the conquest of a new life. Patches of the old carpet remain in place, only to suddenly break off from its moorings, replaced by a new floor. Speculating what lives and what dies in this environment is no longer a question that can be asked. Damaged, the boundaries separating memory from imagination have been flooded by an oceanic melancholy, free-floating in its movement and disconcerting in its refusal to be placed. In a word, *uncanny*.

"One would suppose," Freud writes, "that the uncanny would always be an area in which a person was unsure of his way around: the better orientated he was in the world around him, the less likely he would be to find the objects and occurrences in it uncanny" (2003, 125). This conflation between orientation and the uncanny has a side effect: Without orientation, things lose not only their structural bearings, but also their personal content. No longer being placed within the world, a cleft is created where the fabric of the world once existed.

Time and again, it is the sense of being *lost* in place that is invoked through the experience of the uncanny: "One may," so writes Freud again, "have lost one's way in the woods, perhaps after being overtaken by fog, and, despite all one's efforts to find a marked or familiar path, one comes back again and again to the same spot" (2003, 144). Sometimes being lost is the very condition of being found again, thus renewing all that we had so far taken for granted. At other times, the loss becomes instructive, and the fracture that is opened up when memories are effaced becomes a guiding force.

During the uncanny, loss is not a thing to be redeemed. Rather, it is with the conjunction of two or more strange images that the ontological structure of place is fully realized, a realization that reaches its apotheosis with the uncanny. Nowhere is this clearer than in the case of returning to a familiar place. In the return to a remembered place, the familiarity of a preserved memory fuses with the strangeness of an anonymous place. As a result, a struggle ensues: As objective time is dislocated by lived time, a sense of "unreal reality" is introduced. This paradoxical phrase "unreal reality" has two aspects to it. First, the phrase refers to the ambiguity of a place that is at once "real" and objectively present in the world. At the same time, the very reality of that world is the source of an otherness provided by the work of memory and imagination. Second, "unreal reality" hints at the tension between anonymity and desire, memory and imagination, and sameness and difference. Where the uncanny is concerned, these polarities break. Yet the breakage is not unambiguous. Remnants of a particular place continue, only now dwarfed by the broader separation between the place we remember and the temporal discontinuity that disrupts that memory. The formation of place thus becomes a negative operation, in which a new landscape is carved from the erasure of old memory. Losing ourselves in place, we are reminded of what is missing from that place.

Three further examples can be consulted, each of which testifies to modes of this disorientation experienced during the return to place. The first is from Pierre Nora, the second a passage from Simone de Beauvoir's autobiography, and the third from Latvian geographer Edmunds Bunkse.

> Returning across the threshold of one's natal home, one finds oneself
> in the old abode, now uninhabited and practically unrecognizable—

with the same family heirlooms, but under another light; before the same *atelier*, but for another task; in the same rooms, but with another role. (Nora 1989, 18)

The past is not a peaceful landscape lying there behind me, a country in which I can stroll wherever I please, and which will gradually show me all its secret hills and dales. As I was moving forward, so it was crumbling. Most of the wreckage that can still be seen is colourless, distorted, frozen. . . . Here and there, I see occasional pieces whose melancholy beauty enchants me. (de Beauvoir 1972, 365)

My sense of returning home was further dashed by the fact that the crowd swirling around me at the entrance to the station spoke only Russian. I had nowhere to go. . . . And so I stood there, in the cold winter drizzle, with my three pieces of luggage on an airline carry-on cart, a stranger in a foreign land, a land with some familiar emblems in an unfamiliar landscape. (Bunkse 2004, 54)

Paradoxically, what unites these accounts in their radical disjointedness is the subtle reversal of spatial forms. In Nora's evocation of returning, form and content clash, forcing sameness and difference to cross a shared path. It is because the interchange is subtle, so arousing the imagination to stretch itself beyond the role of fortifier of the past, that the distance between time and place is articulated. The same place now reconstituted, now reused, and now dwelt in by the other, transforms the idea of "place" to a vague chimera.

The apparent contradiction is repeated in de Beauvoir's imagined return. Here, time sculpts place rather than place's determining time. We are in a timescape, obscured by the gaze of consciousness. Moving forward means recognizing what has escaped the watch of memory. And what remains is "wreckage," fragments that have been reduced to dissociated detritus, countered only by the "occasional pieces" that fortuitously correspond with the image preserved.

In Bunske's description of his return to Latvia after a considerable period of absence, the same dynamic is met with the awkward rearrangement of memory, hampered by the prosaic details, which, in their insubstantiality, confirm the incidental and obsolescent relationship preserved memory has to indeterminate place.

Figure 21: *Key Food Supermarket, Brooklyn. Photo by author.*

The emphasis on the everyday and the otherworldly is especially clear where liminal and transient places are concerned. A supermarket in a country other than our own does not give itself over to the plenitude of an easily contained memory. Yet such memories do not simultaneously suffer a loss of significance simply because they belong to interchangeable places. Unlike the home, or any other location fixed in both memory and place, returning to a supermarket achieves a level of depth framed by its anonymity. Because of this anonymity, significance is heightened and not effaced. As leveled-out, the emission of memory and self in the midst of an outwardly sterile environment forms an aesthetic gesture, parallel to the displacement of the world from its everyday context. Now, that same world is shown under a different light, a light that does less to enlighten the reality of things in their clarity and more to cast things in a strange, amorphous state. Indeed, there is something intensely spectral about returning to a supermarket, which had once been sedimented in the body as a regular "haunt," but is now simultaneously remote and intimate, leading us irresistibly back to Freud's account of the uncanny as "the species of the frightening that goes back to what was once well known and had long been familiar" (2003, 124). Peculiar to this spectrality is the exchange between sameness and difference. A tension is instilled between the precise yet marginal details of the memory of the place and the now-overturned details that occupy the place of that memory.

Here and there, however, a vast world makes itself known, shattering the pillars of memory and embodiment and flooding the empty space that remains with a numb remnant of the previous environment. All accounts of reciprocity and warmth dissolve in this annihilation of human life. Unflinching, this newly formed outpost fails to accommodate our desires and at the same time does nothing to prepare us for the next life. Instead, a gesture of retreat can be witnessed, forcing so-called "real life" to relinquish its powers.

In temporal terms, it is as though the "primal repression" of which Freud speaks has now buckled. What emerges in this breakdown is the rise of *anonymous materiality*. Whereas we take it for granted that the places we value somehow mirror our identities, what we tend to overlook in this mimetic act is the cosmic indifference lurking beneath that materiality. All along, however, there exists the anonymous space that fails to look back at us, despite our attempts to imbue that world with value and memory.

But where has the "I" gone in the emergence of these anonymous chunks of materiality deposited in the life-world? Somehow the "I" has remained in place, but instead of there being the singular self, what exists alongside this anonymous space is the interplay between myself in the present and myself as I was previously in the memory-laden past.

The question, therefore, is of not *where* I am, but *when* I am. The answer is clear: when "I" begin to repeat myself, establishing a series of internal deaths that, while eroding the "real me," nevertheless produce a series of bodily identities layering one another. The neutralization of the past, experienced when memory's death throe reaches its end, is productive: It produces nothing less than a temporal mirror. Referred to as the "end of memory," this flattening-out of the past spits back scatterings of old selves: I have come to haunt myself, and I do this through recognizing the damaged space where the desire of the present once existed.

THE DARK ENTITY

"Memories and possibilities," so writes Lovecraft correctly, "are ever more hideous than realities" (1985, 158). Hideous because what is thought of has having an irreducible unity—the "I"—is proven to be a composite of discontinuous fragments, anonymous zones of materiality, and whispers of half-lit memories forged in the hidden atlas of the human body. As for reality: Its unbridgeable distance from the site of "home" sets in place a depersonalized, dereal world wholly incompatible with the notion of "dwelling." Yet these possibilities, of which Lovecraft refers, despite their hideousness, are also the source of a truth peculiar to the uncanny. And so it falls to us to extract the contribution the uncanny makes to our understanding and experience of memory and place.

The return to the place of memory is at the same time a return to the memory of place. For in the physical return to a former place of intimacy, the very memory that constituted that place undergoes massive revision, a trait I analyzed in the previous illustrations. In each case, evidence was presented to suggest that the self is dispersed in time through the radical collision between the anonymity of materiality and the memorial value placed on that materiality. Like some creaking flood barrier, nostalgia enters the scene of the fragmented self in order to cultivate a border around the wreckage of place and memory, and thus salvage what time has indiscriminately sought to annihilate. To this end, nostalgia earns its pernicious reputation through retreating from the horizon of an open place, enclosing itself from the world and prohibiting all chances of a critical history.

At the expense of going astray, however, the structure of a hypervigilant place is constructed. Here, Gaston Bachelard becomes a defining figure in the tension between anonymity and intimacy. For Bachelard, such a construction is a victory over the outside, as he writes: "We shall see the imagination build 'walls' of impalpable shadows, comfort itself with the illusion of protection—or, just the contrary, tremble behind thick walls, mistrust the staunchest ramparts" (1994, 5). Against those borders, unfamiliarity is expelled and "homeliness" is secured.

Nowhere is this domestication of anonymous materiality clearer than in Bachelard's account of the house in snow. "Behind dark curtains," he writes, "snows seems to be whiter. Indeed, everything comes alive when contradictions accumulate" (1994, 39). With the outside pressing down on the inside, both domains are sparked by a tense animation. In this geography of snow and ice, Bachelard finds warmth and tenderness. "We feel warm *because* it is cold out-of-doors" (39; italics in original). For him, the very condition of warmth is predicated on contradiction. For this reason, home—*homecoming*—is best suited to the winter months: "Winter is by far the oldest of the seasons. Not only does it confer age upon our memories, taking us back to a remote past but, on snowy days, the house too is old" (41). Thanks to its immemorial time, the house becomes the axis through which the universe is channeled. Yet owing to Bachelard's agoraphobic relation to the outside, snow is conceived only as a thing pressing down and reinforcing the fortitude of the house. Never does he encounter the house as pointing to its own otherness; that is, as viewed from the outside. Indeed, at times he will go so far as to say that winter is a "simplified cosmos," marking a "non-house," which ultimately entails a "cosmic negation" (40–41).

What did Bachelard omit in this refusal to move beyond the inside? The same question can be asked by way of Bachelard's cellar. Before it is "rationalized," the cellar embodies the "dark entity" of the house, "the one that partakes of subterranean forces" (1994, 18). Unlike the attic, the cellar cannot be tamed or mastered: "Darkness prevails both day and night" (19). Of the cellar's relationship to the house up above, Bachelard says very little. The reason for this can be deduced from the cellar's resistance to human desire: It is, after all, a place with a personality of its own, as evidenced by Bachelard's claim that "even when we are carrying a lighted candle, we see shadows dancing on the walls" (19). From a human eye, however, this "buried madness" (20) is seen only as an object of fear. In truth, however, what is "dark" about the house is not its maligned spirit but its anonymity—returning us to Merleau-Ponty's (2006, 376) "resolutely silent Other," which lurks beneath the frost of appearances.

Given its tremendous power to create place, the question of what lies beneath has an irresistible pull to it. Lurking within *The Poetics of Space*, a tension is detectable in the sanguine prose with which Bachelard presents the reader. On the one hand, all that is homely to the evocation of the snow scene depends on the cosmos' being leveled to a blank space for the dreams and memories of the home to come alive. While the house is empowered by this transformation of the world to an empty tabula rasa, in the outside world, "snow covers all tracks, blurs the road, muffles every sound, conceals all colors" (Bachelard 1994, 40).

On the other hand, this dialectic has an uncanniness to it that Bachelard does not acknowledge. At first, the house in the winter is taken to be an ontological center of intimacy. Yet this center is not autonomous, but depends upon Bachelard's contradictory union of warmth and coldness. As such, at the heart of the center is an identity formed by its own immanent negation: Gaining a "refinement of intimacy," the house assimilates the "cosmic negation" of the "non-house" into its hearth. With this, Bachelard plants the seeds of the home's coldness and unfamiliarity in the midst of its apparent warmth and familiarity, thus preparing the ground for an aesthetic of the uncanny and the anonymous. Aware of this danger, Bachelard frames the "non-house" as hospitable to the desires of the "I," affecting an "increased intensity" of intimacy with the "dreamer of houses" (1994, 40–41).

But Bachelard's attempt to curtail the outside from the inside with "dark curtains" and ancestral memories is a short-term solution to the presence of the house's "dark entity." As the "felicitous" orientation of Bachelard's thought reaches its limit through the incursion of phenomena such as returning to place after a prolonged absence, this enclosure exposes itself to horror, not of a house that no longer reciprocates the gaze of the dweller—but of a house that reciprocates the gaze of the dweller with *different eyes*. Out of this abject gaze, a croaking uncanniness is founded, where the character of the house is proven to be fundamentally anonymous: an impersonal creaking in the middle of the night before subduing at the first sight of a white dawn.

And here, the cellar and the snow unite in their relationship to the unconsciousness in its refusal to be "civilized." Precisely what evades civilization, as Freud notes in his essay on the uncanny, is "the idea of our own mortality" (2003, 148). Bachelard's (1994, xxxv; italics in original) passionate commitment to *"felicitous space"* is less a cultural statement about modernity and specific forms of architecture and urban life, and more an existential position with regard to memory and death. For what is understood by this commitment is a "topophilia," which "[defends] against adverse forces, the space we love" (xxxv). Indeed, at the heart of this defense is the work of imagination, which, in its preemptive action, forever points toward the restoration of memory's fallout. As such, for Bachelard, "hostile space is hardly mentioned" (xxxvi). But while Bachelard points out this focus as having the "advantage of being well circumscribed" (xxxv), this thematic oversight is far more than a methodological orientation. The reason being: Bachelard's entire ontology of memory and place depends upon the substantiality of the memory of home, against which "memories of the outside world will never have the same tonality" (6). Even were he to incorporate "hostile space" into his thought, the same centrality of home would retain its place unless Bachelard revised his entire ontology.

With this privileged ontology of the home, death, transience, and sickness seldom feature in Bachelard's text. But we need not phrase these themes in literal terms. Rather, the absence of mortality more broadly within Bachelard has a profound effect on his treatment of selfhood and spatiality as a whole. For him, the house "is one of the greatest powers of integration . . . an embodiment of dreams . . . body and soul [from whence] life begins well, it begins enclosed, protected, all warm in the bosom of the house" (1994, 4–7). In a literal sense, this constant overlapping of memory and dream leaves no place for "*ein unheimliches Haus* ('an uncanny house')" (Freud 2003, 148). Yet this omission, far from cordoning off the home from estrangement, only heightens the presence of the home's "dark entity," which has so far been consigned to the relative safety of the cellar.

In the face of the mortality of both self and home, Bachelard simplifies the cosmos, divesting the outside of a reality, which only the inside has access to. With his treatment of snow, we witness the very essence of the atomized house in its removal from coldness and darkness. All along, however, something remains unable to be domesticated in this "universal whiteness" of a snow-covered world: the unconscious sense that what animates the home in its intimacy and warmth is also the same agency engineering the home's own cosmological indifference to our being (Bachelard 1994, 41). That the house should return our gaze with a different set of eyes other than our own confirms the existence of a "resolutely silent Other" embarking on its own occult teleology, and a teleology that will no longer remember us once we've left its icy lair.

True, we seek to bury the strange eyes that occasionally mirror our bodies in the places we dwell. When stirs the phantasmagorical prospect that a home is different from the one we remember, then we align that difference with an error in memory rather than an agency within the house itself. At no point does the house, in its silence and whispering, come to be seen as plotting a life of its own. When shadows creep across hallways, then once more the task becomes one of mastery over raw space, as though to exhume not only the specters long since forgotten in the basement, but also those undead forces that lurk within our own thinking. *And yet.*

"Yet we do not feel entirely secure in these new convictions; the old ones live on in us, on the look-out for confirmation" (Freud 2003, 154). *The old ones live on in us,* thus Freud writes, inadvertently pointing to some macabre cellular or genetic memory, of which thought and consciousness are yet to become fully aware. "Now," so Freud continues, "as soon as something *happens* in our lives that seems to confirm these old, discarded beliefs, we experience a sense of the uncanny" (154; italics in original). The uncanny intervenes, intercedes, and affects the nervous system in such a way that reason stands no chance of assimilating the unreal into the real. A parched fragment is left over, a deterritorialized remnant of a previous order that, through incubation and sheer strategy, has outlasted the domain of civility.

Beyond the "'walls' of impalpable shadows," lies what Henri Michaux terms the "horrible inside-outside that real space is" (quoted in Bachelard 1994, 216). And this space is foreign, alien, and immune to the classification of home and non-home: a mutant, receptive to the warm flesh of the physical body but more or less unresponsive to the desires running through that body. Into this malformed space, Bachelard senses only "a sonorous echo from the vaults of hell" (217). His language testifies to the hellish power the "inside-outside" entity holds over the imagination, as it tears through the protection of oneirism before usurping the very foundations of memory itself: "This spirit, this shade, this noise of a shade which . . . desires its unity, may be heard on the outside without it being possible to be sure that it is inside" (217). Only now, the nothingness of the outside has gained momentum and the inside loses its reserves, producing the "backwash of expiring being" (217).

For Bachelard, despite the fact that outside and inside "are always ready to be reversed, to exchange their hostility," the inside-outside hybrid is a nightmarish scenario plagued by the pain of touching the "border-line surface" (1994, 218). For in that encounter with the surface, there is no place left to hide. That which has been consigned to the cellar of the house—the "dark entity"—is now proven to be constitutive of the house itself: an accumulation of nothingness in the heart of being. Accordingly, before long, Bachelard must close the file on this bit of "experimental folly," citing it as "like a virtual grain of hashish . . . an exaggerated image" (219). And so he resumes his sojourn of "fossilized metaphors" (221). This rationalization of the "horrible inside-outside" cuts short the promise of a house at home in its own unhomeliness.

Despite Bachelard's circumscription of the uncanny, the nightmare of the dark entity is a space of insight. For what surfaces in the relation between memory, spatiality, and the uncanny is an order of inhuman being that re-molds our nominal understanding of "home." Throughout this chapter, this has been evident in at least three ways. First, against the rallying call of the personal ego, with its insistence on discerning a sense of place in the world through the interplay of memory and dream, the uncanny's intervention in this desire draws our attention to the narcissism of the anthropomorphized cosmos. Disruptive and disordering, through its relationship to the "buried madness" that lurks within dark space, the ontological warmth of the *heim-lich*, with its "familiar, tame, dear and intimate" (Freud 2003, 126) tone is damaged by that mysterious agency that just as soon converts the familiar into the unhomely. In this conversion, the centrality of human experience is overturned, and often with an eerie effect. Reaching its apotheosis in the mania of nostalgia, the willful rearrangement of the material world by a nos-talgic body prepares the ground for a dramatic reentry into a world spooked by both anonymity and awe.

Second, with the world of human desire decentralized by the animated indifference of the material world, previous borders demarcating inside and outside no longer hold ground. Insofar as this dissolution disturbs the sedi-ment of human experience, its direction is archetypically phenomenological in origin. By now, the allegiance between the uncanny and the phenomeno-logical method suggested in the introduction will have found expression in things themselves, not least memories and places. Thanks to phenomenol-ogy's receptivity to the birth of appearances, ambiguity is placed central, and the stifled, sedimented cluster of familiar knowledge is renewed and es-tranged from its placement in the world.

Finally, the uncanny brings to light the omnipotence of our own mortality within both memory and place. "In hardly any other sphere," Freud writes of death, "has our thinking and feeling changed so little since primitive times or the old been so well preserved, under a thin veneer, as in our relation to death" (2003, 148). At the heart of our memories of place is the ambivalence of death, which incubates itself as much in the flesh of the human body as it does in the flesh of the childhood home. Death alone is the recurring motif of the uncanny, that which forces an unbridgeable abyss between ourselves and the places that detach themselves from our embrace. When returning to a place from our pasts, the difference we experience between the materiality of the place and the immateriality of our memories attests to the distancing between our own selves and the world as a whole; beyond our own lived pasts, eventually the world will reduce even the most triumphant of memories to a gelatinous mass, whose specificity and value are no longer visible.

Of all the fears of human life, death cannot be mastered by the unconsciousness, since death *is* a part of the very fabric of unconsciousness. Recall Bachelard: "The unconscious cannot be civilized" (1994, 19). Cannot be civilized because the unconscious is immune to the rationalization of space and time. And here Bachelard's sentiment mirrors Freud's: "Our unconscious is still as unreceptive as ever to the idea of our own mortality" (Freud 2003, 148). But we need not maintain a fixed adherence to this psychoanalytic language. For what we have seen in this chapter is the alliance between the unconscious and the lived-body. In advance of thought, the body's own intelligibility paves the way for the self to retain unity through time, a trait I described under the name "spatial morphology."

In between the swollen cracks of memory and imagination, fragmentation and death intercede, placing an injunction on even the body's great powers to heal the wounds of time. Here, the uncanny guides us with its avenues of eerie disquiet and uninhabited vistas, at all times reminding us that however much we attach ourselves to the places in which we dwell, those same places never truly reciprocate the cosmos of our own being. Only by chance, habit, and sheer act of force is the anonymous materiality of the world masked with a warmth and familiarity, of which further effort is required to preserve such a state. Through that force, memory is nullified from reality while place is rendered the object of anthropomorphic narcissism.

Through the uncanny, presence is stripped of its reassuring content and "things" are reduced to their shadows—to some extent, "dead" even before their biological expiration. As dead, things lose their animative quality in the world, becoming overshadowed in the melancholy of Rilke's acute awareness of the "fate of transience" (Freud 2005, 197). This premature death infects our sense of belonging to a place, whereupon place and time are revealed as having a concealed life, hitherto hidden despite our attempts at domesticity. Thinking once more alongside Freud: *The old ones live on in us.* This fundamental dis-ease with ever truly belonging to any given place reminds us that place is forever prepared to reject us from its hold, forever ready to reconfigure our memories, and so augment our very sense of who we are.

For all his perennial nostalgia, it is Rilke who fully crystallizes the elemental value of estrangement, melancholia, and transience:

> To see landscape thus, as something distant and foreign, something remote and unloving, something entirely self-contained, was necessary. . . . It had to be almost hostile in its sublime indifference, if it was to give a new meaning to our existence. . . . For we begin to understand Nature only when we no longer understood it; when we felt that it was the Other, indifferent toward men, which has no wish to let us enter, then for the first time we stepped outside of Nature, alone, out of the lonely world. (1987, xxv)

Slowly, place alters. Under the watchful eye of the home's primitive body, a change occurs. Now, indifference—the very essence of cosmic topophobia—reveals itself as a source of illumination rather than a canvas of pure darkness. From the horror of the "non-house" in the snow-ridden landscape, the frost begins to thaw. In the process, a partially familiar landscape is created in the ruins, from which human life is recognized in a cosmos lit by the "sublime indifference" of a place with no borders.

Part Three
From Black Holes to Specters

. . . .

CHAPTER FIVE

TRAUMATIC EMBODIMENT

But how does the disease perceive us?

—David Cronenberg, *Cronenberg on Cronenberg*

J. G. Ballard presents us with a disarming image. In an unspecified time, we are summoned to an abandoned space center in Florida. Up above, a "strange pilot" is flying in circles, the result of which woke the story's protagonist "Dr Mallory soon after dawn, as he lay asleep bedside his exhausted wife on the fifth floor of the empty hotel in Titusville" (Ballard 2006, 569). Later on, we learn that Edward Mallory is a former NASA employee, who, along with his wife and "the other NASA personnel based in Florida," are all suffering from "space sickness," the symptom of which is the slowing-down of time (573). "One day," Ballard tells us, "[time] would stop, freeze forever on one frame," a movement that has centered "into the eternal present of this timeless zone," Florida (573). Having returned to Florida with the aim of understanding space sickness, Dr. Mallory discovers that the aimless pilot is Hinton, a rogue astronaut who murdered a copilot while in orbit.

The location moves to a deserted highway and Mallory is in pursuit of Hinton. Soon after, the rogue astronaut begins shooting at Mallory from a low-flying Fokker plane above. Escaping into an abandoned motel, Mallory manages to work his way back to Titusville through the desolate landscape and increasingly distorted timescale. Ballard reports:

> Time was slowing now, coming almost to a halt. Mallory hung in mid-step, his bare feet in the air above the ground. . . . The waves were no longer running towards the beach, and were frozen ruffs of icing sugar. Fish hung in the sky, the wise dolphins happy to be in their new realm, faces smiling in the sun. The water spraying from the fountain at the shallow end of the pool now formed a

glass parasol. . . . Time had flowed out of Florida, as it had from the
space age. After a brief pause, like a trapped film reel running free, it
sped on again, rekindling a kinetic world. (2006, 579–81)

Eventually, the conflict between Mallory and Hinton escalates. Embracing
the "destruction of time," Hinton sets about entrapping Mallory's wife,
Anne, into escaping a "time-reft world" (Ballard 2006, 598). Having set fire
to his collection of antique planes, Hinton makes his way with Anne to the
assembly deck of the remaining shuttle in order to "cast them both loose into
space" (598). Meanwhile, Mallory, having now resigned himself to the end of
time, returns to the abandoned hotel. Unlocking a caged tiger, they both lie
and wait, braced for the emergence of a "world beyond time" (601).

Ballard's story "Memories of the Space Age" is a parable on the threshold
of experience. By stripping time of its familiar attributes, Ballard presents us
with a world in which a singular event—spaceflight—can alter the spatiotemporality of the embodied subject, such that the sickness of a "world without
time" is the result. For Ballard, the return to earth after spaceflight does not
simply contend with the physical consequences of zero-gravity isolation and
the atmospheric reentry of the body. Rather, what becomes the leading motif
is the disembodiment of time.

In Ballard, this rupturing of time produces a world of anomalies, littered
by relics of the previous order, both spatial and temporal. The "dream-
time" that encroaches upon the deserted Floridian landscape does so less as
an abnormal incarnation of time and more as a logical consequence of the
"breach of laws" that comes with human flight into space. As Ballard states
in another of his so-called Cape Kennedy stories: "Perhaps the right to travel
through space belonged to another order of beings, but his crime was being
punished just as surely as would any attempt to ignore the laws of gravity"
(2006, 544). It is as though something returned in that voyage—something
that, having incubated itself within the bodies of the astronauts, is now being
discharged into the surrounding environment. Indeed, later on in the story,
we are told that the astronauts' bodies are themselves changing form, for
Hinton, "an atrophied organ that he would soon discard" (589).

Of course, part of the appeal of this spatiocorporeal disintegration for
Hinton is to transgress the ultimate horizon of time, leaving behind the scattered remnants of finitude in his wake. The eventual erosion of time leads
to an atemporal state, which is necessarily devoid of an embodied sense of
being *here* and *now*. Consigned to temporal oblivion, Hinton has come to

associate flight as a freedom, not only from space, but from time, too: "To get out of time we first need to learn to fly. That's why I'm here. . . . I want to fly without wings" (Ballard 2006, 590). This redemption from time requires the decompression of the body, leaving to one side the embedded memories of the past alongside the projected imagination of the future.

Such is the power invested in spaceflight: No less than singular in its formation, the event becomes a marker of differing identities and worlds. Yet despite Florida's being the physical site of this temporal mutation, Ballard's vision is not a realist one. As one character says to Mallory: "The real Cape Kennedy is inside your head, not out here" (Ballard 2006, 582). The statement places the reality of time and space within the subject, disturbing the conception that both realms are strictly linear in their unfolding.

However, Hinton's posttemporal utopia reveals an even darker underside than Ballard's already eerie world lit by the "spectral light over the sombre forest" (2006, 591). For it is a world in which what remains standing is carved like tombs from what has been destroyed in the past. Ballard's figures—Hinton and Mallory—are ghosts of another era, present in their absence. Yet this announcement of a spectral life is in no way a sign of deficiency. Rather, in the tension between time and place, a new life, manifested as a "space sickness," is created. Although fundamentally at odds with the previous order of habit and familiarity—and indeed even going so far as to live off the old order—this new agency is nevertheless just as legitimate a form of life as any other. As such, Ballard's depopulated NASA landscape, with its atrophied bodies, presents itself as nothing less than a living, working organism, striving toward motion at the expense of the previous spatiotemporal regime.

And so Ballard establishes a problem that will become central to the present chapter. The problem can be formulated as a question: *How is it possible for an experience to fragment the course of time, producing two or more embodied timescales, which, in their contact with one another produce a variation of "space sickness," and thus rupture the unity of self-consciousness?* Without time and embodiment, in the figure of Hinton, Ballard presents us with a posthuman subject, anonymous in its presence, estranged to the self, and thus emblematically *traumatized* in its structure.

This turn toward trauma, which will become the focus of the current chapter, is already implicit in my above characterization of Ballard's tale as being on "the threshold of experience." For what is peculiar about the temporality of trauma is a deferred and fragmented manifestation of the past. In "Memories of the Space Age," the dozens of relics and ruins that emerge in this fragmented and misshapen light all gesture toward the uneven erosion of human duration, leaving in its path the uncanny space in which that duration once existed. As Ballard states it: "Each flight to the moon and each journey around the sun was a trauma that warped their perception of time and space. The brute-force ejection of themselves from their planet had been an act of evolutionary piracy, for which they were now being expelled from the world of time" (2006, 545). In what follows I shall attempt to transplant this "brute-force ejection" into the relation between embodiment and trauma.

Insomuch as deferment and fragmentation are said to mark the memory and structure of trauma, then it is perhaps misleading to describe the current chapter as a "turn" to trauma. During the final stages of the previous chapters, the action of body memory absorbing place independently of cognitive memory called upon a movement that will become viscerally expressive in the present chapter. In what follows, the body as a plane of experience, able to register the world in spite of a cognitive failure, will become a central problem. Already we have gestured toward this dynamic in the case of what I described as "alien flesh." There, the tension between corporeal and cognitive experience was mediated by the inability to register an environment lacking heterogeneous properties. In what follows, this tension will be pushed to a threshold, whereby what is given to consciousness as ambiguous and strange will be denied its immediacy. Following the broadly phenomenological structure of the preceding chapters, the chapter will initially plot the problematic structure of trauma. Calling upon on the important work of Cathy Caruth, I will argue that the impasse at the (non)center of trauma can be understood in terms of an asymmetrical emergence of the past. By providing a sketch of Caruth's model of trauma at the outset, I will analyze traumatic memory in a genetic manner, detailing the temporality of memory, as it fails to "give" itself to consciousness. The result of this failure is the symptomatic emergence of the past, which I will proceed to analyze via the body's retention of the traumatic past.

THE EVENT HORIZON

Before we venture directly into the eye of trauma, let us return to a theme I alluded to in the above discussion about Ballard. There, a central theme at stake was the creation of a new spatiotemporal order, manifested as a "space sickness," and developed from the remnants of an older one. Recall, too, that this birth was established by the singularity of an event: spaceflight. Above all, what sparked the dynamism of space sickness was the coexistence of two worlds in the same sphere: that is, the world of lived experience existing alongside the world of "dream-time."

I have placed these realms in a dyadic relation, since at the heart of space sickness is a standoff between the ruins of the pre-spaceflight mode of temporality and the encroachment of a "vivid light" marking the erasure of that remnant. Seen in this way, despite the abundance of abandoned motels and ghostly figures, Ballard's vision is not so much postapocalyptic as it is cast in the shadow of a looming void. The point is important, since it underscores the fact that what comes to light in this world is a zone of conflicting and morphing horizons rather than a dying landscape set far from its living counterpart.

In the transitional interplay between conflicting modes of presence, a precise moment can be formulated—a conceptual event horizon—whereby one world is irreducibly altered through being colonized by another. We witness it here, for example: "Mallory felt the light suddenly steepen, the intense white glare he had last seen as the cheetah sprang towards him" (Ballard 2006, 590). This turn toward the language of the "event horizon" is neither incidental nor solely coincidental with Ballard. Rather, by using the astrophysical language of "event horizons," we can discern a structure of time and space transferable to the limits of human experience. Thus, one of my principal aims in the current chapter is to *apply the findings of an astrophysical account of the event horizon to the human body*. I shall do this by attending to the body memory of trauma. I recognize that by conflating phenomenology and astronomy through the device of metaphor, speculative thought might exceed its welcome status. But I have, I believe, good reason for formulating this relation, and I hope that the risk of testing the reader's patience will be resolved by committing to this voyage.

In astrophysical terms, an event horizon is the boundary demarcating a black hole. Once material enters the event horizon it never returns, is never seen, and no longer affects the external viewer. Rather, through being assimilated by the massive gravitational field of the black hole, into which even light is pulled, all materiality is reduced to a homogeneous void. Moreover, since no light can withstand the pull of the black hole, thus concealing itself in deep space, the light surrounding the event horizon on the other hand assumes a privileged role for the viewer. In this way, the whirlpool of light and gas associated with the black hole is nothing more than a symptom of its core, framed by the border of the event horizon. As a living, breathing void, therefore, the core of the black hole is beyond space and time. All communication with the core is prohibited, all theory speculative.

With no past and no specific spatiality to speak of—since, after all, all black holes must be the same if all matter is null and void within them—the black hole's structure is repeated from one hole to another. This simplicity, however, belies the paradoxical nature of the event horizon's relationship to the black hole. For what is at stake in the structure of the event horizon is not the strangeness of the phenomenon itself, but the event's symptomatic relation to the black hole. In other words, the manifold way in which the event horizon appears cannot be taken as an appearance in its own terms, despite the broad phenomenological framework employed to access it. Rather, what "appears" does so as a reverberation of an inaccessible and invisible force channeling its presence through the nearest visible source. This indirect approximation to the black hole places the event horizon in a privileged position: Through studying its contours and patterns, we are able to observe the unobservable.

On an aesthetic and cultural level, the phenomenon of the black hole occupies a central role in its signification of the "dark entity" at the heart of space and time. Beyond this darkness, the language of black holes tends to refer to that which is beyond representation, formless, nameless, other, unknowable, abject, primal, and, above all, *traumatic*. In each of these terms, there is a tension between the black hole and subjectivity. As pure negativity, the language of black holes is a void carved within the depth of presence, the trace of which is evident only as the absence where something once was. Because of this conceptual and phenomenal elusiveness, the term "black hole" has assumed an almost mythical role in culture, its resistance to definition an invitation for the projection of unconscious desires, from the phantoms of hell to the secrets of the universe.

Consuming everything in its field of force, the black hole entertains the paradox of a horizon within the universe, a sudden departure from space and time, in which "things" cease to be. Yet the black hole cannot be reduced to "nothingness." The void is not simply the absence of being, but the mutilation of being. Through it, things become otherwise. Not a dearth of activity, but an active, dynamic life force in its own right intersecting the invisible laws of the universe. Into this maelstrom of phenomenality, borders collapse, inviting the possibility of the repressed or dormant component of experience to come unbound.

At the same time, from this rupture of order, possibility is forged, new life-worlds created in the establishment of decolonized spaces. The namelessness of the black hole is thus also a space through which the sediment of the past is given room to breathe. Thanks to its capacity to estrange and defamiliarize the world, the black hole's receptivity to the aesthetic of the uncanny is privileged. And like the uncanny, the black hole of experience engineers a peculiar relationship with the unknown and the familiar, at once commanding an anxious affectivity through which trauma coexists with transformation.

How can we make the transition from the infinite domain of cosmological space to the finite world of the embodied subject? My plan is as follows: First, we shall frame the relation between the black hole and the event horizon as a singular entity. In doing so, we shall envision the moment in which an object touches the surface of the event horizon as coinciding with an ensuing act of molecular transformation. Precisely because of this dynamic of transforming matter, a temporary and transitional zone is forged between the morphing of foreign bodies; namely, those outside the black hole and those already vaporized by its gravitational force.

Aligned with this provisional claim, I suggest the following hypothesis: By reconstituting this transitional zone between the event horizon and the black hole within the sphere of memory and trauma, it is the human body—the very embodiment of "space sickness" itself—that acts as privileged portal between divergent and mutually conflicting worlds. Only, unlike cosmological research into black holes, in our speculative investigation into the relation between trauma and embodiment, we shall gain an advantage over astrophysics by witnessing the fallout of materiality *surviving* the black hole. What would this survival mean in forensic terms?

One thing is clear: The body that survives the black hole returns to us a witness, able to testify to the threshold of experience. Here, a curious outcome ensues. If all space and time, having come into contact with the event horizon, is said to be inescapable from the pull of the black hole, and when thrust into the void fundamentally warped beyond all recognizability, then whatever is returned from the hole in a reconstituted form necessarily remains blind to its own experience—necessarily becomes alien. That is, even if we consider the reconstituted body as resembling the previous one, then the very act of having survived the black hole places a rupture at the heart of identity, leaving the unity of selfhood exposed to violent disunity.

Epistemologically, this is a disturbing claim. For what is being suggested is the fusion of two different worlds in the same body, effectively overrunning the body with a duration foreign to lived experience. In turn, this claim will be justified in full. For now, however, it will suffice to pose this problem in hypothetical and formal terms. By framing the relation between memory and trauma in a structurally parallel manner to the event horizon and black hole relation, what I propose is that the body memory of trauma occupies a liminal realm, both revealing and concealing itself simultaneously.

(RE)CLAIMING EXPERIENCE

We have been introduced to a world of "space sickness." It is a world in which space and time are manipulated through the influence of a past event. Our task is to shift this dynamic from cosmic to corporeal space, thus situating the event horizon between our two principal themes, memory and place. To do so, we need to revive the broader context in which the event horizon and space sickness arise.

So far, our treatment of memory and place has treated these two themes as phenomenal appearances in the world. In each of our earlier chapters, the memory of place was in some sense given to consciousness, however ambiguous that act was. In those chapters, memory and place persist through their ambiguities by becoming visible in space and time. With traces deposited in the life-world, memory's call to return us to place was thus fundamentally possible. As we turn to the memory of trauma, the givenness of the past will defy such possibilities. The reason for this is that the phenomenology of traumatic memory withdraws from appearances, binding itself to an event, which, according to Cathy Caruth, "is not assimilated or experienced fully at the time, but only belatedly, in its repeated *possession* of the one who experiences it" (quoted in N. Levi and Rothburg 2003, 193; italics in original). We will stay with Caruth's understanding of trauma, giving particular attention to the temporality of what she terms is an "unclaimed experience" (Caruth 1996, 10–24). In particular, I will consider how givenness and recognition work together in the appearance of the past, an appearance that fundamentally unsettles phenomenology.

For Caruth, what is fundamentally peculiar to trauma is its posttemporal structure. Already this structure is evident in Freud's account of unexpected accidents, such as those of a train collision, whereby the victim is said to register the event only as a "series of grave physical and motor symptoms" a considerable time after the event (quoted in Caruth 1996, 16). This belated recognition of the traumatic event raises the question of whether trauma is an event experienced as it occurs or an experience that is grasped only in its nonoccurrence. For Caruth, "the fact of latency, would thus seem to consist, not in the forgetting of a reality that can hence never be fully known, but in an inherent latency within the experience itself. . . . It is fully evident only in connection with another place, and in another time" (17).

The temporal structure of trauma is singular: Through it, the symptomatic reappearance of the past is possible only in a deferred interval between past and present. In this way, latency acts as a defensive shield, protecting the subject from the traumatic event as it is experienced. But as Caruth argues, "Trauma is not simply an effect of destruction but also, fundamentally, an enigma of survival" (1996, 58). The reason being, the subject that survives trauma does so less through the fortitude of subjectivity and more as the uncanny aftereffect of an event, which in experiential terms, cannot be said to have truly occurred. Structurally speaking, therefore, the deferral of trauma's violence upon the subject establishes a radical split in time, with each side prey to a different subjectivity. Indeed, the traumatic past we find outlined in Caruth's study is a past that encroaches upon the present, as though the persistence of the present were nothing more than a reverberation of that past catching up with its history. In turn, this timescale creates a peculiar relationship between distance and inaccessibility: With trauma, memory belongs to the present precisely through being incommensurable with the past.

There is thus something truly abject about trauma, given that like abjection, it "lies there, quite close, but it cannot be assimilated" (Kristeva 1984, 1). The conflation between inaccessibility and intimacy is notable. For both Kristeva and Caruth, this deferred intimacy does not immunize the subject to trauma, but rather surrounds the self in a relationship of negativity. In the abjection of trauma, what we see is a self defined by its relationship to passivity. No longer acting on the past in order to shape it, it is the traumatic past that acts upon the self. Indeed, Kristeva's characterization of abjection as "neither subject nor object" (1) touches on the epistemological impasse central to the memory of trauma: The memory is not only "ungiven" in its appearance, but also at odds with the self, implying for Kristeva that abjection is "opposed to the I" (1).

The epistemic threshold created by trauma places the notion of experience in an uneasy relation with phenomenology. Central to this disquiet is the theme of recognition. While everyday memory presupposes a previous experience with the object of memory, for the memory of trauma, such an object has yet to be registered by consciousness, so bringing us into a territory of experience outside of time. Not only this, but our experience of remembering as a whole tends to assume a directional familiarity, in which intentionality stretches itself toward a pregiven region, as Casey puts it in his analysis of recognition: "This movement of increasing specificity is the work of recognition. At the same time, a distinct sense of 'nearing' accompanies availability and enhances it" (2000b, 123). Emblematic of everyday memory is thus a position of trust and confidence. In Casey's account, this power is underscored by what he terms "suffusion," a bringing together of distinct objects of memory, such that they in turn mix "to the point of indistinguishability" (126). The idea of suffusion demonstrates a faith in the structure of remembering, able to counter what Casey will term "dim and dawning recognition" (130–32).

Indeed, even in the face of a delayed emergence of mnemonic clarity, the momentary suspension of temporal merging resolves itself through the givenness of a recognized object. In this way, recognition joins force with resemblance, with each aspect establishing a criteria for the work of recognition to proceed. In short, to recognize something means recognizing it *as* the thing we anticipate it will be.

If I were to remember the experience of being lost in a forest, then the stability of that memory would depend upon an already-formed idea of what being lost in a forest is like. This circularity between resemblance and recognition sets in place the temporal unity of the past. The memory of the forest beckons me through its already being incorporated into my remembering worldview. No wonder, then, that Ricoeur is led to characterize recognition as nothing less than a "small miracle [which] coat[s] with presence the otherness of that which is over and gone. In this, memory is re-presentation, in the twofold sense of re-: turning back, anew" (2004, 39). In this way, recognizing myself as part of an already lived experience, I "claim" that experience as my own. The ownership attached to memory attests to the hold the past has upon us; recognizing ourselves within and as part of an experience, that same experience becomes a component of personal identity, securing the coherence of the self in time. Thus, the claiming of experience emerges as a *re*-clamation of originary experience, now rendered temporally and spatially present. Such an inclusion is possible only if past experience retains a porous accessibility, in spite of its temporal recession.

Applying this structure to the memory of trauma, the result is that we can no longer speak of duration in a finite sense, as belonging to "this" or "that" particular time. Nor, indeed, are we able to speak of the traumatic experience as resembling a preformed image. If a language of resemblance is applicable, then it would have to rely on evidence constructed *after* the traumatic event, thus assembled from an external history outside the subject. True to its etymological origins, trauma is thus emblematic of *the wound of experience*. The phrase "wound of experience" is a challenge to phenomenology's onus on the life-world as an experiential horizon of meaning. Trauma intervenes in this horizon, if not destroying the life-world, then in the least diminishing it to a threadbare existence. Pulverized in this life-world is that which is taken for granted in our everyday experience of things: motility, speech, and, above all, a broad ownership over one's experience. In the trauma of selfhood, the traumatic event exceeds its end, producing a crisis mediated through the subject's (dis)continuous survival. For Caruth, the result is an "impossible history," whereby the traumatized subjects "become themselves the symptom of a history that they cannot entirely possess" (quoted in N. Levi and Rothburg 2003, 194). Symptomatic because the identity of the subject carries with it the aftereffects of the event as part of its reconstituted identity. For this reason, the reemergence of the "I" is fundamentally under question where that identity of the subject is traumatized. It is the question of where the "I" is during trauma that we must now pursue.

THE SKIN OF MEMORY

Through Caruth, we have considered the notion of an experience that "is not assimilated or experienced fully at the time, but only belatedly" (quoted in N. Levi and Rothburg 2003, 193). Far from being consigned to the black hole of total inaccessibility, however, an unnameable thing is created through the experience of trauma before manifesting itself symptomatically. Temporally, the memory of trauma subverts our preconscious experience of time by dismantling the continuity of lived duration and replacing it with a constellation of irregular blocks of experience. As we proceed to focus more narrowly on the subjectivity of traumatic memory, we shall be required to consider how an event can materialize itself precisely through being absent. Of course, absence in itself is not problematic for phenomenology. We have, for instance, already seen how the structure of intentionality is guided at all times by a teleology of appearances, in which lack and absence are themselves modes of presentation. With the memory of trauma, a particular mode of absence takes the stage that deviates from phenomenology's receptivity to absent phenomena. Central to trauma's absence is its *unpresentability* to consciousness. Trauma is the missing of experience, the wound that prohibits the work of restoration. Only in its indirection and symptomatic appearance is the memory of trauma "given" to consciousness. But just how trauma is "given" is a complicated affair. Thus, by turning to Jean-Luc Marion's presentation of phenomena that "can be described by their radical irreducibility to any givenness" (2002, 53) I will approach the question of trauma's unclaimed structure from the perspective of what *fails* to be given to consciousness.

How can we say that trauma "fails" to give itself to consciousness? Caruth offers us a clue as she writes: "The shock of the mind's relation to the threat of death is thus not the direct experience of the threat, but precisely the *missing* of this experience, the fact that, not being experienced *in time*, it has not yet been fully known" (1996, 62; italics in original). Through bringing the "missing" of experience into the realm of phenomenology, we situate ourselves directly on the border of appearances, an appearance that is marked by the quality of an experience, in which the subject is now alienated precisely by living through it. This is clear if we consider that throughout the literature on trauma and memory, trauma is presented as a paradox, an event that occurs indirectly. What this means is that the "traumatized subject," to borrow a phrase from Rudolf Bernet (2000), is radically incompatible with its previous incarnation. As Bernet puts it: "The subject which resurfaces after being plunged into the ordeal of a nonrepresentable says at most: 'Here I am, in spite of myself'" (99). The gesture of concealment and self-presencing carries with it a retroactive emergence of the past, allowing "a primitive shock to become present for the subject when it is already long past" (102).

Nowhere is this primitive shock clearer than in the words of Holocaust survivor Charlotte Delbo:

> I have the feeling that the "self" who was in the camp isn't me, isn't the person who is here, opposite you. No, it's too unbelievable. And everything that happened to this other "self," the one from Auschwitz, doesn't touch me now, *me*, doesn't concern me, so distinct are deep memory and common memory. (quoted in Langer 1991, 5; italics in original)

There are at least two salient points to note about this passage. First, Delbo's dualistic account of selfhood establishes a peculiar relationship to the past.

Lacking the means to find "closure" on the past, Auschwitz the event continues to harbor a coexistence with Delbo in the present. This persistence is possible, given that the breakage in Delbo's subjectivity is defined by an absent presence fixed in time, as she writes: "Auschwitz is there, fixed and unchangeable, but wrapped in the impervious skin of memory that segregates itself from the present 'me'" (Langer 1991, 5).

Second, Delbo's distinction between deep and common memory sets in place two distinct ways of receiving the past. On the one hand, "common memory" provides a restorative role to the self in the present, gesturing toward a "detached portrait" of the past. The advantage of this model is that memory is acknowledged and yet retains a sufficient distance so as not to break the continuity of the present self. The "skin" of memory, to use a phrase that Delbo comes back to time and again, remains unaffected by the felt depth of remembering: "In Auschwitz I took leave of my skin" (Langer 1995, 77). This domestication of the past is possible due to the protective skin that enables the self to remain united in the face of the past. The body, as it is lived and experienced, becomes a different way of receiving the past. In its place, a substitute body is established, its function to "consolidate" the past into a manageable whole. "The skin enfolding the memory of Auschwitz," so Delbo writes, "is tough" (78). Yet this skin that renews itself, casting off its own past, is not immune to the past it seeks to bury. As Delbo asks herself: "How does one rid oneself of something buried far within: memory and the skin of memory[?]" (77). Over time, reality intrudes, and "deep memory" creeps in. Deep memory is the memory that circumvents the distance of a nonsensory engagement with the traumatic past. Instead, the depth of deep memory is the depth of its felt experience: "Auschwitz is so deeply etched in my memory that I cannot forget one moment of it" (78). Deep memory's relationship to common memory, therefore, is one of profound entwinement; it "suspects and depends on common memory, knowing what common memory cannot know but tries nonetheless to express" (Langer 1991, 6).

This twofold distinction, thus, carries with it varying levels of Delbo's corporeal and experiential immersion in Auschwitz. If the "underlying memory sensations remain intact" within Delbo's body, then that layer of experience is nonetheless contrary to the stability of selfhood (Langer 1995, 78). The result of this necessary repression of experience is the doubling of selfhood: "To return from [Auschwitz] was so improbable that it seems to me I was never there at all" (78). Only, Delbo *has* returned from that place, and if her experience of identity has undergone radical transformation, then her body nonetheless persists spatially and temporally. To avoid being like those who "survive as ghosts," Delbo's skin of memory thus allows her to feel "that the one who was in the camp is not me, is not the person who is here, facing you" (78).

This bind between the fragmentation of time and of the self frames the question of what is symptomatically given to consciousness as an issue central to a phenomenology of trauma, as Bernet puts it efficiently: "How can a subject apprehend the appearance of something totally inconceivable that, however, concerns it irremediably?" (2000, 104). In response to this question of the phenomenology of symptoms of trauma, let me turn to Jean-Luc Marion's recent *Being Given*.

My reason for bringing Marion into this debate between trauma and phenomenology is to question how it is possible for "nothing" to be given as a "something" without involving an act of conversion. By presenting us with a case for how nothingness and death are given as an appearance, Marion is helpful in directing this debate. Applying this analysis to the case of traumatic symptoms will lead us to a closer consideration of the negative space between the "deep memory" of the body and the "common memory" of cognition.

Here we can join Marion in §5 of *Being Given*. At this juncture, Marion begins to question if a phenomenology of "even nothing" is possible (2002, 53). What concerns me in this discussion is Marion's attempt to reconcile "the universality of givenness" with the "quasi phenomena" that appear to disrupt the "privileges of givenness" (53). Marion's strategy for treating "even nothing" is to argue that the privilege of givenness derives from an intrinsic source, which gives itself "without limits of presupposition because it gives (itself)—it alone—without conditions" (53). In other words, what Marion wants to bring to the relation between givenness and nothingness is the prima facie impossibility of there being a lacuna in phenomenality that is not in the first place taken as a "mode of a *givenness*," as he puts it tersely: "Nothing arises that is not given" (53–54; italics in original).

We can pursue this claim in one of two ways. First, we could follow Marion in taking the possibility of attending to nothingness as being inextricably bound with the privileging of givenness. The strength of this claim is that it appears to "enclose" even the most fragmented mode of givenness as remaining within the space of experience. What this entails is that the nonmeaning of an appearance that fails to give itself in positive terms nonetheless relies on being given in the first instance, albeit as holding a "deferred" meaning (Marion 2002, 55). Marion's thought is to isolate intuition from givenness, allowing ambiguous phenomenon to retain an unconditional presence within an experiential sphere, such that he regards the term "nongivenness" as being entirely legitimate (55). It is the tacit relation between presence and negation that leads me to the second trajectory.

Second, we could accuse Marion of conferring a presence upon nothingness, so reducing "denegation" to a mode of visibility. My concern here is not so much the logical solutions surrounding the relation between something and nothing, but with the presentation of a nonpositive phenomenon as a subcategory of that phenomenon. Indeed, Marion's depiction of "even nothing" as being "characterized by its deficiency of content" would appear to loosen the distinction between what gives itself as a presence and what gives itself through its absence, since the term "deficiency" is always with reference to what the object is deficient *from*. That is, by ascribing a presence to nothing, a danger emerges of conflating "quasi" phenomena with "common" phenomena. For Marion, the result of this is that we are in "the very least [able] to discuss" non-givenness in terms of what is given (2002, 55). The "very least" is perhaps telling, as it implicates the role of representation in givenness.

Equally problematic, Marion refers to a "satisfactory enough" situation, whereby givenness merely "approximates" nongivenness (2002, 56). Marion's positive reference to Heidegger's employment of "the Nothing" as a mode of anxious being attests to the metaphysical experience enabling "the Nothing" to be "embraced" by the self (Heidegger 1977, 97–105; Marion 2002, 56–57). This tendency toward reconciling nothingness with the centrality of the self is contentious, inasmuch as the question of embodied identity appears to have receded into the background. While I am in agreement with Marion and Heidegger regarding the structural positivity of the nothing, what is missing in this account is a description of the relation between the bodily self, temporality, and a less common mode of givenness. Rather, what we have surveyed in Marion is a structural relation that takes nongivenness as an isolated instance.

Applied to the case of trauma, this oversight is especially troubling. If we understand trauma as involving an interplay between the wounded subject and the subject that remains in sight of that wounding, then the distance between those identities would seem to involve something *other* than the bare persistence of the subject in time. How else is the transition from the pre-traumatic subject to the post-traumatic subject possible if not for a common agency binding them?

As we have seen in the words and writings of Delbo and Caruth, the agency binding disparate and conflicting identities is manifested only in a symptomatic and belated way; that is, through self-consciousness of dreams and nightmares. But what is notable about this mode of self-consciousness is that it derives less from abstract reflection and more from the body's perception of the past. If the mind can embalm itself with a wall of protection, then the body, in its pregiven experience of the world, remains far more vulnerable. The body, after all, never leaves us, however much we take leave of our bodies. What is missing in trauma is thus a lacuna that takes place in consciousness. All along, the body remains in place, experiencing what the "common memory" of survival cannot confront.

Through the body, therefore, the phenomenology of traumatic memory gives itself as an instantiation of an event "beyond" the symptom. Beyond the event, and yet simultaneously *of* the event. For what is disclosed in Delbo's experience of traumatic memory is the importance of the body as an expressive organ of the inaccessible past. Conversely, what is lacking in Marion's account of ambiguous phenomenon is the way in which the body speaks on behalf of events that we ourselves are not privy to, except indirectly. The result of this indirection is the existence of two simultaneous objects, the first giving itself as a symptom received through the body, the second giving itself as a cognitive awareness of this bodily absorption. Thus, by appropriating the traumatized body as a vehicle of expression for the fragmented past, we gain sight of the manner in which deep memory and common memory dialectically arrange the spatiotemporal structure of trauma. It is to this end that we now turn.

THE PHANTOM ZONE

Thinking through Marion, we have seen an account of intentionality that privileges what it is for something to give itself in its immediacy. In turn, even nothingness became elevated in this action. But what is missing in this account is the role the body plays in mediating phenomena, especially where the phenomena in question is ambiguous in form and content. As indicated, to combat this lacuna in Marion's work, we shall proceed with the aim of employing Charlotte Delbo's account of traumatic memory as the means of understanding how the body indirectly expresses phenomena that is not immediately accessible to self-consciousness.

In order to make this shift from Marion back to Delbo, I want to turn to Levinas. Especially useful is Levinas's account of death as it figures in *Time and the Other* (2005). For what emerges in this account is a dynamic structurally parallel to that of traumatic memory. In Levinas (69), the relationship between the subject and death is one of the impossibility of nothingness. The result of this is a remote void forged in the midst of lived time, thus relying on a fissure in experience that is repeated in the structure of trauma. The association between death and trauma refers to more than the neutralization of subjectivity: It encompasses an event that is both inaccessible and immanent simultaneously. As such, what I intend to elicit from this correspondence is a constructive rejoinder to Marion's privileging of givenness.

To begin with, let us approach Levinas's account of death by way of its inaccessibility and foreignness:

> The unknown of death, which is not given straight off as nothingness but is correlative to an experience of the impossibility of nothingness, signifies not that death is a region from which no one has returned and consequently remains unknown as a matter of fact; the unknown of death signifies that the very relationship with death cannot take place in the light, that the subject is in relationship with what does not come from itself. We could say it is in relationship with mystery. (2005, 69–70)

Levinas's insistence on the "impossibility of nothingness" leads to a relationship of passivity on behalf of the subject. In contrast to Marion and Heidegger, who understand nothingness as an opportunity for the subject, Levinas wants to position nothingness as fundamentally conflicting with the experience of the self. In turn, this establishes a "relationship with mystery," whereupon death gains a presence only through a preemptive desire to assimilate its mystery to the experience of the self, as he writes: "The object that I encounter is understood and, on the whole, constructed by me, even though death announces an event over which the subject is not master, an event in relation to which the subject is no longer a subject" (2005, 70).

Seen in this context, the Heideggerian account of death as a transformation of the self to discover a "supreme virility" within itself thus falls short (Levinas 2005, 70). Against this glorification of death as freedom, Levinas maintains an imperative to retain the impossibility of nothingness: "Absolutely unknowable means foreign to all light, rendering every assumption of possibility impossible, but where we ourselves are seized" (71). In pursuing foreignness to its limits, Levinas confers a futurity on death that renders it ungraspable, other, and yet immanently present. The peculiarity of death is such that the recognition of the event is estranged from the subject who undergoes it. Here, Levinas poses a critical question: "How can the event that cannot be grasped still happen to me?" (77). The failure to resolve this question thus creates an excess in experience emblematic of trauma. Indeed, it is precisely this disjunction between ungraspability and presence that aligns death with trauma. In both cases, trauma and death give themselves to consciousness through their fundamental ungraspability and anonymity.

The reference to anonymity is central to the tension between ungraspability and presence. For what is common to both Delbo and Levinas is the expression of ungraspable phenomena in its anonymity. We recall Delbo saying: "To return from [Auschwitz] was so improbable that it seems to me I was never there at all" (Langer 1995, 78). This omission of the "I" sets in place another agent of experience: the prepersonal human body, which, in its distance from the self-conscious "I," proceeds to absorb the trauma of Auschwitz to some extent independently from that of the subject, Charlotte Delbo.

In Levinas, the threat of anonymity reappears in the case of death. In an important passage, he asks: "How can the existent exist as mortal and nonetheless persevere in its 'personality,' preserve its conquest over the anonymous 'there is' [il y a], its subject's mastery, the conquest of its subjectivity?" (2005, 77). At least two things are especially important in this passage. First, Levinas places "personality" (or personal identity) in opposition to mortality. Second, the preservation of the personality takes place against the backdrop of what Levinas terms the "there is." In what follows, I want to consider the importance of Levinas's idea of the il y a for our understanding of embodiment and trauma.

Levinas's mention of an "anonymous 'there is'" accounts for the "idea of an existing that occurs without us, without a subject, an existing without existents" (2005, 45–46). The language of existents and existing plays upon Heidegger's celebrated division between being and Being, which, in turn, hinges upon the distinction between the ontic and the ontological. In each case, Levinas's motivation for introducing the il y a is thus to counter Heidegger's claim that there can be no "existing without existents" (45). For Levinas, as for us, this omission merits consideration.

His strategy for describing the appearance of the *il y a* is to invite the reader "to imagine all things, beings and persons, returning to nothingness" (Levinas 2005, 46). "What remains after this imaginary destruction of everything," he writes, "is not something, but the fact that there is [*il y a*]" (46). Not only does the *il y a* survive the removal of existents, but it does so in an anonymous manner: "There is neither anyone nor anything that takes this existence upon itself. It is impersonal like 'it is raining' or 'it is hot'" (47). Arising from this anonymity is a presence marked by a "plenitude of the void, or the murmur of silence" (46). The Levinasian *il y a* is thus dynamic to its core. By relying on a spatiotemporal arc beyond "the fact that there is," the *il y a* at once points to a past and a future, which is coexistent with the silence, absence, and anonymity. The plenitude of anonymity is possible precisely because "being" (*un être*) is displaced from its immediacy, so establishing an "atmospheric density" held apart from a prior mode of experiential awareness.

To illustrate this exchange of phenomenality, Levinas calls upon insomnia as privileged metaphysical instant. Concerning the origin of the *il y a*, in *Ethics and Infinity* Levinas states the following:

> My reflection on this subject starts with childhood memories. One sleeps alone, the adults continue life; the child feels the silence of his bedroom as "rumbling." . . . It is something resembling what one hears when one puts an empty shell close to the ear, as if the emptiness were full, as if the silence were a noise. . . . In the absolute emptiness that one can imagine before creation—there is. (1985, 48)

Let us embody this metaphysics of insomnia. Notably, the continuity of the adult (Bachelard would no doubt speak of the adult as being *downstairs*) marks an event of discontinuity for the child. Is the life of the adult suspended in the child's bedroom? Far from it. It is because of the persistence of a life outside the room that the child's experience of silence proceeds to "rumble" from within the bedroom. Only, the sense of rumbling fails to mark an overlapping of presence between the child and the adult, but rather punctures what remains in the child's bedroom as occupying a presence; namely, *silence*.

How is this silence experienced? Levinas asks that we imagine or remember putting a shell to our ears, the result of which is the formation of an acute presence of a silence that fundamentally vibrates in its singularity. The silence manifest in both the shell and the room of the child is both *after* and *before* appearances. Before and after appearances, Levinas's primordial silence is thus at the ground of an existing without existents. For the child exposed to this brute facticity, the envelopment of silence comes as an incursion, a rupture in which the otherness of the world effectively slides beneath the door. As such, the dialectic of inside and outside that the door delineates is thus firmly entrenched with the felt experience of silence. Only as a contained absence, offset by the broader world, is the invisible anonymity of Levinas's metaphysics of silence possible.

As the anonymity of silence transpires, so Levinas's account of the insomniac body becomes marked by a seizure of something already immanent in the world, which, in turn, overlaps and assimilates the subject within its grasp. Here, the horror of insomnia can be located. For what occurs in the rumbling of the child's bedroom is an invasive silence, a silence that does not end with its own innocuous invisibility, but proceeds to enrapture the body of the insomniac in its own peculiar spatiotemporality. Thus Levinas can write: "Insomnia is constituted by the consciousness that it will never finish—that is, that there is no longer any way of withdrawing from the vigilance to which one is held" (2005, 48). The insomniac body becomes defined by an agency other than its own, transforming that body into something opposed to the "I." With no beginning and no end to speak of, the subjectivity of the insomniac loses ontological security; "nothing moves away or shades off" (48). Instead, impersonal existence and the "absence of all self" take the place of subjectivity (49).

The eventual result of this murmuring silence is a metaphysical impasse with no resolution: "The impossibility of escaping wakefulness," so he writes, "is something 'objective.' . . . This impersonality absorbs my consciousness; consciousness is depersonalized. I do not stay awake: 'it' stays awake" (Levinas 1985, 49). The notion of an "it" that is of the body and simultaneously other than the body returns us to the trauma of Charlotte Delbo.

In both Levinas and Delbo, we are faced with a depersonalized consciousness, apprehended by the anonymity of an agency beyond time and place. At the same time, both Levinas and Delbo present us with an indirect access to this anonymous terrain. For Levinas, the transcendental invisibility of the *il y a* articulates itself by proxy in the body of the insomniac. Doing so, the body becomes other than itself, a dissolution of identity, from which a new "field of force" begins (Levinas 2005, 46). More than this, during insomnia, there is no escape and no "refugee in unconsciousness" (49). Rather, the body is accented in its brute materiality, producing a "vigilance without possible re-course to sleep" (49). And this vigilance over the anonymous body by the wayward subject is where Levinas ends and Delbo begins.

The affinity between Levinas and Delbo becomes clear once we situate the Levinasian *il y a* within Delbo's distinction between common memory and deep memory. As we recall, for Delbo, common memory refers to the self-reflective rationalization of the past, as she puts it, "from intellectual memory, the memory connected with thinking processes" (Langer 1995, 79). It is a mode of memory that is singular in its nonsensuousness. Divested of all but the most cursory sensory properties—"Thirst has turned back into a word for commonplace use"—Delbo's (79) common memory of Auschwitz pushes the body to the background. Yet Delbo does not take leave of her body, recognizing that she "live[s] next to [Auschwitz]. Auschwitz is there, unalterable, precise, but enveloped in the skin of memory, an impermeable skin that isolates it from my present self" (78). In turn, deep memory consti-tutes a different mode of access to the past. "It is," she writes, "the memory of the senses" (79). Because of this felt depth, the affective experience of trauma is of a different order, now matched by a visceral horror equal to the original unclaimed experience. During nightmares, the horror of deep memory is given a space to breathe: "The suffering I feel is so unbearable, so identical to the pain endured there, that I feel it physically, I feel it again through my whole body, which becomes a mass of suffering, and I feel death seizing me, I feel myself die" (78–79).

The dialectic of remembering that emerges in Delbo's memory of Aus-chwitz fulfills the metaphysical abstraction of the Levinasian *il y a* through the establishment of a body, in whose flesh the anonymous "atmospheric density" of a force simultaneously *of* but also *other* than the self coincides (Levinas 2005, 46). Delbo's body, to put it in Levinasian terms, is unable to sleep even when asleep. The reason being that for Delbo, the body assumes a consciousness of its own, and one that "will never finish" (48) so long as there remains an experience unclaimed. This "vigilance without end" allows no escape from the memory that forces a split in the identity of Charlotte Delbo. As she puts it: "I live within a twofold being" (Langer 2005, 78).

But far from positing a radically dualistic account of mind and body, Del-bo's doubling of experience instead points to the incorporation of memory's rupturing within herself as a whole. Mind and body remain bound, and in-deed are amplified in their intimacy with the memory of trauma. Only now, the body speaks of an experience that is not only inaccessible to rational reflection but also opposed to that act of reflection. For Delbo, the history of Auschwitz is thus told in the history of the body. Delbo's deep memory is necessarily hidden within the particular landscape of the body. In speaking of the experience of thirst within Auschwitz, for example, Delbo is placed in an absolute environment, implicating the totality of the self: "If I dream of the thirst that I felt in Birkenau, I see myself as I was then, haggard, bereft of reason, tottering. I feel again physically that *real* thirst, and it's an agonizing nightmare" (quoted in Langer 1991, 8; italics in original). The incursion of a reality that has its roots in the flesh of the body establishes a doubling of history, with each prying for sovereignty over the other.

At the heart of this corporeal drama is a disquiet, in which the body ceases to be an orientating agent in the world and instead becomes a site of estrangement and horror. In such a case, the body gains a material reality of its own, quite outside of the reality experienced subjectively. The flesh gains independence, its desire for unity at odds with the self-consciousness of reason. Against the phenomenological insistence that the body and the mind are but one organ of perception, for the traumatized body, the experience is of a radical bifurcation in the self. Indeed, even within a phenomenological context, there is an admission that in certain bodily experiences, dualism becomes a truth. Merleau-Ponty states: "Our body does not always have meaning, and our thoughts . . . do not always find in it the plenitude of their vital expression. In the cases of disintegration, the soul and the body are apparently distinct; and this is the truth of dualism" (1965, 209).

Merleau-Ponty's admission is telling. With it, a tacit duality is acknowledged despite the fact that phenomenologically speaking, there is nothing metaphysically true about this dualism. Beyond metaphysics, however, the phenomenal appearance of the body during disintegration can no longer be said to be strictly "mine." Instead, a process of dissociation takes place, such that the normal functioning of the body comes to a standstill. Coming to a standstill, suddenly the body's materiality becomes a foreground issue for the traumatized subject: "I feel it physically," writes Delbo of the power of nightmares, "I feel it through my whole body which becomes a mass of suffering" (Langer 1995, 78–79. The visceral reality of the body pushes Delbo the subject elsewhere. In her place, a necessary dissociation ensues, necessary because in order for Delbo to "survive" the event of trauma, her body must be left behind. All the more horrifying, therefore, that the nightmare of trauma should return Delbo not simply to the facticity of the event, but to its bodily reality, a reality that was hitherto "forgotten."

It is no surprise that the shock surrounding the secret history of the body features as a central aspect in the so-called "body horror" genre of film, of which David Cronenberg is the obvious and most significant exponent. Indeed, speaking about the role of "treacherous flesh" in his films, Cronenberg states the following:

> It really is like colonialism. The colonies suddenly decide that they can and should exist with their own personality and should detach from the control of the mother country. At first the colony is perceived as being treacherous. It's a betrayal. Ultimately, it can be seen as the separation of a partner that could be very valuable as an equal rather than as something you dominate. (1997, 80)

Cronenberg's eloquent account of "flesh undergoing revolution" (80) captures the sense of the body opening itself as the space in which an alternative history, with its own series of customs, formations, and growth patterns, develops. It is impossible to escape the question: If the body can decide its own fate, then can I really be said to *be my body*, or is it that I simply have a body but one that I do not possess? These troubled thoughts stand in contrast to our everyday experiences of the body. Ordinarily, bodily movement, both spatial and temporal, is a pregiven layer of experience enabling us to "hold sway" in the world. Here, the body sinks into the background, assuming an inconspicuous role in the stability of the material world. Yet all along, the body is at work behind the scenes, forging layer upon layer of its own veiled history. This is the work of colonization at play in Cronenberg's body horror. Yet Cronenberg is not a Cartesian dualist, and the celebrated notion of "body horror" that is often associated with his films depends on the idea that self is an embodied subject, now experiencing disturbance as corporeality dissents from that unity.

Indeed, what is central to the genre of body horror is the sense of the body's dissolving boundaries between inside and outside, self and other, and the living and the dead (Trigg 2011). In each of these dyads, Cronenberg has crafted an account of identity torn asunder by the motif of "flesh undergoing revolution." Ultimately, Cronenberg hints at a unity in this revolution, evidenced by the constitution of a new relationship with the flesh and affirmed in his celebrated dictum "Long Live the New Flesh!" In the case of the body's memory of trauma, such a recovery is neither treacherous nor unified, but simply divested of the specificity with which common memory can establish a thematic link with deep memory.

In this way, the body of traumatic memory occupies a destabilizing relationship not only to cognitive memory but also to the cognitive perception of the body as held through the prism of self-consciousness. This is the strangeness of the traumatized body: It carries with it its own shadowy other beneath the surface. In effect, two bodies occupy the same space at the same time, disarming a paradox that Freud, above all else, was acutely aware of in his study of the mental preservation of the past as an analogue of "juxtaposition[s] in space" (2001, 70–71). The "new flesh," to appropriate Cronenberg's term, which emerges from this collision, prevents common memory from constructing a self-contained narrative. Rather, the body of deep memory, as it were, undercuts such containment through establishing its own network of interrelated experiences of the past, wholly in conflict with the narrative laid out through the cognitive reconstitution of the past.

The critical question concerns how these two bodies are brought together as a singular entity in the present. How, in other words, does the personal ego of the present catch sight of the anonymous "there is" of the past? The answer, I would suggest, is in the privileged moment whereby common memory becomes aware of the zone of deep memory (emblematically having just awoken from the nightmare), and thus carries out the attempt to, in Delbo's words, repair the "skin of memory" through "refilling" it once more with a common memory. Through this divisive episode, the twilight of deep memory surfaces to the realm of air and light, invoking a phenomenology of shock, as though the anonymity of deep memory had outlasted its presence and was now caught in the cold lens of reason. What is privileged about this emergence is the appearance of the secreted wounds of traumatized flesh undergoing restoration in the present.

Such a relationship between deep memory, conditioned by the trauma of the body, and the experience of awakening from the dream returns us to the realm of the Levinasian *il y a*. Here, the "murmur of silence" that Levinas identifies discovers a parallel structure in the case of the relation between deep memory and common memory. Within the motion of common memory's repairing the "skin of memory," this murmur becomes *felt* as a reality. Being felt as a reality means becoming estranged by the immanence of the body. "It takes days," we recall Delbo saying, "for everything to get shoved back inside memory, and for the skin of memory to mend again" (quoted in Langer 1995, 79). The adjustment experienced in those ensuing days can be thought of as a sustained glance toward the *il y a*. As an experience unable to be shared with others—less even with herself—Delbo's suspension in this spatiotemporal realm represents the horizon of ultimate meaning, in which anything more than the "plenitude of the void" is banished (Levinas 2005, 46).

In bodily terms, the pressurized atmosphere experienced upon waking from the dream captures the moment in which the anonymity of the body's deep memory inadvertently falls in sight of the strictly personal domain of common memory. It is a discovery in which opposing modes of memory and flesh feed upon one another, creating a shock that accounts for the horror Delbo experiences, an experience that is swept into the opening of a history that has otherwise remained hidden.

Indeed, this notion of the self as (re)animated by an anonymous and independent force outside of rational memory brings Levinas, Delbo, and Cronenberg into the same scene. "I do not stay awake: 'it' stays awake," thus we recall Levinas stating (1985, 49). The "it" remains after the "I" has partially dispersed, and the partial dispersion is central in retaining the anonymity of the *il y a* alongside the body's deep memory in this active dynamic. Thanks to this partiality, enough of common memory remains in place to conceptualize the phenomenality of an anonymous *phantom zone* against a wider and more familiar backdrop.

The term "phantom zone" is used to thematize how the memory of trauma is received through the body. What I have suggested is that by applying the absorbing gesture of the *il y a* to the memory of trauma, what follows is a tension between what is registered in time cognitively and what is held in place corporeally. The split between place and time coexists alongside embodied experience breaking away from rational experience, such that the body creates its own history independently from that of the conscious intentionality. When the body's history comes into contact with the rational appropriation of memory, such as waking up after a nightmare, then the production of a fundamentally mutated form of history, comprising the space between embodiment and cognition, fully emerges. At the heart of the phantom zone is the moment whereupon the rational self catches sight of the body being reconstituted for a different history. Here, the word *phantom* marks the uncertainty of selfhood in this malformed history. Having been "absorbed" by the body, what remains is the anonymity of the "I." Neither fully at ease with its own cognition nor yet estranged through and from the materiality of its body, the "I" that withstands this mutation floats adrift, fundamentally traumatized, not only by the event of trauma itself, but by divergent variants of memory that emerge from that event.

Here, the uncanny resurfaces at the center of the phantom zone: "It took a few years for the new skin to fully form, to consolidate. . . . I'm the same too, apparently" (quoted in Langer 1995, 77). Delbo's self-doubt captures the body as an uncanny phenomenon. Through it, the effort to "consolidate" the flesh draws our attention to a fundamental ambiguity at the heart of Delbo's body. For it is a body, in which the duality of common memory and deep memory encounters the singularity of Delbo the self-conscious subject. Within the history of her body, a trace of Delbo forever remains in place despite the continued attempt at "shedding [the] old skin" (77). Through taking leave of her skin, with its "leaden stare out of sunken eyes, the tottering gait, the frightened gestures" (77), Delbo in fact retains an involuntary complicity with the anonymity of her buried body, the isolation of her traumatized flesh encroaching upon waking life. During the phantom zone, when the subject of trauma confronts the materiality of the body's independence, the uncanny intervenes. The uncanny does so not through a complete destruction of the "I," but through establishing the conditions in which the subject recognizes him or herself as a stranger. The uncanny body thus plots a hidden history of the flesh alongside a familiar history, producing a dissociated experience of the body's traumatized facticity.

If the uncanny, traditionally conceived, marries the homely attributes of a place with the forgotten or unhomely realm of that place, then what we see in Charlotte Delbo is this dialectic transported to the body of trauma. Just as the uncanny pertains to that "species of the frightening that goes back to what was once well known and had long been familiar" (Freud 2003, 124), so Delbo lives in a body of which she has at once taken possession while simultaneously acknowledging how that body possesses her. The simultaneity of her possessed body mirrors the doubling of her temporal experience. After all, it is not that she lives "with Auschwitz," but instead lives "*next* to it. Auschwitz is there, unalterable, precise, but enveloped in the skin of memory" (Langer 1995, 78; emphasis added). The sense of living beside Auschwitz prevents Delbo from being at home in her body. For like a house that guards its secrets in the basement, it is a body, in which an entire layer of experience is resistant to all forms of exorcism. At constant threat of being invaded by her own past, thus reduced to "survive as [a] ghost," the traumatized body becomes emblematic of body horror par excellence.

This constellation of different and divergent memories occupying the same body returns us to the phenomenology of the event horizon. If we are to phrase the event horizon as an ultimate threshold, in which identity is cut in half, with the fracture marking a liminal zone inaccessible to everyday experience, then we are clearly placed within the same terrain between deep memory and common memory. The shadowy surface beneath the body of the subject of trauma creates a halo of darkness through the contours of indirect symptoms and "space sickness." This independent world comes to light only as rationality is pushed back into recession. Yet coming to light does not mean being seen. For this exchange to occur, the black hole of trauma needs to collide with the border of the event horizon: a dynamic that occurs on a bodily level when the deep memory of trauma is thrown back into the world of the living. There, we can speak of the subject who witnesses the unnameable, who catches sight of a place beyond place, and who defies the laws of physics through becoming the host of an anonymous silence known only to the deepest recesses of the traumatized body.

As for the phantom zone, it has become clear that if we are to take this term as the opening in which the "self" directly witnesses its own body being colonized by a foreign agency, then we are in the region of an atmospheric reentry, a return to a newly formed strange place. The phantom zone contains all that has returned to haunt the present, seized from beyond the threshold of experience. Into this mass of different and colliding timescales, the notion that beyond the event horizon all materiality is dispersed is proven to be wrong. Rather, the incubation of the black hole within the human body reveals itself to be vividly *alive*. Only now, the living force as witnessed in the phantom zone is shown to be anonymous, and thus a threat to human life. Delbo again: "I feel death seizing me, I feel myself die" (Langer 1991, 7).

For this reason, the psychoanalyst Nicolas Abraham is apt to describe the phantom as an "invention of the living" (1987, 287). The relationship between Delbo's concept of common memory and deep memory is mediated at all times via the former. As such, that which punctures the appearance of a rational appropriation of the past becomes a phantom only from the perspective of the living and lived-body. Given that adopting the perspective of the prepersonal body is impossible, the materialization of Delbo's deep memory within the body assumes a spectral affectivity, crystallizing the existence of the unconscious within the flesh of the body. An invention of the living (body), yet an invention that bridges a void to an already existing world, the phantom thus "works like a ventriloquist, like a stranger within the subject's own mental topography" (Abraham 1987, 290). This tension between strangeness and subjectivity is compounded insofar as the phantom does not descend from a remote elsewhere, but ruptures the present *from within* the body.

Delbo's confrontation with her past is uncanny precisely for the reason that the sense of catching one's own body as fundamentally other is at the same time recognizing that otherness is constitutive of selfhood. Abraham writes notably: "The difference between *the stranger incorporated* through suggestion and *the dead returning to haunt* does not necessarily come to the fore at first, precisely because both act as foreign bodies lodged within the subject" (1987, 290; italics in original).

We are in the company of a ghost with no place to haunt. Both the stranger and the dead serve as visceral reminders that Delbo's body memory testifies to the total dissolution of subjectivity, leaving in its place a body that has become the material witness to a phantom, the origin of which is no longer traceable to common memory or deep memory, but to the gap in between.

We are now in a position to see that the relation between corporeal space and cosmic space is less like a dynamic void consuming time and more like a disease entwined with the wounds of corporeality. As such, the black hole of trauma is not an inactive lacuna in space and time. It is not, that is, a dead space bereft of human life. Rather, it takes the form of a strange parasite surviving on the wounded remains of human embodiment.

This relationship between the materiality of the body and a foreign world discharging itself in that body has been a prevalent theme throughout the previous chapters, not least in the idea of alien flesh, where the very structure of being-in-place was shown to be constituted by manifold influences, some of which emerged as divergent to the cognitive experience of that place. In the following chapter, this difference will find its counterpart through an analysis of the materiality of trauma, and in particular the ruins that outlive the traumatic event.

. . . .

CHAPTER SIX

RUINS OF TRAUMA

But if I see before me the nervature of past life in one image, I always think that this has something to do with truth.

—W. G. Sebald, *After Nature*

In the opening scene of Claude Lanzmann's documentary film *Shoah* (1985), we follow Simon Srebnik, a former Polish prisoner, in his return to the ruins of the Chelmno extermination camp. As he approaches the site, Srebnik pauses, surveys the space, and nods. "It's hard to recognize," he remarks somberly, "but it was here. They burned people here" (Lanzmann, 1985). During this opening scene, the camera, so far fixed on Srebnik's devastated expression, cuts to a panning shot of a flat, desiccated clearing, punctuated by the rectangular spaces of what were the camp's structural foundations. "No one can describe it," Srebnik says, now walking around the site. "No one can re-create what happened here. Impossible! And no one can understand it. Even, I, here, now . . . I can't believe I'm here."

How can we approach this tension between place and trauma in a phenomenological sense? On the one hand, we are faced with a scene of recognition, in which specific details are recollected from the past and applied to the spatiality of the present. On the other hand, the same place where Srebnik stands in the present is undercut by the radical singularity of the traumatic past, such that the simple fact of *being there* fails to contribute to reality. The result of this displacement between recollection and experience is the impossibility of re-creating the felt depth of the past.

Phenomenologically, materiality, memory, and time appear to splinter in this ambiguously placed emergence of the past. Far from offering itself as a testimony to the past, Srebnik's witnessing of Chelmno brings to light a fundamentally *spectral* relation trauma occupies to place. Central to this logic of spectrality is the displacement of the body. Despite being in place, during this

opening scene of *Shoah*, Srebnik remains essentially displaced from the materiality of the location. We return to his confession: "Even, I, here, now . . . I
can't believe I'm here." Phenomenologically, this is a startling claim, which
appears to usurp the classical notion of the body as a locus of unity and
movement, evident, above all, in the work of Merleau-Ponty.

Given the temporal and spatial complexity of this experience, it is somewhat surprising to consider how little attention phenomenologists have paid
to the relation between materiality, time, and what might be termed the "spectrality of trauma," where spectrality would mean a presence that is ambiguously placed. How can we account for this oversight? Perhaps one response
is that phenomenology's relationship with place has predominantly relied on
the notion of the environment as reinforcing identity, temporal continuity,
and, more broadly, the harmony between place and memory. This reliance is
clear enough in an explicitly topophilic work such as Bachelard's (1994) *The
Poetics of Space*, where "felicitous" places dominate, but remains implicit in
Merleau-Ponty's (2006) notion of the "absolute here," is central in Husserl's
(1970) account of "kinesthetic" experience, and occupies a pivotal place in
Heidegger's (1996) presentation of the unity of "aroundness," and indeed in
the notion of "Dasein" itself. Yet in pointing out this lineage of omission, my
intention is far from wishing to dispense with phenomenology as a method.
Indeed, phrased in a constructive way, this oversight can be seen as an invitation to assert the dynamism of phenomenology. How, then, can phenomenology assist us in negotiating the tension between the experience of place
in the present and the blocked emergence of a traumatic memory rooted in
the past? It is this question with which the present chapter seeks to contend.

ABNORMAL EMBODIMENT

In the dual subjects of Srebnik and Chelmno, we gain a sense of the tension
between place and trauma. Yet even at a glance the relationship is problematized through the inclusion of the terms "place" and "subject." Are these
terms legitimate if each appears to be incompatible with the other? The frequent usage of the term "site" in relation to the memory of trauma testifies
to the tension between conflating place with trauma (Foote 2003; Huyssen
2003; Adams, Hoelscher, and Till 2005; Tumarkin 2005). But is the term
"site" employed as a methodological device simply to provide a link between
spatiality and subjectivity? For the most part, the connotation of "site" as

being leveled-out, divested of its specificity, and reduced to a non-place serves to distance the remoteness and fragmentation of trauma with the felt experience of place. Further, unlike "place," "site" suggests a location between other places, a liminal space at once incomplete and in transition (as in "grave site"). Yet to what extent the term "site" is better suited to locations of trauma is contentious and deserves attention. Indeed, without wishing to proscribe the term "site" in advance, there is clearly a sense in which the spatiality of trauma merits careful examination, such that both "place" and "site" are brought into the specific impasses traumatic memory invokes.

In order to assess whether these terms can be used legitimately, let me take up the invitation of building upon the work of phenomenology, rather than rebuking that to which it has so far failed to attend. Again, let us turn to Merleau-Ponty with the aim of charting the emergence of traumatized materiality. Thinking back to our discussion of Merleau-Ponty's notion of the "absolute here" in chapter 3, what was presented as a given was the unity of embodied experience, such that movement in the world is "dovetailed into the present," sealing the temporality of the body through a fluid succession of intertwined positions. Alongside this development of fluidity, the continuity and reliability of the body are experienced as the ground for spatial normality, where normality refers to the body in its taken-for-grantedness. The result of Merleau-Ponty's "absolute here" is the elevation of the body to a spatial and temporal locus, absorbing the world from the inside out. Speaking about "motor memory," temporality, and space, this emphasis on synthesis and unity is made clear:

> In so far as I have a body through which I act in the world, space and time are not, for me, a collection of adjacent points[,] nor are they a limitless number of relations synthesised by my consciousness, and into which it draws my body. I am not in space and time, nor do I conceive space and time; I belong to them, my body combines with them and includes them. (Merleau-Ponty 2006, 162)

By making space and time inclusive of the body, rather than either being contained in the world or structured by the transcendental ego, Merleau-Ponty establishes a synthesis, in which the body becomes a center stretching out into the world. The resultant "body image" manages to bind the self and the world through an "incarnate intentionality," an intentionality that prefigures conscious intentionality (2006, 112–15). What this means is that the centrality of the lived-body enables objective space to be positioned in a dimensional manner. I "belong" to space and time, as Merleau-Ponty says declaratively.

As we saw in chapter 3, what emerges from this scene of embodiment and spatiality is a tremendous faith in the power of place as a source of unity. Indeed, seen from the perspective of a lived duration, the above passage underscores the peculiar retention of body memory in (per)forming the experience of the present. The parenthesizing of "per" in performing marks the role of the body in enabling the formation of the self through the body's own action in the world. Thus, it is not simply the case that the body retains the past in a dormant manner. Rather, such a past becomes actualized when the body performs specific actions peculiar to that temporality, conferring a sense of spatial and temporal unity in the present.

How, then, does this status of regularity and normality slide toward what we might call *abnormal embodiment*? In response to this question, let us return to Lanzmann's (1985) *Shoah*. Two points can be made. First, against the unity of Merleau-Ponty's "absolute here," what unfolds in this scene from *Shoah* is the fundamental ambiguity of *hereness*. Permeating this scene is a paradoxical sense of radical estrangement compounded with an intense proximity between Srebnik and the location. "Even, I, here, now . . . I can't believe I'm here": With this statement, the temporality of personal identity collides with the disbelief that the same person is now witnessing the same location, right *here*, right *now*. Recall that "here" and "now" mark the basis of Merleau-Ponty's account of embodiment. Throughout, there is a sense of orientation aided by the lineage of movements stored in the "absolute awareness of 'here'" (2006, 161). Indeed, about the spatiotemporal continuity of the body, Merleau-Ponty states the following: "Just as it is necessarily 'here,' the body necessarily exists "now'" (162). Yet it is precisely because of this necessity of "here" and "now" that the appearance of Srebnik in Chelmno is essentially spectral. As an appearance without a spatiotemporal ground to support it, disbelief intervenes in this scene of return.

Within this context, the term "abnormal embodiment" gains relevance. What is suspended in this scene is the evidence of the body as the primary giver of appearances, thus subtracting the very reality of the lived-body in its spatiotemporal unity. As a cue for this concept of abnormality, it will be useful to consult Anthony Steinbock's reading of Husserl's analyses of normality and abnormality (Steinbock 1995, 132–37). Of particular interest to us, in this discussion, is Husserl's distinction between "concordance"

Figure 22: *Chelmno Death Camp, Poland. Courtesy of Thomas Herrmann.*

and "discordance" (132). In Steinbock's reading, the development of discordance is marked as a "rupture" from the concordance of the lived-body, establishing a disjunction between "the old and the new appearances [which] no longer hang together concordantly" (132). No longer hanging together concordantly means that as the line of continuity is broken, what is pushed to the foreground becomes discordant precisely through altering rather than negating normal experience. Central to this interplay is "the internal coherence of the experience" (133), which is shattered through the emergence of anomalous properties.

In corporeal terms, this dynamic marks the arrival of an ambiguous mode of being "here" and "now" occurring within the scope of the transcendental unity of the body. Treated within the context of Srebnik in Chelmno, such a mode of givenness is inhibited by the pathology of being unable to align place with time. In this way, the phenomenal scene of Srebnik entering Chelmno plays on this interplay of a previously concordant mode of normality being "paused" (to retain the Husserlian terminology) while another mode of experience dislodges and simultaneously fails to encompass that prior mode of intentionality. What is abnormal about the scene of Srebnik in Chelmno is less the destruction of unity and more the failure to produce a new concordance in the phenomenal realm. Indeed, what we witness is the impasse of a rupture that does not resolve itself either materially or temporally.

Phenomenologically, what can we say of the spatiality of Chelmno in relation to Srebnik? We recall that Merleau-Ponty speaks of "belonging" to space and time (2006, 162). This claim is made in relation to the unity of the body as it proceeds to "combine" with space and time. Thanks to the body's "motor memory," movement in space entwines with the past, establishing a spatial instant in the present that "dovetails" temporally. Placed in this context of *Shoah*, the materiality of the environment appears as basically divorced from the temporality of Srebnik as a lived subject. Srebnik's remark that "it's hard to recognize, but it was here. They burned people here," is less about visual recognition and more about the failure to synthesize space and time through the body.

Tellingly, Merleau-Ponty admits that "the synthesis of both time and space is a task that always has to be performed afresh" (2006, 162). During the scene from Lanzmann's film, we witness such a task appear to falter. The failure to align materiality with temporality does not, however, deny the reality of Chelmno as a memory, but affirms that reality through confounding the "absolute here" of the body. The return Srebnik makes is not, therefore, to bear witness to the temporal end of place, but to recognize the dynamic persistence of an event that continues in spite of the absence of its original containment; in effect, conceding to the power of place as fused with a spectral undercurrent.

In what follows, I plan to approach this tension between place and trauma through attending to the appearance of *ruins*. My use of the term "ruins" designates location of memory, where trauma took place and continues to be inextricably bound with that location in both an affective and evidential manner. Note, however, that a ruin does not have to involve a relationship with the built environment. If this appears contradictory, then consider how certain "natural" environments can become materially altered by the events that occurred there, not least fields and forests shaped by human intervention. What is central here is the identity of a location marked by the events that are constitutive of that identity. At the same time, clearly there is an intimate relation between physical remains and the building that existed prior to that stage of dissolution. It is in this sense that ruins have come to assume an aesthetic presence, inviting the viewer to fill out the broken form through the active dynamism of the imagination (Ginsberg 2004). In both cases, the term "ruins" refuses to fall neatly into either the region of place or site, encouraging at each stage of its evolution an ambiguous spatiality at odds with our understanding of domestic place (Trigg 2006a).

At stake in this evolution is the parallel development of questions of testimony and temporality. One way in which this development is rendered explicit is with the magnetism places of trauma hold for visitors, survivors, and even those complicit with propagating the traumatic event. Such magnetism is by no means self-explanatory, despite the symbolic import of mourning frequently being conferred upon traumatic places. While themes of mourning, closure, and remembrance are all clearly at stake in the relationship between the material remains of trauma and the need to witness those remains, just how this relationship is possible is harder to define.

Despite the difficulty, eliciting a description of this interaction between the physical appearance of trauma and the subject experiencing that appearance is the plan for the remainder of this chapter. I propose to achieve this in the following way: Rather than beginning with materiality itself, I will, instead, chart the emergence of traumatic space from the standpoint of the traumatized subject. In this way, I hope to emphasize the structural parallels binding embodiment, identity, and materiality. To gain an entrance into this structure, I shall return to Charlotte Delbo. Already, Delbo has lucidly captured the traumatized subject as characterized by an "unclaimed experience," the effect of which produces a double identity, at all times held apart by the deferred emergence of memory (*Nachträglichkeit*). Returning to Delbo, I will employ the theme of nightmares of trauma alongside Giorgio Agamben's (1999) account of testimony as presented in his *Remnants of Auschwitz*. The purpose of constructing this dialogue between Agamben and Delbo is to extract the testimonial attributes common to both the surviving subject and the surviving place.

MEMORIES OF NIGHTMARES

The task that falls to us is to align the structure of the traumatized subject with the traumatized place, a goal we can achieve by returning to the writings of Charlotte Delbo. Whereas I consulted Delbo in the previous chapter to draw out the bodily structure of traumatic memory, what I aim to do presently is apply this structure to the relation between testimony and place. As we have seen, for Delbo, the appearance of the nightmare is presented as a disruption of the rational appropriation of trauma, a tension we explored previously in terms of "deep" memory and "common" memory. As an unconscious presence, the nightmare of trauma embodies what reason seeks to maintain at a distance. As such, the structural importance of the nightmare within the broad scheme of traumatic memory is to reunite two selves divorced by experience. In this light, the nightmare returns Delbo to herself, producing at once an alienated and familiar self. She writes:

> Over dreams the conscious will has no power. And in those dreams I see myself, yes, my own self such as I know I was: hardly able to stand on my feet, my throat tight, my heart beating wildly, frozen to the marrow, filthy, skin and bones; the suffering I feel is so unbearable, so identical to the pain endured there, that I feel it physically, I feel it throughout my whole body which becomes a mass of suffering; and I feel death fasten on me, I feel that I am dying. (quoted in Langer 1995, 78–79)

What is occurring in this passage is a reunion of two selves, a chance encounter emblematically framed as an instant of death, and thus mediated by the memories of nightmares. The result of this action is the creation of a space between other identities, a space that opens only as the conscious and unconscious selves stand in tense proximity to each other. Central to this space is the moment of recognition in the nightmare, whereby Delbo sees herself once again. Yet the reunion is not simply a case of two selves retaining a temporal distance from each other. Rather, what we witness is an amorphous fusion of those selves, constituted by parts of Delbo that simultaneously belong and do not belong. Enclosing time, the nightmare catches sight of memory catching up with self-presence. Indeed, this is precisely what is terrifying about the dream: The event returns in its absolute fullness, as was never experienced in the instance of its occurrence or in the rational recollection that took place afterward. It is into this return that Delbo's feeling of "dying" occurs. *Who* is dying, however, is less clear.

The lack of certainty surrounding the question of whose death is at stake in the nightmare is indicative of the testimonial impasses central to the memory of trauma. Constituted by divergent dimensions of the self, the voice emerging in the darkness of memory refuses a direct entrance into the narrative of recollection. Rather, what unfolds is "a mass of suffering" taken up through the body and in turn muting verbal articulation. Because of this disturbance, the appearance of the dream occupies a privileged position where testimony is concerned, forging an indirect opening into the disjunction between two selves divorced in time. Such a tension is realized in the writings of Agamben.

As we turn to Agamben, a worry unfolds. On the one hand, we wish to conduct a phenomenology of Delbo's nightmare. On the other hand, we wish to employ Agamben's (1999) account of the aporetic structure of testimony, an account that is decidedly unphenomenological in approach. In response to this tension, my method will be to focus on only those aspects from Agamben's writings on testimony that lend themselves to our overall aim: eliciting the testimonial attributes of sites of traumatic memory. If this approach constitutes a disservice to Agamben, then I hope that by importing his writings on testimony into a phenomenological context, that disservice can be countered. For Agamben, what is peculiar to the relation between witnessing and testimony is an aporia that entails the impossibility of completion. More specifically, what this dynamic revolves around is the incompletion determined by the impossibility of materially surviving, in Primo Levi's words, "the destiny of the common prisoner" (quoted in Agamben 1999, 33). How can we approach this limit?

In the least, we can say that a relationship between voices in the past and those in the present emerge. Moreover, we can go on to say that such a relation constitutes a dynamic of inside and outside, in which the indirect opening into the memory of trauma becomes facilitated with the standoff between what is heard in the present and what remains to be said in the past. To speak of what is heard in the present and what remains to be said in the past means to confer an afterlife upon the temporality of trauma, one that outlives the immediacy of the event. Rather than simply recollecting the past into the present or otherwise allowing that same past to disperse of its own accord, it is only when conflicting temporalities are brought together, so constituting a single nonlinear timescale, that trauma becomes pronounced, as such. Here, let us turn to Agamben:

> Not even the survivor can bear witness completely, can speak his own lacuna. This means that testimony is the disjunction between

two impossibilities of bearing witness; it means that language, in order to bear witness, must give way to a non-language in order to show the impossibility of bearing witness. (1999, 39)

Agamben presents us with an impasse, whereby "a non-language" establishes the impossibility of bearing witness, which itself becomes the very act of testimony. "Two impossibilities of bearing witness," stretched out between spaces in time. For Agamben, such a relation is exemplified in the figure of the "muselmann," a term taken from Primo Levi (1996, 88) referring to the "drowned" human being. The figure of the muselmann, according to Agamben, marks a "limit situation," whereby "the non-place in which all disciplinary barriers are destroyed and all embankments flooded" (1999, 48). Distinct to this "non-place" is a fundamental indefiniteness, a deep ambiguity that renders the muselmann both human and non-human simultaneously. Indeed, the proximity to the non-human divides the muselmann from "the common prisoner." Such a paradoxical tension with the appearance of being human is contested by the refusal of that human state. To refer to Levi, what characterizes the muselmann is a basic absence of presence: "An anonymous mass, continually renewed and always identical, of non-men who march and labour in silence, the divine spark dead within them, already too empty to really suffer" (1996, 90).

For Agamben, such a lacuna renders the testimony of the muselmann fundamentally unapproachable, presupposing the destruction of lived experience. As such, Agamben's confrontation with this inapproachability results in a synthesis between the survivor and the muselmann.

Given this structure of disjunction and dislocation, how can we find a thematic link from the subject of testimony to the place of that experience without imposing a bond in advance? By posing this question, what is at stake is not simply the testimonial attributes of a place understood in forensic terms, but the implicit relation between "place" and "witnessing" (taking both terms in a provisional sense).

I would suggest that one way in which we can approach this transition from memory to materiality is with the notion of "superstes." For Agamben, the word *superstes* "designates a person who has lived through something, who has experienced an event from beginning to end and can therefore bear witness to it" (1999, 17). With this notion, we fold back to the figure of the muselmann, since it is with the muselmann that the temporal conflict between the end of the event and the deferred continuity of that end fuses. This peculiar juncture between a formal end and a protracted end places us once more in sight of Levinas's *il y a*. At the heart of Agamben's interpretation of superstes is the dynamic of an *afterlife*, a life that has outlived its own duration and yet persists through that expiration. In a similar way, the basic action of the *il y a* is a resurfacing of "an atmospheric density," which, as we recall, Levinas takes to be the anonymous "fact of existing" (2005, 46–47). Because this force is said to "reappear," it occupies an immanent relation to the nonanonymous world, indeed goes so far as to "survive" the nonanonymous world. This structure of reappearance and disappearance binds the idea of superstes firmly within the region of the *il y a*, marking both with a presence that depends on an act of spatiotemporal displacement.

Coexistent with this return to the *il y a* is a double return to Charlotte Delbo's memory of the nightmare. This is made clear if we consider that both the muselmann and the nightmare not only present themselves as symptoms of the event, but also structure themselves in such a way that their presence is always deferred. With this deferral, the muselmann and the nightmare materialize as objects seized from what Delbo has termed "deep memory." The significance of this is that the muselmann and the nightmare share the borderline absence, in which two selves become divorced. That the muselmann was cited as a "void" supports this view insofar as he is positioned on a peripheral border. Similarly, Delbo's nightmare is an exposure of the deep memory, which stands as an indeterminate void in the region of "refilled memory" and rational ordering. Indeed, Delbo goes so far as to say that the dream "gives [memory] back its contents" (quoted in Langer 1991, 6). The act of giving content to a voided space is an invitation for us to consider testimony in material terms.

TRAUMATIZED MATERIALITY

By employing the idea of "superstes," I have suggested that what is peculiar to the muselmann and to Delbo's nightmare is the role they play in bringing two realms together through acting as a dynamic void. This role becomes amplified if we consider that the identity of the traumatized subject is thought of as being radically divergent, to the extent that before the event and after the event mark two selves. In the case of Delbo's nightmare and Agamben's muselmann, two selves broken in time were maintained by the void between them. As a result, the void gained the privileged position of forming an intercession between time and place. I would suggest that a parallel intercession occurs in the appearance of ruins, whereby we witness a *reciprocity between the destruction of the past, the lapse in time thereafter, and the unexpected persistence of damaged materiality in the present.*

We can think of this process in two ways. First, we can understand the persistence of a ruin in evidential terms; that is, as the forensic remains of an event, the understanding of which was blocked as it occurred. In such a case, the physical remains of the event become the raw material for the work of history to enrich its understanding of trauma and materiality. Second, the mediation can refer to the interior trace of voided experience, thus suggesting that the materiality of the place somehow "absorbs" the world lived through its flesh. This second mode of testimony brings the ruin into the realm of the nightmare and the muselmann. After all, what is peculiar to the ruin is that it manages to attend to both the "unclaimed experience" of trauma and the impossible "limit situation," whereby the identity of the traumatized subject discovers an environmental counterpart.

To defend this claim, let me pose a question: If place is symbolically imbued with the texture of a past that is particular to that place, and if, moreover, the housing of memory is said to involve the surfacing of architectural space, then how, given their fragmentation and incompleteness, can the ruins of disaster testify to the events that took place there? Taken from a textual angle, we say that we are able to "read" a place for the reason that memory gains its identity through withdrawing and returning to a spatial center. The spatiality of ruins, however, challenges the assumption of spatial centrality and thus temporal narrativity.

This challenge to conventional spatiality is clear at the outset. Unlike the "felicitous" space that characterizes domestic place, which allows time and place to coincide as unitary phenomena, the formal features of the ruin are situated in a negative zone, whereby what remains is defined by what is absent. Beyond its time, the ruin appears for us as being of a different era. As of a different era, the ruin's temporality is decidedly polymorphous, at once rooted in the past and dispersed into the present. For this reason, Mikel Dufrenne describes the aesthetic experience of ruins as "stirring," noting that "it partakes of that profundity of time from which it arises. The ruin's prestige comes both from the allure of the distant, to which man is always responsive because the distant is like an image of what is primordial, and from the ruin's ability to illustrate time in submitting to and surmounting it" (1979, 163–64).

The ruin's deep relationship with time situates it in a unique place. "Submitting to and surmounting" time, the ruin operates with a strange logic, in which immobility sits side by side with mobility and constant flux. In this way, the ruin's history is also its presence. The ruin does not part with its history through becoming a relic. Nor does the ruin suffer from a lack of aesthetic vibrancy through its physical dissolution, a point I have labored elsewhere (Trigg 2006a). Dufrenne's claim, therefore, that the "object which bears a date of origin must also show that it has faced time bravely" has a scope limited to classical aesthetics (1979, 164). Withstanding the forces of time, the ruin may well awe the viewer with its grandeur and resistance to time. But such awe remains within the realm of aesthetic discourse as having a unique relationship to human "affectivity." When trauma intersects in the ruin, then aesthetic discourse becomes problematic—a subsidiary of the very phenomena of the place, which may be interpreted with a suspicious glance. That the ruins of trauma "outlive" the event that initiated their existence is not an aesthetic gesture, but an ontological gesture demonstrating the singularity of traumatic events. Speaking of the remains of disused war bunkers, Paul Virilio writes how "this architecture floats on the surface of an earth which has lost its materiality" (2004, 12). The detachment of place from its site points to the ruins' strange relationship with the world, as though the ruins were somehow freed of the burden of being placed.

Ruination is thus not simply the erosion of materiality, but also the preservation of a past, manifest not by the fulfillment of that past, but through its decay. This is especially true of traumatic ruins. For what is at stake in the category of "ruin" is not a particular configuration of materiality. Nor does "ruin" simply refer to a place that has been left to the elements. Rather, the inclusion of "ruin" points to a broader dynamic within the fabric of space and time, such that the place in question will forever remain scarred by the events that occurred there, irrespective of what actually remains of the physical fallout of that event. This paradoxical conflation between absence and presence means that the phenomenality of ruin loses nominal clarity. Do the history and memories of a place slide into obscurity as the same place undergoes erasure? In the case of the ruins of trauma, the relationship between materiality and time is prised apart, a breakage we have seen in the case of Srebnik returning to Chelmno. For what he sees is not the place as it was, but a wholly modified landscape, divested of all but a fraction of its material relationship to history. Does this modification undermine Srebnik's memory? The answer is clearly the opposite: His refusal to believe he is once again there attests to a spatial continuity that outflanks the destruction of the place, thus signaling a broader relationship between the ruin as a void and the void as the trace of an event.

We can analyze this relation between traces and voids in two stages. First, through the occurrence of disaster, the relation between event and place adopts an intimate, if disturbed, connection. Consider, in other words, how a place marked by trauma "punctures" the broader region surrounding that event, effectively acting as a spatiotemporal gathering source. Not only this, but through this gathering gesture, the event conversely reaches out in space and time, developing a life independent of the original location. This movement of an afterlife leads us to the second form of voided traces.

Peculiar to the material memory of trauma is the role ruins play in housing what is absent. Such a fundamentally altered form testifies to the negative spatiality of the ruin, and ultimately to the ruin's significance. Phenomenologically, the formation and discovery of the ruin is marked by the fulfillment and embodiment of what is dynamically void. Here, the ruins of disaster paradoxically present themselves in terms of being empty of memory. Instead of monumentalizing what remains, the ruins bring about a nonmemory, a split in spatiotemporal presence, from which the imprint of disaster upon space distorts the formal appearance of materiality.

Because of this distortion, the ruin can be seen as absorbing not only the broader region, but also the previous incarnation of the physical site where the traumatic event occurred. Today, it would be disingenuous to experience the physical site of the World Trade Center in New York City independently of what took place there on September 11, 2001. History intervenes, causing a rippling effect not only within the surrounding area, but also within the very history of the place.

And so, we are faced with a phenomenology of negative space, a location defined not only by what has ceased to exist, but also by what cannot be accommodated spatially. Unable to be accommodated spatially, what emerges in this appearance is a dynamic tension between the desubjectification of "place" and the contrasting emergence of "site." The significance of this tension is that the ruin mirrors the internal terrain of the witness to trauma, and so achieves a testimonial dimension. Indeed, as far as the ruin is reduced to a strange variant of "place," thus shadowing the shift from the human to the inhuman, then we are drawn back to the figure of the muselmann.

Like the muselmann, the ruin urges us to approach testimony as an impossible demand, a break in spatiotemporal presence. "He is truly," writes

Agamben, "the *larva* that our memory cannot succeed in burying, the unforgettable with whom we must reckon" (1999, 81; italics in original). Connecting Agamben to Delbo, we can take the metaphorical term "larva" to mean the "deep memory" that opposes the thin layer of "common memory" rationally applied to that space retrospectively. In this way, the surge of larva, understood metaphorically, establishes a space created in its own unrepressed emergence; namely, the empty space from where the larva appears. Thus, it is not simply that the larva of deep memory overpowers our idea of the relation between trauma and materiality, but that in this collision, a new space is conceived formed through the memory of presence.

A DISTURBANCE OF MEMORY

I have sought to place the structure of the ruined subject alongside the materiality of the ruin. The result of this alignment is the appearance of sites of memory as a symptomatic rather than direct emergence of the traumatic past, contesting the notion of memory as being "contained" by place. Where the ruins of trauma are concerned, the traumatic event exceeds the spatiality governing time and place. For this reason, the relationship between trauma and materiality is thus at the heart of what renders a site of traumatic memory "ruinous." What remains to be said is how such places affect us on an embodied level, a question that will now reunite us with Srebnik. In order to gain entrance into the experiential quality of traumatic ruins, it will be to our benefit to focus more precisely on the relationship between nightmares and ruins.

As we saw above, for Delbo, the nightmare of being in the camp acts as a bridge between identities, each identity distinguished by its modes of experiencing the past. But to say that the return of the repressed is to a space between identities fails to grasp the experiential dimension of the dream in its manifold appearances. To adjust this omission, the symptomatic and nonvolitional aspect of the nightmare stands in contrast to what Delbo described as "external memory." In this way, the return to a space between identities emerges as an attempt to give back a presence, both spatial and temporal, to a nonexperience. To give back a presence to an event means, above all, to *place* the event in time, an event that, as we have emphasized, has no place in time.

Yet if the function of the dream is to give presence to what is temporally displaced, then it is only upon waking that the damaged temporality of the event is realized. Because the nightmare animates the self-estrangement of the trau-matized subject, a disjuncture is positioned between what is seen in the pres-ent and what is felt as a murmur in the past. In a word, the nightmare emerges as a plane of nonexperience, structured around a logic of displacement.

About this movement, Maurice Blanchot writes accordingly: "If it comes to us, it does so only by way of forgetfulness, a forgetfulness which is not only censorship or simply repression. We dream without memory" (1986, 35). To "dream without memory" implies that the dream's temporality is funda-mentally suspended; a void attesting to the singular instant of trauma. Con-sidered in material terms, the suspended temporality of the nightmare refers to the remains of the event leaking into the everyday world. In this sense, to "dream without memory" also means bringing something back from the nocturnal world that is recognized only in the world of nondreaming, albeit indirectly. The nightmare is an opening, not into the presence of trauma and abjection, but into the articulation of the mute void. Blanchot again: "We cannot recall our dreams, they cannot come back to us" (35). With this re-moteness, the dream of presence is thus reduced to a memory, and the trace of an event that passes through its own death.

Figure 23: *Auschwitz, Poland. Courtesy of Hannah Swithinbank.*

To rephrase this in material terms: Insofar as the ruin appears in an ambiguous border between waking life and dreams, then the dream's action of giving presence to a ruptured space is precisely what distinguishes sites of memory from inanimate materiality. Unlike the enclosure of dreams, the ruin has a persistence, in which the sleep of memory collides and coexists with the consciousness of daylight. Where human identity has suffered under the tribunal of an "unclaimed experience," the ruin has survived as a manifestation of this process, and this unexpected survival underpins the ruin's radical spectrality. This spectrality is clear if we consider that whereas the dream entails a struggle between appearance and disappearance, ultimately consigning itself to an impenetrable void, in the present, the ruin, in its fleshy materiality, mediates between these dimensions simultaneously through its attempt to house and give place to what is essentially an unhomely event.

We are placed on the surface of a dark earth. Standing within a gray field, at least four columns stretch above the horizon, each made from blackened bricks. Their presence appears to have been assimilated within the natural landscape, with each stack assuming the color of the ground beneath.

Figure 24: *Auschwitz, Poland. Courtesy of Hannah Swithinbank.*

Surrounding this ground are heaps of broken masonry, large slabs of concrete, and smaller particles of rock and brick. In the background, a row of fences, their tops adorned with barbed-wire, is separated by a train track that carves the land into different factions. Watchtowers, now empty, overlook where the train would have journeyed its cargo to and from the destination. Surrounding the scene, a line of trees rise above the scene of desertion and collapse. Beyond the trees in the mid-distance, trees farther in the background form a double layer. Within this horizon, small remnants mirror those in the foreground, the ominous vertical chimney stacks retreating into the far background.

We have arrived too late, invoking the sense that the presence is defined by a knowledge that the surface of the place is privy to but unable to articulate. Here, the stillness of the place, at once tense and subdued, is amplified. But the stillness is not simply the absence of movement, as though such nonmovement were the result of the place being depopulated. Rather, the particular stillness takes place against a historical backdrop, of which we ourselves are removed: in effect, a stillness played out against a past that is no longer accessible and yet intensely fused with the environment in which we are currently placed. Stepping into an environment as that same environment evades our desire to grasp the place in its totality, the result is one of disorientation and displacement.

This disorientation adopts an overtly uncanny quality as the frozen materiality of the ruin pierces the banality of the daylight, invoking the rupture from the world of dreams to the world of the everyday. Indeed, it is especially in the banality of still daylight that the strange formation of the ruin's attempt to give presence is especially clear. There is, after all, something truly disturbing about an entity from the nocturnal realm that is now captured in the sunlight of a docile afternoon. When some creature from our nightmares ascends from the subterranean world, then we seem to be confronted with nothing less than an *accident in reality*. It is as though a force of the unconscious has unlocked the invisible screen linking the night with the day, thus dismantling the safety of natural light.

"Even, I, here, now . . . I can't believe I'm here," so we recall Simon Srebnik saying among the ruins, in an oddly prosaic environment. Unable to be placed in the present, Srebnik's comment reveals not merely the distance between time and place, but the metaphysical strangeness of a phenomenological appearance of embodied disembodiment; that is, a material emergence without time and stability. In a word, *an architecture of disappearance*. The encounter pushes the ruin beyond place, beyond time, and toward an other-worldly landscape comprising remains that ought to have been confined to the interior of the unconscious, but now stand before consciousness as a left-over in the world of appearances.

In a late essay titled "A Disturbance of Memory on the Acropolis," Freud offers us a parallel case of spatiotemporal disappearing, which is notable for its reference to the "feeling of estrangement." Standing before the Acropolis, Freud makes a shocking confession: *"So this all really does exist, just as we learned in school!"* (2005, 237; italics in original). Freud's response is as striking as it is intuitive. Before the ruins, the facticity of phenomena exceeds its own appearance, establishing a fissure between materiality and experience. Suddenly, it is no longer enough to bear witness to the ruins with the senses alone—something escapes the subject's gaze. Thus, Freud's response mirrors Srebnik's: "According to the evidence of my senses, I am now standing on the Acropolis, but I can't believe it" (Freud 2005, 239). This tension between scientific observation and spatiotemporal mystification belies a faith in the "evidence of my senses" to place Freud at the scene. Yet displacement ensues, despite the abundance of evidence suggesting otherwise. As such, Freud's unnerving response to the Acropolis concerns less a tension between anticipation and experience and more a rupture between place and embodiment.

No longer believing themselves to be placed, where are the bodies of Freud and Srebnik as they undergo spatiotemporal dislocation? Do their bodies lie in wait, with all sensory awareness momentarily suspended? If so, what remains: the bewilderment of an experience without a memory, or a memory with no experience? In each case, the experience of things—the Acropolis or Chelmno—becomes defined as a negative space, suffused with a derealized sensation, in which *"what I am seeing there is not real"* (Freud 2005, 240; italics in original). Just as with Srebnik in Chelmno, Freud's encounter with a derealized world centers on the markings left by ruins. In the traces left behind, an excess in matter is produced, serving to remind the visitor that beyond the appearance of presence, uncanniness and otherness coincide with an abnormal mode of embodiment.

For both Freud and Srebnik, the derealized experience of time and place damages the body's intentionality toward the world, invoking the abnormal mode of embodiment discussed above. The body is seized in its tracks, and a semirealized reality is the result. In such a case, disbelief becomes an epistemically privileged experience, pointing to a tension resistant to logic and reason. "Even, I, here, now . . . I can't believe I'm here." This phrase haunts the experience of derealization, its spectrality codependent on the placid banality of things.

In the words of both Freud and Srebnik, the ruin gives voice to the nightmare of trauma through its own materiality before resituating it in the everyday world of sense and sensibility. And so the appearance of the site shocks our attempts at placing the past through the work of memory and imagination. What is experienced is less a fragment of a broken narrative and more a murmur of the place where that narrative once existed.

In testimonial terms, we discover a parallel to the impossibility of witnessing trauma. Indeed, insofar as the ruin creates the spatial and temporal conditions necessary for the past to be articulated, it is precisely through that gesture the same past prohibits articulation. Surrounded by an aura of spectrality, the tension instills a tension in the viewer: as much as we attempt to commune with the environment, so there is a sense in being watched by the environment. This reversible duality gathers a resonance thanks to the collision of worlds, spatial and temporal, with each diametrically opposed to the other. The reality of the traumatic event is not reinforced in this encounter, but instead *trembles* as a deep void is given a voice between the viewer and the place.

The trembling of traumatized materiality, felt as the experience of unreality becoming real, is evidence of the close relationship between materiality and spectrality. The specter becomes visible as the environment establishes a portal between the past and the present. The result of this opening is the sense of the ruin—in both its natural and built forms—becoming possessed by a past that cannot be reconstructed in a conventional narrative. Instead, the place of trauma vibrates with an indirect language, blocked from interpretation and displacing the certainty of self, memory, and place. In the midst of this dreamscape, the terms "place" and "site" lose their bearings. Whereas the term "place" attests to the desire to orient ourselves in an environment, the incursion of "site" disrupts that desire, leading to a hybrid between the two dimensions. In this way, the ruins of trauma do not redeem time and experience from annihilation and rupture, but help us to understand the structure of "unclaimed experience" by mirroring our own attempts at giving presence to a place that refuses all evidence of presence.

***

Taken together, the last two chapters have attempted to provide a phenomenological account of both the traumatic memory of place and the place of traumatic memory, in this way fulfilling the twofold trajectory set out at the beginning of the book. We have witnessed this relation as one of entwinement and reciprocal correspondence. From memory to place, we have indeed been returned through place to memory. Whereas this twofold gesture has been implicit through the work, it is especially prevalent in the relation between trauma and place, given that our understanding of the materiality of trauma depends upon a previous analysis of the structure of the traumatized subject. Furthermore, this interrelated bond between subjectivity and materiality has been situated in the context of an increasing arc of tension, developing from an account of everyday memory, then on to the realm of transitional memory, and now finally on the horizon of traumatic memory. Having surveyed this broad terrain, how do these final chapters fit within our broad theme; namely: *How are identity and embodiment shaped through being touched by the past?*

Above all else, what these two final chapters have shown us is that the phenomenological premise of the lived-body as being the "zero-point" of orientation, from which the "here" and "now" of materiality and flesh are cast, in a fundamental sense survives trauma. This spatiotemporal limit, in which both place and body return to haunt the self, marks not only the endurance of the lived-body, but also of phenomenology as able to attend to that resistance.

Phenomenology survives trauma? This may sound surprising, given that through these final chapters, it is the push toward a postphenomenological analysis of death and trauma, orientated primarily through Levinas, that has assisted us in making the transition from the nongivenness of trauma to its embodied and symptomatic emergence through the figure of the *il y a*. Indeed, in the end, it is the enigma of the *il y a*, implicit in Agamben's discussion of the "limit situation," that returns to us, marking an embryonic origin as well as an ultimate horizon. Such a double-sided intentionality allows us to remain within a phenomenological analysis while also positioning us in the liminal zone, into which phenomenology itself must ultimately remain silent.

Into this silence, phenomenology and trauma confront each other. Far from the fulfillment of a previously ruined narrative, what these final chapters have shown is that in the strange (and strained) disjunction between intentionality and absence, enough remains of the phenomenal world for phenomenology to articulate the structure of trauma precisely through speaking of that relation as a shadow. In this way, shadows and murmurs emerge as distinctly privileged phenomena, establishing the link from a conventional analysis of what appears for consciousness to be a consideration of how those appearances can simultaneously be void.

Broadly construed, it is this middle ground between presence and absence that unites the chapters as a whole. Time and again, in dealing with how self and embodiment are touched by the past, we have been compelled to walk the line between memory and history, place and body, experience and recognition, and, finally, materiality and time. In each of these cases, the shadow of each counterpart seeps inward, casting an indirect light that is only registered in the space in between. And it is in the space in between that phenomenology, finally, finds its own place.

CONCLUSION
. . . .

THIS PLACE IS HAUNTED

Who am I? If this once I were to rely on a proverb, then perhaps everything would amount to knowing whom I "haunt."

—André Breton, *Nadja*

Why do the dead return? Why, in the darkness of the night, when all activity has been reduced to a trembling in the distance, do the dead disavow their rest and return to the living? What strange beacon is emitted in the world of the living that draws these phantoms to the things of everyday life? When, in some act of elaborate risk, we venture to the basement after hearing a sonorous clanking in the floorboards, what greets us: an immaterial specter sent from the undead, or a memory trapped somewhere between the basement and our imaginations? The living and the dead; the material and the immaterial: Those who pass from the land of the dead to the living carry with them the promise of a place to come, and that place is haunted.

GHOST H(A)UNTING

Considered retrospectively, the contents of this book have been visited by a series of ghosts, which have so far remained largely buried beneath the pages, only occasionally rising above the perceptual horizon. We have, for instance, seen ghosts appear in the case of where objects are uncannily displaced from their native place of memory (such as in the case of Kant's *Critique of Pure Reason* being transported from Las Vegas); where the body reveals itself as embodying a different set of experiences and histories to that of abstract reflection (such as journeying through a harshly lit environment late at night); where our intimate attachments to a place are offset by the anonymity lurking beneath the veil of personal attachment (such as returning to one's childhood home after a long absence); and, finally, where there is a complete suppression of the lived experience of the past, such that the past manifests itself indirectly through the body (such as undergoing a traumatic event).

In each case, something has returned from a state of apparent hibernation to roam the living. Just as we have returned to the past, so the past has returned to us. In doing so, something else was assimilated in the return, a life independent of the event of remembering itself. But what is this "thing" that accompanies our memories, especially our memories of places? As this book has sought to demonstrate, the "thing" in question is nothing less than the force by which our memories are given their strange, unsettling, and unresolved resonance. The "thing" that interbreeds with the recollection of an event is the anonymous life of memory, its animate and vital spark. Because of this dynamic, memories remain irreducible to either empirical or evidential qualities. As has been emphasized, the memory of place is a visceral and primal memory resistant to all modes of rigid abstraction. Above and beyond their status in the world, the returning of memories attests to both their fundamental singularity and their inherent fragmentation. Yet the quality of memories being unresolved and fragmented is not a question of their phenomenal status. Structurally speaking, a memory of trauma is no less irresolute than a benign episode all too familiar to the remembering subject. At stake is not only the question of *what* is being remembered, but the brute fact *that there is remembering at all*.

More thematically, the implicit undercurrent of spectral presences has intensified in correlation with the threefold arc of the book. In the case of everyday memory, we took it for granted that memory had a "place," which was interwoven with the act of remembering. Even within the realm of things losing their bearings—such as the vague quality memories can bring, in which we ourselves are objectified in the scene of memory—there is nonetheless an abiding unity to the event and the place being recalled. This presupposition of unity meant that "things" of the world stood in a roughly harmonious correspondence with one another, with all experiences orientated toward a desired state of concordance.

Yet even here, the incipient germs of disorientation were rooted in the very fabric of what it is to remember. After all, if our account of the structure of place memory as involving a disturbance in the "pregiven stillness of the contextual and everyday world" is right, then the loss of this surrounding world exists in a relationship of estrangement with the subject. Not only this, but at the frontier of the event of place memory, a new life-world begins, in which the previous unity withdraws. Here, the very gesture of withdrawing instigates a significant moment in the genetic origin of the ghosts accompanying all memory. The significance has a location: It is sourced at the point in which place memory and the surrounding world come into contact with each other, establishing a ravine, from which new forms of life emerge.

As if there were any empirical doubt to this claim of new life, then by the time we moved from the region of everyday memory to the sphere of transitional memory, then it was the lived-body that testified to the dawn of a ghostly era. At such a point, the limited clarity grounding everyday memory slowly seeped into a porous region, which placed at the foreground the figure of the "between."

Between place, between memory, between time, between identity, between embodiment: Throughout, the movement of memory was nimble and clandestine, forever unmasking, disrupting, and (re)ejecting the human tendency to fix memories in place. In the zone that outlasted humanized place, the nonhuman and anonymous body gained the upper hand. Only now, the body we encountered lost its reassurance as the locus of all unity and experience. In place of the unified body came a body that departed from the centrality of the "I." In short, "one's own body" became the site of a haunting, a mound of materiality caught up in the "wild being" of the world's anonymous flesh.

Alongside the body, the anonymity of place—a cosmic barrenness destined to overturn all human endeavors on our shared planet—reigned sovereign. Even—no, *especially*—in innocuous places, the barriers bridging organic and synthetic textures were prised apart. The result of this dissolution: Even a supermarket can assume the appearance of a place spooked by inaudible, nameless, and figureless entities. And yet owing to some weakness on behalf of human desire in the face of estrangement, we conferred a name upon those entities, the title "Anonymous Materiality." This baptism of anonymity led to an explicit declaration of the difference between our lived experiences, our recollected experiences, and the wilderness underlying those experiences. Once again, therefore, the space of difference emerged as a privileged location, in which all that has been discarded as incidental to lived experience materialized as being not only central but fundamentally constitutive of that experience.

From the depths of ambiguity, the final movement in this provisional ghost hunt was rendered highly problematic and yet far more pressing given the nature of the body's ability to conceal the past from the present. Here, our topic was the memory of trauma. Especially pressing to this turn was the incompatibility between, on the one hand, human identity as striving toward temporal continuity, and, on the other hand, traumatic memory, which defines itself through a legacy of indirection and discontinuity. The outcome was a flight into abjection of the "phantom zone." As with the abyss between place memory and the surrounding world, the phantom zone structured and instantiated itself through a paradox; namely, the reality of "rational memory" gains its identity only through submitting to the status of a corporeal unreality. Played out in the movement of the flesh "undergoing revolution," the life animating the human body now becomes a thing *felt* as a visceral reality. Here, there was no doubt that a veritable danse macabre of invisible ghouls was being rehearsed within the walls and hallways of the body.

As with the movement of transitional memory, this materialization of traumatic and ghostly agencies eventually found its way into place. Indeed, it was precisely through the reappearance of the traumatic memory within the ruins of the built environment that the ghost was given form and mass. Inaccessible to the body except as a murmur felt symptomatically, through discerning the presence of a specter within the animate void of a ruin, all that was pushed to the margins as immaterial and barren of specificity is given a voice to channel into the land of the living.

What, then, of this strange agency that accompanies all remembering: this ghost of memory, this memory of ghosts? Until now, the figure of the ghost has appeared only in the murkiest light, raising itself to the realm of visibility at critical junctures in the book. But given the significance of this appearance, we would do well to refine our h(a)unt in a more thematically focused manner.

To direct the phenomenological eye toward the thing that precisely disturbs vision? Ordinarily, this altered visibility would not be a problem. As we have seen, a phenomenon such as death gives itself to consciousness through a dialectic of presence and absence. By the force of its absolute absence from lived and *living* subjectivity, the specter of death at the same time constitutes a fundamental definition of subjectivity. Yet the coming of the ghost is nether present nor absent, neither visible nor invisible, to phrase it in the more appropriate language of Merleau-Ponty.

Not only this, but alongside this aporetic structure of defying appearances, the ghost occupies another liminal space, which privileges the language of betweenness. To phrase the problem as a question: Can we readily assign our experiences of ghosts to either memory or imagination? A risk arises from doing so: The experience of paradoxical phenomenon is reduced to a psychic activity, the implication of which would be to pathologize the ghost as a distortion in perception. What does this psychological treatment of ghostly life entail?

On the one hand, conferring a causal relationship between memory and sightings of ghosts suggests a sediment of unfinished personal history discoloring our experience of the world, such that once that history was subtracted, then vision would be restored. To "see" would mean to unconsciously remember that which is dead but has yet to move on. Especially pressing in this reading would be particular kinds of losses, not least those that occur suddenly and remain affixed to a heightened state of pathos. There, the presence of those who passed from life would be felt at a more acute level, the voices of a ghostly presence more audible, sitting aside those who speak in the living. Yet the dialogue would invariably prove to be a solitary act, a summoning of one's own failure to transform the losses of the past into the gains of the present. In this way, the ghost would essentially reinforce the "fundamental narcissism of all vision" (Merleau-Ponty 1968, 139), with the experience of being haunted traceable to a debt the dead still owe to the living.

If this interpretation of ghosts presses too hard on memory as the production of a series of accidents in perception, then leaning toward imagination is equally problematic. Here, the positivist assumption would be that the visitation of a ghost would be nothing more than a speculative apparition spontaneously created from nothing. The seeing of the ghost would thus be parallel to a miss-seeing of things in the world, no different from one of the senses being cloaked in a veil. Does "my mind play tricks on me," as the language would have it, when I see a ghost? Phenomenologically, there would seem to be more ground for uncertainty, ambiguity, and elaboration in the case of imagining the presence of something rather than reintroducing that thing from memory.

As Sartre has pointed out, memory and imagination differ not only in their temporal orientation, but also in their very structure: "The handshake of Peter of last evening in leaving me did not turn into an unreality as it became a thing of the past: it simply *went into retirement*; it is always real but *past*" (2001, 96; italics in original). Always real, always past, remembering is forever guided by an authenticity that imagination lacks, a point we first touched upon in the first chapter. More than its futural direction, imagination thrives on that which is formless and void of definite content. Thus, Sartre is prepared to align imagination with "Nothingness," situating it "beyond reach" (96). Here, there is a detachment in time, such that the future and the present are no longer in contact. What remains is a "hypothesis of unreality" (97), which for Sartre does not mean the absence of intentionality, but intentionality's very constitution.

How are we to take this placement of imagination as sitting within nothingness and unreality? For Sartre, the imagined object is a departure from the world, in the process establishing a world autonomous of reality. Indeed, that imagination need not take into account the reality of the lived world means that the world can, indeed, necessarily *is*, negated as the imagined experience places itself "on the fringe of the whole of reality" (Sartre 2001, 98).

Yet there is a problem with this account. In treating memory and imagination as "two aspects of Nothingness" (96), each with their own discernible relation to reality, Sartre precludes the prospect of ambiguity between memory and imagination. This preclusion is problematic in that it prematurely confers the quality of reality upon memory, while reserving unreality for the imagination. In each case, both domains are purported to be independent from each other, with a "real" world and an "unreal" world mutually opposed.

Applied to the phenomenology of ghosts, the phenomenon of the ghost risks being reduced to a mental activity, which is taken as either an exercise in unreality or a blockage in a previously lived reality. Clearly, there is something unsatisfactory in the attempt to explain the experience of ghostly phenomenon in terms of a derivative of either memory or imagination. This is not to imply, of course, that these aspects occupy an arbitrary relationship with the figure and presence of the ghost. By now, it will be clear that the materiality of the ghost attests to the act of remembering, and indeed remains implanted in the very notion of reprising and reexperiencing an already-extinct event. Time and again, remembering has proven itself to be at home amid spooks and phantoms, both those of the past and those of the future. But to overcome the aporetic structure peculiar to the dynamic of the ghost, we need to think beyond the dichotomous region of memory and imagination.

How to counter this impulse to psychologize the ghost? How, in other words, to give a voice to that which is inherently voiceless? We need, I suggest, to approach this task of speaking on behalf of the ghost by stripping it from certain external attributes. We need, for instance, to stand in direct opposition to the prevalent tendency in philosophy and cultural studies to treat the ghost as an offshoot of Derrida's (1994) much cited concept of "hauntology."

Derrida's neologism refers to the "specter of Marx" looming over academia, a presence that serves to destabilize concepts of history, finality, and temporality. Extending even to phenomenology, Derrida's notion thus presents us with a direct challenge, as he writes: *"There is no Dasein of the specter"* (1994, 100, emphasis added). In what follows, this accusation will be confronted head-on. In the process, I will seek to demonstrate the converse of this claim, which Derrida himself allows us to formulate: "There is no *Dasein* without the uncanniness, without the strange familiarity (*Unheimlichkeit*) of some specter" (100).

Despite hauntology's ability to contest dichotomous modes of temporality, the downfall of this oversaturated "trope" of contemporary theory is that it is commonly used merely to describe a certain mode of cultural effect and production. As such, it retains the limit of being a concept imposed upon experience, rather than giving credence to experience itself. Indeed, one of the results of a concept such as "hauntology" is that it too readily becomes an aestheticized idea, bearing minimal relation to the phenomena it purports to face. As Fredrick Jameson writes about Derrida's concept:

> Spectrality does not involve the conviction that ghosts exist or that the past (and maybe even the future they offer to prophesy) is still very much alive and at work, within the living present: all it says, if it can be thought to speak, is that the living present is scarcely as self-sufficient as it claims to be; that we would do well not to count on its density and solidity, which might under exceptional circumstances betray us. (Sprinker et al. 2008, 26–27)

The porous interpretation hauntology lends itself toward, advantageous in many cultural respects, means that its structure is basically indexical, there to be employed to diverse ends. That a conviction in the actual existence of ghosts is secondary to the overall hauntological project attests to the subordination of the specter to a metaphor, a metonym, or a trope. As an ambassador for another cause, the ghost's voice is lost in the blur of academic discourse, and thus nullified in the realm of commentary and textual analysis.

Similarly, the academic literature on ghostly phenomenon, although impressive in several respects, tends to treat the ghost in a highly metaphorical fashion. Thus in a treatment of the "ghosts of place," Michael Bell cites the ghost as that which "gives a sense of social aliveness to a place," the author himself conceding to his metaphorical use of "ghost" (1997, 815). In turn, this conflation between sociality and ghosts leads Bell to a veneration of the "social experience of place," a thesis at odds with the reality of what he calls elsewhere in his paper a " 'genuine' ghost" (826). Indeed, by the time we get to the end of the paper, Bell admits that the "ghosts of place are, of course, fabrications, products of imagination, social constructions" (831).

This tendency toward the ghost as a second-order concept to be interpreted as a symptom of something other than itself appears time and again in the extant literature. For instance, in Avery Gordon's important *Ghostly Matters*, the reader is told at the outset that the book's use of ghostly phenomenon does not concern subject matter deriving from "the occult or . . . parapsychology," but because the figure of the ghost "highlighted the limitations of many of our prevalent modes of inquiry and the assumptions they make about the social world" (1997, 8). This, of course, is not to say that the examination of ghosts must necessarily have its roots in parapsychology. Nor is it to deny the significance of the ghost as a metaphor of liminal aspects of the social realm, of which Gordon's book is a clear demonstration. But to preclude the ghost as an object of experience from this field of research would be to do an injustice to hauntings more broadly.

Similarly, Tim Edensor, with Derrida in mind, also employs the ghost as a metaphorical device, for him a specter pointing to the working class, the result of which is that confronting "ghosts is a necessary check on grand visions and classifications that fix understandings of place, for they can provide an empathetic, sensual, impressionistic insight into the unseen energies that have created the city" (2008, 331). But within this sociological analysis, the very phenomena of the ghost is itself repressed, legitimized only with recourse to an already-established problem, be it the analysis of class, social injustice, or the social construction of place.

Were we to invoke a phenomenology of hauntings in light of both the hauntological and the sociological treatment of ghosts, then we would begin by stationing ourselves at a location as remote as possible from these milieus of thought. Doing so, we would, first, confer a reality upon the ghost, which considers the ghost *as* a ghost. At the same time, what follows is not a phenomenological defense for the objective existence of ghosts, which would be the concern of another investigation. Rather, our treatment of the ghost *as a ghost* means that we wish to remain open to the experiencing of a ghost as just that—a lived experience that assigns a supernatural category to natural phenomena.

Second, suspending all desire to treat the ghost as a symptomatic expression of an obstruction in time and space, we would cultivate a naïveté toward ghostly appearances, fully holding in suspension the prospect that such figures are simply deviant modes of perception.

Third, not only would we put to one side our theoretical and perceptual prejudices against the ghost, but so, too, must our aesthetic and cultural preferences submit to being bracketed. To be clear, phenomenologically, the ghost is not at the service of some already-formed aesthetic disposition, to be fulfilled through establishing a particular atmosphere. Rather, we must begin by prising apart the intimacy between the human world of institutionalized thought and the primitive experience of the ghost. We must think of a horizon, in which the sedimented world of debate and theory is forsaken. Liberated from subordination, the ghost might stand some chance of coming into the light, so far repressed by the language of deconstructionism. In order to proceed in this venture, therefore, we must truly expose ourselves to the workings of the ghost from the inside of our bodies to the otherness of our selves.

THE DOPPELGÄNGER

To haunt. To be haunted. How to bridge the gulf that lies between these two phrases? How to move from the subject who haunts to the one who is haunted? Let us suppose the conditions were right and I turned to you. What would I confess? *Here is the place I haunt.* We would then turn to each other and agree that we are both in the realm of a shared presence. In such a case, "to haunt" would mean to frequent a given location over a sustained duration of time. Far from being a void in space and time, to haunt this place would mean to keep a vigil over it, forever retaining a presence within its life. Yet this gesture of maintaining a presence of a thing in the world is not without considerable ambiguity. After all, if my act of haunting this specific locale is seen as an attempt at domesticating a small pocket of the earth, then the other side of this site of dwelling is the invisible and invasive force that haunts me, the inhabitant.

To be haunted. A turning occurs in the act of haunting a locale, a turning in which place gains a set of organs that perceive. Suddenly, we, the dwellers of place, become the site of dwelling ourselves. An agency takes over, whose powers are visible only in the trembling of nearby walls and yet wholly felt within the depths of our bodies. We are in a different, denser, darker terrain than that haunting our childhood memories. No longer to haunt, now the place employs us as its locale to visit when and where it deems necessary. Without any warning, the place appears. From a hole in the earth, it ascends to the soil, frozen like some exotic monument left here by an alien civilization. Often, the encounter is by chance. We feel the room slowly vibrate with its own past, the tension in the walls exhaling within our chest cavities. It is as though a voice becomes nearer, felt in the present, and manifests indirectly through being lodged in space. But the voice speaks inaudible words, and its desires cannot be resolved. Can we speak of things still being "here" in this visitation? The room speaks, yet no one speaks behind it. The chairs rattle, yet nothing is moving them. And then there is the nothingness. Silence. An abundance of time passes, veering off toward the solar system,

Figure 25: *Storeroom, Brighton. Photo by author.*

before igniting into a void. A massive space remains, and our memories grow quiet. Freed from the burden of time, we begin to think that our bodies have returned to their nascent state, at once rejuvenated by the immediacy of the present. Essential are those moments in which we suddenly become aware of this emergent state, whereupon the luminosity of a strange visit suddenly departs our bodies. Only then, in the brink of an incipient absence, do we realize that, all along, we were never alone.

How is it possible to attend to that which is simultaneously the site of haunting and the subject conducting that haunt? How, to phrase it another way, does that which emits a familiar presence upon us also dissent from that familiarity, become sentient and thus embarking on a new quest for life? The response to this question can be developed with recourse to the word *sentient*. When our everyday experiences are disturbed by an agency from another time and place, then the thing that comes to us does so deliberately. The object of hauntings is not menacing in its lurking distance, but disturbing in its familiarity, albeit in an augmented form. When we are shocked by things in the night, then it is only because we already have a relationship not only with the night, but also with the things that seek to commune with us from the beyond.

Contrary to folklore, things that come from nowhere (and no-when) appear as such only on first sight—or rather, *first touch*. The sentience in inanimate matter has an orientation that is guided by the embodied life-worlds that cross through that foggy horizon. In a word, we are already in the midst of what haunts us long before that effect vibrates through us. The deliberation inherent in this movement points to a magnetism at the heart of all hauntings, a magnetism that stems from the heart of human life. Ghosts from the "other world" find us. Able to navigate their way to the surface of the world, their appearance is never coincidental but forever timed with our human comings and goings. How is this coincidence of materiality and immateriality possible?

To answer this question, we must turn inward, attending to the role our bodies play in structuring the relationship between memory and hauntings. Already this tripartite relationship between embodiment, memory, and hauntings has been gestured toward in our dealings with such phenomena as alien flesh, nostalgia, and trauma. In each case, the body becomes the site of an experience of itself as a *double*.

For the body of alien flesh, a disjunction between experiences ensues, such that my body becomes the host for a different place memory. Not only this, but the memory in question materializes as being receptive to an experience, which the personal self remains unaware of. As the body memory rises to the surface, an uncanny distance is forged in the midst of subjectivity. Suddenly, I become aware of the prepersonal anonymity at all times guiding me through the world. Far from reassuring, however, this lurking presence constitutes a shadowy underworld to my movement, thus drawing my attention to the existence of a "world more ancient than thought" that dwells within my body (Merleau-Ponty 2006, 296).

Where the nostalgic body is concerned, the unity of my body is offset by the insertion of an experience of my own self as a thing in the past. My body, for me, becomes less the center of lived experience and more the threshold to a place distinct from the one I currently inhabit. Not only this, but thanks to the narcissism of the nostalgic vision, things in the world, both bodies and places, were also consumed by a will to assimilate difference into sameness. Such a power was viscerally clear in our dealings with Rodenbach's *Bruges-la-Morte* but also in the idea of spatial morphology. In both instances, things became doubled, both by themselves and by their other.

Similarly, this doubling of time and place reappears in the case of trauma. Here, the human body becomes the host for an experience that has yet to be fully registered, thus producing two distinct experiences, one cognitive in focus and the other corporeal, both of which dwell in the same body. As we have seen, only in the light of the phantom zone do these two experiences cross into the same path, thus instigating the reality of the traumatized body as prey to its own memories. The motif of two distinct experiences dwelling in the same body leads to an inevitable conclusion: The human body is its own doppelgänger.

Taking the doppelgänger as a conduit to the realm of ghosts, a murky avenue into a different world comes forth. How is it that I come to experience myself as *other*; that is, as my habitual self but simultaneously as a modified and in some sense anonymous self? How, moreover, do I retain existential unity knowing all along that within me lurks another self—a double—to which I have only indirect access? Answers to these questions are necessarily evasive, and the duality of the double resists all dialectical synthesizing. The reason being, the doubling of the self necessarily involves a partial perspective, in which I see "myself" not from the outside, but through a mirror that augments my gaze.

Another self has been produced, one that has split off from an adjoining part of my body. More than this, the other self remains visible only through a fortuitous reflection. That the content of the reflection concerns the past attests to the ambiguous appearance of the double. Never are the two selves truly visible to me, except in strained moments, whereupon I "take leave of my senses," to employ an appropriate idiom. Taking leave of my senses, I retrospectively discern an incursion into my personal body, which carries with it a gesture of the uncanny. And the uncanny is mounting: The figure of the doppelgänger is not harmonious in its structure but "has become an object of terror, just as the gods become demons after the collapse of their cult" (Freud 2003, 143). Thus, my concept of "I" is met not simply with another "I," but instead with a "non-I." The self who purports to visit my body when my life-world is stretched to a liminal sphere is not felt as "an insurance against the extinction of the self," to quote Freud (2003, 142), even though Merleau-Ponty (2006, 97) will have us think of the prepersonal body as lending "itself without reserve to action." The other subjectivity does not come to fortify my being, but to *displace and estrange it.*

This displacement is inevitable, given that the reality of the "I" is put into question once another being assumes residence within my body. Thus, the experience of the double casts a shadow over the materiality of the world, its presence dispatched upon the self with no prior warning. Time and place are dethroned in this arrival, the fabric of the life-world shown to be prey to an abiding sense of otherness. No wonder, then, that the question of where the "I" was appeared and reappeared in different forms throughout the previous chapters. For what this question hints at is the deconstruction of the "I" as a singular thing. In that fragmentation, the self-presentation of the "I" as occupying a particular place is overturned by the gaze of another "I." "*I feel myself looked at by the things*" (Merleau-Ponty 1968, 139; emphasis added). Merleau-Ponty's claim has a profundity that extends to the flesh of the world before returning to the corporeality of the lived-body. Not only do I feel things look at me, but I also feel myself looked at *by my own self*. Only, this self who is looking at me is not my "alter ego," nor is this self a mechanism of my psychodynamic activity, which results in "the function of self-observation and self-criticism, [exercising] a kind of psychical censorship, and so becomes what we know as the 'conscience'" (Freud 2003, 142). Attempts at explaining the causality of the doppelgänger—and indeed, of all supposedly "supernatural" phenomena—through the lens of psychoanalysis alone, as though such entities were the "mere" manifestation of hidden motives, demonstrates an arrogance consistent with an anthropomorphic worldview.

In the three primary ways that the double has appeared—the alien flesh, the nostalgic body, and the memory of trauma—the ambiguity of the "non-I" is central. Indeed, the felt experience of this anonymous presence comes alive only through a gesture of metamorphosis; that is, when the occult teleology of my prepersonal body strives toward an end that "I" the personal self remain hitherto unaware of. Yet disquiet ensues, and beyond the frontier of my immediate existence, a host subject can be felt moving from within. In this respect, the reality of the doppelgänger points toward an archetypically uncanny aesthetic. Through its emergence, the other self that arrives is horrific, not because it is an abject mutation of personal ego, but because it lacks all intimacy with my own being.

As proof of this lack of intimacy, the double is from another age, to quote Merleau-Ponty again, "more ancient than thought" (2006, 296). That which is more ancient than thought is necessarily divested of a "human" presence, necessarily a challenge to reading the double through a psychoanalytic eye (Webber 1996). Against the psychoanalytic and Derridean tradition, in our liminal phenomenology, the body of the subject can no longer be taken for granted as being unassumingly "here." "It may be said," as Merleau-Ponty does, citing Binswanger, "that the body is 'the hidden form of being ourself'" (Merleau-Ponty 2006, 192). Hidden from sight, the body constitutes an experiential foundation that is absent to appearances yet visible to the subterranean world, whose entrance is barred by volition.

Immeasurable in its history and secret in its ambiguous presence, the very condition of being embodied establishes an intensity of uncanniness, which, as Freud writes, "can surely derive only from the fact that the double is a creation that belongs to a primitive phase in our mental development" (2003, 143). At the heart of the horror of the doppelgänger is the discoloration of the self as a coherent and unified thing, transparent to its own nature and indivisible in its structure. This peculiarly human attendance to identity is damaged by the anonymous "*one* [who] perceives in me" (Merleau-Ponty 2006, 250; italics in original), overruling the instinctive basis that the "*corps vivant*" is identifiable with the "I."

If my body is subject to another self, and a self whose ends are unknown to me, then do I retain possession of my body? After all, do I really "experience" the prepersonal body that forms a double of my own presence? Any such answer to this question appears retroactively, by which time the anonymous body has sunk into invisibility. Even within the very fabric of my physiological being, unified possession remains evasive, as Erwin Strauss puts it:

> My hands are parts of my body. Yet other parts—the heart, the adrenal glands, the reticular activating system—are not mine in the same sense, for two reasons: (1) Not immediately acquainted with them I only know them through anatomical studies and instruction; (2) I do not master them; *as a creature, they possess me*. (Strauss and Griffith 1967, 107, emphasis added)

They possess me. With this, Strauss invites us to consider how this benign possession extends not only to the organs of which I am composed, but to their very prepersonal being.

PHANTOM MEMORY

Stretching the possessed body to the realm of ghosts more broadly, a critical question descends in this liminal phenomenology: When shadows lurk on the walls and wild groans reverberate from the floor, when hands slither through cold flesh and voices whisper inaudible words in keen ears, and when, finally, we are able to discern a "figure in pale, fluttering draperies, ill-defined" (James 2007, 73), appear on the shoreline, then are we in the company of a ghost without mass, or a ghost whose dwelling is assumed in things other than its own immaterial being? The importance of the question is central. For what is at stake is the issue of whether or not the appearance of the ghost has an existence beyond the lived-body.

In the midst of *Ideas*, Husserl draws us to a striking passage concerning the concept of "I as man" (1990, 99). About the relationship between the body and the I, he writes:

> When the soul departs, then what remains is dead matter, a sheer material thing, which no longer possesses in itself anything of the I as man. The Body, on the contrary, cannot depart. Even the ghost necessarily has its ghostly Body. To be sure, this Body is not an actual material thing—the appearing materiality is an illusion—but thereby so is the affiliated soul and thus the entire ghost. (100)

On one level, Husserl looks as though he is presenting us with a materialistic account of ghostly phenomenon. The human dies, the soul leaves the body, but the body remains, now consigned to a world without its living counterpart—a mere corpse. From that corpse, movement is detected, and a movement that remains bound to the materiality of the body. In this respect, Husserl is right: The sight of the ghost is necessarily spatial. The ghost assumes a perspective in space and time, occupies mass, even if that mass is no more than "an intensely horrible, face *of crumpled linen*" (James 2007, 80; italics in original). However ethereal the ghost, ethereality is still a phantom of the phenomenal world. Far from the customary association of being beyond materiality, as though a figment of the imagination, the figure of the ghost is as much embodied in place as is the "visible" observer of that ghost. Indeed, the idea of a haunted place depends upon the very materiality of a ghost assuming a habitual routine in place. A placeless ghost is, after all, as inconceivable as a placeless memory; the shadow in the hallway does not linger aimlessly, but dwells in a specific place, indeed, if not specific things within that place. The sense, therefore, of a presence intensifying and diminishing in proximity to particular things is entirely consistent with the idea of the ghost as retaining a phantom relationship to the same world it did when alive.

For Husserl, however, the ghost is ultimately phrased as an "illusion," which nevertheless does not detract from its phenomenal reality. As a thought experiment, Husserl proceeds to contend with the idea of a "psychic being [appearing] and be actual while lacking a *material* Body" (1990, 100; italics in original). Even here, within this clearly delineated realm of the supernatural, Husserl draws us back to a "spatial phantom" (100), thus affixing the ghost to a negative energy, whose presence is to be discerned in a "phantom Bod[y]," possibly even a "purely visual" body (101). Thus, despite his conviction that the "possibility of actual ghosts is granted, [given that] a psychic subject without a material Body is indeed thinkable," Husserl ends by assigning an "entirely empty" reality to the ghost (101).

This strange tension between logical and actual existence belies a sedimented commitment to the visual perception of the undead, and thus marks a point of departure for our own phenomenological investigation into the supernatural. How do we find the dead? The question invites a reversal: How do the dead find *us*? Lacking the necessary sensory organs we associate with the living, the supernatural are forced to make recourse to the surface of their natural habitat, at which point human life is thought of as intervening with the otherworldly. Yet this is an illusion. The realm of the supernatural does not exist in an "elsewhere," far removed from human habitation. Nor does human life fortuitously encounter the experience of being haunted, as though ghosts dwelled in a dormant province, awakened only by the creeping dread of human fear. Rather, when the dead come, they do so alongside the living who reciprocate their desires and memories, which fuse the living with the dead.

The proof of this already-established correspondence between the living and the dead is demonstrated in Merleau-Ponty's account of the phantom limb, which we provisionally surveyed in the introduction. At stake in that discussion was evidence that the feeling of an absent limb was made possible thanks to the body's preemptive orientation toward unity and continuity, which Merleau-Ponty terms the "intentional arc." Striving to preserve the unity of selfhood, the intentional arc manifests itself as the sense of a thing that is now absent. Absent, yet still constitutive of a dynamic life-world. In this way, what the phantom limb thematizes on a local scale is the mingling of the living and the dead, with absent phenomena overlapping into the body and forming the flesh of the present.

Here, we can resummon Merleau-Ponty's account of the phantom limb with the aim of expanding its scope beyond the boundaries of the body and into the materiality of the world. This extension of the self in and through the world allows us to account for the reality of phenomenon such as ghosts without ascribing a reductive, causal analysis to their existence, be it from psychoanalysis, sociology, or any other branch of thought that contends with the ghost as a figure belying a hidden depth. In order to demonstrate this claim, it will be necessary to align ghosts and phantom limbs through a unified experience. In so doing, we will see that the experience of being haunted, of sensing ghosts, and communing with the undead is a particular manner of being-in-the-world rather than an abnormal deviation from the world.

In the first instance, let us remind ourselves that the boundaries of the lived-body do not end with its own materiality. As I have sought to show throughout, being-in-the-world involves an anonymous intentionality, in which the body incorporates and absorbs the surrounding environment in a precognitive manner. From chairs to ballrooms, from cars to walking sticks, things are exposed to a reversibility between my body and the world, with both being made from the same "stuff." As we have also seen, after a period of habituation, the boundaries demarcating the body from those things is diminished, such that an invisible force descends upon worldly things, affecting their very being, to the extent that the point where the body begins and the object ends becomes ambiguous. Extended beyond the realm of habit, objects not only become an extension of the body, they also become *possessed*

Figure 26: *Apartment, Pittsburgh. Photo by author.*

by the bodies that dwelled within them. Here, "possession" capitalizes on the double meaning of ownership and otherness. Indeed, precisely through its habitual occupancy is the other side of possession possible. When worldly things exist for long enough alongside the owners, then a reversal of nature occurs: The thing assumes the controlling role, preserving the identity of the owner long after the owner has died.

Long after physical extinction, the clothing worn by those who have since died retains an aspect of their personal being within the texture of the cloth. This is more than an imprint of the body shedding its skin upon wool, cotton, and linen. In the synthesis between the living and the dead, the invocation of a presence that has fused with a piece of cloth cannot be reduced to the empirical fact that the clothing simply smells of the person. Nor can the persistence of spirit be rationalized in terms of that same article of clothing reminding the living of the dead. In each case, a particular life is assumed *from within* the clothing. The clothing embodies the person, expresses their being, and signifies an elemental mystery in which the invisible is clothed in the visible. Yet this mystery is dynamic. When left in a closet untouched for years, a piece of clothing is not unaffected by the passing of time, but instead morphs, distancing itself from its owner before facing a new life possessed by a different presence. In his short story *Tony Takitani*, Haruki Murakami reports the following:

> These shadows had once clung to his wife's body, which had endowed them with the warm breath of life and made them move. Now, however, what hung before him were mere scruffy shadows cut off from the roots of life and steadily withering away. What were they now but worn-out old dresses devoid of any meaning whatsoever? Their rich colors danced in space like pollen rising from flowers, lodging in his eyes and ears and nostrils. The frills and buttons and epaulets and lace and pockets and belts sucked greedily at the room's air, thinning it out until he could hardly breathe. (2006, 189)

Murakami's tale of a widower seeking to commune with his dead wife is an invitation for phenomenology to place clothing alongside the importance of the lived-body. In so doing, the clothing adorned by the living becomes less a costume to shield the nakedness of the flesh and more a world in which the flesh is expressed and extended, as Merleau-Ponty states: "If I did not take off my clothes I could never see the inside of them, and it will in fact be seen that my clothes may become appendages of my body" (2006, 104). At such a point, the divisibility of body and clothing becomes ambiguous, as the possessor of the garment in turn becomes possessed by the garment.

This transition from habit to possession is consistent with the idea that the mind is not contained within the upper area of my body known as the "head," nor is the mind simply the phenomenon of my brain. Indeed, beyond phenomenology, this idea has been well covered in the "extended mind" account of consciousness (Clark 2008). Phenomenologically, the mind's being is distributed within objects of the world, generating an affective texture upon the world, as Merleau-Ponty writes: "The things of the world are not simply neutral *objects* which stand before us for our contemplation. Each one of them symbolises or recalls a particular way of behaving" (2008, 48; italics in original). This twofold axis between recollection and symbolism serves to infuse objects with a spirit that evades their own materiality, just as "the objects which haunt our dreams are meaningful in the same way" (49). In each case, objects must contend with a language that is also understood by human discourse. And this language is dynamic. In the years of a life, the objects that are seized with warmth in turn fall into an anonymous ravine, their inner attributes divested of familiarity, thus "they dwell within us as emblems of forms of life we either love or hate" (49).

That things in the world—vases, mirrors, trees—are taken up with a personal presence is beyond doubt. The critical question is: Can we detect the mind of *another person* dwelling within an object or place? True, sometimes we feel the presence of another body behind us, even though we have yet to see the person. When such an event occurs, then it is invariably the case that the person's attention is neither random nor passing. Rather, with their eyes affixed to our backs, some kind of invisible communion is activated, of which the visual sight plays only a part. It is as though the sensing organs implanted in our bodies become aware of a field of force, warning us of an approaching presence. Here, there is no physical contact, yet our minds clearly exceed the bounds of fleshy materiality. But in the case of experiencing a person or presence through things in the world, that intuitive apprehension is problematized. For what this question hints at is the detachment of embodied experience from a subject, thus producing a *phantom memory* that lurks within things, even if the person to whom those memories belong is no longer of this world.

We have already seen phantom memories materialize in the case of the ruins of trauma. There, it was possible to witness an experience without an experiencer. Part of this act of witnessing is made possible thanks to a symbolic order encoded in the language of ruins, remnants, and revenants. The sense of a place as coming alive before our eyes depends upon the bind between spatiality and hauntedness. Yet the experience of traumatic ruins remains incomplete, necessarily dispersed into a vague fog. What remains is a nocturnal murmur cast in the horror of daylight. As we know from Levinas, the shadowy murmur is a privileged phenomenon. Feeling things in our bones, we are reminded of an invisible correspondence with the world, primitive enough to send a shiver down our spines yet sufficiently elusive so as to elude being tied to a particular place. Attending to this phantom, the question concerns how we can experience a thing precisely through *not* experiencing it. The indirection of this search attests to the need to capture the invisible at work before it becomes tied down by visual perception.

The inclusion of "visible" is deliberate. Were we to speak of encountering a ghost in a place, then we would have to do so in a solely prepersonal way. Our bodies would have to speak on behalf of things that our eyes can no longer see, as one of the characters from Shirley Jackson's bewitching *The*

Haunting of Hill House tells us: "Nothing in this house moves . . . until you look away, and then you just catch something from the corner of your eye. Look at the little figurines on the shelves; when we all had our backs turned they were dancing" (2009, 110). When visual perception establishes contact with the dead, then already the moment has elapsed; the nameless thing has been assigned a name, enriched with the wealth of human value and culture, and so the specter vanishes.

AN UNCANNY MOOD

With the body extended beyond its own materiality, it becomes possible to mount a case for experiencing immaterial things through the medium of material objects. This is possible if we take seriously the idea that lived memory can detach itself from the experiencer, establishing a phantom appearance receptive only to the living body that reciprocates and recognizes that immaterial presence. Here, we must pause to distill this notion. When we think of the ghosts that have haunted the contents of this book—from Hugues Viane's "sighting" of his dead wife in *Bruges* to the experience of one's own body as being doubled by an anonymous presence—in each case, there already existed a desire to attend to the world in a particular way. Above all, this manner was characterized by a heightened sensitivity toward the lacuna in our sense of self, as Merleau-Ponty writes when discussing the phantom limb: "What it is in us which refuses mutilation and disablement is an *I* committed to a certain physical and inter-human world, who continues to tend towards his world despite handicaps and amputations" (2006, 94). Confronted with sudden discontinuity, the "I" does not relinquish the quest for continuity, but only throws a halo of significance upon those things that further its sense of fortitude. When faced with his wife's closet of clothes, Haruki Murakami's protagonist experiences her presence pulse through his body, the clothes partaking of both the wife and the widowed husband. The moment carries with it a poignancy certified by the fragmentation of identity, leaving in its wake a residual sense of self that remains part of a no-longer-existing life.

Such an experience presupposes the existence of Merleau-Ponty's "intentional arc": worldly things—derelict houses, rusty trinkets, a pair of gloves discarded on the floor—remain alive because the prepersonal body is still tied up with their being. All bodily existence is governed by this arc, "which projects round about us our past, our future, our human setting, our physical,

ideological and moral situation, or rather which results in our being situated in all these respects" (Merleau-Ponty 2006, 157). The spirit that dwells
within such experiences is thus brought alive through *a particular kind of
prepersonal longing.*

The longing is necessarily prepersonal, as the desire for continuity is not
something that can be consciously mediated. If that were the case, then the
sense of one's self as being fragmented would forever be explicit as a specific lack. Merleau-Ponty states: "The refusal of mutilation in the case of
the phantom limb . . . [is] not [a] deliberate [decision], and do[es] not take
place at the level of positing consciousness" (2006, 94). Rather, thanks to
the body's unconscious desire to "lend itself without reserve to action" when
I am in "danger" (97), a preemptive correspondence with the world is established, in which things speak to me. To this extent, the affective sense of being
haunted by objects attests to a structure inhabiting our bodies, of which we
ourselves are for the most part unaware. The body communes, possesses a
world, from which the possession is reversed.

In a moving passage concerning the knowledge of another person's death,
Merleau-Ponty writes:

> We do not understand the absence or death of a friend until the time
> comes when we expect a reply from him and when we realize that
> we shall never again receive one; so at first we avoid asking in order
> not to have to notice this silence; we turn aside from those areas of
> our life in which we might meet this nothingness, but this very fact
> necessitates that we intuit them. (2006, 93)

Aligning the loss of a friend with the loss of a limb, Merleau-Ponty draws our
attention to the "will to have a sound body" that structures each event (2006,
94). The encounter with the dead arrives only when the body's sedimented
sense of orientation and continuity draws us toward a mode of experience
that no longer reconciles with the objective world. Under the watch of the
prepersonal body, rupture ensues, and the immateriality of the dead materializes. Only then is the work of giving presence to nothingness—in a word,
grieving—visible. In the meantime, the status of the world in objective terms
does nothing to undermine the body's memory of its own being; the body
carries on, sensing the existence of a world that is now irrevocably lost.

The condition of being haunted, therefore, depends upon what might be
termed a "cryptic teleology" guided at all times by the body's unwavering

refusal to face the edge of its own existence. Through its retention of the "I," the body expresses a longing for unity that evades even the most persistent intellectual inquiry. For what is demonstrated in the phenomenology of hauntings is that the haunted body is the crystalline illustration of the ambivalent middle ground between world and self, simultaneously bridging both realms.

If I have so far suggested that the condition of being haunted depends upon recognizing the body's longing for unity, then the adjoining matter arises as to how the body corresponds with objects other than those from its own past. How, in other words, does the body experience an immaterial presence—a ghost—in an environment other than its own? The tension inherent in this question is stipulated on Freud's sense of the uncanny as "nothing new or strange, but something that was long familiar to the psyche and was estranged from it only through being repressed" (2003, 148).

Repressed from the self, the notion of a genuinely unfamiliar presence can be understood only in contrast to an already familiar context. In this respect, Freud's (2003, 148) consideration of the "acme" of the uncanny as being "represented by anything to do with death, dead bodies, revenants, spirits and ghosts" plays upon a doubling of the self, previously seen in the account of alien flesh, the dark entity, and Charlotte Delbo's division within inside her flesh. In each case, a logic of trauma exposes the self to another side of its being, shadowy to the core. And the logic is traumatic because the exposure to the otherness of selfhood is involuntary; the ghost resists introspection, resists reason. We know nothing more of the habit and dwelling of ghosts through archaeological excavations than we do from parapsychology. Presupposed in the methods of science is a conviction that ghostly phenomena lie in wait, their existence measured through careful quantitative analysis. All of which is based on the misjudgment that the ghost has already detached itself from the living investigator, be it the scientist or the philosopher.

But as we have seen throughout, the other side of being, in which the self experiences itself in another guise, is established not through the accumulation of evidence but through loss—more precisely, through *being lost*. Exposed to the anonymity of memory, the self does not experience plenitude, but its own estrangement and concealment. And for good reason: That which has been repressed from the surface necessarily opposes the unity of the I, necessarily risks overruling the sense of self as being a presence in the world. When "something that should have remained hidden" does come to the opening, then the shock of the uncanny becomes a battleground between possession of oneself and oneself as being possessed. In such an instance, the body has returned from its incubation, and thus speaks on behalf of a nameless, voiceless entity that assumes a voice by dint of its effect upon the material and corporeal realm. And what is witnessed in that turn to the other side of being is a spectral image of the self, occupying the same form but lacking the familiar content. A relic of a different era, but a relic that retains a fundamental spirit of otherness, from which nothing is either genuinely new or strange.

Nothing new or strange. Does the ghost ever exceed the dark core of the self, declaring itself to be known by others? The question is not simply spatial. For the adjoining issue central to this matter concerns the temporality of ghosts. Confronted with the ghosts who double our own experience, who lurk within childhood homes, before leaving their shadows on the things we love but now cease to be, then Jean-Claude Schmitt is surely right to suggest that "the time of ghosts was the time of living memory" (2000, 16). The notion of the ghost as finite certifies its occupancy of the material realm, carrying with it a specific teleology, the code to which resides within the living. In this respect, establishing a life span to the undead is arbitrary; just as the ghost's presence in space is not an incidental lingering, so its occupancy of time is governed by a purpose and a specific end. So long as the end remains unresolved, then the ghost's presence is one of restlessness and anxiety.

To engage with the question of how it is possible to be haunted outside of one's own haunt, we need only remind ourselves of the body's remarkable hold on the places it not only inhabits, but also passes through. At every instance, our bodies carry the remains and reminders of a lived past, fulfilling the original meaning of the sense that *we carry places with us*. Ordinarily, the places we carry with us sediment themselves in our bodies innocuously, establishing a fluid "intentional arc" that reinforces the singularity of the self's being-in-the-world. Yet, as we have seen, when the I is confronted with what Merleau-Ponty terms "mutilation and disablement," a certain mode of being is forged, which thematizes a prepersonal longing for unity.

That the experience of encountering ghosts depends upon a certain way of being-in-the-world should not surprise us. As we have seen above, identifying with phenomenon such as alien flesh, un-place, and the home's dark entity depends in each case upon a heightened sense of affectivity in the world. Access to the world is not conceptual but taken up in a particular affective framework. Such an affective intentionality is made possible thanks to a certain *mood* accompanying that framework.

The term "mood" deliberately gestures toward Heidegger's (1996) use of the concept in *Being and Time*, as *Stimmung*. Of particular interest to the experience of ghosts is the idea that certain moods augment the structure of being-in-the-world. For Heidegger, a mood is not a subsidiary aspect of experience, which disturbs rationality of its calm. Nor is mood solely the province of the senses, and thus assigned a transitory status. Rather, mood is a manifestation of the transcendence of our being-in-the-world. Mood is fundamental; it shapes the very "thereness" of a given thing. In this way, Heidegger sees mood as the mise-en-scène of how things appear for us. The world is shaped in accordance with the mood that attends to it, and in doing so colors the mode of intentionality that stretches forth from that mood: "*Mood has always already disclosed being-in-the-world as a whole and first makes possible directing oneself toward something*" (Heidegger 1996, 129; italics in original). What this means is that things are always already affected by my being long before those things are experienced in the flesh.

More than this, things are experienced in specific ways, ranging from serene to terrifying. In this way, mood presents itself as being ontologically more primordial than the abstract conceptualization of thought, as Heidegger writes: "Ontologically mood is a primordial kind of being for Dasein, in which Dasein is disclosed to itself *prior* to all cognition and volition, and *beyond* their range of disclosure" (1985, 175; italics in original). Heidegger's emphasis on the *prior* points back to Merleau-Ponty's sense of the prepersonal body as being *beyond* the realm of phenomenality, accessible only indirectly. Yet precisely through that indirection is the primordiality of the prepersonal body understood. Accordingly, by joining Heidegger's account of mood with the prepersonal body of Merleau-Ponty, we begin to get a sense of how a particular kind of embodied mood shades, affects, and sculpts the very fabric of the world on a transcendental level.

My hypothesis is that the mood that will lead us closer to the experience of the haunting falls under what Heidegger terms "angst" (1996, 176). Although the context of Heidegger's account of angst—also translated as "anxiety"—is well known, it is worth surveying this terrain given its privileged ontological status. The reason for the privileging of this mood is twofold. On the one hand, for Heidegger, angst instigates a disruption in our experience of the world. In contrast to fear, which is directed toward an object, anxiety's intentionality is essentially without ground, lacking a distinct object of perception. Because of this break in intentionality, in the mood of angst, the world itself obtrudes, as he writes: "*That about which one has Angst is being-in-the-world as such*" (174; italics in original).

Angst, therefore, is not a mood peculiar to the privacy of the self. It is not, in other words, a mood that points to the contents of subjective experience, and that alone. As such, angst retains an indefiniteness, in which "the world has the character of complete insignificance" (Heidegger 1996, 174). Yet insignificance does not signify a diminishing of presence. Quite the opposite. As we know from Heidegger's celebrated "tool analysis," when things go missing in the world, or are otherwise broken, their presence becomes conspicuous, obtruding from the world. In the mood of angst, this logic of circumspection extends to the world as a whole. Doing so, conspicuousness becomes a formal feature of the world, such that being-in-the-world is thematized as an instant of rupture: "Being anxious discloses, primordially and directly, the world as world" (175). In such a mood the security of being is disturbed, and our everyday absorption in the world collapses.

Second, in light of angst's rupturing movement, a particular affective mode of intentionality arises, to which Heidegger assigns the term "uncanny": "Here the peculiar indefiniteness of that which Dasein finds itself involved in with *Angst* initially finds expression: the nothing and nowhere. But uncanniness means at the same time not-being-at-home" (1996, 176).

Heidegger's alignment between uncanniness, angst, and not-being-at-home is notable. Through the experience of angst, the surface of the world is shown from the outside, in the process infecting "tranquillized self-assurance" with an insecurity, of which Da-Dasein is now aware. Aware of its own being-in-the-world, the fundamental movement of Heidegger's uncanny is to individuate Dasein from "everyday familiarity" (1996, 176).

Just what Dasein is being individuated from is Heidegger's notion of "tranquillized familiarity" as being the province of "the they" (*das Man*), by which he refers to a generalized, impersonal "one," able to shield Dasein from its own facticity (1996, 176–77). Through angst, the uncanny intervenes, articulates itself with an unequivocal presence, and thus dislodges Dasein from its "everyday lostness in the they" (177). Yet this intervention does not neutralize the world as a referential whole; to be clear, the world persists just as it did before angst. The world does not suddenly descend into an amorphous, homogeneous mass, from which human life is wrought by a ceaseless state of torment. Indeed, Heidegger's "angst" need not entail the common usage of the term, which tends to accent anxiety as a mode of incipient panic. Heidegger: "*Angst* can arise in the most harmless situations. Nor does it have any need for darkness, in which things usually become uncanny to us more easily. In the dark there is emphatically "nothing" to see, although the world is *still* "there" *more obtrusively*" (177; italics in original).

Through angst, worldliness persists, as do the ontic lives of beings. Only now, the world recedes from Dasein, with all avenues of absorption blocked by a mood of anxiety and unhomeliness, and thus assuming a peculiar aura to it. Indeed, precisely because the world persists as it did before angst, thus establishing a frame of context, is its unhomeliness possible.

In such a light, things lose their bearings, become unhomely. The world presents itself with a sense of being dereal, forever distanced from the subject in the midst of it. The network of meaningful correspondences between things collapses, and so they lose their depth. Yet this experience of lack is not a subsidiary of familiar being-in-the-world, nor is it an abnormal instance of the everyday. Rather, what is shown through Heidegger's analysis of angst is that not-being-at-home "belongs to the essential constitution of Dasein," given that the uncanny is transcendental to being-in-the-world, even when "tranquillized" (1996, 177).

Considered broadly, therefore, what emerges from Heidegger's account of the uncanny is a mood that has less to do with the psychology of the individual and more to do with a particular way of being-in-the-world, into which the world appears in a specific manner. What transpires is a type of mood that is particularly attuned to a pervasive and yet innocuous sense of oppression. It is a mood of vague disquiet, in which the world undergoes a subtle shift in its presence. That the shift is subtle means only that estrangement from the everyday is amplified. As such, the uncanny does not descend from afar, nor does it violently intervene within the fabric of the world. Instead, "it is already 'there'—and yet nowhere. It is so near that it is oppressive and stifles one's breath—and yet it is nowhere" (Heidegger 1996, 174). This ambiguity between the familiar and the unfamiliar recalls Freud's dialectic of the uncanny, in which a prior knowledge of the uncanny thing is a condition of its eerie affectivity. Only, in Heidegger, it is not individual things that become imbued with an uncanny aspect, but the world as a whole.

If we align Heidegger's account of angst with our phenomenological foray into ghostly and haunted phenomena, then what comes to the surface is the centrality of not-being-at-home. In each case, a particular type of mood unfolds, in which the unity of the self (and here, we can deviate from the Heideggerian terminology) is put into question. For Heidegger, the uncanny is a rupture of "tranquillized familiarity," a summons to individuation and authenticity. For us, the uncanny is an instant of heightened affectivity, in which self-awareness of the body's prepersonal longing for that which no longer exists comes to the foreground.

The prepersonal dimension of longing peculiar to the uncanny, which we have identified in Merleau-Ponty's account of the phantom limb and in which the body orients itself toward a no-longer-existing world, can now be seen as extended to more than a specific limb of the lived-body, and thus infused into the mood of being-in-the-world as a totality. What bridges these experiences is the thematic sense of mood and world reconciling through the rubric of the *unheimlich*. In the shadow of the uncanny, the world itself becomes unhomely.

The mood of the uncanny thus sets in place—in a concrete sense—a reciprocity between subject and world, in which both are cast in an unhomely light. Thanks to this shared correspondence, the uncanny subject—the subject for whom not-being-in-the-world is existentially realized—is necessarily more attuned to uncanny phenomena than the subject immersed in his or her "entangled absorption in the 'world'" (Heidegger 1996, 176).

That the history of ghost sightings, from Hamlet to Roderick Usher, coincides with a melancholy mind-set is consistent with a mode of being in which hypersensitivity aligns with existential and physical disturbance. Far from mere symptoms of a "disturbed mind," however, the intimacy between hauntings and melancholy attests to a creative renewal of the world rather than a retreat from it. Indeed, the very notion of being "ill at ease" in the world means that subjectivity becomes imbued with a world that can no longer be taken for granted, thus accessing portals that are otherwise inaccessible. Because of this heightened affectivity, things are affected with a thematic and experiential content that aligns with the uncanny subject, such that world and self are each mirrored in the other's mood. From the "nothing and the nowhere," things protrude from their silent anonymity, and thus carry with them a germ of strangeness accessible only in a mood of unhomeliness.

No wonder, therefore, that in grimoires dealing with necromancy, contact with the undead is phrased in terms of a communion, in which the trapped souls are purported to dwell within the living, as nineteenth-century occultist Eliphas Levi states: "The beings in question, for the most part, cannot speak except by a ringing in our ears produced by the nervous shock to which I have referred, and commonly they can reason only by reflecting our thoughts and our reveries" (1975, 121). The continuity between Heidegger's account of angst as a mood and Levi's notion of the undead communicating via the living is not as arbitrary as it might first appear. For what Levi is drawing our attention to is the notion that liminal phenomenon speaks through the lived-body, and indeed is articulated only from the experience of one's own body. This is possible only through the two worlds joining together in an altered state, which Levi will refer to as a "waking somnambulism" (121).

By underscoring the role of the body in the uncanny—which itself is con-spicuously absent in Heidegger's account—we begin to get a sense of the extent to which the embodied subject becomes the means for otherworldly phenomena to emit a presence. Similarly, discussing the dialectic of the *heim-lich* and the *unheimlich*, Freud offers us a quotation: "I sometimes feel like a sleepwalker who believes in ghosts: every corner seems to him eerie and frightening" (2003, 134). This conscious sleep allows the body to be em-ployed as a medium, quite apart from its own self-awareness of that use. From encountering the ghost in its haunt, we thus cross into a shared realm, whereupon the living becomes the voice of the dead, mirroring the distur-bances from beyond.

When asked, therefore, how the body can experience a ghost in an environ-ment other than its own, the answer emerges: *through developing a chiasmatic*

Figure 27: *Bandstand, London. Courtesy of Mark Dodds.*

relationship with place, in which the haunt and the haunted become one thanks to a shared mood. Already in our analysis of Merleau-Ponty's ideas of "flesh" and "wild being," we have seen how the chiasmatic fold marks an entwining, whereby "we become the others and we become the world" (1968, 160). This reversibility between self and world establishes a point of contact for the flesh of the living to touch that of the undead. Exposed to the unhomeliness of its own mutilation, the haunted body expands its loss of security to the broader world rather than retracting into an insular domain. In much the same way that the body of the nostalgic adapts certain features of the world to accommodate spatiotemporal discontinuity, so the body of the haunted extends to a world that corresponds with its own spectral disquiet.

THE HAUNTING

You love the night. From the jagged canvas of this dark space, an immense space unfolds. Infinite in its depth, the space stretches from the alcove in the childhood home to fossilised patches of water found on planets other than your own. You stand at the shore of this space, its immensity felt through the flesh. Often, the space appears vacant, a barren cosmos, already expired. At other times, the space murmurs with a shadowy presence, humming in the dark sky. Things gather within this presence, a half-dreamed memory, of which only glimmers are accessible to the conscious body. But the fragments are buried deep within the human body, their light extended far beyond the limits of the flesh. Guided by these corporeal morsels, you reach further out to this world, allowing the fog of memory to shape the world into a recognisable scene. Long before you are in touch with the world, the world is already with you, overlapping with the unresolved desires and melancholy dreams that prevent your senses from falling into a state of harmony. And you are haunted by this absence of harmony. At night, you dream of the residue that outlasts the day. Your body refuses to give up on the sorrow that your waking self cannot contain. The senses do not sleep, even when we you are no longer conscious that there is a world. Your body persists beyond the night, salvaging at the dark walls of the unconscious for a unity that was destroyed in the waking world. When waking, the image becomes clear: The haunted house, in which you find yourself time and again, at once a composite of the old and the new, the intimate and the anonymous, is nothing less than *the human body itself.*

Our excursion into hauntings has discovered the life of a ghost, the prox-imity of which does not dwell in some foreign land, nor does it reside in derelict mansions and dilapidated factories, waiting to be conjured from dormancy by human intervention. Rather, the ghost expresses itself primar-ily through its native haunt, the human body. The result of this synthesis between the ghost and the body is the unity of the haunt and the haunted, an interplay that is possible thanks to the fact that "the body," so writes Merleau-Ponty, "is the vehicle of being in the world, and having a body is, for a living creature, to be intervolved in a definite environment" (2006, 94). Given this inseparable relation between embodiment and place, our final task in this phenomenological work is to facilitate the movement of the ghost from the body to place, thus establishing the basis of a topography of haunt-ings. For what we have seen in these final pages is the genesis of a body, whose heightened affectivity and existential drama are sufficiently visceral in pres-ence so as to mold the world in the shape of the body's own being. But what of this haunted world, this ontology of absence? If, as we have said, experi-encing a ghost is less a question of "seeing" things in the world, and more an issue of a particular mood, in which the anonymity of the prepersonal "I" strives toward a world that no longer exists, then how does materiality become expressive of this unhomely mode of being-in-the-world?

We know from experience that the body remains in the world, despite the contingencies of existence. Indeed, beyond its own dissolution, the body has but no choice except to persist in the world, and thus to strive toward a unity within it. As such, the experience of ghosts and hauntings is not confined to an interior space held within the physical organs of flesh and blood. Already we know that the relationship between ghostly phenomenon and subjectivity is possible through developing a chiasmatic relationship with place, in which the haunt and the haunted become one thanks to a shared mood. Through this relationship, we have touched upon the role of place as a force of expression for the haunted body. Indeed, following Merleau-Ponty, the body's necessary rela-tionship with an environment means that place becomes the voice of the body's own being. More than a physical site to contain me, more even than Bach-elard's "psychologically complex" oneiric house that guards my daydreams, place as an expression of the body allows me to experience a unity, in which I "retain the practical field . . . enjoyed before mutilation," that would be quite impossible were my relationship to place static (Merleau-Ponty 2006, 94).

As Merleau-Ponty writes, "For if it is true that I am conscious of my body *via* the world, that it is the unperceived term in the centre of the world

310 CONCLUSION

towards which all objects turn their face, it is true for the same reason that my body is the pivot of the world" (94). As the center of the world, place adapts to the body rather than vice versa. As such, when the body's being undergoes existential mutilation—be it when the subject is possessed by another subjectivity, or through the experience of anonymity within intimacy, or even through the total bifurcation of identity through traumatic memory—then, the world does not remain unaffected by the body's suffering. The world subordinates itself to the prepersonal body's repression of its own disturbance. Likewise, when an insect loses a limb, it "simply continues to belong to the same world and moves in it with all its powers" (90). Only now, this phantom limb produces a phantom world, a world that only the disabled insect experiences in accordance with its broken body.

The fluidity between phantom limbs and phantom memories is entirely coherent, and the term "mutilation" is thus applicable to both a physiological and an existential context. In both cases, the body responds to the world in accordance with the absence at the center of its being. In the corporeal realm "the reflexes themselves are never blind processes: they adjust themselves to a 'direction' of the situation, and express our orientation towards a 'behavioural setting' just as much as the action of the 'geographical setting' upon us" (Merleau-Ponty 2006, 91). This is the underside of the body's prepersonal being at work, the anonymous background movement of the reflexes adjusting the body to a world, whose meaning has shifted in light of damage afflicted upon the body.

Through this silent vigilance, things that are not objectively present— above all, the premutilated body—are posited in the world. As such, the protraction of the premutilated body carries with it a side effect: The temporality of place is altered, and things cease to be "of the past" and instead disembark on their own timescale. The limb "continues to count in the insect's scheme of things" (Merleau-Ponty 2006, 90). Thus, the insect experiences a part of itself where objectively speaking that life is now over. But the insect's mourning is deferred, its acceptance of loss repressed.

Along with the insect, the broken subject experiences the world not only in a spatially dis-eased manner, but with a temporal fracture, too. We recall Kierkegaard speaking in proxy of the nostalgic body: "He is always absent, never present to himself" (1971, 220). The logic is amplified in the case of the haunted body. Thanks to the body's tremendous power of repression, the unchartered realm of a world void of ghosts is seldom revealed. Thus, repression does not disperse the phantom, but only displaces it. As Merleau-Ponty explains, repression consists of the subject "encountering on this course [of action] some barrier, and, since he has the strength neither to surmount the obstacle nor to abandon the enterprise, he remains imprisoned in the attempt and uses up his strength indefinitely renewing it in spirit" (Merleau-Ponty 2006, 95). Remaining imprisoned within the schematic of an old order, this melancholy mood begins to project beyond the flesh of the body to that of the world. In doing so, time "does not close up on traumatic experience; the subject remains open to the same impossible future, if not in his explicit thoughts, at any rate in his actual being" (95). How this "impossible future" is played out spatially is the final task that now awaits us.

*∗∗

Eleanor Vance's death at the end of Shirley Jackson's novel *The Haunting of Hill House* is the last in a series of uncanny events in the book, in which the possessor becomes the possessed and the possessed becomes the possessor. After all, the uncertainty surrounding the protagonist's death centers on the question of: *Who* caused her to "send the car directly at the great tree at the curve of the driveway" (2009, 245): herself or Hill House? Indeed, by the time we get to the end of the novel, prising Eleanor Vance apart from Hill House becomes problematic, as she remarks to herself while attempting to flee the house: "They can't turn me out or shut me out or laugh at me or hide from me; I won't go, and Hill House belongs to *me*" (245; italics in original). The character's "disappearance" into the house is the logical outcome of what Eliphas Levi (1975, 121) termed a "waking somnambulism," a process in which the dead coexist alongside the living, in turn forming a unified phenomena. Whose hands are driving the wheel that plunges her into a tree, killing her on the spot? The reader is just as unsure as Eleanor Vance is: "This is me, I am really really really doing it by myself. In the unending, crashing second before the car hurled into the tree she thought clearly, *Why am I doing this? Why am I doing this? Why don't they stop me?*" (Jackson 2009, 245–46; italics in original).

Jackson's novel is an exemplary treatment of the ambiguity of hauntings, and thus serves to viscerally demonstrate the chiasmatic relationship with place, in which the haunt and the haunted become one. At the heart of the novel is the drama of Eleanor Vance, who has spent the majority of her adult life caring for her disabled mother, until her death. Freed from the burden of attending to her mother, Eleanor accepts an invitation from an anthropologist, Dr. Montague, to investigate paranormal activity through residing in Hill House. Joined by two other participants, the narrative plots their collective experience of hauntings within Hill House, with the psycho-dynamics of Eleanor at the forefront. Throughout the novel, the reader is never entirely clear if the "sightings" of ghostly phenomenon at Hill House are a symptom of Eleanor's guilt that she feels for her mother's death or a facet of the house itself. Indeed, at times we are led to believe that the manifestation of hauntings is nothing more than an expression of Elea-nor's already heightened vulnerability. At other times, assigning responsibil-ity for the hauntings to Eleanor's psychology is at odds with the fact that those same spectral mirages are witnessed by the group as a whole. As such, the ambiguity between the possessed and the possessor blurs the notion of the haunting as a "reality" outside of subjectivity but also bound to subjec-tivity. Speaking of the formal character of the house, Dr. Montague remarks: "Hill House, whatever the cause, has been unfit for human habitation for up-wards of twenty years. What it was like before then, whether its personality was molded by the people who lived here, or the things they did, or whether it was evil from its start are all questions I cannot answer" (Jackson 2009, 70).

In the shadow of this dark uncertainty, what unfolds is a constant overlap-ping of the materiality of the house with the flesh of Eleanor, eventually result-ing in a Dionysian self-implosion, led by a "self" whose identity is unclear.

How do we get to the point where the haunt and the haunted become one, so rendering the experience of ghostly phenomenon possible? In Jack-son's novel, this development is surveyed with an acute sensitivity to the genetic unfolding of a place's possession of the subject. At first sight, Elea-nor's relationship to the house is one of resistance and abject terror: "The house had caught her with an atavistic turn in the pit of the stomach . . . listening to the sick voice inside her which whispered, *Get away from here, get away*" (Jackson 2009, 35). Yet even at the outset this revulsion is met with an ambivalence: "But this is what I came so far to find," we are told on the same page (35). Eleanor's sense that the house holds something more than its own materiality is predicated on a tacit determinism that runs through the novel, as Dr. Montague says by way of warning: "Hill House has a reputation for insistent hospitality; it seemingly dislikes letting its guests get away" (67). In turn, this conflation of the abjection of the home's power and Eleanor's desire to have her existence authenticated establishes a literally uncanny relation, whereupon the experience of being homesick is also an expression of homecoming.

Figure 28: *Kitchen, Brighton. Photo by author.*

Nowhere is the unhomely haunt of Hill House clearer than in a scene halfway through the novel. Exploring the nooks and crannies of the house, the group spot some writing on a wall, apparently written in a chalk and "incredibly real, going in broken lines over the thick paneling of the hallway" (145). Moving closer, they discern the message: "HELP ELEANOR COME HOME" (146). Eleanor's reaction is bewilderment: "*Why*—?," which in turn converts to an anxious affirmation: "That's it. . . . It knows my name, doesn't it? It knows *my* name" (146; italics in original). This sense of the house recognizing Eleanor as belonging to it as Eleanor recognizes the house belonging to her implies a sentience that is the province of neither subject in isolation from the other. What emerges in this correspondence between the house and the character is the simultaneity of consciousness, with the house as expressive of Eleanor's being as she herself is. Far from abject terror, the communication between house and human points to a strange entwining, in which the "autonomous" subject finds herself traced within the walls of the house.

As if to disprove that the writing on the wall is an occult manifestation of Eleanor's "neurosis" and nothing more (especially given that Eleanor is

inducted into Hill House because of her purported power of telekinesis),
soon after the chalk writing, another inscription appears, this time written in
blood: "HELP ELEANOR COME HOME ELEANOR" (155). That the plea is written in
blood points to the allegorical absorption of Eleanor within the flesh of the
house, as though the plea were carved into her own body. At this point, Eleanor has entered a state of rationalized engagement with the writing: "I was
supposed to be *much* more frightened than this, I think, and I'm not because
it's simply *too* horrible to be real" (156; italics in original). The implicit
suggestion that there is something unreal about Hill House gestures back
to an earlier remark she makes in respect of Hill House's "disjointed" design: "What happens when you go back to a real house?" (107). Hill House's
status as "unreal" accords with its ontological status as being haunted. For
what is unreal about Hill House is its expressive corporeality, which, in turn,
reflects the corporeality of the bodies within it.

This union of flesh and materiality is made possible thanks to the fact
that both aspects partake of the same "mood." This is clear if we recall that
for Heidegger, mood is not something inside a person, but something that
a person—or *persons*—can be in. The inclusion of "persons" points to the
fact that a mood need not be solitary, but instead can assume a general atmosphere, or ambience. Indeed, *Stimmung* carries with it an association of
mood within a musical sense, as that which establishes a general atmosphere
in which the mood becomes an interpersonal phenomenon, forever vibrating
against each individual being. That there is such a thing as a "public mood"
attests to the natural idea of a mood existing beyond the solitude of the individual. Alongside its public structure, the adjoining use of "attunement"
reinforces the point that mood is not an incidental side effect of being-in-the-
world, but the very means by which we attune ourselves *to* the world.

If attuning ourselves to things in a particular way shapes the manner in
which our being-in-the-world is given, then what we see throughout Jackson's novel is the mood of hauntings structure both the bodies of the guests
and the body of the house. This interplay between a collective haunting
and the house precludes the accusation that the experience of supernatural
phenomena within Hill House is nothing more than a symptom of Eleanor
Vance's overactive imagination, thus consigning the "ghosts" to a fictitious
appearance.

Indeed, this claim is clearly disproved in a scene from the book in which
both Eleanor and another of the participants, Theodora, hear banging on
the walls. At first, we are made to think of this banging as nothing more

than a symptom of Eleanor's conscience inducing guilt from within: "Coming, mother, coming," she says with a start (Jackson 2009, 127). But this is a misdirection, as Eleanor is in Hill House, and her mother is dead: "It is a noise down the hall, far down at the end, near the nursery door, and terribly cold, *not* my mother knocking on the wall" (127; italics in original). The noise intensifies, and Theodora hears it, too: "Like something alive. Yes. Like something alive" (128). Eleanor makes an assessment: "It sounded . . . like a hollow noise, a hollow bang, as though something were hitting the doors with an iron kettle, or an iron bar, or an iron glove" (128). Eventually they both force the noise to subside, but only after Eleanor instructs it to "go away, go away!" (129).

That both Eleanor and Theodora hear the noise is a testament to Jackson's urge for us to approach ghostly phenomenon in a relational manner, rather than ascribing a causal explanation to the psychology of the characters. Moreover, even if we assign the existence of the phantom sound to Eleanor's unconscious memories, this is all the more evidence that Theodora's hearing of the sound is a result of a mood shared between them. For what we are witness to in this scene is an affective intentionality, which is expressive of both characters in what Heidegger terms *"a disclosive submission to world out of which things that matter to us can be encountered"* (1996, 129–30; italics in original).

Prior to cognitive abstraction, the mood imbuing a place and its people establishes a meaningful series of correspondences that is framed by a field of force not instantly accessible. This is why Eleanor's experience of Hill House is uncanny: the mood catches her unaware and "would never be able to discover anything like what is threatening" (Heidegger 1996, 130), even though she belongs to the mood and is expressive of it.

Even at the beginning of the novel, there is an invitation to consider the mood of persons alongside the mood of the house: "No live organism can continue for long to exist sanely under conditions of absolute reality; even larks and katydids are supposed, by some, to dream" (Jackson 2009, 3). Far from a dream, however, Eleanor's experience of Hill House expresses the burgeoning of "absolute reality," the piercing clarity that fails to domesticate both the house and its subjects. That she should then claim that Hill House "makes me sick, but it doesn't frighten me" (157) only reinforces the point that Eleanor Vance was already a part of Hill House long before she actually entered its domain: "It is already 'there,'" so we recall Heidegger remarking, "and yet nowhere" (1996, 174).

The ambivalent con-fusion of sickness and fright attests to the involvement of Hill House within the structure of Eleanor's mood of *angst*. For what is visible within her experience of being absorbed by the place is the gradual erosion of her "entanglement" within the world (Heidegger 1996, 174). In a literal way, the materiality of Hill House embodies that for which she is anxious: "being-in-the-world" (176). This is clear if we remind ourselves that up until the point of arriving at Hill House, Eleanor "could not remember ever being truly happy in her adult life; her years with her mother had been built up devotedly around small guilts and small reproaches, constant weariness, and unending despair" (Jackson 2009, 6).

Only this initial despair has, in Heidegger's (1996, 164) terminology, "fallen prey to the 'world,'" forever directed at things rather than the ground(lessness) of its own being. And the world of Eleanor prior to Hill House is structured by subordination, guilt, and a flight into the "tranquillized self-assurance" of the figure of her mother as *das Man*; that is, the other for whom "*disburdens* Dasein in its everydayness [and] accommodates Dasein in its tendency to take things easily and make them easy" (Heidegger 1996, 120; italics in original). Heidegger's claim that "the they" renders everyday as "easy" for Dasein reminds us that the experience of "unending despair" is also a bridge to homely familiarity and reinforced borders, even if those borders are essentially pernicious. Thus, the indictment of "easy" refers less to a carefree being and more to the refusal to resist the hold of "the they." Having disowned her own responsibility, it turns out that "Eleanor had been waiting for something like Hill House" in order to summon her from a directionless existence (Jackson 2009, 7).

Read in this Heideggerian way, Eleanor's act of caring for her mother, and thus experiencing the guilt and unhappiness that coexisted with that life, is more than a case of being imprisoned by her duties. Rather, the eleven years spent caring for the disabled mother are manifestly an expression of Eleanor's attempt at rendering "tranquillized familiarity" homely. In the shadow of her mother's death, this homely manner of being-in-the-world ruptures, making it clear that "entangled flight *into* the being-at-home of publicness is flight *from* not-being-at-home, that is, from the uncanniness which lies in Dasein as thrown, as being-the-world entrusted to itself in its being" (Heidegger 1996, 177; italics in original). Heidegger draws our attention to the intimacy between being-at-home and not-being-at-home. Fleeing into the "easy" world of *das Man* is at the same time a recognition of that which Eleanor is fleeing from: the primordiality of not-being-at-home.

Figure 29: *Stanmer House, Sussex. Photo by author.*

It is for this reason, therefore, that Eleanor Vance's sickness within Hill House is also a returning, a recognition of and struggle with the nothingness and "unending despair" that structured her adult life until now. In this respect, the affective polarities of Hill House, from cold to warm, inside to outside, serene to terrifying, signal Eleanor's own attunement to the parallel mood. "*I don't like it here*," she remarks when first entering the house (Jackson 2009, 37; italics in original). As she feels herself "disappearing inch by inch" (201) into the house, so she believes that she has "broken the spell of Hill House and somehow come inside. I am home, she thought, and stopped in wonder at the thought. I am home, I am home, she thought" (232). But this unhomely home does not serve to cut the uncanny short. At no point in Jackson's story do the characters domesticate the ghosts that inhabit Hill House, thus "tranquillizing" not-being-at-home. That the story concludes with the protagonist's death should confirm the uneasy resolution of the book. Rather, what we witness is a destabilizing of perceptual, experiential, and ontological norms, such that assessing what belongs to Hill House and what is superimposed on it from afar is undermined by the collapse of a "real house" (107). But this incursion of sedimented norms carries the reader into this rupturing, too. For in its refusal to redeem the uncanny of its strangeness, the reader is also drawn into the materiality of the haunt, alienating us not only from the home we have so far dwelt in, but also from the distance between the living and the dead.

The synthesis of mood and materiality in Shirley Jackson's *The Haunting of Hill House* helps us understand how the relation between the haunt and the haunted is possible. Thanks to the prereflective power of mood, things in the world become imbued with a particular atmosphere before they are apprehended in abstraction. By extending itself into the world, the body expresses itself in the places it inhabits, experiencing the drama of its loss from the inside out. For the haunted subject, the very phenomenality of the world becomes an avenue of expression for that which is hidden to perceptual experience. Place summons the body's mood, of which cognitive thought is not yet aware, and when the materiality of the world corresponds with the teleology of the body, so a disturbance is felt within the flesh: "A shadow flits before me, not thou, but like to thee" (Tennyson 1991, 164).

But are those things shadows of the undead? Are they dismembered revenants terrorizing the living through their own disharmony? Are the groans and wails heard at night immaterial manifestations from beyond? Of these questions, there are no clear answers, and those that have been formulated have a rich history that is beyond the scope of the current work (Davies 2009; Finucane 1996). At the heart of ghostly phenomenon is a fundamental obscurity, which precludes a genealogical analysis of the ghost's exact origin in space and time. Partly this obscurity is due to the fact that the ghost presents itself as a trace of that which no longer exists. More important, however, the origin of the specter is of subsidiary interest to a phenomenological investigation of ghostly matter. Our concern is not with diagnosing the source of what is experienced, as though to prove or disprove the experience of supernatural phenomenon, but instead of remaining open to the possibility that an experience of ghostly phenomenon is both natural and supernatural simultaneously.

In positive terms, we are now able to assert that the condition of being haunted depends upon a certain manner of being, a certain way of experiencing the world, which I have outlined above. In contending with the experience of hauntings as a particular bodily mode of being-in-the-world, we have sought to demonstrate the phenomenal nature of ghosts rather than their appearance as a symptom of something other than itself. Far from the repressed ailments of an ill society, the ghosts we hear and experience within place are as much a part of the world as are our memories and dreams. Likewise, the experience of the ghost is not a side effect of nocturnal fantasies nor a misdirected mode of perception, but a condition of our being-in-the-world in a particular way.

As we have seen, the mood that draws us to the "species of the frightening that goes back to what was once well known and had long been familiar" is angst (Freud 2003, 124). Because of its attunement to the world as un-homely, angst establishes a correspondence between a subject haunted by his or her self-discontinuity and a world that persists despite that discontinuity. As such, the tension between discontinuous and continuous modes of time is at the genesis for the experience of being haunted, and, as we have also seen, is played out in both corporeal and material terms. Corporeally, the prepersonal body strives to retain its belonging in a world, which, logically speaking, no longer exists. Materially, this blockage of time spills over into the fabric of place, suffusing the world with an uncanny atmosphere filtered through the subject's own discontinuity.

Speaking once more of the phantom limb, Merleau-Ponty is instructive: "The traumatic experience does not survive as a representation in the mode of objective consciousness and as a 'dated' moment; it is of its essence to survive only as a manner of being and with a certain degree of generality" (2006, 96). The generality peculiar to the traumatic experience leaves enough room for ambiguity to casts its ray over a still-forming world, in the process augmenting that world to the shape of the subject's (mutilated) being. Affixed to a static date, both personal time and impersonal time would decompose. Instead, the body goes on, longing for a unity that is constitutive of its very being-in-the-world. The result of this dialectic between continuity and discontinuity is an "abstraction of that existence, which lives on a former experience, or rather on the memory of having had the memory, and so on, until finally only the essential form remains" (96).

The communication between the haunted body and the world serves to "place" the ghost that would otherwise disperse were the world the habitat of disembodied spirits alone. That human bodies inhabit the earth means that communion with less-embodied entities is possible. Thus, the ghost occupies a particular relationship with the place it haunts, in the process articulating its desires in and through space. In this way, the ghost's dwelling-in-place shatters the linearity of time, its legacy one of repetition and returning.

Beyond the ambiguity of its presence, the very sighting of the ghost makes one thing clear: *Its work is not yet done.*

The excess of life that drips slowly into the dead, so reviving them one last time, disrupts the course of time. The ghost returns, carrying with it the promise to amend the damage either it incurred upon the living or the living incurred upon it. Thanks to this legacy, a correspondence is established between immaterial and material realms, such that the routine of the dead is resurrected by the haunted body in the present.

In a key paragraph, Merleau-Ponty writes: "The ruin of the objective world, abandonment of true action, flight into a self-contained realm are conditions favouring the illusion of those who have lost a limb in that it too presupposes the erasure of reality" (2006, 99). Merleau-Ponty's correlation between the alteration of reality and the mutilation of the body demonstrates the role of the body as not only being expressive of a mood, but also serving as a receptacle for a strange reality, in which the present mingles with a half-lit past, and where the division between natural and supernatural becomes increasingly ambiguous. In this altered reality, the "ruin of the objective world" is presented as a residue, but a residue that is governed from the perspective of a sedimented past.

The intersection of the ghostly figure of the past that circumvents the destruction of time and the materiality giving voice to that past is at all times expressed through the centrality of the body. As proof of this bind, often the entwining between the visibility of the haunted and the invisibility of the haunter becomes ambiguous. In a section from James Thomson's *The City of Dreadful Night*, this ambiguity is writ large:

> I have seen phantoms there that were as men
> And men that were as phantoms flit and roam;
> Marked shapes that were not living to my ken,
> Caught breathings acrid as with Dead Sea foam:
> The City rests for man so weird and awful,
> That his intrusion there might seem unlawful,
> And phantoms there may have their proper home.
> (1993, 43)

Given this reversibility between the human body and the phantom, with each incorporated into the other's world, it follows that the relation between embodiment and haunting becomes less a question of eliciting certain features from the world—archetypically, "old houses, with resounding galleries, and dismal state-bed-chambers, and haunted wings shut up for many years, through which we may ramble, with an agreeable creeping up our back, and encounter any number of ghosts" (Dickens 2010, 242)—and more an issue of the kind of relation we have with place. That environments as diverse as supermarkets, castles, airplanes, and childhood homes have the ability to haunt us testifies to the multifarious relationship between hauntings and place. The ghosts that frequent places do not consign themselves to abandoned asylums on the edge of the city, nor is their sole haunt lonely and rugged landscapes far from civilization. Rather, in the landscape of ghosts, revenants, and specters, it is the human body, still alive and yet to some extent already grieving in its death, that serves as the guide.

With the body as the original haunted house, an uncanny parallel to Bachelard's oneirism unfolds. For just as Bachelard's (1994, 13) oneiric house overlaps, folds, and secretes itself into the world, so establishing a thread of continuity for the dreamer of place, so the haunted body sets in place its own home-less wanderings and unhomely secrets. If we are to entrust our thoughts to Bachelard, then we must agree that the body's memories and dreams of the places it once inhabited are not restricted to the night. Those same dreams that flash before us when the world has turned quiet and the earth has become nothing more than an eerie night reappear when waking. For Bachelard, memories place the dreamer, and so afford repose to the anxiety of being. As they achieve this monumental task, continuity is won, and the ineffable grip of the past is preserved: "The odor of raisins! It is an odor that is beyond description, one that it takes a lot of imagination to smell" (13).

We take Bachelard's oneirism seriously; we admire his topophilia in the sincerest terms. Because of this pledge to his thought, we must be prepared to account for an oneirism that is conceived not in the language of repose and intimacy, but in the troubled dreams of mutilation and estrangement. The body that no longer belongs to a natural world now stands adrift, its desires for home matched only by its awareness of the anonymity of a different body, the origin of which precedes the existence of the self, as such: "These terrors are of older standing. They date beyond the body—*or without the body, they would have been the same*" (Lovecraft 1994, 99; italics in original). Thus the body carries with it a foreign life, whose invisible carvings produce a phantom memory upon the visible world. Bachelard is right in this respect: the body's memory of place marks a "group of organic habits," forever pushing at "the successive houses in which we have lived" (Bachelard 1994, 14–15). Only now, those same habits engender themselves not to intimacy, but to spectrality—to the formation of *ghosts*.

In so doing, the body's sense of being lost forces the silent dwelling of anonymous ghosts to materialize in places that appear incongruent with the very notion of hauntings. The human body, conceived of habit and desire, torn by plenitude and lack, gives itself over to the world in a particular mood, and thus carries with it a prepersonal longing that exists not solely in relation to the childhood home, with its latches, alcoves, and nooks, but instead extends to the compartments and aisles of the world more broadly.

Whereas we previously witnessed this prepersonal intervention in our study of alien flesh, whereupon the body is summoned to reconstitute the flesh of the world when that flesh is undercut by disembodiment, what we are now seeing is an extension of this model of transcendental embodiment. For in the case of our previous study, an appeal to alien flesh took place only in certain modes of anxious embodiment, particularly those that threatened the unity of the subject. Not only was this incursion of the body's anonymity limited to particular liminal experiences, it was also to be understood in a strictly retrospective fashion. In such a case, the flesh of the world disclosed itself through the deferred expression of the body's memory of place. Suddenly, the experiences I thought of as being peculiarly "mine" were proven to be constituted by a manifold field of forces, not all of which were coincidental with "my" experience.

Applying the structure of alien flesh to the haunted body, what we see is not only one aspect of the body subjected to the possession of another consciousness. Nor do we simply see the anonymous body as being activated retroactively as a deferred memory. Instead, an entire transformation of the body occurs, such that the "captive or natural spirit [, which] is my body" (Merleau-Ponty 2006, 296), foreshadows my personal being *in the present*. The emphasis on the prepersonal body as foreshadowing my personal body in the present means that the division between the two aspects becomes ambiguous, no longer distanced by a void in time. The result: experience of the world is "shared" with an anonymous self who sets in a certain place a certain mood, the tone of which is attuned to the uncanny and weird.

The weirdness of the prepersonal body is structurally implicated by its relation to the personal body. For what is peculiar to the prepersonal body is its sheer *immateriality*. After all, as we have seen from Merleau-Ponty, this is not a body that can be detected through an autopsy, at once laid out on the surgical table for inspection. The prepersonal body does not hide itself within the internal organs of the physical flesh. Nor is the prepersonal body peculiar to my own lived experience. Instead, this invisible agency is a condition of there being a body in the first instance, impersonal, anonymous, and thus fundamentally a *specter*. As a specter of corporeal experience, the prepersonal body materializes only through its proximity to the lived flesh, which Merleau-Ponty takes to be "one's own body." The anonymity of the prepersonal body speaks through me, possesses me—*I am it, but it is also me.*

Yet the weirdness of the prepersonal body is not only structural, but in its relationship to hauntings, experiential, too. Given that the affective experience of being haunted is characterized by a mood of unhomeliness, in which the world-as-haunted becomes incorporated into the body, then the weirdness of the anonymous body is wholly amplified through the materialization of its longing for unity. At the heart of this longing is an explicit declaration of the body's work in the world, with the world adopting an eerie tone in light of the absence that now protrudes into things.

Into this enlightened absence, the solidity of things wavers, at once invoking a porous boundary between the material reality of the personal body and the immaterial unreality of the body from beyond. Sensing an immaterial

Figure 30: *Venice, Italy. Photo by author.*

body lurking behind the flesh, the haunted body in turn projects that immaterial lurking to the world as a whole, augmenting the inanimate sphere with a certain clandestine aura. Through the haunted body, the relationship we have with place becomes infused with an incongruity between the personal and the prepersonal experiences of the same phenomenon, the former oriented in the "natural" realm, the latter gesturing toward a "supernatural" vision.

If the haunting of place is less a question of the particular attributes of a place and more a question of the sort of relation we have with those attributes, then we can begin to sense an alternative to the reading of hauntedness as assuming a particular aesthetic, be it Gothic decay, industrial ruins, or hauntological nostalgia. Instead of adhering to these models of aesthetic discourse, what the phenomenology of hauntings exemplifies is the emergence of the *everyday uncanny*.

Such a dynamic has been covertly present throughout our earlier dealings with ghostly bodies. Glowing below the threshold of perception, "a resolutely silent Other" dwells, whose presence is unmasked only in the confrontation with a reality that is now augmented with an appeal to the uncanny (Merleau-Ponty 2006, 376). Such is the proximity of this silent agency, which, for the most part, absorbs itself into the fabric of the everyday realm, thus becoming constitutive of that realm. Because of this absorption, the "hostile and alien" (376) force that structures the possibility of experience also underpins the radical spectrality of everydayness. Thus when the silence is shattered, then the everyday uncanny becomes defined as *reality emancipated of its "naturalism" and unreality divested of its "supernaturalism."*

The result of this deformation of the natural and the supernatural is a symbiotic fusion of the prosaic and the spectral, a blurring of divisions, in which the occult sits side by side with the banal. Through this ontological friction, simple objects in the world—"such beings as the collar stud, the inkstand, the fire, the razor, and, as age increases, the extra step on the staircase which leads you either to expect or not to expect it" (James 2006, 201)—shudder with a formless vibrancy, their supposed inanimateness now possessed by an unhomely aura. Heidegger writes: "We believe we are at home in the immediate circle of beings. That which is, is familiar, reliable, ordinary. Nevertheless, the clearing is pervaded by a constant concealment in the double form of refusal and dissembling. At bottom, the ordinary is not ordinary; it is extra-ordinary, uncanny" (1975b, 54).

Heidegger's evocation of the everyday as a haunted house returns us to Derrida's criticism, according to whom "there is no *Dasein* of the specter"

(Derrida 1994, 100). Derrida's allegation overlooks phenomenology's ability to estrange the relation between "being" and "there." Against Derrida's claim that being-in-the-world privileges a coherent unity, in which "being" is forever "placed," what our analysis has proved is in fact consistent with Derrida's counterclaim that "there is no Dasein without the uncanniness, without the strange familiarity . . . of some specter" (100). Far from offering us untiring familiarity, in which uncanny phenomenon dwells in a place far beyond, the world-as-haunted coincides with the ritual of everyday life, its eerie avenues of anxious quiet forever plagued not with the unmasking of perceptible terror, but instead with the subdued threat of terror, as though there were a presence that had yet to be placed. And into this lurking threat, things are never taken as they are given but always point to "a resolutely silent Other" undercutting their presence.

Of this interceding otherness, it is the body's memory of place that proves to be central. For nowhere is the conjunction of familiarity and unfamiliarity, absence and presence, intimacy and impenetrability clearer than in the body's hold on the places it has inhabited and passed through. As the body appeals to the memory of a place that is no longer available, save as the felt experience of absence, so the natural world reveals itself as being subject to an extraordinary, supernatural realm. Somewhere in the recesses of the lived-body, the obstinacy of the "I" not only survives but refuses the tribulations of a life marked by loss and rupture. Continuing to inhabit the world, the prepersonal body expresses itself as a longing for unity, which, in its anonymity, disrupts the naturalism of the everyday. In its place, the everyday world becomes the site of an attempt at resolving the body that withstands loss and the loss that withstands the body. But the world falls short, its brutal objectivity an enemy to grief, and where the materiality of things fuses with the immateriality of loss, so the memory of place thrives.

Far from providing a linage of plenitude and stability, the absorption of place within the flesh, instead, alerts us to a different order of space and time, conceived through the body's memory of place. If we are to speak of immaterial things lying in wait, attuned to our presence, before emerging from the cloak of a pre-ancestral time, then those nameless things are already with us, or rather, *in us*. What returns from a state of dormancy to roam the living (body), is pregiven to experience, and so contained deep within the anonymity of the prepersonal body.

Beyond its own fragmentation—be it through the loss of a beloved, the desolation of the childhood home, or the mutilation of its own materiality—the body persists in space and time, its experience of things now cast upon the surrounding world. In doing so, the genius loci at the heart of place comes alive. In the ruins where the home once stood, in the place where the beloved once spoke, gazing toward the "dark house, by which once more I stand, here in the long unlovely street" (Tennyson 1991, 8), the body, with its collection of memories and desires, touches a world that is retained only in the alcoves of phantom flesh. Possessed by its own anonymity, the world assumes an un-nerving presence, familiar but other, and at all times apprehended by the vigilant but nameless watch of an eye without a face, whose shadow articulates the knowledge that *this place is haunted.*

REFERENCES

Abraham, Nicolas. 1987. "Notes on the Phantom: A Complement to Freud's Meta-
psychology." Translated by Nicholas Rand. *Critical Inquiry* 13:287–92.

Abram, David. 1997. *The Spell of the Sensuous: Perception and Language in a More-
Than-Human World*. New York: Vintage Books.

Adams, Paul C., Steven Hoelscher, and Karen E. Till, eds. *Textures of Place: Exploring Humanist Geographies*. Minneapolis: University of Minnesota Press.

Agamben, Giorgio. 1998. *Homo Sacer: Sovereign Power and Bare Life*. Translated by
Daniel Heller-Roazen. Stanford, CA: Stanford University Press.

———. 1999. *Remnants of Auschwitz: The Witness and the Archive*. Translated by
Daniel Heller-Roazen. New York: Zone Books.

Antze, Paul, and Michael Lambek, eds. 1996. *Tense Past: Cultural Essays in Trauma
and Memory*. London: Routledge.

Aristotle. 1941. *The Basic Writings of Aristotle*. Edited by Richard P. McKeon.
Translated by J. I. Beare. New York: Random House.

———. 2004. *Physics*. Translated by Edward Hussey. Whitefish, MT: Kessinger.

Augé, Marc. 1995. *Non-Places: Introduction to an Anthropology of Supermodernity*.
Translated by John Howe. London: Verso Books.

Augustine. 1961. *Confessions*. Translated by R. S. Pine-Coffin. London: Penguin.

Auster, Paul. 2004. *The New York Trilogy*. London: Faber and Faber.

———. 2005. *The Invention of Solitude*. London: Faber and Faber.

———. 2006. *The Music of Chance*. London: Faber and Faber.

Bachelard, Gaston. 1988. *The Flame of a Candle*. Translated by Joni Caldwell. Dallas: Dallas Institute Publications.

———. 1994. *The Poetics of Space: The Classic Look at How We Experience
Intimate Places*. Translated by Maria Jolas. Boston, MA: Beacon Press.

Backhaus, Gary, and John Murungi. 2005. *Lived Topographies: And Their Media-
tional Forces*. Lanham, MD: Lexington Books.

Ballard, J. G. 1995. *Crash*. London: Vintage Books.

———. 2006. *The Complete Short Stories*. Vol. 2. London: Harper.

Barthes, Roland. 1982. *Camera Lucida: Reflections on Photography*. Translated by
Richard Howard. New York: Farrar, Straus and Giroux.

Baudrillard, Jean. 1989. *America*. Translated by Chris Turner. London: Verso Books.

———. 1990. *Cool Memories*. Translated by Chris Turner. London: Verso Books.

———. 1995. *Simulacra and Simulation*. Translated by Shelia Faria Glaser. Ann
Arbor: University of Michigan Press.

Beauvoir, Simone de. 1972. *The Coming of Age*. New York: Putnam.

Behnke, Elizabeth A. 1997. "Ghost Gestures: Phenomenological Investigations of Bodily Micromovements and Their Intercorporeal Implications." *Human Studies* 20:181–201.

Bell, Michael M. 1997. "The Ghosts of Place." *Theory and Society* 26:813–36.

Benjamin, Walter. 1977. *Illuminations*. Translated by Harry Zohn. London: Fontana.

Bergson, Henri. 2004. *Matter and Memory*. Translated by Nancy Margaret Paul and W. Scott Palmer. New York: Dover.

Bernet, Rudolf. 2000. "The Traumatized Subject." *Research in Phenomenology* 30:160–79.

Blanchot, Maurice. 1986. *The Writing of the Disaster*. Translated by Ann Smock. Lincoln: University of Nebraska Press.

Bloomer, Kent C., and Charles W. Moore. 1977. *Body, Memory, and Architecture*. New Haven, CT: Yale University Press.

Bontana, Mark, and John Protevi. 2004. *Deleuze and Geophilosophy: A Guide and Glossary*. Edinburgh: Edinburgh University Press.

Boym, Svetlana. 2001. *The Future of Nostalgia*. New York: Basic Books.

Breton, André. 1999. *Nadja*. Translated by Richard Howard. London: Penguin.

Brown, Charles S., and Ted Toadvine, eds. 2003. *Eco-Phenomenology: Back to the Earth Itself*. Albany: State University of New York Press.

Bunkse, Edmunds V. 2004. *Geography and the Art of Life*. Baltimore: Johns Hopkins University Press.

Carr, David. 1991. *Time, Narrative, and History*. Bloomington: Indiana University Press.

Caruth, Cathy. 1996. *Unclaimed Experience: Trauma, Narrative, and History*. Baltimore: Johns Hopkins University Press.

Casey, Edward S. 1987. "The World of Nostalgia." *Man and World* 20:361–84.

———. 1993. *Getting Back into Place: Toward a Renewed Understanding of the Place-World*. Bloomington: Indiana University Press.

———. 1997. *The Fate of Place: A Philosophical History*. Berkeley: University of California Press.

———. 2000a. *Imagining: A Phenomenological Study*. Bloomington: Indiana University Press.

———. 2000b. *Remembering: A Phenomenological Study*. Bloomington: Indiana University Press.

———. 2001a. "Between Geography and Philosophy: What Does It Mean to Be in the Place-World?" *Annals of the Association of American Geographers* 91:683–93.

———. 2001b. "Body, Self, and Landscape: A Geophilosophical Inquiry into the Place-World." In *Textures of Place: Exploring Humanist Geographies*, edited by Paul C. Adams, Steven Hoelscher, and Karen E. Till, 403–25. Minneapolis: University of Minnesota Press.

———. 2004. *Spirit and Soul: Essays in Philosophical Psychology*. Putnam, CT: Spring Publications.

———. 2007. *The World at a Glance*. Bloomington: Indiana University Press.

———. 2008. "Edges and the In-Between." *PhaenEx* 3:1–13.

Cataldi, Suzanne L., and William S. Hamrick, eds. 2007. *Merleau-Ponty and Environmental Philosophy*. Albany: State University of New York Press.

Cazeaux, Clive. 2000. *The Continental Aesthetics Reader*. London: Routledge.

Chang, Amos Ih Tiao. 1981. *The Tao of Architecture*. Princeton, NJ: Princeton University Press.

Clark, Andy. 2008. *Supersizing the Mind: Embodiment, Action, and Cognitive Extension*. Oxford: Oxford University Press.

Connerton, Paul. 1996. *How Societies Remember*. Cambridge: Cambridge University Press.

Cresswell, Tim. 2004. *Place: A Short Introduction*. Oxford: Blackwell.

Cronenberg, David, director. 1996. *Crash*. Based on the novel by J. G. Ballard. DVD. Toronto: Alliance Communications.

———. 1997. *Cronenberg on Cronenberg*. Edited by Chris Rodley. London: Faber and Faber.

Crowell, Steven. 1999. "Spectral History: Narrative, Nostalgia, and the Time of the I." *Research in Phenomenology* 29:83–104.

Davies, Owen. 2009. *The Haunted: A Social History of Ghosts*. Hampshire: Palgrave Macmillan.

Deleuze, Gilles. 2000. *Proust and Signs*. Translated by Richard Howard. London: Athlone Press.

———. 2005. *Cinema 1: The Movement-Image*. Translated by Hugh Tomlinson and Barbara Habberjam. London: Continuum.

Derrida, Jacques. 1994. *Specters of Marx: The State of the Debt, the Work of Mourning, and the New International*. Translated by Peggy Kamuf. London: Routledge.

———. 1998. *Of Grammatology*. Translated by Gayatri Chakravorty Spivak. Baltimore: Johns Hopkins University Press.

Dickens, Charles. 2010. *A Christmas Carol and Other Christmas Writings*. London: Penguin.

Doel, Marcus. 1999. *Poststructuralist Geographies: The Diabolical Art of Spatial Science*. Lanham, MD: Rowman and Littlefield.

Donohoe, Janet A. 2002. "Dwelling with Monuments." *Philosophy and Geography* 5:235–42.

Dreyfus, Hubert L. 1997. *Being-in-the-World: A Commentary on Heidegger's Being and Time, Division I*. Cambridge, MA: MIT Press.

Duany, Andres, Elizabeth Plater-Zyberk, and Jeff Speck. 2001. *Suburban Nation: The Rise of Sprawl and the Decline of the American Dream*. New York: Farrar, Straus and Giroux.

Dufrenne, Mikel. 1979. *The Phenomenology of Aesthetic Experience*. Translated by Edward S. Casey. Evanston, IL: Northwestern University Press.

Duncan, James S., and Nancy G. Duncan. 2001. "Sense of Place as a Positional Good." In *Textures of Place: Exploring Humanist Geographies*, edited by Paul C. Adams, Steven Hoelscher, and Karen E. Till, 41–54. Minneapolis: University of Minnesota Press.

Edensor, Tim. 2008. "Mundane Hauntings: Commuting Through the Phantasmagoric Working-Class Spaces of Manchester, England." *Cultural Geographies* 15:313–33.

Entrikin, J. Nicholas. 1991. *The Betweenness of Place: Towards a Geography of Modernity*. Baltimore: Johns Hopkins University Press.

Evans, Fred, and Leonard Lawlor. 2000. *Chiasms: Merleau-Ponty's Notion of Flesh*. Albany: State University of New York Press.

Finucane, Ronald C. 1996. *Ghosts: Appearances of the Dead and Cultural Transformations.* New York: Prometheus Books.

Foote, Kenneth E. 2003. *Shadowed Ground: America's Landscapes of Violence and Tragedy.* Austin: University of Texas Press.

Foucault, Michel. 1986. "Of Other Spaces." Translated by Jay Miskowiec. *Diacritics* 16:22–27.

Freud, Sigmund. 1967. *Moses and Monotheism.* Translated by Katherine Jones. New York: Vintage Books.

———. 1984. *Introductory Lectures on Psycho-Analysis.* Translated and edited by James Strachey. London: Penguin.

———. 2001. *Civilization and Its Discontents.* Translated and edited by James Strachey. London: Penguin.

———. 2003. *The Uncanny.* Translated by David McLintock. London: Penguin.

———. 2005. *On Murder, Mourning and Melancholia.* Translated by Shaun Whiteside. London: Penguin.

Gadamer, Hans-Georg. 1977. *Philosophical Hermeneutics.* Translated and edited by David E. Linge. Berkeley: University of California Press.

Ginsberg, Robert. 2004. *The Aesthetics of Ruins.* New York: Rodopi.

Gordon, Avery F. 1997. *Ghostly Matters: Haunting and the Sociological Imagination.* Minneapolis: University of Minnesota Press.

Harman, Graham. 2008. "On the Horror of Phenomenology: Lovecraft and Husserl." In *Collapse: Philosophical Research and Development.* Vol. 4, edited by Robin Mackay, 333–64. Falmouth: Urbanomic.

Harries, Karsten. 1993. "Thoughts on a Non-Arbitrary Architecture." In *Dwelling, Seeing, and Designing: Toward a Phenomenological Ecology*, edited by David Seamon, 41–60. Albany: State University of New York Press.

———. 2000. *The Ethical Function of Architecture.* Cambridge, MA: MIT Press.

Hart, James G. 1973. "Toward a Phenomenology of Nostalgia." *Man and World* 6:397–420.

Hayden, Dolores. 1997. *The Power of Place: Urban Landscapes as Public History.* Cambridge, MA: MIT Press.

Heidegger, Martin. 1973. "Art and Space." *Man and World* 6:3–8.

———. 1975a. "My Way to Phenomenology." In *Existentialism: From Dostoevsky to Sartre*, edited by Walter Kaufmann, 234–41. New York: New American Library.

———. 1975b. *Poetry, Language, Thought.* Translated by Albert Hofstadter. New York: Harper Perennial.

———. 1977. *Basic Writings.* Translated and edited by David F. Krell. New York: Harper and Row.

———. 1982. *The Basic Problems of Phenomenology.* Translated by Albert Hofstadter. Bloomington: Indiana University Press.

———. 1985. *Being and Time.* Translated by John Macquarrie. Oxford: Basil Blackwell.

———. 1996. *Being and Time.* Translated by Joan Stambaugh. Albany: State University of New York Press.

———. 2002. *On Time and Being.* Translated by Joan Stambaugh. Chicago, IL: University of Chicago Press.

Houellebecq, Michel. 2008. *H.P. Lovecraft: Against the World, Against Life.* Translated by Dorna Khazeni. London: Orion Books.

Hubbard, Phil, Rob Kitchin, Brendan Bartley, and Duncan Fuller. 2002. *Thinking Geographically: Space, Theory and Contemporary Human Geography.* London: Continuum.

Husserl, Edmund. 1967a. *Cartesian Meditations: An Introduction to Phenomenology.* Translated by Dorion Cairns. The Hague: Nijhoff.

———. 1967b. *Ideas Pertaining to a Pure Phenomenology and to a Phenomenological Philosophy: Studies in the Phenomenology of Constitution, Book 1.* Translated by W. R. Boyce Gibson. New York: Humanities Press.

———. 1970. *The Crisis of European Sciences and Transcendental Phenomenology.* Translated by David Carr. Evanston, IL: Northwestern University Press.

———. 1999. *The Essential Husserl: Basic Writings in Transcendental Phenomenology.* Edited by Donn Welton. Bloomington: Indiana University Press.

———. 1990. *Ideas Pertaining to a Pure Phenomenology and to a Phenomenological Philosophy: Studies in the Phenomenology of Constitution, Book 2.* Translated by Richard Rojcewicz. New York: Springer.

Hutton, Patrick H. 1993. *History as an Art of Memory.* Hanover, NH: University Press of New England.

Huyssen, Andreas. 2003. *Present Pasts: Urban Palimpsests and the Politics of Memory.* Stanford, CA: Stanford University Press.

Jackson, Shirley. 2009. *The Haunting of Hill House.* London: Penguin.

James, M. R. 2006. *The Haunted Dolls' House and Other Ghost Stories.* Edited by S. T. Joshi. London: Penguin.

———. 2007. *Collected Ghost Stories.* London: Wordsworth.

Janz, Bruce B. 2005. "Artistic Production as Place-Making Imagination." Accessed August 4, 2006. http://pegasus.cc.ucf.edu/~janzb/papers/pmitowson1.htm.

Jaspers, Karl. 1997. *General Psychopathology.* Translated by J. Hoenig and Marian W. Hamilton. Baltimore: John Hopkins University Press.

Jentsch, Ernst. 1996. "On the Psychology of the Uncanny." *Angelaki* 2:7–21.

Jewison, Norman, director. 1971. *Fiddler on the Roof.* Adaptation of the play by Joseph Stein. DVD. Los Angeles: MGM Entertainment.

Jung, Carl G. 1965. *Memories, Dreams, Reflections.* Edited by Aniela Jaffé. Translated by Richard and Clara Winston. New York: Vintage Books.

Katz, Peter. 1993. *The New Urbanism: Toward an Architecture of Community.* New York: McGraw-Hill.

Kaufmann, Walter, ed. 1975. *Existentialism: From Dostoevsky to Sartre.* New York: New American Library.

Kierkegaard, Søren. 1971. *Either/Or.* Edited by Howard A. Johnson. Translated by David F. Swenson. Princeton, NJ: Princeton University Press.

Kolb, David. 2008. *Sprawling Places.* Athens: University of Georgia Press.

Kristeva, Julia. 1984. *Powers of Horror: An Essay on Abjection.* Translated by Leon S. Roudiez. New York: Columbia University Press.

Kunstler, James H. 1994. *The Geography of Nowhere: The Rise and Decline of America's Man-Made Landscape.* New York: Simon and Schuster.

Langer, Lawrence L. 1991. *Holocaust Testimonies: The Ruins of Memory.* New Haven, CT: Yale University Press.

————. 1995. *Art from the Ashes: A Holocaust Anthology*. Oxford: Oxford University Press.

Lanzmann, Claude. 1985. *Shoah*. DVD. Directed by Claude Lanzmann. London: Eureka Entertainment.

Lefebvre, Henri. 1991. *The Production of Space*. Translated by Donald Nicholson-Smith. Oxford: Blackwell.

Legg, Stephen. 2005. "Contesting and Surviving Memory: Space, Nation, and Nostalgia in *Les Lieux de Mémoire*." *Environment and Planning D: Society and Space* 23:481–504.

Le Goff, Jacques. 1992. *History and Memory*. Translated by Steven Rendall and Elizabeth Claman. New York: Columbia University Press.

Levi, Eliphas. 1975. *Transcendental Magic*. Translated by Arthur E. Waite. London: Rider and Company.

Levi, Neil, and Michael Rothburg, eds. 2003. *The Holocaust: Theoretical Readings*. Edinburgh: Edinburgh University Press.

Levi, Primo. 1996. *Survival in Auschwitz*. Translated by Stuart Woolf. New York: Touchstone.

Levinas, Emmanuel. 1969. *Totality and Infinity: An Essay on Exteriority*. Translated by Alphonso Lingis. Pittsburgh: Duquesne University Press.

————. 1985. *Ethics and Infinity: Conversations with Philippe Nemo*. Translated by Richard A. Cohen. Pittsburgh: Duquesne University Press.

————. 1994. *Otherwise Than Being: Or Beyond Essence*. Translated by Alphonso Lingis. Dordrecht: Kluwer.

————. 2005. *Time and the Other*. Translated by Richard A. Cohen. Pittsburgh: Duquesne University Press.

Light, Andrew, and Jonathan M. Smith. 1998. *Philosophy and Geography III: Philosophies of Place*. Lanham, MD: Rowman and Littlefield.

Lovecraft, H.P. 1985. *Omnibus 2: Dagon and Other Macabre Tales*. London: Grafton.

————. 1993. *Omnibus 1: At the Mountains of Madness*. London: Grafton.

————. 1994. *Omnibus 3: The Haunter of the Dark*. London: Grafton.

Malpas, Jeff E. 2007. *Heidegger's Topology: Being, Place, World*. Cambridge, MA: MIT Press.

————. 2008. *Place and Experience: A Philosophical Topography*. Cambridge: Cambridge University Press.

Mann, Thomas. 1994. *Death in Venice*. Translated by Clayton Koelb. New York: Norton.

Marion, Jean-Luc. 1998. *Reduction and Givenness: Investigations of Husserl, Heidegger, and Phenomenology*. Translated by Thomas A. Carlson. Evanston, IL: Northwestern University Press.

————. 2002. *Being Given: Toward a Phenomenology of Giveness*. Translated by Jeffery L. Kosky. Stanford, CA: Stanford University Press.

Massey, Doreen B. 2005. *For Space*. London: Sage.

Merleau-Ponty, Maurice. 1965. *The Structure of Behaviour*. Translated by Alden L. Fisher. London: Methuen Books.

————. 1968. *The Visible and the Invisible*. Translated by Alphonso Lingis. Evanston, IL: Northwestern University Press.

————. 1979. "Eye and Mind." In *Aesthetics: Oxford Readings in Philosophy*, edited by Harold Osborne. Oxford: Oxford University Press.

———. 1993. *The Merleau-Ponty Aesthetics Reader: Philosophy and Painting.* Edited by Galen A. Johnson. Translated by Michael B. Smith. Evanston, IL: Northwestern University Press.

———. 2006. *Phenomenology of Perception.* Translated by Colin Smith. London: Routledge. First published 1945 by Gallimard, Paris.

———. 2008. *The World of Perception.* Translated by Oliver Davis. London: Routledge.

Millet, Marietta S. 1996. *Light Revealing Architecture.* Hoboken, NJ: Wiley.

Moran, Dermot, and Timothy Mooney, eds. 2002. *The Phenomenology Reader.* London: Routledge.

Mugerauer, Robert. 1993. "Toward an Architectural Vocabulary: The Porch as a Between." In *Dwelling, Seeing, and Designing: Toward a Phenomenological Ecology,* edited by David Seamon, 103–28. Albany: State University of New York Press.

———. 1994. *Interpretations on Behalf of Place: Environmental Displacements and Alternative Responses.* Albany: State University of New York Press.

Murakami, Haruki. 2006. *Blind Willow, Sleeping Woman.* Translated by Jay Rubin. New York: Knopf.

Nietzsche, Friedrich. 1997. *Untimely Meditations.* Edited by Daniel Breazeale. Translated by R. J. Hollingdale. Cambridge: Cambridge University Press.

———. 2000. *Basic Writings of Nietzsche.* Translated by Walter Kaufmann. New York: Random House.

Nora, Pierre. 1989. "Between Memory and History: Les Lieux de Mémoire." *Representations* 26:7–24.

———. 1996. *Realms of Memory: The Construction of the French Past.* Vol. 1 of *Conflicts and Divisions.* Translated by Arthur Goldhammer. New York: Columbia University Press.

Norberg-Schulz, Christian. 1974. *Existence, Space, and Architecture.* New York: Praeger.

Osborne, Harold, ed. 1979. *Aesthetics: Oxford Readings in Philosophy.* Oxford: Oxford University Press.

Pallasmaa, Juhani. 2007. *The Eyes of the Skin: Architecture and the Senses.* West Sussex: Wiley.

Plato. 1987. *Theaetetus.* Translated by Robin A. H. Waterfield. London: Penguin.

———. 1993. *Sophist.* Translated by Nicholas P. White. Indianapolis, IN: Hackett.

———. 2003. *The Republic.* Translated by Desmond Lee. London: Penguin.

Plotinus. 1991. *The Enneads.* Translated by Stephen MacKenna. London: Penguin.

Plutarch. 2001. *Plutarch's Lives.* Vol. 1. Edited by Arthur H. Clough. Translated by John Dryden. New York: Random House.

Proust, Marcel. 1967. *Within a Budding Grove.* Translated by C. K. Scott Moncrieff. London: Chatto and Windus.

Relph, Edward C. 1976. *Place and Placelessness.* London: Routledge.

———. 1993. "Modernity and the Reclamation of Place." In *Dwelling, Seeing, and Designing: Toward a Phenomenological Ecology,* edited by David Seamon, 25–39. Albany: State University of New York Press.

Ricoeur, Paul. 1990. *Time and Narrative.* Translated by Kathleen McLaughlin and David Pellauer. Chicago: University of Chicago Press.

———. 2004. *Memory, History, Forgetting.* Translated by Kathleen Blamey and David Pellauer. Chicago: University of Chicago Press.

Riegl, Alois. 1982. "The Modern Cult of Monuments: Its Character and Its Origin."
    Oppositions 25:20–51.
Rilke, Rainer Maria. 1987. *The Selected Poetry of Rainer Maria Rilke*. Translated
    and edited by Stephen Mitchell. London: Picador.
Rodenbach, Georges. 2005. *Bruges-la-Morte*. Translated by Mike Mitchell and Will
    Stone. Cambridge, MA: Daedalus.
Sack, Robert D. 1997. *Homo Geographicus: A Framework for Action, Awareness,
    and Moral Concern*. Baltimore: Johns Hopkins University Press.
Sartre, Jean-Paul. 1969. *Nausea*. Translated by Lloyd Alexander. New York: New
    Directions.
———. 2001. *Basic Writings*. Edited by Stephen Priest. London: Routledge.
Schmitt, Jean-Claude. 2000. *Ghosts in the Middle Ages: The Living and the Dead in
    Medieval Society*. Chicago: Chicago University Press.
Schopenhauer, Arthur. 2000. *Parerga and Paralipomena*. Translated by E. F. J. Payne.
    Oxford: Clarendon Press.
Scott, Charles, E. 1999. *The Time of Memory*. New York: SUNY Press.
Seamon, David. 1979. *A Geography of the Lifeworld*. London: Croom Helm.
———, ed. 1993. *Dwelling, Seeing, and Designing: Toward a Phenomenological
    Ecology*. Albany: State University of New York Press.
Sebald, W. G. 2002a. *After Nature*. Translated by Michael Hamburger. London:
    Penguin.
———. 2002b. *The Rings of Saturn*. Translated by Michael Hulse. New York: New
    Directions.
See, Anik. 2008. *Saudade: The Possibilities of Place*. Toronto: Coach House Press.
Sokolowski, Robert. 2000. *Introduction to Phenomenology*. Cambridge: Cambridge
    University Press.
Sprinker, Michael, Terry Eagleton, Fredric Jameson, Antonio Negri, et al., eds. 2008.
    Ghostly Demarcations: A Symposium on Jacques Derrida's Specters of Marx.
    London: Verso Books.
Steeves, H. Peter. 2006. *The Things Themselves: Phenomenology and the Return to
    the Everyday*. Albany: State University of New York Press.
Steinbock, Anthony J. 1995. *Home and Beyond: Generative Phenomenology after
    Husserl*. Evanston, IL: Northwestern University Press.
Strauss, Erwin W., and Richard M. Griffith, eds. 1967. *Phenomenology of Will and
    Action*. Pittsburgh: Duquesne University Press.
Tanizaki, Junichiro. 2001. *In Praise of Shadows*. Translated by Thomas J. Harper
    and Edward G. Seidensticker. London: Vintage Books.
Tarkovsky, Andrei A., director. 1983. *Nostalghia*. DVD. London: Artificial Eye.
———. 1986. *Sculpting in Time: Reflections on the Cinema*. Translated by Kitty
    Hunter-Blair. Austin: University of Texas Press.
Tengelyi, László. 2004. *The Wild Region in Life-History*. Translated by Géza Kállay.
    Evanston, IL: Northwestern University Press.
Tennyson, Alfred. 1991. *In Memoriam, Maud, and Other Poems*. Edited by John D.
    Jump. London: Everyman.
Thomson, James. 1993. *The City of Dreadful Night*. London: Canongate Classics.
Till, Karen E. 2005. *The New Berlin: Memory, Politics, Place*. Minneapolis: Univer-
    sity of Minnesota Press.

Toadvine, Ted. 2009. *Merleau-Ponty's Philosophy of Nature*. Evanston, IL: North-western University Press.

Trigg, Dylan. 2006a. *The Aesthetics of Decay: Nothingness, Nostalgia, and the Absence of Reason*. New York: Peter Lang.

———. 2006b. "Furniture Music, Hotel Lobbies, and Banality: Can We Speak of a Disinterested Space?" *Space and Culture* 9:418–28.

———. 2006c. "Memories in Site: Toward a Renewed Understanding of Starbucks." *Environmental & Architectural Phenomenology* 17:5–10.

———. 2011. "The Return of the New Flesh: Body Memory in David Cronenberg's The Fly." *Film-Philosophy* 15:82–99.

———. 2012. "Bodily Moods and Unhomely Environments: The Hermeneutics of Agoraphobia and the Spirit of Place." In *Interpreting Nature: The Emerging Field of Environmental Hermeneutics*, edited by Forrest Clingerman, Martin Drenthen, Brian Treanor and David Utsler. New York: Fordham University Press.

Tuan, Yi-Fu. 1977. *Space and Place: The Perspective of Experience*. Minneapolis: University of Minnesota Press.

Tumarkin, Maria M. 2005. *Traumascapes: The Power and Fate of Places Transformed by Tragedy*. Melbourne: Melbourne University Press.

Unwerth, Matthew von. 2005. *Freud's Requiem: Mourning, Memory, and the Invisible History of a Summer Walk*. New York: Penguin.

Virilio, Paul. 1998. "Dromoscopy: of The Ecstasy of Enormities." Translated by Edward R. O'Neil. *Wide Angle* 20:11–12.

———. 2004. *The Paul Virilio Reader*. Edited by Steve Redhead. Edinburgh: Edinburgh University Press.

———. 2005. *City of Panic*. Translated by Julie Rose. Oxford: Berg.

Warf, Barney, and Cynthia Waddell. 2002. "Heinous Spaces, Perfidious Places: The Sinister Landscapes of Serial Killers." *Social and Cultural Geography* 3:323–45.

Webber, Andrew J. 1996. *The Doppelgänger: Double Visions in German Literature*. Oxford: Oxford University Press.

Webber, Melvin M., John W. Dyckman, Donald L. Foley, Albert Z. Guttenberg, William L. C. Wheaton, and Catherine B. Wurster. 1964. *Explorations into Urban Structure*. Philadelphia: University of Pennsylvania Press.

Winterson, Jeanette. 2006. "Guidebooks." *Times* (London), August 6.

Yates, Frances A. 1978. *The Art of Memory*. London: Penguin.

INDEX

· ·

ghosts, (*cont'd*)
   and memory, 281–84, 295, 319
   and mood, 303, 305
   and phenomenology, 287, 293
   and photography, xx
   and place, 294, 298, 321–22
   of *The Memory of Place*, 299
   and trauma, 242, 254, 256
   as a trope of cultural studies,
     285–86
   See also hauntings; phantoms;
     spectrality
Ginsberg, Robert, 263
Golden Nugget (casino), 54–55

habit, 7, 9, 11–12, 16–17, 26, 46,
   49–51, 58, 97, 105, 225
Harries, Karsten, 89–92
Hart, James, 175–77, 184, 188, 206
hauntings, xx, xxvii, 33, 35, 61, 206,
   281, 286–87, 288–89, 301,
   303, 306, 309, 311–12, 314,
   318, 320–24
   See also ghosts; phantoms;
     spectrality
hauntology, 285–86, 324
Heidegger, Martin, xxiv–xxv, xxvii,
   18–22, 24–25, 39, 40–42, 52,
   64, 75, 133, 183, 194–95,
   243, 245–46, 258
   on anxiety, 153, 316
   "Art and Space," 86–88
   being-in-the-world, 118–19
   on monumentality, 94–96
   on mood, 302–7, 314, 315
   on the uncanny, 324
   on world, 57–58, 182
history, xix, 34, 39, 67, 90, 179, 219,
   237, 239, 268–69, 278, 283,
   285
   of Auschwitz, 250
   of the body, 2, 12, 35, 42, 163,
     165, 168, 251, 253–54, 292
   of ghosts, 306, 318
   of the house, xv
   of lighting, 147

   and memory, xxv, 70, 72–75,
     77–79, 96–97, 269
   and monumentality, 85, 92, 94
   of nostalgia, 199
   of phenomenology, 18, 121
   of philosophy, xvi
   of place, xxix, 17, 124, 129, 131,
     168, 270
   and space, xxv, 33, 107
   See also prehistory
home, 5, 7–8, 25, 36, 69, 108,
   116–18, 135, 145, 150, 160,
   163, 178–79, 189, 216–17,
   219, 304–5, 312, 316–20,
   326
   childhood, xiii, 37, 209, 211–15,
     280, 302, 308, 321–22, 325
   and homesickness, 194–96, 198
   and memory, 9, 71
   and the uncanny, 28, 30, 61, 155,
     220–24, 226, 254, 284, 324
   See also unhomeliness
homelessness, 1, 188, 196
homesickness, 36, 178, 190, 193–96,
   198–99, 312
horror, 166
   of the childhood home, 221
   of contingency, 153–54
   of daylight, 298
   of the doppelgänger, 292
   of insomnia, 248
   of the non-house, 226
   as phenomenology, 29
   the traumatized body, 249–50,
     253–54
   See also body horror
Houellebecq, Michel, 32
Husserl, Edmund, 13, 18, 20–22,
   28–29, 33, 38, 51, 89, 130,
   160, 192, 258, 260, 262
   on the body, 14, 157–58
   on the epoché, 18–19
   on ghosts, 293–94
   on the life-world, 23–25
   and Lovecraft, 31–32
   on memory, 48–49

CPSIA information can be obtained
at www.ICGtesting.com
Printed in the USA
FFHW020942311019
55884936-61769FF